Science,
Medicine
*and*
Society
*in the*
Renaissance

# Science, Medicine *and* Society *in the* Renaissance

## Essays *to honor* Walter Pagel

EDITED BY

### Allen G. Debus

*Director*
The Morris Fishbein Center
for the Study of the
History of Science and Medicine
University of Chicago

VOLUME TWO

Heinemann · London

Heinemann Educational Books Ltd.

LONDON   EDINBURGH   MELBOURNE   AUCKLAND

HONG KONG   SINGAPORE   KUALA LUMPUR

IBADAN   NAIROBI   JOHANNESBURG

NEW DELHI

ISBN 0-435-542354

Published by Heinemann Educational Books Ltd.
48 Charles Street, London WIX 8AH

*Printed in the United States of America*

# The Essays

20   ERNA LESKY
Paul de Sorbait (1624-1691), Anti-Paracelsian and Harveian ..... 1

21   PETER H. NIEBYL
Galen, Van Helmont, and Blood Letting ...................... 13

22   AUDREY B. DAVIS
The Circulation of the Blood and Chemical Anatomy ........... 25

23   JEROME J. BYLEBYL
Cesalpino and Harvey on the Portal Circulation ............... 39

24   KARL E. ROTHSCHUH
Cardiac Function, Blood Volume and the
Circulation of Blood in Antiquity ........................... 53

25   CHARLES B. SCHMITT & CHARLES WEBSTER
Marco Aurelio Serverino and His Relationship to William Harvey:
Some Preliminary Considerations .......................... 63

26   RICHARD TOELLNER
The Controversy between Descartes and Harvey
Regarding the Nature of Cardiac Motions ................... 73

27   PAUL F. CRANEFIELD
On the Stupidity of the Boeotians and the Batavians ............ 91

28   J. R. RAVETZ
Francis Bacon and the Reform of Philosophy ................. 97

29   D. P. WALKER
Francis Bacon and *Spiritus* ................................121

30   PAOLO ROSSI
Nobility of Man and Plurality of Worlds .....................131

31   WALTHER RIESE
On Symbolic Thought in Cartesianism .......................163

32   P. M. RATTANSI
Newton's Alchemical Studies ...............................167

33   RICHARD S. WESTFALL
Newton and the Hermetic Tradition ........................183

34   I. BERNARD COHEN
Newton and Keplerian Inertia:
An Echo of Newton's Controversy with Leibniz ................199

35   ROBERT P. MULTHAUF
The Constitution of Saltpeter, According to Becher and Stahl .....213

36   HUGH TREVOR-ROPER
The Sieur de la Rivière, Paracelsian Physician of Henry IV ........227

37   JOSEPH NEEDHAM
A Chinese Puzzle: Eighth or Eighteenth? .....................251

38   CARLO CASTELLANI
The Problem of Generation in Bonnet and in Buffon:
A Critical Comparison ...................................265

MARIANNE WINDER
A Bibliography of the Writings of Walter Pagel ................289

The Contributors .........................................327

Editor's Acknowledgements ................................335

Illustration Acknowledgements ............................337

# 20

## Paul de Sorbait (1624-1691), Anti-Paracelsian and Harveian

### ERNA LESKY

EDWARD BROWNE (1644-1709), the son of Sir Thomas Browne and later President of the Royal College of Physicians, was quite correct when he wrote, in his travel report of 1673,[1] about the professors of the University of Vienna: "They follow here the old beaten way of Knowledge: and I met with few who had any good insight in new Philosophy."

Indeed, with few exceptions, Viennese medical practice in the 17th century had not yet caught up with the *nova scientia* flourishing in southern and western Europe. Among the few men of marked distinction, Sir Edward mentions Paul de Sorbait, a native of Belgium who had studied in Padua and whose tombstone in St. Stephan's cathedral bears the following inscription: *Paulus de Sorbait in Belgio natus hic denatus, musicus, orator philosophus, miles, medicus, professor, archiater, rector magnificus, mendicus, nihil.* Paul de Sorbait has been called with justice the Abraham a Santa Clara of medicine. The words inscribed on his tombstone and, more significantly, his addresses at university graduations indicate the manner in which he, when describing his own personality, joined the baroque era's delight in down-to-earth antitheses to the strong religious faith of a physician.

We should like to know more about his youth and his education than either his biographer Leopold Senfelder[2] or Ernest Matthieu in his *Biographie nationale de Belgique*[3] has transmitted to us. Some elements of legend have here evidently combined with the truth. In any event, it appears certain that de Sorbait was born on January 25, 1624, the fifth child of a woodcutter in Montbliard, near Mons. The statement by Matthieu that de Sorbait left his father's home when he was fifteen and made his living as an itinerant musician, agrees with the designation *musicus* on his tombstone. Further than that, so far as this period is concerned, we must content ourselves with the few data included in de Sorbait's works and in the *Epicrisis gratulatoria*[4] of the Westphalian

I

physician Joannes Christophorus de Prato. According to these sources, de Sorbait must have completed his studies of the arts in Paderborn and those of medicine in Padua; later he seems to have practiced as a physician in Cologne, in Arnhem, along the Netherlands coast, and in Rome.

We reach indisputable ground only at the start of his career in Vienna, in the year 1652. Like many others who had obtained a degree elsewhere—generally in Padua—during this period of decline of the Viennese school, he complied with the Acts of Repetition, the procedure for the Vienna Medical Faculty's recognition of his Paduan degree,[5] on August 26, 1652. It was not until this procedure has been completed that de Sorbait could display the richness of his sanguine and combative nature in the Imperial city; he rose to become the dominant personality of university life and public health during the reign of Emperor Leopold.

In his capacity as professor of theoretical (1654-1666) and practical medicine (1666-1682), he attempted to convey to his students something of the spirit of Paduan medicine, particularly in relation to anatomy, as this account will show. As dean and rector, he fought successfully against the arrogance of bureaucratic authorities. Significant in this respect is his attitude when he assumed the burdensome office of head of the public health service in the plague-ridden Vienna of 1679[6]:

*Fateor ingenue me haec dignitatis officia illubenter assepisse, ut tamen facultati medicae viam aliquam ad extraordinarias dignitates imposterum sternerem essetque semper aliquis ex facultate apud regimen, qui eam protegere posset, adductus fui, ut onera potius quam dignitates hasce meis imponi humeris sinerem.*

If, in 1679, de Sorbait fought both the plague and the authorities, he proved, in 1683, to be a true *miles,* as was also inscribed on his tombstone. When the Turks stood before the gates of Vienna, the 59-year-old de Sorbait took command of a student company and fought as their colonel on the city walls. The verses written by a student of jurisprudence on that occasion may be somewhat awkward, but they do convey some feeling of the impact this powerful medical personage had on Vienna of the baroque era:[7]

> Our colonel-chief, the noble knight
> Abandoned books, as was his right
> The brave knight, leaving art to rest
> Sever'ly put by bravery to the test
> Pallas' favourite sons.

His martial ardour kindled bright the flame
His ample heart all doubt soon overcame
The Muses' sons by him inspired
Fought heartily, their courage ne'er tired....

It might seem likely that a fighting and innovative person such as de Sorbait would soon leave the "old beaten way of Knowledge" and introduce a new way of thinking into Viennese medicine. This development would have been even more probable because de Sorbait, since 1671, had been a member of the most progressive scientific society in the German language area, a society attempting to achieve an exchange of observations and experiments along the lines of *nova scientia*. De Sorbait had been accepted into that society, the *Academia naturae curiosorum*, under the cognomen of Machaon, the son of Asclepias. But it was Walter Pagel himself, in his basic study on the history of science in the baroque era, "The Reaction to Aristotle in Seventeenth-Century Biological Thought",[8] who demonstrated the close relationship between ideas and their contradictions during that tumultuous century. Just as Harvey could simultaneously be an Aristotelian and a quantifying experimentalist, so de Sorbait well knew how to combine his support of traditional Hippocratic and Galenic medicine with his recognition of Harvey's discovery.

As he stated in the preface to his principle work, the *Praxios medicae*,[9] de Sorbait's combative mind aimed to cleanse traditional medicine completely of the new heresies. An *Epicrisis gratulatoria*[10] further explains just who these heretics are; in this work, de Sorbait simply assumes the position of a vindicator of Hippocratic and Galenic medicine, strongly opposing and ridiculing Paracelsus' claim as the inventor of medicine *per se*. The author does not even refrain from the crudest invective, calling the Paracelsians a plague of murderers and robbers.

Although *Praxios medicae* was published in 1680, de Sorbait had formulated his Anti-Paracelsian views eight years earlier in his textbook *Universa medicina*.[11] If we look for the principal features of his opposition to Paracelsus, we may distinguish two patterns of argument—typical of de Sorbait—which, at the same time, reflect some of the history of Paracelsian thought in the 17th century. Whenever, as we will show, de Sorbait directly assails Paracelsus by attacking the magic elements in the latter's medicine, he presents himself as a faithful and straightforward Catholic. When he is, to some extent, forced to allow for chemical medicament in his therapy, he becomes the down-to-earth,

PAVLVS DE SORBAIT Philo: & Medicinæ Doctor, Sac: Imperatricis Medicus Cubic. Praxios Med. Professor Primarius Regni Hungar. eques & P. T. Vniuersitatis Vienn. Rector Anno 1669.

Gerhart Bouttats Vniuersi. Vienn: july. fe.

sober practitioner who does not disdain to borrow from the "chymists" whatever he deems useful for the welfare of his patients—even though this may conflict with his Hippocratic and Galenic principles.

Let us, then, examine the specific polemics against Paracelsus. In his chapter *De variis methodi medendi principiis,*[12] de Sorbait asks why Paracelsus effects cures by characters and words, by magical therapy when he claims to possess the true *arcanum;* would this preference imply that characters and words are more effective than "universal medicine"? Even worse, would this not imply using the devil's assistance and "transplant" diseases (*transplantare*) rather than cure them—methods unworthy of a Christian physician? In pursuing this concept, de Sorbait refers to Paracelsus as *impius ille magus* and complains that, contrary to the tenets of Hippocrates and Galen, Paracelsus again allows considerable latitude for diseases of magic origin. De Sorbait regards as particularly reprehensible Paracelsus' indifference as to whether a cure is effected by God, by angels, or by unclean spirits.

This raises the question as to what extent de Sorbait's invective does justice to Paracelsus. We need only look into the chapter *De causis morborum invisibilium,*[13] in which Paracelsus speaks about characters in connection with superstitious rites on Mount Venus, to read: "...also wissent, das ir auf solche ding kein glauben sellent sezen, dan es ist der grunt in diser kunst sonder ein ablasz gesucht on tugent und kraft." On the other hand, in the chapter *De characteribus* of the *Archidoxa magica,*[14] Paracelsus expressly confirms his belief in characters and recommends their use in the treatment of magic supernatural diseases. Once more we see the many levels in the character of this being—full of contradictions, suspended between two worlds, the man who made it so difficult for the dogmatic physicians of the 17th century to judge him fairly. It is, therefore, understandable why the problem of *An verborum et characterum aliqua vis sit* occupies so much space in their accounts. As for de Sorbait's chapter on this question—and, therefore, his opinion of Paracelsus—we must ask whether he consulted the original writings of Paracelsus or merely followed the preconceived views of contemporary physicians. Fortunately, at the place here de Sorbait uses the epithet *impius ille magus,* he names his informant: the Spanish physician, Gaspare Bravo de Sobremonte Ramirez. In this author's *Disputatio apologetica pro Dogmaticae Medicinae praestantia* (Lugd., 1671, p. 199), we read: *De reliquis impiis propositionibus et imposturis, quas Paracelsus iniunxit suae sectae, non ipse tanquam sectae Medicinae Au-*

*thor protulit illas, sed tanquam impium Daemonis mancipium, qui
illud non elegit Medicum; sed ut sub praetextu Medicinae plures detestabiles spargeret propositiones blasphemicas, impias, et diabolicae ma-
lignitatis plenas, quae ideo ut detestabiles, et damnatae sunt fugiendae.*
In making Bravo's judgement his own, de Sorbait joins the large group
of Anti-Paracelsians that begins with Erastus (1523-1583) and continues with the many upholders of dogmatic medicine well into the
17th century.

One might expect that this Anti-Paracelsian attitude would be reflected in his medicative therapy, to the extent that de Sorbait would
refuse to consider all chemical therapeutic agent introduced by Paracelsus.
On this supposition, it is all the more astonishing to receive his assurance[15]
*a Chymicis remediis non abhorremus, sed et nos ea cum fructu praescribi-
mus.* Of course, these should not be prepared by a rude empiricist, but
rather by a *prudens Artifex* who knows how to eliminate the dangerous
and violent elements contained in these remedies.[16] In spite of this reservation, the statement does raise a basic issue, revealing the wide gulf
between dogmatic and Paracelsian medicine. In his standard work on
Paracelsus, Walter Pagel,[17] in the chapter on "The Homeopathic Principle," stated with admirable lucidity: "If remedy and disease are attuned to
each other like lock and key, the ancient principle 'Contrario Contrariis
Curentur' cannot hold." Or, to speak in the words of Paracelsus: "Never
hath a hot disease been cured with cold, nor a cold one with heat."[18]

It is obvious that de Sorbait, in order to make his application of
chemical remedies credible, had to take a position on this fundamental
discrepancy between the therapeutic principles of Hippocratic and
Galenic, and of Paracelsian medicine. After clearly defining the homeopathic principle of the "chymists" in the words[19] *morbos ex sale ortos
medicamentis ex sale praeparatis, sulphureos sulphureis, Mercuriales
Mercurialibus curari tradunt,* he goes on to say (and this is surprising,
considering his Anti-Paracelsian attitude): "If there were no more profound discrepancy between chymists and Galenians, agreement could be
reached without any difficulty."

After this statement we may, with some degree of anticipation, look
forward to learning by what means the arch-Galenian will bring about
this accord: it is the Scholastic differentiation between *indicatio vitalis*
and *indicatio curatoria* on which de Sorbait bases his argument, maintaining that we must distinguish strictly between these two indications.
One, he states, refers to the maintenance of natural powers, whereas

the other applies to anything that is against nature (*contra naturam*). Both Galenians and "chymists" seek to preserve the natural powers of the body and thus agree, whereas the Hippocratic axiom *contraria contrariorum esse remedia* only applies to the curative indication. In addition, no Paracelsian would be insane enough to believe—for example—that an already dried-out body should be further desiccated.

However, this argument is not original with de Sorbait. A reading of Daniel Sennert's[20] *De Chymicorum cum Aristotelicis et Galenicis consensu ac dissensu liber* (Wittenberg, 1629, p. 377 ff.) makes evident that de Sorbait has used verbatim—with a few omissions—Sennert's attempt at reconciling these viewpoints. The comparison also reavels something else: Sennert does not refer to the *cardo controversiae* until page 380, where he uses subtle argument to resolve the difficult problem of reconciling homeopathic and allopathic principles with regard to the action of sulfur, salt, and mercury on the cause of the disease, as assumed by Paracelsus. It shows a gross oversimplification on de Sorbait's part to overlook completely this cardinal problem of Paracelsian or dogmatic medicine. Instead, in subsequent chapters, he continues for page after page, attempting to explain to his public the subtle differences between *Indicatio* and *Indicans*, according to the rules of the Scholastic art of quotation. Indeed, Edward Browne's statement in his travel report of 1673 seems to apply to de Sorbait, too: "They follow here the old beaten way of Knowledge...."

However, this same man who was so committed to Galenic thought successfully rejected his idol on one critical issue: an acknowledgement of Harvey's discovery and the renewal of anatomical study which the discovery brought about in Vienna. In the same *isagoge*,[21] filled to the brim with Galenianisms, there is, in the chapter on anatomy, a description of the hepatic vessels with a tribute to Harvey's discovery, plainly revealing de Sorbait's disapproval of the polemics directed against Harvey. This indicates that de Sorbait had personally convinced himself of the truth of Harvey's discovery: *hinc Harvejana Circulatio. Quam et nos oculari inspectione et experimentis frequentissimis detectam et comprobatam ambabus ulnis, una cum celeberrimis Europae Universitatibus, amplectimur putamusque eos duntaxat hanc negare, qui cadaverum foetorem nauseantes, verae Anatomiae fundamenta ignorant. Sic vera scientia et doctrina nullos habet Inimicos nisi ignorantes et turpiter unus multis contradicit Regiaque aberrat via.*

Of course, the laudatio *Harveiana Vindobonensis* came somewhat late. De Sorbait himself stated that he had, by this act, joined the ranks of the *celeberrimae Europae universitates*. However, he did seize the first available opportunity—prior to 1672, none of his writings had appeared in print—to acknowledge Harvey's work. The following circumstances indicate he had probably become convinced in the forties that Harvey was right. The road led by way of Padua, Padua of the forties, where in all likelihood Johann Vesling (1598-1649) had been de Sorbait's teacher of anatomy. Vesling, who had met Harvey as early as 1637, corresponded with him and, in his letters, took Harvey's part against the critics Parisanus and Primrose.[22] The first Paduan edition of Harvey's works was published in 1643. How heatedly Harvey's doctrine was discussed in Padua in those days—a fact reflected in the writing not only of such medical men as Cecilio Folli (1639), but also of natural philosophers such as Claudio Berigardo (1643), and even such astrologers as Andrea Argoli (1644)—has been shown by Walter Pagel and F. N. L. Poynter[23] in their joint publication, as well as in the work of L. Premuda.[24] It is therefore reasonable to assume that, in this pro-Harveian milieu and under the guidance of Johann Vesling, the young Belgian medical student de Sorbait not only became familiar with Harvey's teaching but had already formed an opinion of it—one that he was to state after 1654 during his career as teacher of anatomy in Vienna, and later, as Professor praxios, 1678, when he affirmed these teachings so unequivocally in his *isagoge*.

The story of the reception of Harvey's work in Vienna has not yet been written. When the account is written at greater depth than is possible in this outline, attention will have to be given to the note in the *Acta facultatis medicae Vindobonensis* (5,364) which states that, even prior to de Sorbait's arrival in Vienna on November 28, 1650, by the *Magister Carolus Kniel, medici filius et majestatis musicus, de circulari motu* was discussed. Primarily, however, the personality of one young man will have to be studied—the man of whom Edward Browne wrote in his travel report:[25] "During my stay at Vienna, I went unto a publick Anatomy of a Woman that was beheaded...It was performed by a Learned Physician, Dr. Wolfstriegel, who read in Latin to the satisfaction of all persons...." This was the Viennese, Laurenz Wolfstriegel, whom de Sorbait paid, from his own funds, for work as anatomical assistant until Wolfstriegel was made full professor of anatomy[26] in 1668. It is high praise indeed that Vienna's great expert in the history of anatomy, Joseph Hyrtl,[27] expressed of Wolfstriegel: "I revere in this man the first Austrian who deserved the name of anatomist and bore it with honour." In the context of our subject, it is important to note that this anatomist received his training in Padua. Even more important for the response to Harvey's teaching in Vienna is a report by Hyrtl,[28] that, one year after Harvey's death, Wolfstriegel defended a thesis entitled *De merito inventi Harveiani contra omnes et quoscumque opponere volentes;* this treatise was published the same year by Johannes Grunnelius. To date, all efforts to locate the thesis have failed. Let us hope that these lines will assist in the discovery of this lost thesis and so serve to complete the picture of the reception of the *inventum Harveianum*—a subject to which Walter Pagel devoted one of his fundamental works.

## References

[1]Browne, Edward, *A brief account of some travels in Hungaria, Styria, Bulgaria, Austria, Servia, Carinthia, Carniola, Friuli,* London, 1673. Quoted according to Neuberger, Max, "Die Wiener Universitätuund die Wiener medizinische Schule im 17. Jahrhundert", *Mitteilungen zur Gesch. d. Med. u. d. Naturwissenschaften,* 16 (1917), 144 ff.

[2]Senfelder, Leopold, "Paul de Sorbait. Ein Wiener Arzt aus dem XVII. Jahrhundert (1624 bis 1691)", *Wien. klin. Rundsch.,* 20 (1906), nr. 21-27, 29-30. By the same author, *Acta facultatis medicae Vindobonensis,* VI, 1677-1727, IX ff. The funeral oration, unknown to Senfelder, by P. Emericus Pfendtner, *Austrian Galenus, this is the eulogy, funeral oration and laudatio for his Magnificence the well-born and learned Pauli de Sorbait,* Vienna, 1691, is written in the style of the time and contains practically no biographical data. The other acknowledgments of de Sorbait's work by J. Schaffran (1909), M. Neuberger (1917), and Chr. Bittner (1954) are all based on the source studies of Senfelder and do not include any additional details.

[3]Matthieu, Ernest, "Paul de Sorbait", *Biographie nationale de Belgique,* vol. 23, Bruxelles, 1921-4, 227-230.

[4]Paul de Sorbait, *Praxios medicae auctae et a plurimis typi mendis ab ipso auctore castigatae tract. I-VII,* Vienna, Leopoldus Voigt, 1680.

[5]*Acta facultatis medicae Vindobonensis,* V, 1605-1676, published by Leopold Senfelder, Vienna, 1910, 376.

[6]*Ibid.,* VI, 12.

[7]Joh. Constant. Feigius, *Adlerskrafft...,* Vienna, published by Joh. Jak. Kürner, 1685, 39 ff. Quoted by L. Senfelder (see note 2), *op. cit.,* 22.

[8]*Science, Medicine and History,* Oxford Univ. Press, 1953, vol. I. 489-509.

[9]Paul de Sorbait, *op. cit.* (quoted in note 1), *praefatio.*

[10]*Ibid.* (refer to note 4): Inventum medicina tuum est: Paracelse quid inquis,
Helluo quid loqueris Tune Monarcha? probrum es.
O vos fullones; vos estis pessima pestis,
Quisque manet vestrum trux homicida, Latro.

[11]Paul de Sorbait, *Universa medicina tam theorica quam practica...*, Nuremberg,
Sump. Michael et Jo. Frid. Endterorum, 1672. We quote the following according
to the *Nova et aucta Institutionum medicarum isagoge,* Vienna, Joannes Baptista
Hacque, 1678, or according to the *Praxios med.,* cited in note 4.

[12]*Isagoge,* 194, or *Praxios med.,* 447.

[13]*Theophrast von Hohenheim, gen. Paracelsus, Sämtliche Werke. I. Abt. Medizinische, naturwissenschaftliche und philosophische Schriften,* published by Karl
Sudhoff, vol. 9, Munich, 1925, 348.

[14]*Ibid.,* vol. 14, 518.

[15]*Isagoge,* 254, or *Praxios med.,* 447.

[16]Bravo (*op cit.,* 37 ff.) also does not wish to exclude the spagyric remedies
from the armamentarium of dogmatic medicine.

[17]Pagel, Walter, *Paracelsus. An Introduction to Philosophical Medicine in the Era
of the Renaissance,* Basel and New York, 1958, 146 ff.

[18]*Theophrast von Hohenheim,* vol. 9, 236, as quoted by W. Pagel, op. cit.,
146, note 54.

[19]*Isagoge,* 192, or *Praxios med.,* 446.

[20]Pagel (*op. cit.,* 330) assesses his attitude toward Paracelsus as fairly judicious.
Also see Pagel's chapter "Daniel Sennert's Critical Defence of Paracelsus", *ibid.,*
333-343.

[21]*Isagoge,* 51. On page 30 of the *Universa medicina* quoted in note 11, we find
only the beginning of this quotation. Furthermore, Bravo supported Harvey as
early as 1649. Compare J. J. Izquierdo, "On Spanish neglect of Harvey's De motu
cordis", *Journ. Hist. Med.,* 3 (1948), 105-124.

[22]Keynes, Sir Geoffrey, *The Life of William Harvey,* Oxford, 1966, 277.

[23]Pagel, W., and Poynter, F. N. L., "Harvey's Doctrine in Italy. Argoli (1644)
and Bonacorsi (1647) on the circulation of the blood", *Bull. Hist. Med.,* 34
(1960), 419-429. Menini, C., "Il moto circolare del sangue in un' opera astrologica padovano 1648", *Acta Med. Hist. Patavinae,* 4 (1957-8), 121-133. Also see
the tables in E. Weil, "The Echo of Harvey's De Motu Cordis (1628) 1628 to
1657", *Journ. Hist. Med.,* 12 (1957), 169, and Keynes (quoted in note 22),
*op. cit.,* 449 ff.

[24]Premuda, Loris, "Filosofia de circoli, Aristotelismo Padovano e Guglielmo Harvey", *Guglielmo Harvey—nel tricentenario della morte*, Rome, 1957. See Pagel and Poynter, *op. cit.*, 420, note 8.

[25]Browne, Edward, quoted by Neuburger, Max, *op. cit.*, 144 ff. (refer to note 1).

[26]*Acta fac. med. Vindob.*, V, 1663, 470 ff. Wolfstriegel was admitted to the Vienna Medical Faculty in 1663 (*ibid.*, V, 435).

[27]Hyrtl, Joseph, *Vergangenheit und Gagenwart des Museums für menschliche Anatomie an der Wiener Universität*, Vienna, 1869, XX.

[28]*Ibid. However,* Hyrtl does not state where this thesis was published.

# 21

# Galen, Van Helmont, and Blood Letting

## PETER H. NIEBYL

THE medical writings of J. B. van Helmont contain speculative and original ideas, but they also contain traditional knowledge. Venesection had been a pillar of therapeutics since antiquity, and Van Helmont's opposition to it was certainly one of the most revolutionary and controversial aspects of 17th century medicine.[1] Georgio Baglivi, a more conservative iatromechanist, had no hesitation in awarding Van Helmont the dishonorable priority.

> Many physicians of this age reckon bleeding, blistering, purging and other Galenick remedies, at once superfluous and pernicious. This puny thought was first launched by Helmont.[2]

Thomas Willis called those followers of Van Helmont who totally rejected blood-letting "fanatics."[3] Yet much of what Van Helmont had to say in this regard was traditional and Galenic.

According to Willis the "ridiculous" reason Van Helmont opposed venesection was its great injury to nature and her effort to overcome the offensive thing.[4] Indeed, Van Helmont had said:

> But it is not permitted him to hurt nature, who ought to heal and restore the same,...For by a sudden emptying out of the blood made by heaps, nature for the most part neglects the expulsion of her enemy;[5]

But Van Helmont went on to identify this view with the traditional "crisis" at which time blood-letting was not permitted.[6] Galen in commenting on a Hippocratic aphorism had said venesection should be used at the onset of the disease rather than during the time of crisis when the faculties are exhausted by their vigorous efforts.[7] Van Helmont generalized this contraindication to the whole course of the disease including the beginning. Thus to prostrate the faculties by repeated venesections was to "take away the hope of a crisis."[8] Van Helmont believed the crisis was due to an intelligent being rather than due to the traditional digestive process (concoction), but he did believe that venesection disturbed the crisis.[9]

13

Van Helmont was not the first to oppose the use of venesection. According to Galen Chrysippus the Cnidian opposed venesection and was followed by his student Erasistratus.[10] Galen quoted Erasistratus as having said that Chrysippus considered venesection dangerous because it impaired the strength of the patient.[11] Hippocratic authors had previously warned against bleeding weak patients for this reason.[12] Chrysippus apparently expanded this specific contraindication into a general rejection. In this respect Van Helmont was following in the footsteps of Chrysippus. Thus Van Helmont said of his contemporaries:

> they render the strength of a weak man weaker, and pull it back, as if they were willing to destroy him by repeated venesection.[13]

Apparently Van Helmont and Chrysippus considered most patients weaker than did other physicians. Van Helmont even accused these physicians of "murder."[14] But even this strong language was not unique. Galen noted that excessive blood-letting had been called "murder."[15]

Sprengel has suggested that Chrysippus opposed blood-letting because he was influenced by the Pythagorean belief that the soul was in the blood.[16] If true, it would be analogous to Van Helmont's Biblical argument against venesection. Van Helmont considered the vital strength of the patient and the blood to be "correlatives." As evidence he cited the Biblical statement that the Soul, or vital spirit, is in the blood.[17] Galen of course considered the heart to be the source of the innate heat and vital spirit, but this was distributed by the arterial system rather than the veins.[18] It is doubtful if Galen believed in a natural spirit distributed by the veins, and if he did, he did not consider it very important.[19] Galen considered the blood "useful to nature." On the other hand, it could also be "harmful to nature" and her strength by virtue of its quantity or quality.[20] Galen thus did not identify the blood itself with nature, and the vital strength of the patient. He could therefore justify venesection as aiding nature in a way that Van Helmont could not.

Van Helmont, on the other hand, concluded that venesection was "a pernicious wasting of the treasure of blood and strength."[21] Galen seems to have thought the heart attracted blood as a "treasure."[22] Avicenna had apparently interpreted Galen's contraindication of venesection during a crisis to mean that blood was to be considered a "treasure" during a febrile paroxysm.[23] Similarly, Henri de Mondeville had considered blood to be a "treasure" when there was a relative increase in one of the other humors.[24] This is consistent with Galen's tendency to use venesection for the excess of blood rather than for an excess of one humor.[25] Van Helmont considered blood in general to be a "treasure" *all* the time. He was thus generalizing from specific Galenic contraindications to venesection.

Aside from the previously mentioned speculation about Pythagorean influence, ancient opposition to venesection was based largely on quantitative considerations. A therapeutically effective amount of blood-letting was too close to a harmful amount of blood-letting.[26] The therapy was not wrong in principle, it was merely too dangerous. Galen himself acknowledged that more patients would perish when treated by venesection carried out by physicians with insufficient knowledge of how to use it than would perish in the hands of those physicians who do not use venesection.[27] It never occurred to Galen to carry out a clinical trial to prove this point, much less to put his own approach to such a test. Ancient thought was more concerned about the harmful side-effects of venesection that its lack of efficacy. Galen noted that those physicians who never employed venesection used other evacuative remedies to accomplish the same thing as venesection.[28] Erasistratus used starvation instead of vene-section, but the purpose was still to evacuate the excess blood.[29] Van Helmont, on the other hand, objected to the very idea that one could be harmed by too much good blood. Because he had more closely identified the blood with the vital strength itself, such a plethora would be a plethora of strength. He thus rejected the concept of plethora in principle as a disease.[30]

While Van Helmont may have rejected the concept of plethora, he did not quite reject the Galenic concept of bad humors. In his desire to turn Galenic doctrine against the Galenists Van Helmont was not always perfectly clear just how much he himself accepted. He apparently did accept the traditional idea that the blood was not uniform throughout the body but rather undergoes a gradual process of perfection from the crude, impure state in the first stages of digestion in the region of the stomach to the more pure blood around the heart.[31] Venesection would thus disperse the bad blood from its more localized source.

> For the more crude, and dreggish bloud is in the meseraick [mesenteric] veins: but the more refined bloud is that which hath the more nearly approached unto the court of the heart.[32]

Since the blood was generally withdrawn from the cubital fossa of the arm, Van Helmont said the good blood from the heart was removed leaving the bad behind.[33] Galen had specifically contraindicated venesection in the case of excess undigested humors for just these reasons. Said Galen, confident in his anatomical reasoning:

> For venesection removes the good blood, but disperses into the whole body the noxious element which is chiefly collected in the primary veins of the liver and mesentery.[34]

Van Helmont in effect generalized this specific contraindication to apply to *all* cases in which the Galenists use venesection. Said Van Helmont:

> Let them prove, that the good bloud being diminished, and the strength proportionally, that there is a greater power in the impure bloud that is left,...Let them likewise teach contrary to the sacred Text: that the Life and Soul are rather, and more willingly in the remaining defiled bloud, than in the more pure bloud which was taken away by the cutting of a vein. Otherwise regularly the drawing out of good bloud includes an increased proportion, and unbridled liberty of the bad bloud remaining.[35]

The Galenists probably would have denied the significance of this effect unless there be an excess of the crude humors.[36] One should note that Van Helmont's Biblical association of the blood with the soul and life itself exaggerated the differences between good and bad blood, thus paving the way for his sarcastic remarks.

Van Helmont noted that a state of bad humors (cacochymia) requires purgation rather than venesection since the former can selectively remove the bad humor while leaving the good.[37] This was Galen's dictum.[38] Yet Van Helmont went on to use this concept of bad humors to argue against venesection in general. Thus he stated that blood-letting cannot separate the good from the bad because it acts without the purpose and will characteristic of nature, whereas menstruation does.[39] Galen, on the other hand, had advocated venesection as an imitation of nature. But here Galen said nothing about separating good and bad blood. Menses evacuated plethora, not cacochymia.[40] Van Helmont thus slightly altered Galen's concept of nature so that venesection would no longer be an imitation of it. Both still believed that nature acted in a purposeful way.

A major indication for venesection had been pleurisy, and here Van Helmont made his opposition to it a special issue. He noted that blood-letting was generally used in pleurisy *as if* plethora were its cause.[41] As already mentioned Van Helmont rejected plethora but was less clear about his own views concerning cacochymia. He saw an internal contradiction in the position of the "Schools." The bad humor was supposedly derived from the habitus of the whole body but also from the source of the humors in the first stages of digestion.[42] As already mentioned, Van Helmont himself used the latter view to argue against venesection. In the case of pleurisy one can see Van Helmont use this same trend of thought in a modified version.

Van Helmont attributed pleurisy, and indeed all internally caused apostems, to an acid expelled from the stomach into the veins, and thence into the flesh. If the acid happens to enter the azygos vein, then pleurisy will result.[43] Although the acid was normal in the stomach, elsewhere in the body it was like an enemy and gave rise to apostems.[44] He acknowledged that venesection might have some temporary effect on the pleurisy, but he claimed that there would be a relapse since the root cause remained. Although he apparently felt that venesection would remove some of the acid indigestion in the veins, he did not think venesection would remove it from the apostem or its source in the stomach.[45] Van Helmont further noted that the evacuated veins would soon fill up again.[46] Since in Van Helmont's view the expulsive process and apostem formation were an active effort of the healing power of nature and depended on the material and vital strength of the blood, he thought venesection would relieve the symptoms by depriving nature of her blood and strength.[47] He called this merely a "palliative cure" because it failed to remove the causative acid.[48] By suppressing nature's reaction to the cause, the existence of the cause was masked. Van Helmont did not deny the traditional belief that venesection was effective against inflammation, he merely denied that it removed the cause. Thus he felt a relapse would occur. However, it should be kept in mind that according to Galen himself, when the cause is an excess of undigested humors rather than plethora, the treatment is a specific purgative rather than venesection although there are exceptions.

In his reaction against academic medicine and their use of venesection Van Helmont turned to the opposite extreme for his treatment of pleurisy. He glorified the common man and his folk medicine.

I have seen a country man curing all pleuritical persons at the third draught. For he used the dung of an horse for a man, and of a nag for a woman, which he dissolved in Ale, and gave the expressed strayning to drink. Such indeed is the ignorance of physicians, and so great the obstinacy of the Schooles; That God gives knowledge to rusticks, and little ones, which he denyes to those that are blown up with heathenish learning.[49]

Van Helmont's pro-rustic, pro-Bible, anti-plethora and anti-venesection views are features less in keeping with Galenic thought than some of his specific arguments. In these respects he stands in sharp contrast to William Harvey, who said:

> Now when I maintain that the living principle resides primarily and principally in the blood, I would not have it inferred from thence that I hold all bloodletting in discredit, as dangerous and injurious; or that I believe with the vulgar that in the same measure as blood is lost, is life abridged, because the sacred writings tell us that the life is in the blood.[50]

Harvey may well have been directly responding to Van Helmont. Van Helmont's views first appeared in 1642 while Harvey's appeared in 1651.[51] According to Robert Boyle, Harvey had tried some of Van Helmont's remedies.[52] Be that as it may, Harvey came out as a strong supporter of venesection, calling it "foremost among all the general remedial means." This was not an arbitrary decision but was based on a firm belief in the concept of plethora which he considered responsible for many diseases from headache to small pox.[53] With respect to venesection Harvey thus stood firm on those issues where Van Helmont showed the greatest deviation from traditional thought.

In one sense Van Helmont had taken specific Galenic contraindications to venesection and applied them to all cases. This was true for the time of crisis, the strength of the patient, the risk of iatrogenic murder, the existence of evil humors, and situations where blood is a "treasure." Yet Van Helmont's approach to venesection was more than a reorientation of Galenic thought. It also differed in a larger, almost methodological sense. Galen's approach was quantitative in that his analytical categories all varied dimensionally as a continuous function. The magnitude of plethora and the magnitude of strength determined the magnitude of blood to be let. The magnitudes of disease and strength were determined by the magnitude of the signs and symptoms.[54] In fact Galen was sufficiently reductionist in his thinking to maintain that when the magnitudes of the disease and strength are large enough, then venesection would be indicated even if the excess humor be undigested.[55] In other words, in the last analysis the qualitative distinction between plethora and cacochymia is not as decisive as the sheer magnitude of the disease. For Galen all the harmful results from the use of venesection were merely "errors of measurement."[56] The difficulty with this approach was that the variables, disease and strength, were inferential. Any attempt by the

physician to translate clinical observations into these inferential quantities made medicine appear more as an art than a science. Thus it is not
surprising to find great variation among physicians in the amount of
blood-letting. Errors of measurement were inherent in their approach.

Van Helmont's concept of a cause was just as inferential as Galen's
and indeed bore some resemblance to Galen's undigested humor. But
Van Helmont did not assume a direct relationship between the symptoms
and the cause. Indeed removal of the symptoms with venesection "masked"
the persistence of the cause—"palliative therapy" as it was called by Van
Helmont and is still called today. This type of reasoning was based on
discontinuous variables rather than the Galenic continuous variables.
Either the cause was present, or it was not present. Blood was good or it
was bad. Venesection was beneficial or it was harmful. Van Helmont
wanted yes-no type answers rather than quantitative qualification, such
as a little more of this and a little less of that. Van Helmont's type of
reasoning demands enumeration rather than dimensional mensuration.[57]
It may have been responsible for what is perhaps the most original
aspect of his attack on venesection. To my knowledge Van Helmont was
the first to suggest a prospective clinical trial in which the two groups of
patients to be compared were to be randomly selected from the same
population. Said Van Helmont:

> Let us take out of the hospitals, out of the camps, or from elsewhere, 200,
> or 500 poor people, that have fevers, pleurisies, etc. Let us divide them
> into halfes, let us cast lots, that one halfe of them may fall to my share,
> and the other to yours: I will cure them without blood-letting and sen-
> sible evacuation; but do you do, as ye know (for neither do I tye you
> to the boasting, or of phlebotomy, or the abstinence from solutive
> medicine) we shall se how many funerals both us shall have.[58]

Van Helmont wanted this clinical trial to be done for the "public good"
in order to show which of the two methods was correct. Since one group
received no blood-letting while the other group received it only when the
Galenic physician considered it appropriate, the Galenic physician could
not claim afterwards that the deaths were due to the use of blood-letting
when it was not indicated, or that too much or too little blood-letting had
been used in this or that case. Van Helmont's "new math" numerical
method had many virtues. It counted discrete observables, namely patients,
and funerals. The possibility that one group might by chance receive a
larger number of severely ill patients would be largely eliminated by the

large number of patients. The random division insured that other factors would not interfere with the comparability of the two groups. Unfortunately Van Helmont and his readers do not seem to have generally exploited this method. Nevertheless, it probably did reflect a new way of thinking.

Perhaps Van Helmont's first suggestions of a numerical method did not go wholly unnoticed. One of the more moderate 17th century French Helmontians, Abraham Bauda, wrote a tract against the abuse of bloodletting in which he used statistical data.[59] Bauda did a retrospective clinical study of the case histories in the Hippocratic *Epidemics*. He found 42 cases of acute disease, the type of disease for which blood-letting was generally recommended. Of these 42 cases of acute disease Bauda found that Hippocrates mentioned the use of venesection only once, and that only on the 8th day of the illness.[60] Thus he concluded that Hippocrates himself rarely used blood-letting. It is also interesting that Bauda was very apologetic in his attitude towards Galen's use of blood-letting. He stressed that Galen did not always use blood-letting and when he did he always carefully weighed all the various factors involved.[61] Both the Helmontians and Van Helmont himself show that Galen's influence was not limited to Galenists. But the ability to draw new conclusions from old data shows that they were using ancient thought rather than passively accepting it.

## References

[1]For a concise discussion of Galenic venesection see the introduction in *Andreas Vesalius Bruxellensis: The Bloodletting Letter of 1539*, introd. & tr. J. B. deC. M. Saunders and C. D. O'Malley, New York, 1947. For a general history of bloodletting see Bauer, Joseph, *Geschichte der Aderlässe*, München, 1870 [reprinted by W. Fritsch, 1966]. An unpublished English translation of Galen's *De venae sectione adversus Erasistratus, De venae sectione adversus Erasistrateos Romae degentes*, and *De curandi ratione per sanguinis missionem* by R. M. Green is in the Historical Library, Yale University School of Medicine. For a general assessment of Van Helmont's thought see Pagel, Walter, *J. B. van Helmont*, Berlin, 1930.

[2]Baglivi, Georgio, *The Practice of Physic*, 2nd Engl. ed., London, 1723, 23.

[3]Willis, Thomas, *Practice of Physick, being the whole Works*, London, 1684, 2nd pt., Sect. III, ch. 1, 131.

[4]*loc. cit.*

[5]Van Helmont, J. B., *De feb.*, 23 #33, in *Opuscula medica inaudita*, Amsterdam, 1648; *Oriatrike or, Physick Refined*, tr. J. C., London, 1662, 954.

⁶*Ibid.*, #35.

⁷Galen, *In Hippocratis aphorismos commentarius,* in *Opera Omnia,* ed. Kühn, 20 vols., Leipzig, 1825, XVII, ii, 522-524.

⁸Van Helmont, *De feb.,* 24 #38; *Oriatrike,* 955.

⁹Van Helmont, *De feb.,* 29 #25-26; *Oriatrike,* 961.

¹⁰Galen, *Adv. Erasist.,* ed. Kühn, XI, 151-2, 197.

¹¹Galen, *op. cit.,* XI, 175-176.

¹²*Oeuvres Complètes D'Hippocrate,* ed. & tr. E. Littré, 10 vols., Paris, 1846, II, 399; VII, 113, 131.

¹³Van Helmont, J. B., *Pleura furens in Ortus medicinae,* Amsterdam, 1648, 396 #31; *Oriatrike,* 398.

¹⁴Van Helmont, *De feb.,* 23 #35; *Oriatrike,* 954.

¹⁵Galen, *op. cit.,* XI, 151.

¹⁶Sprengel, Kurt, *Versuch einer pragmatischen Geschichte der Arzneikunde,* 5 vols., Halle, 1793-1803, I, 473.

¹⁷Van Helmont, *De feb.,* 19 #5-7; *Oriatrike,* 950.

¹⁸Galen, *De methodo medendi,* ed. Kühn, X, 635-636.

¹⁹Temkin, O., "On Galen's Pneumatology," *Gesnerus,* VIII (1951), 180-189.

²⁰Galen, *De meth. med.,* X, 640.

²¹Van Helmont, *De feb.,* 25 #44; *Oriatrike,* 957.

²²Matthew Curtius in his *Lectures on Anatomia Mundini* (c. 1536) stated that Galen said the heart does not permit the blood as a treasure to flow from it, in *Andreas Vesalius' First Public Anatomy at Bologna 1540 An Eyewitness report by Baldasar Heseler,* ed. & tr. Ruben Eriksson, 1959, 265.

²³Avicenna, *Liber canonis,* Venice, 1507 [reprinted G. Olms, 1964], fol. 74 r.

²⁴de Mondeville, Henri, *Chirurgie* (1306-1320), tr. & ed. E. Nicaise, Paris, 1893, 534-535; *Die Chirurgie des Heinrich von Mondeville nach Berliner, Erfurter und Pariser Codices,* ed. Julius Pagel, Berlin, 1892, 367.

²⁵Galen, *De meth. med.,* X, 891-892. However it should be noted that here Galen considers the blood to be an equal blend of all the humors rather than one of the four.

²⁶Galen, *Adv. Erasist.,* XI, 151-152.

²⁷*Ibid.*, 223.

²⁸*Loc. cit.*

²⁹Galen, *Adv. Erasist.,* XI, 157.

³⁰Van Helmont, *De feb.,* 19 #4-7; *Oriatrike,* 950.

[31]Van Helmont, *De feb.*, 12 #31; *Oriatrike*, 942-943.

[32]Van Helmont, *De feb.*, 25 #43; *Oriatrike*, 956.

[33]*Van Helmont, De feb.*, 19 #19; *Oriatrike*, 950.

[34]Galen's *Hygiene*, tr. R. M. Green, Springfield, 1951, 160; *De sanitate tuenda*, ed. Kühn, VI, 263. Here Galen made no mention of the attractive power of the heart to retain the good blood. See above ftn. 22.

[35]Van Helmont, *De feb.*, 23-24 #37; *Oriatrike*, 955.

[36]Galen says that when the excess humor is largely blood, venesection should be used, but with increasing caution as the proportion of faulty humor rises, so that it should not be used at all if the proportion of faulty humor is great. See Galen's *Hygiene*, 156; ed. Kühn, VI, 256.

[37]Van Helmont, *De feb.*, 19 #7; *Oriatrike*, 950.

[38]Galen, *De meth. med.*, X, 891-892; see also Galen's *Hygiene*, 272; *De sanitate tuenda*, VI, 443.

[39]Van Helmont, *De feb.*, 24 #39; *Oriatrike*, 956.

[40]Galen, *Adv. Erasist.*, XI, 158, 164, 165, 167.

[41]Van Helmont, *Pleura furens*, in *Ortus*, 395 #28; *Oriatrike*, 398.

[42]Van Helmont, *De feb.*, 14 #6; *Oriatrike*, 945.

[43]Van Helmont, *Pleura furens*, in *Ortus*, 393 #13-14; 394 #22-24; *Oriatrike*, 395, 397.

[44]Van Helmont, *A sede anima ad morbos*, in *Ortus*, 294-295 #4-5; *Oriatrike*, 290.

[45]Van Helmont, *Pleura furens*, 393-395 #16, 20-24, 29; *Oriatrike*, 396-398.

[46]Van Helmont, *Pleura furens*, 391 #7; *Oriatrike*, 394.

[47]Van Helmont, *Pleura furens*, 391-2 #8-9; *Oriatrike*, 394.

[48]Van Helmont, *Pleura furens*, 395-6 #30; *Oriatrike*, 398.

[49]Van Helmont, *De feb.*, 25 #42; *Oriatrike*, 956.

[50]Harvey, William, *Works*, tr. Robert Willis, London, 1847, 391.

[51]Van Helmont, J. B., *Febrium doctrina inaudita*, Antverp, 1642, cap. IV.

[52]Keynes, Sir Geoffrey, *The Life of William Harvey*, Oxford, 1966. Pagel, Walter, "Harvey and the 'Modern' Concept of Disease," B.H.M., XLII (1968), 506.

[53]Harvey, *Works*, 391.

[54]Galen, *Adv. Erasist.*, XI, 217; *De curand. rat.*, ed. Kühn, XI, 268.

[55]Galen, *Adv. Erasist.*, XI, 289-290.

[56]Ibid., XI, 174.

[57]On the importance of enumeration as opposed to dimensional mensuration in modern medicine see, Feinstein, Alvan R., *Clinical Judgment*, Baltimore, 1967, 61 ff.

[58]Van Helmont, *Ortus*, 526-527; *Oriatrike*, 526. [Professor Debus has kindly called my attention to: Debus, Allen G., *The Chemical Dream of the Renaissance*, *Cambridge*, 1968, 27].

[59]Bauda, Abraham, (1613-1680), *Discours Curieux contre l'Abus des Saignées*, Sedan, c. 1672. Bauda also wrote a *Helmontian Chirurgie*. I have discussed Bauda and other Helmontians in relation to blood-letting in my doctoral dissertation: Venesection and the Concept of the Foreign Body (Yale University, 1969).

[60]Bauda, *Discours*, 10-11.

[61]*Ibid.*, 46-53.

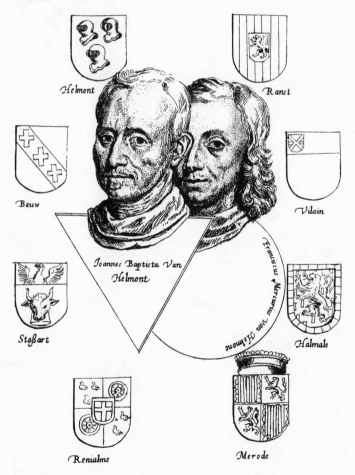

# 22

# The Circulation of the Blood
# and Chemical Anatomy

## AUDREY B. DAVIS

ANATOMY and chemistry shared the brunt of medical censorship and criticism as less than essential studies contributing to medical knowledge at the beginning of the seventeenth century. However, physicians defended the study of anatomy and chemistry increasingly throughout the century. Some, who defended the application of these disciplines to medicine, chose to stress the similarities between anatomy and chemistry in their application to medicine. They placed emphasis on the identification of structural components of the body and its fluids, that is the organs and the chemical elements, thereby finding a link between these two forms of investigation, principally on a methodological basis.[1] Anatomists and chemists, who emphasized the methodological affinity between anatomy and chemistry at this time, made some of their most explicit statements in a physiological connection stemming from the circulation of the blood theory.

Among those who combined anatomy and chemistry in their physiological explanations were physicians, who set as their primary goals the solution of problems like the role of the blood in disease and the nature and cure of blood diseases, the most common of which they termed fevers. Thomas Willis,[2] the celebrated English anatomist and medical chemist, who tried to find the consequences of the circulation for explanations of these diseases, described a host of physiological and pathological doctrines based on chemistry and anatomy. Underlying these doctrines are his methods, which reduce to several forms of anatomy. These are the anatomy of the gross structures of the body and the anatomy or analysis of the chemical components within the body fluids.[3] In the period between 1660 and 1700, theories promoting the integration and application of these two forms of anatomy received extensive recognition among physicians. Here, our remarks will be con-

25

fined to the adoption of the concept of chemical anatomy as it was related to the composition of the blood at mid-century in England.

Anatomy in the sense of looking at the body section by section, organ by organ, tissue by tissue, began in antiquity. It is one of the pervading doctrines of medical science, according to the medical historian E. Bouchut, who stated that anatomy is a "...doctrine which has rendered the greatest service to medical science and which has helped to remove the chaos of unuseful abstraction..." that began with the anatomical studies of Erasistratus and Herophilus.[4] In providing a means to correct ancient errors, in revealing hitherto unknown structures or confirming and suggesting theories of physiological functions, anatomy rose to a new level of significance in the seventeenth century, due, in part, to its association with chemistry.

With much less of a distinguished heritage of application to medicine, the role of chemistry in medicine also reached a higher level of sophistication in the seventeenth century. This development occurred within two categories: chemical therapy and the chemical theory of disease. Masked by the clamor of issues over the use of drugs, whether chemicals like antimony and mercury or derived from other sources like weapon salve and cinchona, some theoretical aspects of chemistry for medicine received less notice, but were nevertheless important. Among chemical theories that emerged in the mid-century was the anatomy of chemical elements, which had been delineated by Paracelsus by the terms *anatomia elementata* and *anatomia essata*. By these terms Paracelsus meant the anatomy or analysis of substances into their chemical components; *anatomia elementata* revealing the elements or principles in the world and *anatomia essata* revealing the minerals and metals in the body.[5] Paracelsus distinguished the search for the elemental similarities between organic and inorganic substances from the usual anatomical studies of the body, and stressed the supreme value of the former investigations. Employing the *anatomia elementata* and *anatomia essata* concepts, Paracelsus envisaged that the physician would be a keen student of both the animate and the inanimate. The physician's success would be measured by his ability to discover the causes of disease. Metal and mineral mines were to be explored for the clues they could disclose to understand the "mine" within the living body. This Paracelsian doctrine was formulated on his belief that the chemical elements or principles common to all substances were mercury, sulphur and salt. Presumed to be the substrata of both organic and inorganic matter, these principles were also assumed to have a major role in the etiology of disease.[6] Generally, the macrocosmic world was reflected in the microcosmic being of man, and upon inspection the macrocosm could be expected to yield yet undetected properties and causes of disease, obscured by their occurrence within the innermost regions of the body.

Of the vicissitudes of the *anatomia elementata* concept in the seventeenth century, when applied to the composition of the blood it provided a description of this fluid, which had since antiquity been described as containing the humors, black bile, yellow bile, phlegm and blood itself. The origin, collection and transfer of these humors among the organs came to be seen as the result of exceptional circumstances when the continuous and circular motion of the blood was disclosed. Willis explained that blood was not generally stored up in any one part, although it was susceptible to change when it was retained, and, depending on its location and characteristics, took on the properties of one of the humors.[7] It appeared more reasonable to believe that the blood contained subdivisions of its own, which circulated with it as a unity, and whose individual parts manifested their presence under abnormal conditions.

The idea of distinguishing elements or principles within the blood was traced in the seventeenth century to Paracelsus, and was a source of criticism of his doctrine by chemists including Daniel Sennert[8] and van Helmont. Paracelsus associated disease with the deposition of the elements mercury, sulphur and salt in various parts of the body. In particular, Paracelsus had commented upon the circulation of the element salt within the body. He explained his "discovery" of the third principle salt as a product obtained upon distillation or circulation of sea water in a pelican, and then argued for the similarity between sea water and blood. After disapproving of the Paracelsian endeavor to associate disease with mercury, sulphur and salt, especially when Paracelsus insisted that salt circulated in the body, van Helmont wondered why Paracelsus, the childish dreamer, although respected chemist, had not realized that the blood does not circulate.[9] Van Helmont's rejection of the blood's circulation, though intended primarily in a chemical sense, and his refusal to link the phenomenon with the movement of salt within the body, provides one clue in trying to understand how the new physiological vista opened up by Harvey's discovery of the blood's circulation included re-emphasis of the Paracelsian principles and the anatomy of the fluids from which these principles were extracted.

The English remarked upon this Paracelsian theory of chemical anatomy, and its relation to the cause of disease, intermittently from the sixteenth century,[10] but in the seventeenth century the discovery of the blood's circulation revived interest in the doctrine.[11] At this time some inadequacies noted in Paracelsus' chemical analogies were ascribed to his ignorance of the circulation. Henry Power (1623 or '26-1668) remarked: "Had Paracelsus known this mystery, (the circulation of the blood) hee might farre better have made out his Analogical philosophy and his Crocosmicall Conceits, then by those lank and farre fetch'd parallelisms which hee Sometimes uses." Power, who studied medicine at Cambridge, became interested in the circulation physiology, prompted by the medical professor Francis Glisson's advocacy of anatomy and physiology in keeping with the circulation doctrine. Power's own explanations of human physiology were expressed in terms of the chemical philosophy and Renaissance medical thought.[12] He described the internal functions of the body such as digestion and blood formation as chemical alterations. He adopted the materialistic spirits and the Paracelsian chemical elements. Thus in two forms (by the singular material spirits and their cumulative interaction resulting in chemical change) Power adapted chemical explanations to human physiology. Although the evidence is inconclusive, it appears that Francis Glisson's adoption of the chemical elements was encouraged by Power's adherence to this type of chemical philosophy.[13]

Pervasive and pivotal to successive chemical theories of the blood were those ideas of Glisson that were recorded in his monograph, *Anatomia hepatis* (Anatomy of the liver), which originally comprised the Gulston Anatomy lectures delivered to the Royal College of Physicians in 1641, but not published until 1654. A manuscript of other anatomy lectures which he gave after the publication of *de hepatis* indicates Glisson's separation of the practical nature of anatomy from its more speculative aspects. Glisson felt that the chemical elements were among the more "abstract and other curious and generall divisions of this art," [which] rather belongs to such as speculate about it, or to such as are in a way of preparation to it; then to such; as are actually in the practice or exercise of the same",[14] that is, anatomy. At the time he published his anatomy of the liver, and after having been in contact with Power, who was extremely interested in his studies related to the circulation, Glisson had visualized a much wider scope for anatomy, one which the anatomist should pursue as Glisson himself was to do. In a prolegomenous chapter to *de hepatis* he outlined the studies with which an anatomist should be involved. Anatomy provides a comprehensive knowledge of the human frame through an exploration of the body, by dissection in conjunction with special techniques such as injection, ligaturing or chemical analysis. The structures, their proportions and defects, the elements, and even the elusive and intangible sympathies, antipathies and faculties were all to be uncovered by the methods of anatomy.[15] The remainder of his book is a testimony to this enlarged study of anatomy applied to the liver and its relationship with other organs and fluids, particularly the blood. By including the chemical analysis of the blood within the study to be undertaken by the anatomist, Glisson extended the discipline that Harvey had raised to a new significance with his investigation of the structures that contained and pumped the blood throughout the body. Harvey's own recognition of the greater importance of the blood in his last publication, *De Generatione,* provided support for those interested in further analysis of the blood. The anatomy or analysis of the blood revealed to Glisson that it contained the five principles spirit, sulphur, salt, earth and water, in addition to the other more obvious components, which were extruded from the blood that had been removed from the body. Why did Glisson believe these elements existed in the blood?

Moderate and conciliatory in his chemical philosophy, overcoming Aristotle's tendentious belief in the reality of the four elements, Glisson sought an equivalence between the ancient elements and the spagyrical principles. Glisson's unoriginal concept of the chemical elements in the blood was dictated by practicality. By conceding that the fourth classic element was a combination of salt and earth (caput mortum), Glisson obtained the spagyrical principle salt as a by-product of the Aristotelian element earth, and thereby ended up with five elements. Glisson explained:

And so, it seems to me possible to reconcile the Aristotelian elements and the principles of the chemists and to lead them back into mutual esteem, so indeed the Aristotelian element fire (ignis) proportionately corresponds to spirit, air to oil (oleum), water to phlegm and earth to both salt and caput mortuum. Indeed the Aristotelians have not been accustomed to separate after things have burned and left ashes in order to elucidate their elements.[16]

Both combination and separation of the various chemical elements had previously been proposed by physicians, including the celebrated medical chemist Daniel Sennert, Quercetanus and Angelo Sala, all of whom tried to reconcile the existence of the Peripatetic elements with the Paracelsian principles. Reconciling the ancient and Paracelsian principles was in order, since Paracelsian doctrine presented no clear evaluation and distinction between these element systems.[17] However, by the 1650's the corpuscular theories of matter, especially the Cartesian system, added another dimension to explanations, which some Paracelsian chemists and medical chemists incorporated into their theories. Thomas Willis brought the chemical and corpuscular theories to bear on circulatory diseases, thus setting a pattern for formulating medical theories that became known as iatromechanism. Willis was a member of a group dedicated to defending Harvey's doctrine and explaining its importance in relation to the problem of disease. His first contribution consisted of his treatises on fermentation and fever, published in 1659. He began by abandoning the Humoral Doctrine, which Harvey had not found necessary. Willis delineated three doctrines of matter—the Epicurean, Peripatetic and chemical.[18] His evaluation of these three theories of matter lay in determining the one preferred for describing the blood's composition. Unlike Glisson, he excluded the four elements because they were too general and therefore impractical for describing the constitution of fluids. Comparing the four elements to the stone and wood of a house, he illustrated the inexplicitness of using these elements to describe the components of a fluid. He then considered, but, unlike other English philosophers with whom he was closely associated, held in abeyance, the atomic philosophies,[19] although his scepticism of atomism was to be modified even further in his final publications.

Anatomists seeking the substructure of the blood had the opportunity of accepting one of several forms of atomism or corpuscularianism, all of which had been proposed in antiquity. Discussed by a growing number of natural philosophers in English and French circles,[20] these atomic philosophies seemed to afford less conspicuous, yet more specific, descriptions of the behavior of fluids. A theory of generation illustrates the value of atomic explanations apparent to seventeenth century investigators. Generation was one physiological function that a physician, who took issue with Kenelm Digby's description of the process, found explicable in terms of atoms. Nathanial Highmore, cousin to William Petty, who received his medical education at Oxford about the time of

Willis, decided that generation could best be explained by a large number of atoms, rather than by chemical elements circulating within the
blood. "Our chemists assure us," he reasoned,

> that in the dissolution of all mixt bodies they find other Elements besides
> those four, we received from the Ancients. And Perhaps could their
> separations and putrefactions be as accurate to distinguish, as Nature
> is in the mixing wee might find many more, from whence these strange
> effects in several Bodies should arise.[21]

Highmore, who could not offer a method to settle the question of how
the number of the elements was to be resolved, resorted to a variety of
atoms as depicted by Cartesian theory to describe the composition and
function of the generative fluid. Gassendi also explained generation in
atomistic terms at this time.

However, other physicians refrained from adopting fully atomic
theories, for like Francis Bacon they found the atomic theories useless for
practical ends. Bacon had complained that even if the atomic doctrines
were true, they had sterile consequences for medicine.[22] Willis, one of
these physicians, hinted that the atomic philosophy might serve as a foundation for the chemical explanations he was about to propose, but, not
completely satisfied, and not willing to relinquish his emphasis on observation in order to promote a theory of matter, Willis suggested that
the atomic hypothesis be examined by others more qualified to speculate
on its veracity.

Willis employed the doctrine of the five chemical elements to
describe the blood. In part influenced by his personal experiences with
chemistry as a member of the Oxford "Clubbe", he concluded as Glisson
had, although for different reasons, that the blood was composed of
spirit, sulphur, salt, water and earth. By the principles Willis meant:
"...not simple and wholly uncompounded Entities, but such kind of
Substances only, into which Physical things are resolved, as it were into
parts, lastly sensible...In the meantime, what Particles are gathered
together in the Subjects, or depart away from them, will appear under
the form of Spirit, Sulphur, Salt, or one of the rest."[23] These principles
were observable by those who distilled blood according to the usual
procedures of the chemist.

These principles in constant motion, labelled an intestine or internal
motion, produced fermentation of the blood. Willis brought the notion
of the blood as a fluid with chemical properties within the compass of

corpuscularianism by emphasizing the intestine motion of these chemical principles. In abetting the traditional effort to associate physiological functions with chemical processes like fermentation, which he redefined, he extended corpuscularianism to the theory of blood flow. Fermentation of wine had long been used as an analogy to describe the various phases of digestion or concoction and blood formation or sanguification. In the Paracelso-Helmontian doctrines, the chemical nature of fermentation was ascribed to the effect of ferments and the reaction between acids and alkalis. Willis, in reassessing the chemical explanation of fermentation, concluded that is was due to chemical elements, especially spirit, rising and opposing sulphur and salt, thereby creating the tumult of fermentation. Fermentation therefore came to be regarded as a motion complementary to the circulation of the blood and became the index for delineating diseases of the blood. For it was blood in excessive or preternatural fermentation that produced fever. Thus, Willis provided a rational explanation for the blood's susceptibility to disease, which was derived from the leading contemporary philosophies of matter.[24]

Willis' description of fermenting blood combined aspects of the Baconian, Cartesian and chemical philosophies and made explicit the methodology common to anatomy and chemistry. By his assumption that a particulate explanation, as prescribed by Cartesian philosophy, might be proven satisfactory, but by holding corpuscularian ideas in reserve, and therefore not violating the tenets of Bacon's chemical philosophy, Willis proposed that the fermentation of the blood rested on the interaction between the chemical principles. The principles were the chemists' anatomical units, and appeared to meet the limitation set by Bacon for the investigation of those processes which included concoction and fermentation. Bacon was dissatisfied with the terms used to describe physiological and chemical changes, since, to him, they merely reflected nominalism. Bacon encouraged research into the "anatomy" of concoction and fermentation, particularly as these processes occurred in the body fluids, part of his general program for "dissecting and anatomizing the world". Classified as a "species of anatomy", distinct from the usual anatomy of the organs, Bacon referred to this greater scrutiny into the "nature" of fluids including blood as "the real anatomy of latent conformation in bodies..."[25] To him it appeared that all substances were composed of invisible material spirits and visible parts of matter, that were continually interacting.[26] Specific elements, whose characteristics were revealed upon their segregation, provided the basis for understanding the behavior as well as the composition of blood and other internal fluids.

One of the important reasons for trying to define the composition of the blood also developed out of a reassessment of its role in the treatment of disease. In addition to fermentation, which described the blood in the throes of fever, the general transporting function of the blood required some re-evaluations of the mechanisms of drug behavior. Chemical anatomy was seen to have a bearing on explanations of the effect of medicinals. A series of pamphlets on the benefits to be gained from using mineral water medicinally display the reasoning employed by an advocate of chemical anatomy. The English physicians George Tonstall and Robert Witty wrote mutually retaliatory tracts, in which Tonstall defended the use of water supplied by a Scarborough spring for treatment of disease and Wittie opposed it. Tonstall, in 1670, lauded the many recent "improvements of knowledge" discovered through anatomy, and wondered "why must the usefulness of this nobel Art be confined to the Animal Kingdom only? For the grounds of Anatomy in the vegetable and mineral Kingdoms...neerly conduces to the discovery of the Nature, Cause and Cure of diseases."[27] The Scarborough spring was found to contain both medicinally active and inert constituents which were revealed by "spagyrick anatomy". Spagyrick anatomy was accomplished by distilling the water and collecting the components as they separated from the fluid. Tonstall's recognition of the medicinal properties of mineral water was associated with the elements he extracted from the water. However, he encouraged further analysis of these waters,[28] for he was not convinced of the thoroughness of the chemical extraction which revealed so few elements.

The physician in the pursuit of his profession persisted in searching for the chemical elements or principles within the fluids. Anatomists continued to be involved in this investigation. James Drake, controversial politician and physician, wrote in a posthumous anatomical text published in 1707:

> That the Resolution of Bodies into their Visible Elements or the most Simple Parts...is of great use to Physicians is past Controversy as well from the constant use which Physicians both in their Theory and Practice make of such Bodies, as from the necessity they have of Recourse to such things as they can upon occasion produce and apply with some knowledge of their operations and effects. They have such constant and

regular effects, and are the ultimate results of the minutest Analysis we have been hitherto able to make...[29]

## Conclusion:

Chemical analysis of the elements had become by the end of the seventeenth century an integral part of anatomy, especially because of the value of chemically based explanations to doctrines of physiology. To assign functions to the body fluids then known, it appeared that a small number of elements was needed; identification of the chemical elements and their properties helped physicians elucidate the mechanisms of the vital functions. The internal fluids appeared to have only a few uses, thereby encouraging the belief that they contained relatively few elements, each possessing unique properties. This practical and physiologically-inspired use of chemistry permitted the physician to dwell on the fact that there existed only a few chemical elements, which were released under the conditions provided by human physiology.

## References

[1]Emile Callot described anatomy as a science of organization which is at the same time analytic and synthetic, i.e. analytic in separating the constituent parts of the organism and synthetic in considering the liasons between these parts. See Callot, E., *La Renaissance des Science de la vie au XVI siècle*, Paris, 1951, 104. Here we will consider the analytic phase of anatomy.

[2]See Isler, Hansruedi, *Thomas Willis, 1621-1675, Doctor and Scientist*, Stuttgart, 1965 (German) and New York, 1968. Translation into English by the author.

[3]William Petty, in an anatomy lecture given before the Dublin society in 1676, expressed the twofold aspect of anatomy. In addition to studies of the muscles, bones, and visceral organs he commented that "Wee might add unto the parts last mentioned others, which I rather call analysis than anatomy: The first whereof is the Description of the matter of bones, teeth (parts whereof are rather stones than bones), cartilages, the Tubes of vessels, the severall parenchymas, fatt, marrow, Blood, milk, sperma, urine, gall, spittle, tears, sweat, earwax, snott, etc." This is taken from an unfinished manuscript which was first published in 1927. See *The Petty Papers: some unpublished writings of Sir William Petty*, ed. from the Bowood papers by the Marquis of Lansdown II, London, 1927, 177. Two papers by Allen Debus are important in understanding 17th century chemical analysis. They are: "Solution Analysis Prior to Robert Boyle," *Chymia*, VIII (1962), 41-62, and "Fire Analysis and the Elements in the 16th and 17th Centuries", *Annals of Science, XXIII* (1967), 127-145.

[4]Bouchut, E., *Histoire de la Médecine et des Doctrines Médicales*, Paris, 1873, I, 5.

[5]Pagel, Walter, *Paracelsus: An Introduction to Philosophical Medicine in the Era of the Renaissance*, Basle and New York, 1958, 133-140. See also an article by Pagel, which he wrote with Pyarali Rattansi, for the other meanings which Paracelsus attached to the term anatomy: "Vesalius and Paracelsus", *Medical History, VIII* (1964), 309-328.

[6]Pagel, *Paracelsus*, 133-135.

[7]"For in truth the Blood is an only humor not one thing about the Viscera, and another in the habit of the Body. The watry humor, fixed in the Bowels, or solid parts, is it which is called Phlegm; some Reliques of adust Salt and Sulphur, being separated in the Liver, and received by the Choleduct Vessels are called choler; the Earthy feculencies being laid up in the spleen, are termed Melancholy. In the meantime, the Blood, if rightly purified ought to want Choler, Phlegm and Melancholy."

Willis, Thomas, "Of Fevers", *Dr. Willis' Practice of Physick being the Whole Works*...trans., S. Pordage, London, 1684, 48. In the *Opera Medica et Physica*, Leyden, 1676, this appears on pp. 64-5. "Of Fevers" was first published with "Of Fermentation" and "Of Urines" in Latin in 1659.

[8]Multhauf, Robert, *The Origins of Chemistry*, London, 1966, 236.

[9]"The Three Principles of the Chymists, nor the essences of the same are of the Army of Disease". van Helmont, Joannes B., *Oriatrike*, trans. J[ohn] C[handler], London, 1662, 404-5.

[10]For example, the earliest known comment was made by Bostocke in 1585: "That by the knowledge of the three substances...Sal, Sulphur and Mercury and by their several properties, vertues, and natures, by palpable and visible experience... The right Anatomie" of each disease could be known. Debus, Allen, *The English Paracelsians*, London, 1965, 60-61.

[11]Robert Fludd, whose relationship to Harvey and the discovery of the circulation has been noted by Allen Debus in his article "Robert Fludd and the circulation of the Blood", *J. Hist. Med., XVI* (1961), 374-393, had proposed a mystical anatomy of the blood in 1623. He described blood as a single humor formed from the concoction of air and claimed that blood "is divided into elements in the common way", [which] explain mysteries in medicine from those of the same. See Fludd, *Anatomiae Amphitheatrum effigie triplici more et conditione varia*, Frankfurt, 1623, 219, 227.

[12]Cole, F. J., "Henry Power on the circulation of the blood", *J. Hist. Med., XII* (1957), 324.

This appears in Power's manuscript entitled "Circulatio Sanguinis Inventio Harveiana", dated 1652.

[13]For an assessment of Power's philosophical beliefs and their sources see Webster, Charles, "Henry Power's Experimental Philosophy", *Ambix XIV* (Oct. 1967). 150-178.

[14]*Ibid.*, 173, 174. Webster believes that Glisson contributed to Power's acceptance of the materialistic spirits, and indeed, this may have been the case, but this

statement in the manuscript of another of Glisson's anatomical lectures appears to indicate a certain reluctance on Glisson's part to be concerned with the elements or spirits. The manuscript of Glisson is preserved in the British Museum and is number 3306 of the Sloane collection, entitled "Medical Collections" II, f.2.

[15]Glissen, Francis, *Anatomia Hepatis,* 2nd ed., Amsterdam, 1659, 6. "Anatomia est ars, quae per artificiales dissectiones, commensurationes, ponderationes, inflatus, injectiones per siphonem, ligaturas, aliasque utiles operationes, corporis humani singularumque ejus partium structuram, proportiones, complementa, desectus, elementa, communitates, differentias, sympathias, antipathias, facaltates, actiones, atque usus luculenter explicat; quantum saltem ingenio humano assequi conceditur."

[16]*Ibid.,* 39.

[17]Debus, "Fire Analysis." Debus remarks on Quercetanus, Sennert and Sala and others who questioned the number and form of the chemical elements revealed through heating or distillation. Robert Boyle's treatise, the *Sceptical Chymist* appears to have marshalled contemporary opinions.

[18]Willis, "Of Fermentation", 2.

[19]*Loc. cit.*

[20]Kargon, Robert, *Atomism in England from Hariot to Newton,* Oxford, 1966.

[21]Highmore, Nathanial, *History of Generation,* London, 1651, 2.

[22]Bacon's rejection of atomism was not complete. His view extrolling the virtues of atomism were published for the first time, posthumously in 1653. For Bacon's fluctuating views on atomism see Kargon, *op. cit.,* 43-53. Bacon at one point claimed that "Men cease not from abstracting nature till they come to potential and unformed matter not on the other hand from dissecting nature till they reach the atom; things which even if true, can do but little for the welfare of mankind." Bacon, Francis, *Works,* ed. J. Spedding, R. Ellis and D. Heath, Boston, 1860-64, VIII, 97.

[23]Willis, "Of Fermentation", 2.

[24]My dissertation traces the development of Willis' concept of fever as a blood disease. *The Circulation of the Blood and Medical Chemistry in England, 1650-1680,* unpublished dissertation, The Johns Hopkins University, Baltimore, 1969.

[25]Bacon, Works, IV, 385-386.
    See also Wolfe, David E., "Sydenham and Locke on the Limits of Anatomy. *Bull. Hist. Med. XXXV* (May-June 1961), 193-220.

[26]Kargon, *op. cit.,* 49-51.

[27]Tonstall, George, *Scarbrough Spaw spagrically Anatomized;* London, 1670, preface. On the controversy, see Poynter, F. N. L., "A 17th Century Medical Controversy: Robert Witty vs. William Simpson", *Essays in Honor of Charles Singer,* ed. E. A. Underwood, II, 72.

[28]Tonstall, *op. cit.,* 18.

[29]Drake, James, *Anthropologia Nova; or a New System of Anatomy, describing the Animal Economy,...*, London, 1707, I, 115-116. For similar views on the utility of the chemical principles to the physician's understanding of the body fluids, see also Beddevole, Dominique, *Essais d anatomie, où l'on explique clairement la construction des organes et leurs opérations méchaniqûes selon les nouvelles hypothèses*, Leyden, 1686, and Collins, Samuel, *System of Anatomy, treating of the Body of Man, Beasts, Birds, Fish, Insects and Plants...*, London, 1685, 2 vols.

¶ Libri quarti de causis generatiue sunt capitula x.
¶ Capitulum primum de elementis et naturis corporum et de compositis ex ipsis et de modis suæ coniunctionis proportionaliter ad artificialia;

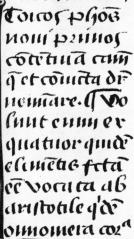

totos physio-
nomini primos
continua cum
q et continua di-
nominare. ¶ Vo-
sunt enim ex
quatuor quæ
elementa ficta
ce vocata ab
aristotile quæ
omnimoda cor-
generata primo a compositione. ¶ Ex hijs aut
corpora alia componi. ¶ Elementorum quædam quædam

# 23

## Cesalpino and Harvey on the Portal Circulation

### JEROME J. BYLEBYL

NOTEWORTHY among Walter Pagel's scholarly achievements is his thoughtful analysis of the ideas of Andreas Cesalpino on cardiovascular physiology and their relationship to the work of William Harvey.[1] After centuries of rather fruitless arguing over the narrow issue of priority in the discovery of the circulation, Pagel has provided us with a broader perspective on the thought of both men which reveals an historical situation too complex to be summed up by awarding the laurel of discovery to one and dismissing the views of the other. Pagel has presented Cesalpino and Harvey as two men of their time who shared a deep respect for the biological teachings of Aristotle tempered by a willingness to go beyond these older ideas through reasoning and observation, and who both had interesting and original insights into the functions of the heart and blood vessels. The traditional and innovative elements were perhaps present in Cesalpino and Harvey in different proportions, but as Pagel has shown, it is at the expense of fuller understanding that we ignore either facet of their respective ideas.

In assessing Cesalpino's views on cardiovascular physiology, historians have focused considerable attention on the passage from his *Medical questions* (1593) where he discussed the idea that heat and blood which had flowed out of the heart through the arteries could return to the heart through the veins.[2] Granted that this passage is fraught with ambiguities, that Cesalpino failed to make clear just how general this process is, and that he continued to ascribe other, non-centripetal, patterns of flow to the venous blood, this nevertheless remains a remarkable and unprecedented insight into the relationship of the heart, arteries, and veins to each other. Our respect for Cesalpino's powers of inference is increased when we consider that he probably arrived at this idea primarily through his knowledge of the anatomy of the heart and blood vessels, and not to any significant degree through vivisectional observations. We may not wish to credit Cesalpino with the discovery of the circulation on the basis of these statements, but this

39

should not prevent us from acknowledging that they amount to more than just a lucky guess.

In this paper I shall discuss a passage from Cesalpino's last work, the *Ars medica,* in which he again took up the idea of a flow of blood from arteries to veins at the periphery.[3] The discussion concerns only the gastric and mesenteric vessels and is therefore less general than that in the *Medical questions,* but it has the virtue of being much more straightforward than the earlier statements. In addition, it closely resembles a passage from Harvey's *De motu cordis* and thus sheds further light on the question of Harvey's direct familiarity with the works of Cesalpino.

In this passage, Cesalpino presented his resolution of a series of controversies which had arisen during the preceding century over Galen's doctrines on the blood vessels of the stomach and intestines. In the Galenic system, the arteries extending to these parts primarily served the common arterial function of maintaining their heat and spirits. The veins, on the other hand, served the special function of conveying prepared nutriment, or chyle, from the stomach and intestines to the liver for conversion to blood. The anatomical arrangement of the portal veins lent strong support to the idea that they transport nutritive material in this way, while the red color of the liver seemed to be a clear sign of its role in the preparation of blood. These two ideas were, in turn, the main bulwarks of the Galenic doctrine that the venous blood flows outward from the liver to nourish all the parts of the body.

But despite its cogency, Galen's functional interpretation of the portal veins was not without its difficulties. The most serious of these was pointed out by Vesalius during an anatomical demonstration at Bologna in 1544, as reported by Gabriele Cuneo: "Vesalius asked everyone if perchance they had ever found the branches of the portal veins which are visible near the stomach, in the mesentery, and along the intestines filled with anything other than red fluid, that is, with blood. For he said that in spite of his careful investigations at various times, he had never come across an animal in which he had observed anything other than blood [in these vessels]."[4] The problem to which Vesalius was calling attention was that although the portal veins are supposed to convey chyle from the gut to the liver for conversion to blood, they are always found to contain red blood rather than white chyle.

Galen had explained this anomaly by saying that the portal veins themselves concoct the chyle into a crude form of blood even before it reaches the liver,[5] but this was not a very satisfactory solution to the problem. Galen made much of the idea that sanguification is essentially a process of assimilation in which the red, bloodlike parenchyma of the liver converts chyle to blood.[6] Indeed, as Vesalius noted in the *Fabrica,* in the *Teachings of Hippocrates and Plato* Galen himself had explicitly rejected the idea that the veins are responsible for sanguification on the grounds that they are composed of a white, membranous substance and are therefore not suited for assimilating chyle to red blood.[7] Yet to explain the presence of blood in the portal veins Galen now ascribed to them the power to change the color of chyle from white to red, and however much additional concoction might remain to be carried out in the liver, it would seem that the essential step in sanguification had actually been performed by the veins.

One way out of the dilemma was proposed by Laurent Joubert, who accepted Galen's explanation of the presence of blood in the portal veins but eliminated the inconsistency in Galen's position by openly maintaining that the veins, rather than the liver, are the principal agents of sanguification.[8]

Vesalius, however, rejected the idea that the portal veins are able to carry on sanguification, though in devising an alternative explanation for the presence of blood in these vessels he probably took his inspiration from Galen's treatise *On the natural faculties.* Here Galen argued at some length that although the normal flow of materials through the portal veins is from the stomach and intestines to the liver, occasionally (perhaps once every few days) there is a reverse flow from the liver to the stomach and intestines.[9] This is because the latter parts are ordinarily nourished by some of the food which they contain, but during periods of fasting, when they contain no food, they provide for themselves by drawing back nutriment which has already passed to the liver. Thus Galen pointed to the possibility that the blood in the portal veins might come from the liver, though the occasional reverse flow which he envisioned would not account for the constant presence of blood noted by Vesalius.

The conclusion reached by Vesalius and others was that at all times there is a two-way passage of materials through the portal veins, of chyle from the gut to the liver and of blood from the liver to the gut.[10] The reason given for this reverse flow of blood was that the stomach and intestines could not be properly nourished by chyle alone, but like all other parts of the body require a constant supply of nutritive blood from the liver. Indeed, this theoretical question of the nutritive requirements of the stomach had been widely discussed for several centuries, long before interest came to be centered on the more practical question of the source of blood in the portal veins.[11] For those who accepted the principles of Galenic physiology the idea of a simultaneous flow of materials in two directions through the same vessels did not present a major difficulty since the qualitative specificity of the natural faculties would permit the stomach and intestines to selectively attract blood from the liver while the liver draws chyle in the opposite direction. Arcangelo Piccolomini compared this process to mixing flour with fine iron filings and then separating the two by placing an electric on one side of the mixture and a magnet on the other.[12]

Vesalius was also puzzled by certain features of the gastric, intestinal, and splenic arteries, as he noted in the second edition of the *Fabrica*:

> Certainly almost no vein extends to the stomach, intestines, and spleen without an accompanying artery, and almost the entire portal vein has a companion artery with it on its course....By no means can we say... that such large arteries were inserted into the stomach, intestines, and spleen only for the sake of their innate heat.[13]

Thus what troubled Vesalius was the relative size of these arteries. Presumably his point was that the accompanying veins are unusually large and numerous because they have the special function of conveying nutriment to the liver for the sake of the entire body in addition to the ordinary venous function of supplying nutritive blood to the stomach and intestines. But why should the arteries of these parts be correspondingly large and numerous if they only serve the common arterial function of maintaining the innate heat? As Vesalius noted, some special function appears to be indicated for the gastric and intestinal arteries as well.

Once again, a possible explanation was to be found in the writings of Galen, who had mentioned the idea that the mesenteric arteries might also take up chyle from the intestines, though he said that the amount would be negligible.[14] But Vesalius and others came to attach increasing importance to arterial resorption as an explanation of the size of these vessels.[15] Costanzo Varoli even went so far as to maintain that direct absorption from the intestines by the mesenteric arteries is the exclusive source of the arterial blood:

> I say that because two kinds of blood were necessary for man, on that account not only veins but also an abundant supply of arteries extend

to the intestines, in order to take up suitable aliment, in the manner of roots. And do not tell me that so many arteries extend to the intestines [only] in order to impart vital heat to them.[16]

In his *Ars medica* Cesalpino proposed a brilliant new theory which provided a unified explanation for all these phenomena:

> But there arises a doubt concerning the nutrition of the stomach and intestines. For it is necessary for all parts to be nourished by blood, but the mesenteric veins cannot supply these parts with blood because they were made to take up chyle and carry it to the liver; it would be absurd to suppose that at the same time and through the same [vessels] chyle is borne upward and blood downward. Nor can this take place at diverse times, since the mesenteric veins are never found filled with chyle, but always with blood. How, therefore, can the mesenteric veins take up chyle as everyone says?[17]...The reason why blood is always found in those veins but never white material is that the arteries distributed together with the veins pour blood into the veins through anastomses, and therefore the chyle is converted into blood in the same way as when wine is mixed with water. In this view, no difficulty remains, for the stomach and intestines are nourished from the chylous substance which they derive from the food during concoction, but with an admixture of arterial blood, without which no nutrition can take place.[18] Thus there is a continuous passage of the material of blood upward through the mesenteric veins to the liver, and of perfect blood downward through the arteries. For this reason more numerous arteries were supplied to these parts than to others, and the omentum was woven from them in the manner of a network, not only to nourish the stomach and intestines, but also so that in them can begin the generation of blood, which cannot be accomplished by the white flesh of the veins, arteries, stomach or intestines, but only by the substance of the arterial blood emanating from the font of the innate heat.[19]

Thus the nutrition of the stomach and intestines, the occurrence of blood in the mesenteric veins, the beginning of sanguification, and the large size of the gastric and mesenteric arteries all find all their explanation in Cesalpino's theory that these arteries supply blood to the portal veins.

This theory represents a major change in Cesalpino's earlier views about the portal veins and the process of sanguification, as set forth in his *Peripatetic questions* (1571).[20] As an Aristotelian he had been concerned with establishing that the heart, rather than the liver or veins, has the primary responsibility for the generation of nutritive blood. He held that this takes place in two major stages. First, the veins take up nutritive material from the intestines, and throughout its passage through the veins this material undergoes a preliminary concoction into a crude form of blood. This concoction is brought about by heat which flows out through the veins from the heart, so that the latter organ is indirectly responsible for this initial stage of the process. In the liver the fine branches of the hepatic veins are directly continuous with those of the portal vein, so that heat from the heart reaches the latter vessel and begins the process of converting chyle to blood as soon as it enters the mesenteric veins. After passing through the liver the crude blood enters the vena cava and its branches, from which some of it is consumed by the parts. More important, however, is that part of the blood which passes through the heart and lungs, where it is concocted into perfect nutriment, and then distributed through the arteries to provide the main nourishment for the body. This theory stands in contrast to the views of most of Cesalpino's contemporaries, who considered the venous blood to be perfect aliment which is primarily responsible for nourishing the body, while the more spirituous arterial blood is chiefly concerned with the maintenance of heat and life rather than nutrition.

In this earlier discussion Cesalpino did not explicitly raise the question of why the portal veins contain blood rather than chyle, but presumably his explanation would have been that the heat from the heart begins the conversion to blood as soon as the chyle enters the veins. We naturally wonder what led him to the new explanation of the presence of blood in the portal veins set forth in the *Ars medica*. As was noted above, in the *Medical questions* he had raised the possibility of a flow of blood from arteries to veins throughout the body, and it may have been this more general theory that suggested to him the idea of a regular passage of blood from the gastric and mesenteric arteries to the accompanying veins. But in the *Ars medica* he makes no reference to the broader theory, and even seems to suggest that the arteries of the stomach and intestines are unusually large because they are exceptional in constantly supplying blood to their companion veins in addition to nourishing the parts to which they extend.

A more likely possibility seems to be that the concept of the pulmonary circuit provided the model for Cesalpino's explanation of the gastric and mesenteric vessels. He was the staunchest Italian advocate of the passage of blood through the lungs during the later sixteenth century, and repeated his endorsement of the idea in the *Ars medica*.[21] A possible veiled criticism of his views which directly linked the two issues may have led him to see an analogy between the flow of blood through the lungs and that through the mesentery. In 1587 Giulio Cesare Aranzi of Bologna proposed a compromise version of the pulmonary circuit in which allowance was made for a reverse flow of vital spirits from the left cardiac ventricle to the lungs through the pulmonary veins, in addition to the flow of blood from the lungs to the left ventricle.[22] In anticipation of criticism of this theory, Aranzi declared, "But immediately those men will cry out who deny [the occurrence of] contrary motions in natural actions, as if examples [of such motions] were lacking, as in the portal vein, where chyle is conveyed [to the liver], blood is supplied to the stomach and intestines, and melancholic humor is excreted to the spleen, all through the same duct."[23]

Galen had also ascribed a diversity of motions to the pulmonary veins and their contents, and in the *Peripatetic questions* Cesalpino had sharply criticized Galen's views on this subject specifically on the grounds that Nature does not permit "contrary motions."[24] Thus it seems quite possible that Aranzi's barb was aimed at Cesalpino, though far from leading him to abandon the principle of no contrary motions, Aranzi's argument may only have stimulated Cesalpino to extend its applicability to the portal veins. It is true that Cesalpino's own earlier views on the latter vessels did not involve contrary motions, but as we have seen many of his contemporaries preferred to accept such motions rather than hold, as Cesalpino did, that blood could be formed within the portal veins themselves. Thus by linking the two problems as he did, Aranzi may have led Cesalpino to a more satisfactory way of eliminating contrary motions from the portal veins, namely the idea that the blood which they contain comes from the gastric and mesenteric arteries, just as the blood of the pulmonary veins comes from the pulmonary arteries.[25]

Additional motivation for this change in Cesalpino's views may have come from criticisms of his theory of sanguification published by Nicolaus Taurellus in 1597. Taurellus maintained that however much the heart might perfect the blood which it distributes through the arteries, the substance which it receives from the veins is already blood to begin with so that the heart cannot be said to generate blood directly.[26] Furthermore, he argued that the heart is not even indirectly responsible for the conversion of chyle to blood in the way that Cesalpino proposed, namely through the agency of the heat which it dispenses. All parts of the body receive the same heat from the heart, yet only parts such as the liver and possibly the veins can carry on sanguification. Thus although the presence of heat may be a necessary condition for sanguification, it is the qualitative specificity of the parts directly involved that is most essential to the process.[27] Taurellus also doubted whether heat from the heart could actually reach the more remote veins of the body, in particular the portal veins which are not directly continuous with the heart.[28] He was uncertain whether sanguification actually begins in the latter vessels, but thought that if it did they would more likely obtain this power from the nearby liver than from the distant heart.[29]

Cesalpino's new theory eliminated all of these objections, for the preliminary conversion of chyle into blood is brought about not by the stomach or intestines or portal veins or liver, nor even by heat from the heart, but by pre-existing blood supplied by the heart through the gastric and mesenteric arteries. From the portal veins this imperfect mixture would pass through the liver and into the systemic veins, from which some of it would be consumed by the parts.[30] But another portion would be perfected by passing through the heart and lungs to the aorta, from which some of the perfect blood would return to the gastric and mesenteric arteries to repeat the process.[31] Thus do the heart and blood together bring about the constant generation of new blood.

Cesalpino's views on the mesenteric vessels and the process of sanguification bear a strong resemblance to the discussion of these topics in Harvey's *De motu cordis*:

> In the mesentery, blood which enters through the celiac and superior and inferior mesenteric arteries proceeds to the intestines, from which it returns to the porta of the liver through the numerous branches of the veins of the intestines, together with chyle attracted into the veins, and then passes through the liver to the vena cava. This occurs in such a way that the blood in these veins [i.e., the mesenterics] is imbued with the same color and consistency as that in the other veins, contrary to what is thought by many. Nor is it necessary to admit the awkward and improbable occurrence of two contrary motions in all the capillary branches, of chyle upward and of blood downward. But does this not take place in accordance with the highest providence of nature? For if chyle were mixed with blood, the crude with the concocted, in equal proportions, the result would not be concoction, transmutation, and sanguification, but rather (since they are mutually active and passive) a mixture of the

two, an intermediary substance, as when wine is mixed with water. But as it is, when a small portion of chyle is added to a large amount of passing blood, so that it represents no significant proportion [of the whole], the outcome is rather like the situation described by Aristotle in which a drop of water is added to a cask of wine, or vice versa; the resulting whole is not a mixture, but either wine or water. Thus when the mesenteric veins are dissected, we do not find in them chyme, or chyle and blood, either separate or mixed, but blood which has the same appearance of color and consistency as that in the rest of the veins. But since [this blood] contains a certain unconcocted portion of chyle, however imperceptible, nature has interposed the liver, in whose meandering channels it undergoes delay and acquires a fuller transmutation, lest the crude material arrive prematurely at the heart and disrupt the vital principle.[32]

Thus Harvey, like Cesalpino, sees the mesenteric vessels as having been arranged to permit a mingling of blood and chyle, and attributes to the pre-existing blood the main role in transforming fresh chyle into blood.[33]

Did this similarity result from Harvey's direct familiarity with Cesalpino's writings? The same question is posed by a number of other tantalizing parallels between the ideas of the two men.[34] We cannot answer the question with certainty, for Harvey nowhere referred to Cesalpino in his writings, not even after contemporaries had drawn attention to the similarities in their views.[35] But as Pagel has argued, when we add to these similarities Harvey's thorough knowledge of previous literature, his shared interest with Cesalpino in the restoration of Aristotelian physiology, and the prominence of Cesalpino in Italy during Harvey's student days there, it becomes highly unlikely that Harvey did not know the works of Cesalpino.[36]

We must, however, distinguish the possibility that Harvey had read Cesalpino and was even influenced by him in some ways from the idea that Harvey's concept of the circulation was a direct borrowing from Cesalpino, for the latter conclusion would be entirely unwarranted. The case of Caspar Hofmann shows that to read Cesalpino was not necessarily to be made aware of the circulation, for despite his avowed admiration for Cesalpino's teachings Hofmann not only did not have an inkling of the circulation prior to 1628, but later resisted the idea even after witnessing a personal demonstration by Harvey.[37] It seems to me unlikely that Harvey would have paid any more attention than did Hofmann to the few passages in Cesalpino that seem to foreshadow the idea of the circulation unless he already had the latter idea in mind, or at least had been prepared for it by his own thinking and observations.

There is a fundamental difference which distinguishes Harvey's firm grasp of the circulation from Cesalpino's fleeting glimpses of the idea, namely Harvey's attention to quantitative considerations, for which there is no parallel in the work of Cesalpino. Even their respective discussions of the mesenteric vessels reflect this difference, for whereas Cesalpino sees sanguification as resulting simply from the mixture of chyle with blood, Harvey emphasizes that minute quantities of chyle must be mixed with large quantities of circulating blood to permit the process to occur. It would, I think, be fair to say that Cesalpino came about as close to the recognition of the circulation as was possible on the basis of anatomical evidence alone. In contrast to most of his contemporaries who thought of the systemic veins as leading outward from the liver, Cesalpino stressed that they lead inward to the heart. He even saw that it would be possible for blood which had flowed out from the heart through the arteries to return through the veins. But his reasons for having the blood follow that pathway were essentially qualitative and teleological in nature. In the more general discussion in the *Medical questions* his main aim was to explain the Aristotelian doctrine that heat flows out from the heart under certain conditions and back to the heart under others. In the discussion of the mesenteric vessels he was concerned with accounting for the presence of blood in the mesenteric veins and the size of the mesenteric arteries, and with explaining the process of sanguification. What he did not have was a compelling reason for thinking that the return of blood from arteries to heart might be the principal and constant function of the venous system.

Harvey was to find such a reason through his numerous vivisectional observations, which provided him with a concrete sense of the rate at which blood is transmitted from the veins to the arteries by the heart. As he tells us in the *De motu cordis,* it was his reflection on the quantitative problems inherent in that rate that first led him to conceive of the circulation, and it was primarily by the development of these quantitative arguments that he sought to bring his readers to accept the constant and rapid circulation of the blood as an inexorable necessity.[38] But although he insisted on the primacy of vivisectional evidence for the demonstration that the circulation occurs, Harvey was also the "lifelong thinker upon the meaning of the circulation"[39] who tried to find teleological justifications for what he had discovered. It was when he went beyond the mechanics of the blood flow to discuss the purposes of the pulmonary, systemic, and portal circulations that his aims most nearly overlapped those of Cesalpino, and not surprisingly it is in these passages that his ideas most closely resemble those of his great predecessor.

## References

[1] Pagel, Walter, *William Harvey's biological ideas*, Basel/New York, 1967, 169-209.

[2] Cesalpino, Andreas, *Quaestionum medicarum libri II*, Venice, 1593, fol. 234 r. This passage has been analyzed in detail by Pagel in *Harvey's biological ideas*, 171-178.

[3] The passage occurs in book 7 ("De morbis ventris"), ch. 1, of the *Ars medica*. The first edition, *Artis medicae pars prima, de morbis universalibus*, Rome, 1602, contains only the first four books, and therefore not the passage under discussion. In 1603 book 7 (together with book 8) was published separately at Rome as *Artis medicae liber VII. De morbis ventris*, in which the passage is found on pp. 9-11. The entire work was published as *KATOPTRON, sive speculum artis medicae Hippocraticum*, Frankfurt, 1605, and again as *Praxis universae artis medicae*, Tarvisii, 1606, in which the passage under discussion occurs on pp. 489-490 and 522-523, respectively.

[4] Cuneo, Gabriele, *Apologiae Francisci Putei pro Galeno in anatome, examen*, Venice, 1564, 74-75.

[5] Galen, *On the usefulness of the parts of the body*, tr. M. T. May, Ithaca, N.Y. 1968, IV, ii, iii, xii, 204-206, 223.

[6] E.g., *ibid.*, IV, xii, pp. 222-223.

[7] Galen, *On the teachings of Hippocrates and Plato*, VI, vii, in *Opera*, ed. Kühn, V, 566; Vesalius, *De humani corporis fabrica libri septum*, Basel, 1543, 267 *bis*. See also Vesalius, *Epistola, rationem modumque propinandi radicis Chynae decocti, ...pertractans*, Basel, 1546, 169, where he repeats the point.

[8] Joubert, Laurent, *Paradoxorum decas prima atque altera*, Lyons, 1566, Dec. I, par. iv, 78-109, esp. 81, 99-100.

[9] Galen, *On the natural faculties*, tr. A. J. Brock, London, 1952, III, xiii, 289-315. See also *On the usefulness of the parts*, IV, xix, 242.

[10] Vesalius, *De humani corporis fabrica libri septem*, Basel, 1555, 615, 617; Cuneo, *Examen*, 68-69, 72. See also Colombo, Realdo, *De re anatomica*, Venice, 1559, 164-166; Piccolomini, Arcangelo, *Anatomicae praelectiones*, Rome, 1586, 96-98; du Laurens, André, *Historia anatomica*, Frankfurt, 1599, 99-102.

[11] Peter of Abano, *Conciliator controversiarum quae inter philosophos et medicos versantur*, Venice, 1565, Diff. LIII, fols. 77 v-79 r. See also Joubert, *Paradoxorum*, Dec. II, par. v, 414-435; Valles, Francisco, *Controversiarum medicarum et philo-*

*sophicarum libri decem,* Frankfurt, 1582, 41-42; Piccolomini, *Anatomicae Prae-lectiones,* 110-111; du Laurens, *Historia anatomica,* 238-239.

[12]Piccolomini, *Anatomicae praelectiones,* 97.

[13]Vesalius, *Fabrica* (1555), 746.

[14]Galen, *On the natural faculties,* III, xiv, 317.

[15]Vesalius, *Fabrica* (1555), 614; Cuneo, *Examen,* 75, 102-103. See also Eustachi, Bartolomeo, *Opuscula anatomica,* Venice, 1563, 98; Varoli, Costanzo, *Anatome, sive de resolutione corporis humani,* Frankfurt, 1591, 54-55, 72-73; Spach, Israel, *Theses medicae physicae de homine sano,* Strassburg, 1593, 57-61; Bauhin, Caspar, *Anatomes: liber primus...editio tertia, et liber secundus...editio altera,* Basel, 1597, 455-456; Hofmann, Caspar, *Disputatio de usu venarum et arteriarum mesaraicarum,* Nuremberg, 1615.

[16]Varoli, *Anatome,* 73.

[17]I have omitted a subsidiary argument: "Besides, if concoction is carried on by each part so that it can benefit by the material which is concocted, then the stomach and intestines would be nourished by chyle, which is indeed admitted by some. For infants in the womb are found to have phlegm in their stomachs, and the author of the book *On principles,* ascribed to *Hippocrates,* thought that this is because the infant sucks from the womb with its lips, an opinion which Aristotle attributes to Democritus. But phlegm of that kind is derived from the head so the mesenteric veins will have material for blood, which is carried to the liver."

[18]As is discussed below, Cesalpino was unusual among his contemporaries in attributing to the arteries the function of nourishing the parts rather than simply sustaining their life.

[19]Cesalpino, *Artis medicae liber VII* (1603), 9-11.

[20]Cesalpino, *Quaestiones peripateticae,* Venice, 1571, fols. 104v-106r.

[21]Pagel, *Harvey's biological ideas,* 169-170; Cesalpino, *Praxis,* 502-503.

[22]Aranzi, Giulio Cesare, *Anatomicae observationes,* published together with the third edition of his *De humano foetu liber,* Venice, 1587, 92-96.

[23]*Ibid.,* 95.

[24]Cesalpino, *Quaestiones peripateticae,* fol. 108. This passage is discussed by Pagel in *Harvey's biological ideas,* 202-203.

[25]Cesalpino reversed Galen's doctrine that the pulmonary artery is actually a vein while the pulmonary vein is actually an artery. See, e.g., *Praxis,* 503.

[26]Taurellus, Nicolaus, *Alpes cesae,* Frankfurt, 1597, 857.

[27]*Ibid.,* 853-856, 879.

[28]*Ibid.,* 859, 868, 881.

[29]*Ibid.,* 857, 868, 872, 879.

[30]Cesalpino, *Artis medicae liber VII* (1603), 6-7.

³¹Cesalpino, *Praxis* (1606), 501-503.

³²Harvey, William, *Exercitatio anatomica de motu cordis et sanguinis in animalibus,* Frankfurt, 1628, ch. 16, 61-62.

³³It is interesting to note that in his earlier anatomical lecture notes Harvey had accepted the idea of a two-way flow of chyle and blood through the portal veins, and had alluded to the question of whether the mesenteric artries also take up chyle from the intestines. See *The anatomical lectures of William Harvey, Prelectiones anatomie universalis,* ed., with intro., tr., and notes by Gweneth Whitteridge, Edinburgh and London, 1964, 81, 91.

³⁴See Pagel, *Harvey's biological ideas,* 200-209 for further parallels.

³⁵*Ibid.,* 195 and n. 3.

³⁶*Ibid.,* 196.

³⁷Ibid., 196-198; Ferrario, E. V., Poynter, F. N. L., and Franklin, K. J., "William Harvey's debate with Caspar Hofmann on the circulation of the blood. New documentary evidence," *Jl. Hist. Med., XV* (1960), 7-21.

³⁸Harvey, *De motu cordis,* chs. 8 and 9, 41-46.

³⁹Curtis, John G., *Harvey's views on the use of the circulation of the blood,* New York, 1915, 152.

# APPENDIX

Andreas Cesalpino, *Artis medicae liber* VII. *De morkis ventris,* Rome, 1603, 9-11.

Sed oritur dubitatio circa Ventriculi & Intestinorum nutritionem. Cum enim necessee sit omnes partes nutriri sanguine, Venae meseraicae non possunt illis sanguinem tribuere, quia datae sunt ut sugant Chylum, & ferant ad Hepar: simul autem per easdem ferri sursum Chylum & sanguinem deorsum, absurdum est; neque diversis temporibus: numquam enim Venae meseraicae repertae sunt chylo plenae, sed semper sanguine: quomodo igitur sugunt Chylum ut omnes fatentur? Praeterea, si concoctio ab unoquoque fit, ut fruatur materia quae concoquitur: Ventriculus & Intestina nutrientur Chylo: quod a quibusdam conceditur. Nam infantes in utero reperiuntur pituitam in ventriculo habere: quod ab auctore, qui librum de Principijs conscripsit, adscriptum Hippocrati, putatum est, quia infans ex utero labijs sugit: quam sententiam Aristoteles tribuit Democrito./ad marg., 2 Ge. an. 5/Sed pituita huiusmodi ex capite colligitur, ut Venae meseraicae materiam sanguinis habeant, quae feratur ad Hepar. Quod autem sanguis semper reperiatur in venis illis, numquam autem materia alba: causa est, quia Arteriae cum Venis delatae per anastomasim sanguinem in Venas transfundunt, unde Chyli fit conversio in sanguinem, ut vinum facit aquae mixtum. Hoc modo nulla difficultas relinquitur: nutritur enim Ventriculus & Intestina ex chylosa substantia, quam in concoctione eliciunt ex cibis, sed admixtione sanguinis arterialis, sine quo nulla fit nutritio. Continue autem fertur sursum per Venas meseraicas ad Hepar materia sanguinis, & doresum per Arterias sanguis perfectissimus. Huius gratia Arteriae numerosiores hi datae sunt, quam ceteris partibus, & Omentum retis similitudine ex ijs contextum est, non solum ut nutrirentur Intestina & Ventriculus, sed etiam ut in illis inciperet sanguinis generatio, quam neque Venarum tunicae, neque Arteriarum, neque Ventriculi, & Intestinorum substantia alba efficere possunt: sed sola sanguinis arterialis substantia ex fonte caloris innati emanans.

# 24

# Cardiac Function, Blood Volume and the Circulation of Blood in Antiquity

## KARL E. ROTHSCHUH[1]

### Translated by GUENTER B. RISSE

*Introduction and formulation of the problem*

THE profound gulf between the traditional Galenic concepts of blood circulation and those mechanical views enunciated in the early seventeenth century on the basis of anatomical, clinical and vivisectional considerations, was dramatically exposed by William Harvey. Writing in the prologue of his work circa 1628,[2] he expounded the various incompatabilities between the two viewpoints. Among Harvey's most prominent doubts was Galen's so-called "attractive faculty." According to the Roman physician, the arteries were filled during an active period of diastole which consisted of the emission of blood, heat and spirit from the left ventricle and the absorption of external air from the distal arterial endings through certain pores. Galen also declared that a single vessel, the pulmonic vein, was the only one in which air, blood and vaporous wastes circulated side by side in opposite directions.

Furthermore, Galen maintained that the finest blood particles flowed across small pores located in the interventricular septum from the right to the left cardiac ventricle without an opposite transit of spiritual blood. Did Galen see any contradictions in such a scheme, as we now do? How could Galen, a clever and shrewd observer, develop such concepts? How was it possible that other highly intelligent physicians such as Fernel (1543) and Bartholinus (1641) continued to defend and convincingly represent these ideas for over 1400 years? The circulation theory was even rejected by some of Harvey's contemporaries, like Primerose (1630), and certainly not out of malice.[3] A fundamental factor in the elaboration of the old concept of blood circulation can probably be ascribed to Galen's ideas regarding the *volume of blood*. Therefore, such viewpoints will be examined in detail.[4]

53

## Aristotle and Galen

Aristotle was probably the first to develop a cardiocentric theory of the organism. The heart became the principle of life, the origin of blood formation as well as the source of a life-giving heat and the seat of the "sensorium commune." However, blood was also needed for the nutrition of the bodily parts. Food was necessary for the formation of blood, and also to furnish material for the source of vital heat in the heart, whereas respiration merely served to maintain and temper the cardiac furnace.

According to this scheme, the motion and distribution of blood emanated from the heart. A cardiac contraction originated when the moist blood began to simmer within the walls of the ventricle dilating it and boiling over into the arteries. Following such an eruption, the cardiac heat was tempered by the cool air absorbed through the lungs, an action which increased the density of the volatile blood and allowed heart and lungs to collapse until the next systole ("Of Respiration," chapter 10). These Aristotelian interpretations seem more inclined to *explain the purposes* of the cardiopulmonary events rather than to depict causally the observed relationships.

Such a conviction of the immanent goal-oriented quality of all organs and bodily parts ("ab *usu* partium") also looms foremost in Galen's physiological interpretations. Moreover, with a teleological view guiding his reasoning, Galen attempted to erect a system of vitality in health and disease from the anatomical data. However, on the basis of his improved anatomy, Galen differed from Aristotle, transferring the blood-forming capacity from the heart to the liver and placing the "sensorium commune" in the brain. Thus, the heart's remaining mission was to elaborate the body's vital heat and distribute it together with the spirit, the Halitus, and a small amount of left ventricular blood to the arteries.

The structure of the blood as well as the functions taking place in the chambers are viewed more as instruments in the service of the heart's primary task. In this context the lungs maintain their assignment to sustain and cool the cardiac fire with air. The pulmonary veins, in turn, furnish the outside air and allow for the elimination of vaporized wastes.

The liver continually produces blood from the available elements furnished by the ingested food. Most of the new blood flows peripherally, without a detour through the heart, in the veins for the nourishment of the various organs where it is absorbed and consumed. Only a small amount of blood travels from the vena cava to the right side of the heart, attracted by the larger cardiac chambers and a cardiac "force of attraction": "Cor...unicum enim id ex iis, quae post jecur habentur, in dextrum sinu suum alimentum trahit."[5] Such an attractive power "primam ferme naturalium facultatum hanc esse."[6]

Since the orifice of the vena cava into the right auricle is larger than that of the pulmonary artery, it is clear that only a portion of the incoming blood flows to the lungs for their nourishment. The rest has only one alternate route, to circulate through the septum into the left ventricle. "Ergo manifestum est, quod in sinistrum sinum transmittitur."[7]

Thus, Galen decided to accept the notion of a passage of blood across the porosities of the interventricular septum. The process was envisioned as a sort of distillation or permeation whereby the more subtle blood particles were *attracted* by the left ventricle during diastole. Simultaneously with such a diastolic distention of the left chambers caused by a "vis pulsifica," the arteries experienced an active dilatation. Under those circumstances, the vessels attracted some of the components of the left ventricle into their lumen; first the subtle spirits, then vapors, and finally some blood.[8] The small volume of blood obtained by the arteries had previously filtered across the septum and was therefore composed of fine particles. In addition, the arteries received another small amount of blood which had been suctioned from the minute openings of the pulmonary arteries and conducted in the pulmonary veins to the left cardiac chambers.

Galen did not talk about the function of the ventricular blood ejection. The cardiac walls, distended during diastole, merely returned to their previous position in systole. The "venae arteriosae" (pulmonary arteries) also drew a certain amount of thin blood from the right ventricle during their period of distention which occurred on inspiration.

From the above, it is clear that the phenomenon of attraction plays a major role in Galen's cardiovascular physiology and that the heart is not viewed as a pump expelling blood.[9] Obviously Galen only considered the transit of very small amounts of blood to the heart which were elaborated from the daily absorbed food after deducting the wastes of fecal matter and urine. Although he did not give any specific quantities, Galen believed that only a thin trickle of blood was actually attracted by the heart.

Hence, Galen's heart was quite a differently working organ than the one we conceive of today. It had primarily an *absorbing* rather than an *ejecting* property. The veins contained a stream of blood while the arteries had more spirit and vapor than blood and were half empty. This fact explains the prevalence of attractive forces: "Majore enim vi cor dilatatum attrahet (!) necesse est, quam contractum expellat."[10]

The arteries do not pulsate because they are being filled. Instead the vessels' distention (*elevantur*) causes such filling.[11] Thus the essential aspects of Galen's ideas of cardiac function were based on anatomical findings, a teleological interpretation and the concept of a very small amount of blood flow.

### From Fernel to Sennert

Galen's somewhat strange theory—for modern standards—concerning the amount and movement of the blood can be found virtually intact in Jean Fernel's *De Naturali Parte Medicinae* of 1543,[12] as well as in the writings of Jacobus Sylvius in 1555.[13] As did Vesalius, Theodor Zwinger declared in 1610[14] that the right auricle and ventricles were wider and larger than the left cardiac chambers. Zwinger was only peripherally interested in the expulsion of blood from the heart: "The blood in the arteries does not move like the water or the blood in veins, but behaves as fire. The blood has a natural movement across the lungs and because of its subtle particles, tends to be carried like the wind moves the ocean."[15]

In the same year, Jean Riolan, Sr., viewed the heart as the center of the microcosm: "Cor...habet rationem in microcosmo quam sol in universo. In corporis oeconomia non aliter praeest, quam Rex in re publica...ut sol mundum, sic corpus nostrum vivificat."[16] To be sure, Riolan talks only about the importance and usefulness of the heart. No commentaries about the amount of circulating blood nor changes of Galen's scheme can be detected in his writings.

In 1616, Caspar Bauhinus also talks much about the purpose but little about the actual work of the heart: "Usus cordis, cum caloris nativi, quo animal regitur, quasi fons sit, totius corporis partes motu suo assiduo a putridine conservare, sanguinem pro pulmonum nutritione et spiritum vitalem elaborare."[17] These praises of the heart are even more accentuated by Riolan, Jr., who in his anthropography of 1626 writes: "Cor... nobilissinum totius corporis partem, irascibilis animae sedem, facultatis et spiritus vitalis fontem, caloris nativi focum atque ut uno verbo dicam, nostri corporis Solem, cujus influxu omnia viscera calent et recreantur."[18] Nothing is said about the amounts of blood and very little about its circulation. One has the impression that the anatomy of the organs involved is somewhat more accurately described than in Galen. However, the physiological questions with descriptions concerning the usefulness of the various parts are all dealt with satisfactorily within the Galenic framework.

In D. Sennert's writings, one already finds the acceptance of a passage of blood through the lungs whereby the left ventricle attracts both air and blood during diastole, "ad spiritus et caloris vitalis generationem et refocillationem attrahit."[19] In systole, however, the vital spirit and arterial blood are distributed throughout the entire body. Thus, the left ventricle seems to expel blood even though its filling is accomplished through attraction. The heart is "in perpetuo motu seu dilatando et contrahendo."[20]

Although the systole of the heart coincides with that of the arteries, both structures do not hinder each other in any way, since, as Sennert declared, the arteries "comprimuntur et clauduntur, ut plane nihil possunt recipere, sed sufficiens adhuc in contractis est cavitas ad id, quod cor transmittit, recipiendum."[21] Therefore, it is clear that the amount of blood furnished by the heart cannot be very great. The cardiac dilatation remains, nevertheless, the determining factor: "Dilatatur autem cor a peculiare facultate sibi insita, quam vitalem et pulsificam nominant."[22] The so-called "vis pulsifica" is more a force of attraction than expulsion.

## Harvey and Descartes

The year 1628 in which Sennert's *Institutiones* appeared in print coincided with the publication of Harvey's book on the circulation of the blood. Taking into consideration the contemporary views on the subject, it is not surprising that Harvey found cardiovascular physiology to be so inscrutable. The English physician was almost inclined to believe that "the movement of the heart can only be known by God."[23] Although already known, it should be stressed that Harvey's line of argument for a new circulatory scheme relied on the idea of a stroke volume and a shift from cardiac attraction to a more prominent function of blood ejection.

Harvey's concepts and demonstrations were already being criticized by James Primerose in 1630.[24] Primerose reproached Harvey writing that "for you the blood is not moving through attraction but expulsion."[25] He went on to declare that Harvey's blood volume determinations were erroneous since the heart only drew enough blood from the liver to fill the right chambers. The amount was to be small, since blood expanded under the prevailing cardiac heat just as milk and honey. Therefore, both the heart and the arteries were mainly occupied with a foamlike, frothy mass which yielded very little blood after cooling off in the arterial tree.[26] When milk was heated, it could experience an eight-fold increase in volume. Hence, one could anticipate that one grain of venous blood would convert to foam during each cardiac contraction.[27] Furthermore, if one would assume that each stroke does not necessarily carry blood, a cardiac contraction would actually average about a quarter grain of blood[28] or one ounce every two hours. Such a conclusion proves that there is very little blood in the arteries.

Primerose's ninth chapter deals extensively with the question of blood expulsion, hitherto never explained in detail. His description is very objective and he uses good arguments for his conclusions. From these writings it appears as if Primerose was the first to establish the hypothesis of a very small stroke volume during cardiac systole.

However, Primerose was not the only author to enunciate such a concept. The same idea reappears in the fifth essay of Descartes' *Discourse* (1637) which represented excerpts of the unpublished work "L'Homme" of 1630. Descartes refers to one large drop of blood for such cardiac contraction.[29] It is known that Descartes learned about Harvey's new circulation scheme in 1630, although he read Harvey's work some years later.[30] Therefore, there are reasons to suppose that Descartes acquired his knowledge of Harvey's discovery from Primerose since he also declared, in 1630, that the blood entering the warm heart experienced, as does milk, a great expansion.[31]

Such an effervescence expanded the cardiac walls, as Aristotle had proposed, opened the valves and drove the vapor of blood into the arteries.

Descartes adopted Harvey's circulation theory. He combined it with the Aristotelian concept of cardiac motion and perhaps the volumetric considerations of Primerose in order to achieve a new thermodynamic model of cardiac function. In any event, the question regarding the amount of blood ejected from the heart acquired a decisive importance following the works of Harvey and Descartes. Moreover, scholars now seriously dealt with the question whether attractive forces are important in cardiac activity.

In the ensuing years, the arguments about stroke volume and the amount of blood circulating through the vessels became a central concern in the disputes about Harvey's new discovery. If, indeed, the blood only flows in small drops through the heart and the vascular system, as Riolan repeatedly stressed in his writings of 1649[32] and 1652,[33] then all the Galenic ideas remain viable. This includes the replacement of used blood by the liver, the general transportation of blood by the power of attraction as well as the passage through the cardiac septum and the parallel occurrence of various phenomena in the vessels.

If the stroke volume is much greater, about half an ounce up to two drachms, then it is impossible for the liver to furnish adequate replacements and expulsive forces will have to be considered in addition to suction. Moreover, the passage across the intra ventricular septum as well as the vascular phenomena would be impossible.

P. M. Schlegel (1650)[34] and Herman Conring (1643)[35] postulated such a greater amount of blood, together with the Cartesian author Cornelis ab Hoghelande (1646),[36] who proposed a systolic volume of a half ounce to one drachm. All three were proponents of the Harveyan circulatory scheme.

Unfortunately, as mentioned above, Descartes had arrived at the idea of one drop of blood per cardiac contraction without reading Harvey. He believed in an Aristotelian effervescence because such a thermodynamic explanation of the systolic contraction could be substituted for the pulsatile faculty. Even Vop. F. Plempius,[37] initially opposed to Harvey, accepted the larger amount of blood in 1644 and thus the circulation theory. F. de le Boe Sylvius[38] publicly accepted Harvey's circulation in 1660 together with the Cartesian variation.

The whole topic was considerably clarified by Richard Lower in his *Tractatus de Corde* (1669).[39] Lower convinced himself that there was no special heat in the heart,[40] and that the ebullition conceived both by Aristotle ond Descartes was indeed false.[41] Moreover, Lower denounced the idea of a drop by drop circulation,[42] believing instead that the diastole was a passive phenomenon allowing blood inflow while systole represented contraction and forceful expulsion into the arteries.[43] In this conception, Lower declared that both ventricular cavities had similar stroke volumes: "Utrique cordis sinus aequalem contingent et distribuunt mensuram."[44]

With G. A. Borelli (1680), pure mechanical views came to dominate the cardiac motions, and a faculty of attraction operating in the heart and other organs was no longer accepted.[45] The movements of the heart were now a "motus naturalis" not derived from the soul or other mysterious sources.[46] The blood vessels were like tubes filled with fluid with a certain pressure in them. The pulse originated because the blood was being impelled into the arterial system.

The mechanical views pertaining to the motion of the blood are completely spelled out in the writings of Friedrich Hoffmann (1730). He wrote: "Cordis machina motoria affabre constructa est, ut ejus systole diastolen arteriarum, quae pulsus est, producet, et diastole arteriarum rurus provocet earum systolen, quae causa postea rursus diastoles cordis evadit, et sic motus fit perpetuus. Quam ob rem non inepte perpetuus. Quam ob rem non inepte perpetuum mobile cor dici potest."[47]

The introduction and improvement of those methods used in the measurement of the stroke volume and blood pressure begin with Stephen Hales (1733).[48] By filling the cardiac chambers with liquid wax and measuring the displaced volume of fluid, he came close to ascertaining the correct amount of blood per stroke. Moreover, the use of glass tubes led to a correct determination of the blood pressure within the vessels.

In retrospect, one can see that there were primarily interpretative changes from antiquity and the Middle Ages until the gradual growth of mechanical causality in the seventeenth century. At this time, the previous contradictions suddenly became immense and intolerable, especially if one went from the older to the more recent viewpoint, as Harvey was first to realize. This was true because Galen's acceptance of a minute amount of circulating blood was consistent and logical with his conceptions of cardiac action and circulation.

## References

[1]My incentive to write this study was a correspondence, during which W. Pagel drew my attention to certain sources. This work is dedicated to him with gratitude and veneration.

[2]Harvey, William, *Exercitatio anatomica de motu cordis et sanguinis,* Frankfurt, 1628. (German edition, *Klassiker der Medizin, Vol. 1: Die Bewegungen des Herzens und des Blutes,* Leipzig, 1910. In this book, Preface, 15-26.)

[3]Cf. Rothschuh, K. E., "Jean Riolan jun. (1580-1657) im Streit mit Paul Marquart Schlegel (1605-1653) um die Blutbewegungslehre Harveys," *Gesnerus* 21 (1964) 72-82.

[4]The source for Galen was *Claudii Galeni. Opera,* Ed. Kühn, Tom. I-Tom. XX, Lipsiae, 1821-1830.

[5]Galen, *De naturalibus facultatibus* (Ed. Kühn, Tom. II, Lipsiae, 1821), Liber II, Cap. I.

[6]*Ibid.,* Liber III, Cap. XII, 113.

[7]*Ibid.,* Liber III, Cap. XV, 208-209.

[8]*Ibid.,* Liber III, Cap. XIV.

9Siegel, R. E., *Galen's System of Physiology and Medicine,* Basel and New York, 1968.

10Galen, *De usu partium corporis humani* (Ed. Kühn, Tom. III, Lipsiae, 1822), Liber V, Cap. XV.

11*Ibid.,* Liber VI, Cap. VII.

12Ambicini, Joannis Fernellii, *De naturali parte medicinae,* 1543, in *Universa Medicina* (1581), *Physiologiae,* Liber VI, Cap. IV. In Cap. XVIII, 296, he says that from the lungs "spiritus in sinistrum cordis ventriculum aeripitur, ex que accedente etiam sanguinis vapore, qui ex dextre ventricule permanavit, vi cordis insita...procreatur spiritus vitalis, qui demum in omne corpus per arterias effusus, salutarem impartit toti calorem."

13Sylvius, Jacobus, *In Hippocratis et Galeni Physiologiae Partem Anatomicam Isagoge...,* Paris, 1555.

14Zwingeri, Theodori, *Physiologia Medica,* Basel, 1610, Cap. XVII.

15*Ibid.,* Cap. XVII, 337.

16Riolani, Joannis, *Opera Omnia,* Paris, 1610, *Physiologiae Sectio I,* 266.

17Bauhini, Caspari, *Institutiones Anatomicae,* Ed. Quinta, Frankfurt, 1616, 127.

18Riolani Filii, Joannis, *Anthropographia,* Paris, 1626, 360.

19Sennert, Daniel, *Institutiones Medicae,* Liber V, Third Edition, Wittenberg, 1628, 101.

20*Ibid.,* 612.

21*Ibid.,* 613.

22*Ibid.,* 614.

23Harvey, William, *op. cit.,* 1. Cap.

24Primirosus, Jacobus, *Exercitationes et animadversiones in librum de motu cordis et circulatione sanguinis* (*adversus Guilielmum Harveum*), London, 1630, 73.

25*Ibid.,* 72.

26*Ibid.,* 76.

27*Ibid.,* 77.

28Descartes, René, *Discours de la méthode,* Leiden, 1637, Cinquième Partie, "ces gouttes, qui ne peuvent être que fort grosses."

29Descartes, mentioning, in a letter to Mersenne in December, 1632, that he had read Harvey's book.

30Descartes, René, *L'Homme.* (German edition, *Uber den Menschen,* 1632..., Ed K. E. Rothschuh, Heidelberg, 1969, 47.)

[31]Riolani, Joannis, *Opuscula anatomica nova,* London, 1649, Cap. 11, 25-27.

[32]Riolani, Joannis, *Opuscula varia et nova in primis de motu sanguinis.* Paris, 1652. Riolani speaks of the droplike progression of the blood on 247, 326, 327, of the septum passage on 283, and of the simultaneity of many processes on 288.

[33]Slegelii, Pauli Marquarti, *De sanguinis mot commentatio,* Hamburg, 1650.

[34]Frisii, Hermanni Conringii, *De sanguinis generatione et motu naturali,* Helmstadt, 1643, 284-286.

[35]ab Hoghelande, Cornelis, *Cogitationes, quibus Dei Existentia; item Animae Spiritalitas et possilibus cum corpore unio, demonstrantur,* Amsterdam, 1646, 191-195.

[36]Plempius, Vopsicus Fortunatus, *Fundamenta Medicinae,* Ed. altera, Louvain, 1644, 115, estimates the heart action of hanged people at almost 2 ounces.

[37]de la Boe Sylvius, Franciscus, *Disputationum Medicarum Decas,* 1660, especially *Disp. III, De Chylis mutatione in sanguinem* ..., in *Opera Medica,* Geneva, 1681, 5, especially § XV, XVI, 6, § XXX, XXXIII.

[38]Lower, Richard, *Tractatus de corde.* Quoted from *Bibliotheca Anatomica,* Ed. Le Clerc and Mangetus, Tom. II, Geneva, 1685.

[39]*Ibid.,* Cap. II, 93.

[40]*Ibid.,* 91

[41]*Ibid.*

[42]*Ibid.,* 94.

[43]*Ibid.,* 87.

[44]Borelli, Giovanni Alphonso, *De motu animalium,* Rome, 1680-1681, Ed. Le Clerc and Mangetus, Tom II, Geneva, 1685, 932.

[45]*Ibid.,* 950.

[46]Hoffmanni, Friederici, *Medicina Rationalis Systematica,* Tom. I, Venice, 1730, 70.

[47]Hales, Etienne, *Haemastatique ou la Statique Des Amimaux.* Ed. Mr. de Sauvages, Geneva, 1744, 16-33.

# 25

## Marco Aurelio Severino and His Relationship to William Harvey: Some Preliminary Considerations

### CHARLES B. SCHMITT
### CHARLES WEBSTER

I N recent years scholarly research has shed much light upon the sources of William Harvey's thought, as well as upon the controversies which arose from his important discoveries. Though one still finds him characterized as a crude mechanist or as an anti-Aristotelian empiricist, the weight of evidence shows him in a far different light from that in which he was commonly viewed several decades ago. In many ways this re-evaluation is due to the numerous detailed studies of Dr. Pagel, which have illuminated the wide range of philosophical, theological, mystical, as well as scientific elements which went into Harvey's thought. In addition to the studies which have done much to clarify Harvey's debts to earlier traditions, there remains much work yet to be done before we can have a full understanding of the numerous controversies which were initiated by the publication in 1628 of the *De motu cordis*. These controversies continued unabated until the end of the seventeenth century and indeed spilled over into the next century.

We have a very incomplete understanding of the debates which followed the publication of *De motu cordis*. Among the most respected of the participants was Marco Aurelio Severino (1580-1656) of Naples, whose relations with the great English physician have been largely overlooked. Not only is there a correspondence connecting the two men, but there are also numerous references to Harvey and his doctrine of circulation in Severino's published works, as well as in Severino's voluminous unpublished writings. Owing to a variety of circumstances, Severino has never been studied by later scholars as carefully as he deserves, and even his role in developing a rational basis for the science of comparative anatomy during its formative years in the seventeenth century has only recently been adequately recognized.

Severino was almost an exact contemporary of Harvey. He ranked among the most renowned medical men of his age and his fame both as a teacher and as a medical authority, particularly in anatomy, surgery, and pathology, spread to all parts of Europe. Among his friends and correspondents are to be counted Danes such as Thomas Bartholin, Johan Rhode, and Ole Worm; Germans such as Hermann Conring, Caspar Hofmann, and Johannes Georg Volkamer; the learned Dutchman, Nicolaus Heinsius; Frenchmen such as Jean Riolan (The Younger) and René Moreau; Englishmen such as Harvey and George Ent; as well as numerous distinguished Italians from all parts of the peninsula. He was a true member of the seventeenth century's international intellectual community, one of the scientific *socii* of the *Respublica literaria*. Perhaps more honoured outside Italy than in his own country, where he fell foul of the still vigorous Neapolitan Inquisition, his medical textbooks were printed time and again north of the Alps well into the eighteenth century.

Born early in November, 1580, at Tarsia, a small Calabrian village, he was the son of a prominent lawyer, and the young Marco Aurelio's early education was directed towards preparing him for a legal career like that of his father. After an early education near home, he moved to Naples for more advanced studies. It was there, during his university days, that his attentions turned in the direction of medicine. While a student in the medical faculty, he studied with, among others, Quinzio Buongiovanni, Giulio Cesare Romano, and Latino Tancredi. Also during his student days at the southern Italian capital, Severino came into contact with Tommaso Campanella from whom he learned, among other things, the rudiments of the exciting new *Philosophia Telesiana*, then flourishing in the south. Though from all indications he was never officially enrolled as a student of the Dominican friar, Severino referred to him as *meus praeceptor* throughout his life. And, indeed, he exhibited many of the same unconventional and anti-authoritarian turns of mind as did the unfortunate Campanella.

After taking his degree from the still famous medical school of Salerno, Severino returned home to take up medical practice. This apparently was not to his liking, and he came back to Naples three years later for further studies in surgery with Giulio Iasolino. He was an apt student, for he began his own private teaching of surgery and anatomy a year later. When the University chair in these subjects became vacant in 1615, Severino was called to fill it. A few years later he was also named to become "first surgeon" in the important *osepdale degli incurabili*. For the remaining forty years of his life, Marco Aurelio worked and taught at Naples, ultimately becoming one of the brightest stars in the rich seventeenth-century Neapolitan culture, which gained worldwide fame. His renown as a teacher was such that it was said that he was able to draw students away from the famous medical school at Padua to fill his own lecture room. John Houghton of England, George Volkamer of Germany, Thomas Bartholin of Denmark, among many others, came to study with him or to visit him. Severino's attracting of fame to Naples at the time is clearly brought out in Bartholin's *De peregrinatione medica,* where Marco Aurelio's presence in that city is considered to be of tantamount interest to the seventeenth-century medical tourist.

Severino's published writings are quite voluminous, including the important *Zootomia Democritea,* published at Nuremberg in 1645, called by Cole 'the earliest comprehensive treatise on comparative anatomy.' Also influential on later developments in physiology was the *Antiperipatias* of 1655-59, a polemical work directed against the Aristotelian doctrine on the respiration of fishes. More widely popular were his *De recondita abscessum natura,* first published in 1632, and reprinted nine times by 1763; his surgery textbook, *Synopseos chirurgiae libri sex,* published in 1664, and reprinted four times by 1711; and *De efficaci medicina,* published in 1646, and reprinted seven times by 1708. In addition to these and other printed works, Severino left behind many volumes of manuscripts, most of which (77 volumes) remain preserved in the Biblioteca Lancisiana in Rome, where they have lain largely unstudied from his day to ours. Here are included, besides a vast correspondence, many medical works of great interest, some dealing specifically with Harvey's doctrine of circulation and others treating various important medical and scientific problems of his day.

Though Severino's career was successful, it was not without its difficulties. Besides coming into conflict with the Inquisition over matters of religious practice, he was criticised by colleagues and enemies for the use of excessive cruelty in his surgical practice. His fame and influence seem to have ultimately been greater in northern Europe than in his native Italy. Many of his more important works were published north of the Alps, through the intervention and help of his many friends there. The publication of some of his works was unduly delayed, as we shall see, perhaps partly through the efforts of his Italian opponents and enemies. Numerous other important writings by Severino were never published and thus escaped being in the mainstream of medical discussions of the decades after his death. All in all, however, his medical career was quite successful and his death on July 12, 1656, when he fell victim to the plague at Naples, was mourned throughout Europe.

Having thus sketched briefly Severino's life and activities, let us now turn to his relations with Harvey and his involvement with the theory of circulation. The full story cannot be told until we have been able to study Severino's manuscripts with the care which they deserve, but even from the printed sources the main lines of the Severino-Harvey relationship seem clear.

Inevitably Severino, as one of the leading Italian medical theorists and teachers, was quickly drawn into the debate on circulation which ensued upon the publication of *De motu cordis*. This unpretentious work was brought forcibly to the attention of the Italian medical public by Emilio Parigiano, whose *Nobilium exercitationum de subtilitate pars altera de cordis et sanguinis motu singularis certaminis lapis Lydius* appeared in Venice in 1635 and again in 1639. This reprinted a major portion of Harvey's work, interspersed with Parigiano's polemic against circulation. Initially it is probable that Severino was caught up in the wave of criticism which greeted Harvey's discovery. Indeed he was prompted to compose a lengthy critical dissertation on circulation, which was periodically modified but never published.

Like Gassendi and Plemp, Severino's motives for opposing Harvey were empirical rather than dogmatic. Thus they all became converted to Harvey's point of view once the empirical superiority of his discovery was demonstrated. Circulation was then integrated into their antiperipatetic natural philosophies as it had been into Harvey's neo-Aristotelianism.

Severino's conversion to Harvey was certainly accelerated by his association with the medical students who were increasingly attracted to the medical school at Naples. This generation, particularly the north Europeans, enthusiastically greeted Harvey's work and played an important role in its dissemination and in the development of a new system of physiology based on circulation.

Among Severino's visitors may well have been Harvey himself. After taking part in the Earl of Arundel's diplomatic mission to Prague, in 1636 he undertook a detour which led him to Rome, where he initiated a life-long friendship with George Ent. Ent had left Cambridge to complete his medical studies in Italy, having taken his M.D. at Padua shortly before becoming acquainted with Harvey. After Rome, Ent and Harvey visited Naples, where they almost certainly met Severino. Indeed this may well have been one of the main purposes for their visit. Whatever the precise details, Severino had a direct association with Harvey and Ent from about this date. This was maintained by correspondence, during which Harvey presented Severino with the only known presentation copy of the first edition of *De motu cordis*. At this time Severino was visited by two more Cambridge medical students, John Houghton and Samuel Remington, both of whom were supporters of Harvey. The former became Severino's main informant on English affairs and was credited with producing the conclusive arguments which led to the complete conversion of the Neapolitan professor to the doctrine of circulation.

Thus by 1640 Severino was firmly in the Harveian camp. Nevertheless his physiological standpoint was sufficiently distinctive for his views to be sought on the physiological implications of circulation. Particularly active in stimulating the exchange of ideas on the new physiology was the Dane, Thomas Bartholin (1616-1680) who arrived in Italy in 1643 for a visit which culminated in a prolonged period of study with Severino at Naples. At Padua Bartholin gave new impetus to Harveian studies by publishing in 1643 a revised edition of his father's *Institutiones anatomicae* which not only brought this work into line with the new theory, but also reprinted for the first time the complete text of *De motu cordis,* and published Walaeus' important *Epistolae duae de motu chyli et sanguinis.* Bartholin went on to solicit further material in support of Harvey, writing in 1643 to request an essay from Severino.

Severino's reply, published in 1663 in Bartholin's *Epistolae medicinales*[2] and entitled "De Harveo judicium", has been universally misinterpreted as an adverse opinion of Harvey. In fact the tone of the letter is one of unrestrained admiration for both Bartholin and Harvey, whose approach to biology through the scrupulous direct study of animals was regarded as typifying his own attitude. Rather than being critical of Harvey's theory, his letter expresses a modest reservation about the value of actually publishing his own views on the subject. He nevertheless sent his own essay on circulation to Bartholin with permission for the Dane to publish it, provided that 'it seems worthy of Harvey'. This essay which had previously been submitted to Harvey himself by letter, was gratefully received by Bartholin, who promised to give it maximum publicity.[3] However it was never published and has not yet been traced.

Yet another visitor to Naples during this period was Johann Georg Volkamer (1616-1693) a prominent member of the Nuremberg Society of *virtuosi,* who undertook the publication of Severino's major work,

*Zootomia Democritea.* This foundation work of comparative anatomy had been composed over many years and was probably virtually complete by the time of Severino's conversion to Harvey's theory. Nevertheless it contains significant but hitherto unnoticed references to Harvey and circulation. The Introduction, composed by Volkamer in September 1645, wrote of the prophetic significance of this work which had been vindicated by the recent successes of those following comparative anatomy. Volkamer singled out Aselli's discovery of the lacteals in dogs and Harveian circulation, recently expounded by Severino's friend Hermann Conring, as the main achievements of zootomy.

In general spirit *Zootomia Democritea* was an ideal complement to Harvey's work, elaborating a methodology and view of structural and physiological unity of animal life which was implicit in *De motu cordis*. Not only was reference to lower organisms advocated for the solution of problems relating to man, but Severino illustrated his thesis with a rich collection of observations and details of novel technical procedures. *Zootomia Democritea* was therefore a valuable handbook for the practitioners of the new physiology and comparative anatomy. Among other things, the book served to reinforce the attribution of the science of comparative anatomy to Democritus, creating a climate of opinion favourable to the revival of biological explanations based on Democritean atomism.

Aselli and Harvey were foremost in Severino's lists of exponents of compartive anatomy,[4] most of the other figures mentioned being followers of Harvey. It was argued that the comparative approach was ideally suited to solve the disagreements over cardio-vascular physiology.[5] While he was not explicit in explaining the detailed path of blood flow, it was described as a process of distillation or circulation *(destillaria, circulatio)*, following the terminology borrowed from the iatrochemists and the general analogy between body and state. As in *De motu cordis* the primacy of the heart was greatly emphasised.

Two further works by Severino, *Antiperipatias* and *Phoca illustrata*—composed by 1645, but not published until 1659, several years after his death—indicate more explicitly Severino's debt to Harvey. *Antiperipatias* is an erudite monograph on respiration in fishes, based on detailed studies of the gill arches. Harvey himself had been aware of the relevance of this problem to circulation, as witnessed by frequent references to respiration. He promised a treatise on respiration as a supplement to *De motu cordis*, probably intended to supplant his teacher Fabricius's *De respiratione*, a work which had provided the occasion for *De motu cordis*. Severino applied the comparative approach to solving the long-debated question of the necessity and role of air in the support of life. On this question Harvey came nearer to the Aristotelian point of view, arguing that respiration served primarily a cooling function; it was not drawn into the bloodstream and its functions in aquatic animals were performed by water. Hence, air was not thought necessary for fishes.

On the basis of comparative anatomy, Severino followed Pliny and Rondelet, arguing that the gills were analogous to lungs and that both absorbed air. This air was not only a cooling agent but the fuel for the vital flame of life. Consequently, the view of circulation adopted by Severino, along with George Ent, was alien to Harvey's in allowing air, or its nitrous component, to enter the circulating blood. No doubt Harvey's opposition to this idea was founded on his rejection of the Galenic theory, which allowed ill-defined gaseous components to play a considerable role in the blood stream. Harvey's insistence that the blood stream contained blood alone was of considerable importance in his proof of circulation. In his later writings, however, when searching for a characterisation of the vital principle of the heart and blood, he came nearer to the position of Ent and Severino.

In Severino's *Antiperipatias* the heart was described as the "vitae principium, Vestalis igniculi nostri focus in animalibus omnibus".[6] Harvey spoke of the vital agency in similar terms, "focus, Vesta, lar familiaris, calidum innatum, Sol microcosmi, igni *Platonis*...quod vago ac perpetuo motu se ipsum conservet, nutriat et auget."[7] Both authors selected Aristotle's analogy with boiling milk to characterise the vitalisation of the blood in the ventricles, whereas Ent preferred a more explicit chemical analogy.

In accordance with his views on the uniformity of animal structure, Severino asserted that fishes had respiration and circulation. However, his appendix on circulation described a pathway which would have been correct only for aquatic mammals. Elsewhere, he was in error in his speculations about the circulation between the heart, gills and swim bladder. Such confusions were avoided in *Phoca illustrata,* which appeared at Naples in 1655. This was an account of the anatomy and physiology of the seal, published inexplicably without illustrations! It was presented as a tribute to Harvey, Ent, Thomas Bartholin, Nathaniel Highmore, Hermann Conring, Johannes van Horn, Fortunatus Plemp, Werner Rolphinck, Wilhelm Ernst Scheffer and Pietro Castelli. The preface, dated 9 December 1645, contains a eulogy of Harvey and his adherents. Severino writes of the universal opposition which the theory of circulation had incurred throughout Europe from those determined not to depart one hair's breadth from the ideas of antiquity. But these dogmatic critics such as Parigiano, Primrose and Birckner had been overcome by Harvey's able supporters, who had rigorously applied themselves to experiment and comparative anatomy. Severino knew that Bartholin had modified his father's textbook to accord with the Harveian doctrine of circulation. Plemp, like Severino, became a convert to Harvey and in 1644 corrected his own textbook, *Fundamenta medicinae* to fit in with the new theory. Conring's lengthy and erudite defence, *De sanguinis generatione et motu naturali*, published in 1643 was the first presentation of Harvey's theory in Germany. Severino was particularly impressed by Ent, author of *Apologia pro circulatione sanguinis*, which appeared at London in 1641. In a letter to Houghton, he described Ent as the 'very soul of the Harveian camp.' The other defenders of the Harveian position had not published in favour of circulation by 1645, but most were to do so within the next new years. One wonders whether Severino, like Harvey, had forewarning of the publication in 1651 of Highmore's *History of Generation,* a pioneer work in which the findings of comparative embryology were given an explanation in terms of Democritean atomism.

The description of the physiology and anatomy of the seal made very frequent reference to Harvey, in deference to whom Severino withdrew his former ideas on the entry of gaseous air into the bloodstream. Now it was suggested that a portion of air was dissolved into the blood to serve as the nutrient for the vital fire in the heart. Consequently, Severino was anticipating the combustion and fermentation theories of respiration which were elaborated by the younger generation of Harvey's followers. However, although plans for the publication of *Phoca illustrata* were well advanced in 1645, when Severino's letters mentioned imminent publication by Conring at Helmstadt, its actual publication was delayed until 1659. This year was marked by the appearance of two other works expressing a similar approach to physiology and comparative anatomy, also containing views on respiration ahd circulation in line with Severino. These were Walter Charleton's *Oeconomia animalis* and Thomas Willis's *Diatriba duae Medico-Philosophicae...De fermentatione...altera de febribus*, works which had a considerable influence in the later seventeenth century. These authors, although inspired by Harvey, departed considerably from his neo-Aristotelian approach to physiology. At every point Harvey had resisted the reductionalist biological theories, whether emanating from Descartes, the ancient materialists, or the iatrochemists. Severino had no such inhibitions. Inspired by the iconoclastic instincts and new philosophies of Telesio and Campanella, he turned to Democritus for insight into methodology and explanation. Descriptive comparative anatomy, the analysis of bodies into their sets of analogous smallest constituent parts, was a prelude to ultimate explanations in terms of atoms. Thus, in the decades which saw the rapid rise of atomism primarily in the context of the physical sciences, Severino was developing a similar approach based on his biological and medical experiences. Although his works were deprived of their full impact by delay in publication, Severino's prestige as a teacher and his wide correspondence suggest that he may have had a considerable influence on the inter-related schools of comparative anatomy and mechanical physiology which had such a dramatic rise in England and Italy within a few years of his death.

The Harvey-Severino relationship is instructive in several ways. Firstly it draws attention to the neglect of certain major biological thinkers at the time of Harvey. It also indicates that scientific correspondence involving a large community of intellectuals played an important role in evolution of scientific opinion. Such olympian figures as Harvey cannot be understood without reference to this background. Finally, the example of Severino powerfully substantiates the view so long expressed by Walter Pagel, that the emergence of scientific physiology in the seventeenth century can only be properly understood by reference to underlying philosophical debates. There was a reciprocal and fruitful interaction between experimental work and philosophical speculation. The poles of opinion represented by Harvey's neo-Aristotelianism, Severino's neo-Democriteanism, Cartesian mechanical philosophy and Helmontianism, engendered a fertile debate on basic questions of explanation which provided a crucial factor in success of mid-seventeenth century biology.

## References

[1]In this paper we have tried merely to sketch out the bare essentials of a.series of questions which we plan to treat in much greater detail elsewhere. For a fully documented and much expanded version of the present paper, which includes a detailed bibliography of Severino's works, a list of the more important secondary works concerning him, and a discussion of the extant manuscript sources, see our "Harvey and M. A. Severino: A Neglected Medical Relationship," *Bulletin of the History of Medicine* XLV (1971), 49-75. We plan to publish with introduction, notes, and translations Severino's correspondence of more than thirty letters with English medical men—viz. George Ent, William Harvey, John Houghton, Richard London, Theophilus May and Samuel Remington—in a forthcoming volume.

[2]Bartholin, Thomas, *Epistolae medicinales,* Copenhagen, 1663, No. XXXI.

[3]*Ibid.,* No. XXXIV.

[4]Severino, Marco Aurelio, *Zootomia Democritea,* 150, 259-60.

[5]*Ibid.,* 151.

[6]Severino, *Antiperipatias,* Naples, 1659, 102.

[7]Harvey, *Exercitationes de generatione animalium,* London, 1651, Ex. 70.

# 26

# The Controversy between Descartes and Harvey Regarding the Nature of Cardiac Motions*

## RICHARD TOELLNER

*Translated by* GUENTER B. RISSE

## A. EXPERIMENTUM ET RATIO

### 1. *The general problem*

EXPERIMENTUM ET RATIO, or experience and reason, are keywords for the understanding of modern science. They reflect two approaches to knowledge which, since the 17th century, have been pitted against each other as representing empiricism and rationalism, respectively. However, such a gross distinction between them has not blunted the realization that neither pure experience nor pure reason can exist alone. New observations and experiences cannot be made without some preexisting rational principles while postulates of pure reason are, to quote Kant, "nothing but mere semblances."[1] In other words, all *a priori* knowledge presupposes a certain understanding of reality while *a posteriori* cognition aims at a rational representation of reality.

Therefore, empiricism is essentially determined through rational elements and rationalism by empirical factors which it always subsumes. Hence, modern empirical science will be able to make more precise statements inasmuch as it understands and remains conscious of its postulates: to restrict its pronouncements to the results obtained with the scientific method here under analysis.

### 2. *The specific problem in its historical and intellectual aspects*

The problem of the relationship between experience and reason, of great importance for the history of science will, to some degree, concern us today. We will deal with the question as to what extent "experimentum" (observation, experience and experiment) and "ratio" (reason and its conclusions) play a role in the dispute between William Harvey and

*Inaugural lecture, after being appointed Professor of the History of Medicine, given on November 12, 1968, at the Westphalian Wilhelms University of Muenster in honor of Walter Pagel.

73

René Descartes regarding the nature of cardiac motion. This debate represents only a minor episode in the history of 17th century medicine and has not hitherto received much attention in the Harveyan or Cartesian literature.

However, problems and insights may emerge from the study of a single historical event which could have a more general and lasting character and may still affect us today. Such a connection with the present must remain a secondary and subordinate goal to the historian but it explains our interest in history.

In this sense, we shall attempt to illustrate how Descartes and Harvey, two great scientists, deal with experience and reason for the correct description and explanation of a physiological phenomenon. Furthermore, we will also try to show how the dispute between the founders of modern philosophy and physiology heralds the great controversy over the proper reason-experience relationship which Kant brought to a temporary conclusion.

Finally, the seemingly paradoxical facts will be elucidated whereby Harvey empirically investigating but deeply rooted in late medieval Aristotelianism in the end was correct in contrast to Descartes, the creator of the modern scientific world-view. Harvey's theoretically less-than-revolutionary circulation scheme started—as Rothschuh has convincingly demonstrated—the "process of autocatalytic increase in knowledge and unfolding of problems." Such a development radically changed a two-thousand-year-old medicine "so that we can properly speak of a post-Harveyan era in medicine."[2]

By contrast, Descartes' physiological conceptions were quite revolutionary but soon abandoned by his closest followers because they were impossible to prove experimentally. Therefore, Leibniz would speak of Cartesian physics and Haller of Descartes' physiology with contempt, both regretting the formulation of such "physical fables."[3] However, Leibniz, the founder of German rationalism, and Haller, the originator of modern experimental physiology, would be inconceivable without Cartesianism. Moreover, Descartes' influence was decisive in the establishment of the new theory of blood circulation.

In order to understand the prevailing conditions under which the dispute on cardiac motion took place between Descartes and Harvey, it is essential to describe the points of departure of both authors. The Venetian humanist Cesare Cremonini has become, at least since Bertold Brecht, a symbol for those people who refuse to accept empirical facts because they do not fit into their world-view. In a letter written to Kepler and dated August 19, 1610, Galileo mentions that Cremonini has steadfastly refused to take even one look through the telescope to see the planets and their satellites.[4] Whether the Aristotelian Cremonini, conscious of the unpredictable consequences associated with the introduction of the Copernican system, acted wisely or not is unimportant. He certainly closed his eyes to a sensually perceptible proof of the new astronomy, "seeking the truth not in the world or in nature...but in his acquaintance with texts,"[5] as Galileo reproachfully stated.

In refusing to recognize a certain relationship, one has in a sense, already tacitly accepted it. This point is made clear by the Bolognese mathematician Magini, who in the interests of the old cosmology simply demanded from Kepler: "The four new satellites of Jupiter must be eliminated and forgotten."[6] The aim was not to deny the observed circumstances and attempt to label the perception of the phenomena erroneous. Rather, the suggestion was to disregard such facts because "nothing can possibly exist which must not be."

The example emphatically demonstrates the strength of the new insight which emerges in the early 17th century. Such a novel concept proposed that observations and experiments derived from nature were more valid than the knowledge derived from books and schools. The sentence "No other proof can be more convincing than perception and personal observation,"[7] reflects the conviction of a man who replies to "those who believe it to be a crime to doubt the authority of the ancients." The answer is "that no dogmas can suppress the obvious facts and no old traditions stifle the work of nature because nothing is more ancient and of greater authority than nature herself."[8] The man who spoke these words and appears to be, like Galileo, an adversary of Aristotle, is no other than the Aristotelian William Harvey.[9]

## B. THE NATURE OF THE CARDIAC MOTION

### 1. *Harvey's position*

Harvey was a contemporary of Francis Bacon and Galileo Galilei, men whose names we link with the introduction of the empirical and inductive method, and thus the beginnings of modern scientific research. Although Harvey must have encountered Galileo at Padua and, as a court physician to James I, could not have ignored the activities of Lord Bacon, there is no proof that they ever influenced him directly.[10]

The appreciation of experiments, observations and experience was, therefore, a general characteristic of a period in this history of science deeply polarized by the followers and detractors of Aristotle. Harvey's preferences for the "sensus" (perception) and "autopsia" (personal observation) as contrasted with "ratiocinium" (the fruits of reason) are not so much characteristic of the man himself but rather of his time. Harveys confidence in experience was therefore more a contemporary presupposition than a self-acquired insight which allowed him to become the immortal discoverer of the circulation.

The discovery was aided by Harvey's preference for anatomical studies. These investigations were carried out during his student days in Cambridge and Padua, and continued until his death. From the notes which Harvey made and the manuscripts of his anatomical lectures—in 1615 he held a chair of anatomy and surgery in London—the stages of his discovery become apparent.

At first, Harvey carried out careful anatomical observations of the venous valves which his teacher Fabricius ab Aquapendente had described in Padua. Then he went on to study the anatomical differences between arteries and veins, the structure of the heart and especially the cardiac valves, which made him question the traditional physiology ascribed to the central organ.

Performing many animal experiments, Harvey attempted to observe carefully the cardiac motions, noting that the auricular contractions alternated with those of the ventricles. Moreover, he realized that the ejection of blood did occur during systole when the chambers contracted rather than in diastole when the walls were distended. During systole, the apex of the heart arose, touching the chest wall and generating a beat which was synchronous with the pulsations of the arteries. Therefore, the throbbing of the heart or systole actually coincided with the diastole of the arteries.

The nature of the cardiac motions which could now be divided into an active systolic contraction and a passive diastolic dilatation became the starting point for new inquiries. Taking into account the valvular mechanics already elucidated by Galen, the thought emerged that the blood entered the ventricles from the auricles during the dilatation of the former. This blood was subsequently ejected during the ventricular contraction into both the large artery (aorta) and the arterial vein (pulmonary artery). If one estimated the volume of blood which was discharged to the periphery during each ventricular systole, and multi-plied such an amount by the number of heart beats, the resulting volume was so great that it could not possibly be all used in the periphery of the body for nutrition and structural replacement as postulated by the older physiology.

At this stage of his observations and thinking, Harvey declares: "In consequence, I began privately to consider if it [the blood] had a movement, as it were, in a circle. This hypothesis I subsequently verified, finding that the pulsation of the left ventricle of the heart forces the blood out of it and propels it through the arteries into all parts of the body's system in exactly the same way as the pulsation of the right ventricle forces the blood out of that chamber and propels it through the artery-like vein into the lungs."[11]

The conceptual framework from which Harvey drew such a conclusion is reflected in the passage which follows his description of the circulation. He wrote: "We have as much right to call this movement of the blood circular as Aristotle had to say that air and rain emulate the circular movement of the heavenly bodies."[12] With this sentence, Harvey reveals himself not only as an individual versed in Aristotelian meteorology and cosmology, but, what is more important, he seems to partake of Aristotle's metaphysical foundations.

Harvey's world is still the Aristotelian cosmos in which circular motion occupies a special place among all other movements. Moreover, life is a distinctive process within the sublunar, terrestrial sphere, characterized by birth and death, growth and decay, change and motion, all of which must be understood and derived from first philosophical principles. Thus, as the sun's movements and warmth are the source of all motions, mixtures and transformations of the macrocosmic elements, the heart with its contractions and beat is the fountain, origin and highest principle of the body or microcosm.

Therefore, Harvey can state: "Therein, by the natural, powerful, fiery heat, a sort of store of life, it [the blood] is re-liquified and becomes impregnated with spirits and sweetness. From the heart it is redistributed. And all these happenings are dependent upon the pulsatile movement of the heart. This organ deserves to be styled the starting point of life and the sun of our microcosm just as much as the sun deserves to be styled the heart of the world. For it is by the heart's vigorous beat that the blood is moved, perfected, activated, and protected from injury and decay."[13]

We know from Harvey's notes that he was convinced as early as 1616 "that a steady flow of blood takes place in a circular manner with the help of a cardiac pulsation."[14] However, only twelve years later he finally decided to acquaint the public with his theory. Although repeated observations and experiments had convinced him of the correctness of his conclusions—they coincided with the principles of Aristotelian-Galenic medicine—Harvey foresaw the effects which his new theory was to have. Indeed, one of his early adherents in Germany, Paul Marquard Schlegel, wrote that "the unheard of scheme which was directed against the general concepts prevailing for centuries brought about a great commotion. There were hardly any physicians who, after hearing of Harvey's discovery, did not decry the work as complete nonsense and urge its banning from the schools."[15]

Harvey had expected such a reaction, as reflected in the cautious words he used on the occasion of dedicating his work to the "doctissimis medicis collegis suis amantissimis." The book, entitled *Exercitatio anatomica de motu cordis et sanguinis in animalibus,* appeared in 1628, published by Wilhelm Fitzer in Frankfurt. The publisher excused himself for the numerous printer's errors, adducing "unfavorable times"—the Thirty Years' War which was ravaging Germany.

## 2. *The Cartesian position*

Harvey's delayed publication of the new circulation theory caused not only confusion and fear; one representative of the French landed gentry immediately greeted the book as "by far the most important and useful discovery in medicine."[16] The author of this laudatory statement was the Sieur du Perron, René Descartes, born in Touraine in 1596, who had just emigrated to Holland when the *Exercitatio anatomica de motu cordis et sanguinis* appeared.

Descartes had gone to a country in which both the economy and science were thriving, and tolerance as well as peace prevailed. There, at his leisure and in the seclusion and safety of that land, he proposed to do those things which he had planned as a young man. In his search for truth, Descartes declared: "I intended to spend a great deal of time in necessary preparations in order to eradicate from my mind all previously adopted and detrimental convictions. Moreover, I wanted to collect a lot of experiences as material for subsequent conclusions, always practicing my self-prescribed method so as to acquire greater skills in using it."[17]

Thus, Descartes spent twenty years in Holland establishing a new philosophy and physical science. In 1650, he died in Sweden because Queen Christina did not understand that one should not summon a philosopher at 5 A.M. during wintry Swedish nights in order to receive philosophy lessons. Descartes did not survive such calls. He caught pneumonia and, true to himself and his principles, refused treatment, dying of the disease to the satisfaction of the attending physicians. Nevertheless, they never forgave him for having perished without their assistance.[18]

René Descartes sought the truth with an unequalled seriousness of mind. He looked for unquestioned knowledge, certainty and confidence. Disappointed because of the contradictions and uncertainties inherent in all book-learning and science, Descartes probed in "the book of the world," nature, for more precise and unambiguous answers.[19] However, he discovered that the perceived phenomena, appearances and relationships in nature were just as equivocal and muddled as the theories and interpretations about them. Therefore, Descartes decided to search for truth within himself rather than in nature or in previous authorities.

Descartes defined as true only that which could be recognized as clear and distinct, together with certain statements which could successfully resist any possible doubt. Thus, the philosopher began systematically to doubt everything he had previously considered to be certain and true, including God, the soul and the world." Everything I have hitherto believed to be true," he declared, "I received from or through the senses, but I sometimes discovered that they had deceived me. Now wisdom means that one should never trust those who have cheated us, even when the deception happened only once."[20]

Hence, everything which is possibly certain falls prey to the methodological doubt, for example, the internal and external sensory impressions mediated through body and environment. The empirical sciences and even mathematics, whose principles appear to be clear and true, were included in the sceptical approach. When everything seemingly secure and certain was engulfed in doubt, Descartes reached the "rock of certitude," the "fundamentum inconcussum" which he had set out to find. Descartes declared: "For while I doubt, I cannot doubt that I doubt what I think. Because I think, therefore, I exist."

Taking the certainty of his own existence as a thinking entity— the "res cogitans"—as his basis, Descartes recovers all those elements, such as God and the world, he had previously dismissed in his scepticism. "Archimedes only required a firm and immovable point to mobilize the whole earth," wrote Descartes, "and therefore great things may be expected if I find something firm and unshakable no matter how small."[21]

This so-called "fundamentum inconcussum" which Archimedes searched for, had apparently been found by Descartes who was determined to change the world. With the help of deduction, he wanted to separate the object—*res extensa*—from the perceiving subject. The history of philosophy, much to its detriment, has not hitherto adequately recognized that Descartes' thinking was strongly geared toward practical verification. The great Cartesian polemic with traditional metaphysics is not carried out in order to erect a new metaphysical framework, but to arrive at a new physical science. In truth, the metaphysical foundations of the Cartesian method—"to guide reason properly and search for truth in science"[22]—only serve to fasten his method more securely in order that man may become the "maître et possesseur," the master and owner of nature through recognition of his own autonomous reason.[23]

Descartes succeeds in his efforts to reduce nature, its components and events, into matter and motion. This is accomplished by a rigorous separation and differentiation between the thinking subject and the objective world, subject and object, spirit and matter. Thus, everything in nature can be explained "more geometrico" and controlled as well as constructed by reason.

Descartes' new, purely mechanical physics allows in theory a technical approach to nature, and he was convinced that it was not farfetched to imagine the organism as a mechanical instrument. "I presume," he says, "that the body is merely a figure or machine made out of clay which God casts into a form closely resembling us. Therefore, he not only gives externally such a machine the color and form of our limbs, but furnishes inner parts necessary for walking, eating and breathing. Finally, it is endowed with all our functions which we presume are derived from matter and the disposition of the various organs."[24]

Hence, Descartes constructs his physiology on the basis of mechanical models provided by his contemporaries: the clock, organ, and hydraulic devices. In view of such physiological ideas, one can understand the reasons why Descartes—at first on hearsay only—enthusiastically accepted the discovery of the circulation by the English physician William Harvey. However, after studying in detail the book *De motu cordis,* Descartes discovered that, although the movement of the blood seemed to be confirmed by his own criteria, the cardiac motions were explained quite contrary to his ideas.

Descartes believed in the connection of heart and circulation as one thermodynamic unit which functioned as follows: through the venous openings, two large drops of blood fall into both cardiac chambers where they experience an explosive dilatation thanks to the heat contained in a residual fraction of fermented blood. The ebullition causes the distillation of various blood fractions, the uppermost being that of the fine "animal spirits." The pressure accompanying the explosion closes the venous valves and forces an opening of the arterial orifices, whereby the hot and divided blood is ejected towards the periphery at the height of the cardiac diastole or dilatation. The more subtle fraction reaches the brain through the carotid arteries, traveling from there to the hollow nerves where it becomes the nervous spirit matter responsible for sensation and motion.[25]

## C. THE CONTROVERSY

### 1. *The opposing viewpoints*

From the above description of the Harveyan and Cartesian positions, it is clear that Descartes, in contrast to Harvey, denies the active contraction of the heart. Seemingly traditional, the philosopher holds fast to the idea that the ejection of blood occurs during diastole, and that such diastole is the result of an expansion of heated blood. Descartes also borrows the concept of a "calor innatus"—an innate heat—from the ancients. Thus, he undeniably adopts many ideas from traditional physiology although he attempts to understand them according to his own principles. The "calor" of the heart, which Descartes never calls "innatus," is not the traditionally implanted heat but rather a "lightless fire." This he conceived to be something "that makes the hay warm when it is stored before being dry, and what causes young wines to ferment."[26] Heat is, therefore, a physically concieved ferment, the rapid motion of subtle particles of matter occurring in the undivided world of dead and living things. Heat is the result of motion, not a principle of vitality.

For Harvey, the "pulsating motion of the heart" was the "origin [*principium*] of life."[27] Although Harvey later claimed, on the basis of his embryological studies, that the blood itself was the cause of its own and the cardiac motions, this shift has no bearing on the matter. What is important is that the cardiac capacity for active contraction was, whatever its cause, a substantial form. According to Aristotelian concepts, it was an effect of the soul, a "spiritus vivificus" which Descartes, referring to Harvey, considered an occult quality.[28]

Descartes could not take such an entity, derived from ancient qualitative physics, as the cause of motion for his mechanical system. Rather, he was in need of a mechanical power which he found in heat. Such a cause was sufficient to explain the pressure, boiling, and production of the various blood fractions. At the same time, the thermic theory necessarily molded the Cartesian concept of cardiac motion, a fact freely acknowledged by Descartes: "For, if we presume that the heart is moved in the manner described by Harvey, one has not only to consider a special power causing motion—whose nature is difficult to explain—but also accept the presence of other forces capable of changing the qualities of the cardiac blood."[29]

Thus, the question concerning the correct description of cardiac motions and their cause becomes the cornerstone for the entire Cartesian physiology. Descartes himself declares "that it is of the greatest importance to ascertain the true origin of the cardiac motions. Without them, it would be impossible to learn anything concerning physiology since all other bodily functions depend on the movement of the heart."[30]

Indeed, the entire question becomes the touchstone for Descartes' philosophy. "I explain...everything that belongs to the motions of the heart quite differently than Harvey," Descartes announces on February 9, 1639, to his close friend Mersenne, "but if what I have written is false, I will concede that the rest of my philosophy is likewise an error."[31] What these sentences reflect is the hitherto overlooked seriousness with which Descartes viewed his so-called "fables" or hypotheses, and the reason for his stubborn opposition to Harvey's ideas on cardiac motion which were based on observation and experiment.

If one compares the Cartesian and Harveyan schemes of cardiac movements as well as their origin and effects with those valid today, Harvey's theory emerges as the correct one in all essential aspects, while Descartes' ideas were all erroneous. Such a fact constitutes a devastating indictment of the Cartesian hypothesis. Now, if one asks why Harvey arrived at the correct solution while Descartes blundered, the answer will have to be sought in the relationship between *experimentum et ratio*.

## 2. *The origin of the controversy*

Both Harvey and Descartes, as we have seen, experimented with widely diverging results. One can explain such a discrepancy by stating that Harvey made careful and precise observations at the proper time and on the proper subject while Descartes did not. However, if one scrutinizes the whole question in more detail, both authors appear to have observed similar facts in the same fashion, describing the rhythmical change between cardiac expansion and contraction. Although certain details remained controversial between both authors, one can quickly recognize that the real issue was not about what could be seen or perceived, but how those events were to be interpreted. Therefore, the controversy between Harvey and Descartes concerning the nature of cardiac motions does not arise because of observational discrepancies but lies in the differing interpretations of the perceived phenomena.

This is made plain by Descartes' understanding of two experiments which actually refute the idea of a passive cardiac dilatation, confirming instead Harvey's theory of an active contraction of the heart. In the first experiment, a heart is taken out of the organism and deprived of all blood supply, and continues to contract for some time. Therefore, the pulsation cannot be ascribed to the expansion of blood in the cardiac chambers.

Descartes does not deny the experiment but objects to the conclusion drawn from it. Being fond of log fires, he explains the phenomenon with the help of an analogy. The situation, he says, is similar to the burning of a green piece of wood still quite impregnated with moisture as the heart is saturated with blood. When the log burns, he declares, one can see "that the vapors escaping from the interior of the wood emerge through the narrow crevices of the bark because of the heat. Their escape can be likened to a wind, since the bark begins to swell and show a series of fracture lines. Once the bark breaks at a certain point, the swelling disappears because the trapped moisture has been released. Shortly thereafter, as new vapor is formed, the bark arches again, intermittently releasing the vapor through the existing opening. This phenomenon occurs rhythmically and can be compared to the pulsations of an isolated eel's heart."[32]

In the second experiment, a finger introduced into the cardiac ventricle through a hole at the apex is able to feel the systolic contraction. Again, Descartes does not deny the phenomenon but gives it a different interpretation. He declares that the finger is not squeezed by the contracting walls of the ventricle but rather by the tendinous fibers which exist between the papillary muscles and the valves in the chamber. These fibres are being distended during the ventricular dilatation. It is only logical that Descartes concludes his interpretation by declaring that these experiments prove only "that our experience provides us often with opportunities for error if we do not examine carefully all possible reasons."[33]

Seldom has Descartes expressed himself as clearly about the relationship of experience and reasoning as in the above statements. They also depict the Cartesian viewpoint about observation, experience and experiment. Hence, the conflict between Descartes and Harvey about the cardiac motions proves to be, in the end, a dispute about the proper sequence of experience and reason, *experimentum et ratio.*

Descartes' experiments and observations were obviously only designed to confirm his rational conclusions about the structure and function of the organism, and not to challenge these views. When a certain observation or an experiment seemed to contradict such ideas, Descartes was always prepared—on the basis of his fundamental principles—to doubt those empirically acquired results. For him, only the conclusions which reason clearly and distinctly recognize were true, while the phenomena were by themselves, confusing and ambiguous.

Objects placed before our eyes reveal only their complex secondary qualities. Phenomena can be adequately grasped only if the primary qualities of things—their geometrical characteristics such as motion and form—are clearly distinguished. Such recognition is necessary before one can appreciate the secondary qualities and recognize the existing geometrical and mechanical relationships. Descartes wanted absolute certainty of knowledge and this is only possible through "more geometrico," the method of rational revelation. Descartes does not trust the senses but rather relies on reason.

Because Descartes builds into his system only those observations and experiences which can be mechanically interpreted, he incorporates uncritically and without hesitation many of the old ideas pertaining to anatomy, physiology and pathology. Such an assimilation was carried out without any consideration of the context, diametrically opposed to his own, in which these ideas had originated and been operational. Descartes thus overlooked the fact that his contemporaries, still thinking within these older cosmological frameworks, were bound to misunderstand him. Moreover, he did not realize in his scorn for history that language, the most effective historical tool, would become a Trojan horse for his system. Precisely because he adopted older concepts and ideas, Descartes allowed his opponents to infiltrate his system and attempt to destroy it from within. Therefore, the history of philosophy has been able to demonstrate, step by step, how Descartes remained a prisoner of the history which he believed he had shed so determinedly by his methodological approach. In the end, he became the victim of his own fiction.

In contrast, Harvey based the certainty of his knowledge primarily on "sensus, autopsia et experimentum"—perception, personal observation and experience, which he placed before "ratiocinium" or reason.[34] In so doing, Harvey remained completely within the Aristotelian framework of thought, even though he contradicted individual tenets of the system because he recognized the phenomena more correctly through more precise observations and experimental skill.

However, Harvey used his new insights into cardiac motion and blood circulation the better to illuminate the Aristotelian truth of life as a special process within the entire cosmic activity and the inextricable relationship between form and matter, body and soul, force and motion. The unquestioned acceptance of cardiac contraction as a vital phenomenon particularly allowed the establishment of the new concepts. Harvey, of course, came into conflict with his own physiology because of novel empirical findings, thus creating problems which he himself could not solve.

The theory of the blood circulation contradicted almost all those functions previously ascribed to the blood. Harvey's most serious adversary, the Parisian anatomist Riolan, Jr., clearly pointed out the difficulties for traditional physiology, pathology and therapy which resulted from Harvey's scheme. Riolan's presentation was sharp and made in the spirit of self-righteous conviction which certain people adopt when they are called upon to defend holy, century-old beliefs and theories.

Riolan forced Harvey to answer the question whether traditional knowledge or personal observation and experience had priority. Placed in that position, Harvey took a decisive step, declaring that his observations were correct even though they merely corresponded with some facts of anatomical research. Said Harvey, "Before analyzing the reasons and the purpose of the circulation, one must first make sure that it exists."[35]

## References

[1]Kant, Immanuel, *Prolegomena zu einer jeden künftigen Metaphysik die als Wissenschaft wird auftreten können*, Riga, 1783, A 205.

[2]Rothschuh, Karl Eduard, "Die Entwicklung der Kreislauflehre im Anschluss an William Harvey. Ein Beispiel der 'autokatalytischen Problementfaltung' in den Erfahrungswissenschaften," *Klinische Wochenschrift 35* (1957) 605-612. Cf. 611.

[3]Leibniz and Haller said in criticism of Descartes that he tended constantly toward the speculative. "Mons. des Cartes n'est tombé icy dans l'erreur que par ce qu'il se fioit trop à se pensées." (Leibniz, G. W., *Discours de Métaphysique*, Gerhardt, C. I., *Die philosophischen Schriften von G. W. Leibniz*, 7 vols., Berlin, 1875-1890, t. IV, 443).

"Deux autres romans physiologiques de Descartes démontrent qu'on peut connoître la bonne méthode de rechercher la vérité, et suivre celle qui lui est la plus contraire." (Haller, A., *Art. Physiologie* in *Supplement à l'Encyclopédie par Diderot et D'Alembert, T. IV, Amsterdam,* 1777, 349).

[4]Brecht, Bertolt, *Leben des Galilei*: 4. *Aufzug* (Stücke VIII, 1957 Suhrkamp, 57-73).

[5]Johannes Kepler, in his *Briefe,* Ed. Max Caspar and Walther von Dyk, T. I., Munich, 1930, 353.

[6]Cf. Olschki, Leonardo, *Galilei und seine Zeit (Geschichte der neusprachlichen wissenschaftlichen Literatur III)* Halle, 1927, 220, note 3.

[7]Harvey, William, *Exercitationes duae anatomicae de circulatione sanguinis,* Ed. Kenneth J. Franklin, Oxford, 1958, p. 137 ff.: "Nulla alia certior demonstratio ad fidem faciendam adduci poterit, quam sensus et autopsia."

[8]"Aut approbatas opiniones relinquere indignum putent; et per tot saecule traditam disciplinam, verterumque auctoritatem, in dubium vocari nefas putent; his omnibus respondeam, facta manifesta sensui nullas opiniones naturae opera nullam antiquitatem morari: natura enim nihil antiquius, majorisve auctoritatis." *Ibid.,* 136.

[9]Cf. Lesky, Erna, "Harvey und Aristoteles," Sudhoff's *Archiv* 41 (1957) 289-316 and 349-378. Pagel, Walter, *William Harvey's Biological Ideas. Selected Aspects and Historical Background,* Basel and New York, 1967, 28-47.

[10]Pagel, *op. cit.,* 20-23.

[11]Harvey, William, *Exercitatio anatomica de motu cordis et sanguis in animalibus,* Frankfurt, 1628, Ed. Kenneth J. Franklin, Oxford, 1957, 165: "Coepi egomet mecum cogitare, an motionem quandam quasi in circulo haberet: quam postea veram esse reperi, et sanguinem e corde per arterias in habitum corporis at omnes partes protrudi et impelli a sinistri cordis ventriculi pulsu, quemadmodum in pulmones per venam arteriosam a dextri; et rursus per venas in venam cavam et usque ad auriculam dextram remeare, quemadmodum ex pulmonibus per arteriam dictam venosam ad sinistrum ventriculum."

[12]"Quem motum circularem eo pacto nominare liceat, quo Aristoteles aërem et pluviam circularem superiorum motum aemulari dixit." *Ibid.*

[13]"Ibi calore naturali, potenti, fervido, tanquam vitae thesauro, denuo colliquatur, spiritibus et balsamo praegnans; inde ursus dispensatur: et haec omnia a motu et pulsu cordis dependere. Ita cor principium vitae et sol microcosmi, ut proportionabiliter sol cor mundi, appelari meretur; cujus virtute et pulsu sanguis movetur, perficitur, vegetatur, et a corruptione et grumefactione vindicatur." *Ibid.*

[14]"unde perpetuum sanguinis motum in ciculo fieri pulsu cordis." Harvey, William, *Praelectiones anatomie universalis. De musculis,* Ed. G. Whitteridge, Edinburgh and London, 1964, Fol. 80 v.

[15]Schlegel, Paul Marquard, *De sanguinis motu commentatio, in qua praecipue in Joh. Riolani, V. C. sententiam inquiritur,* Hamburg, 1650, Praef., 1.

[16]Descartes to Beverwick, Egmond du Hoef, 5 July 1643: "Quippe, quamuis circa sanguinis circulationem cum Heruaeo plane consentiam, ipsumque vt praestantissimi illius inuenti, quo nullum maius et utilius in medicinâ esse puto, primum auctorem suspiciam, tamen circa motum cordis omnino ab eo dissentio." Descartes, *Oeuvres*, published by Charles Adam and Paul Tannery, 13 Vols., Paris, 1897-1913, IV (1901), 4.

[17]"et que ie n'eusse, auparauant, employé beaucoup de tems a m'y preparer tant en deracinant de mon esprit toutes les máuaise opinions que i'y auois receiuës auant ce tems là, qu'ent faisant amas de plusieurs experiences, pour estre aprés la matiere de mes raisonnemens, et en m'exerçant tousiours en la Methode que ie m'estois prescrite, affin de m'y affermir de plus en plus." Descartes, *Oeuvres*, VI (1902), 22 (*Discours de la Méthode*, 1637).

[18]For many similar judgments, Haller cited here: "Des D(escartes) Vorurtheile kosteten im das Leben, er wollte im Seitenstiche sich nicht die Ader öfnen lassen." *Göttingische Gelehrte Anzeigen*, 1773, Zugabe, 371.

[19]"Mais aprés que i'en employé quelques années a estudier ainsi dans le liure du monde, et a tascher d'aquerir quelque expérience, ie pris vn iour résolution d'estudier aussy en moymesme, et employer toutes les forces de mon esprit a choysir le chemins que ie deuoir suiure." Descartes, *Oeuvres*, VI (1902), 10 (*Discours*, 1637).

[20]"Nempe quidquid hactenus ut maxime verum admisi, vel a sensibus, vel per sensus accepi hos autem interdum fallere deprehendi, ac prudentiae est nunquam illis plane confidere qui nos vel semel deceperunt." Descartes, *Oeuvres*, VII (1904), 18 (*Meditationes*, 1641).

[21]"Nihil nisi punctum petebat Archimedes, quod esset firmum et immobile, ut integram terram loco dimoveret; magna quoque speranda sunt, si vel minimum quid invenere quod certum sit et inconcussum." *Ibid.*, 24 (*Meditationes*, 1641).

[22]Subtitle of *Discours de la Méthode*: Pour bien conduire sa raison, et cherche la vérité dans les sciences."

[23]Descartes said of the foundation of his physics: "elles m'ont fait uoir qu'il est possible de paruenir a des connoissances qui soient fort vtiles a la vie, et qu'an lieu de cete Philosophie speculatiue, qu'on enseigne dans les escholes, on en peut trouuer vne pratique, par laquelle connoissant la force et les actions de feu, de l'eau, de l'air, des astres, des cieux, et tous les autres cors qui nous ennivonnent, aussy distinctment que nous connoissons les diuerses mestiers de nos artisans, nous les pourrions employer en mesme façon a tous les vsages ausquels ils sont propres, et ainsi nous rendre comme maistres et posseseurs de la Nature." Descartes, *Oeuvres*, VI (1902), 61-62 (*Discours*, 1637).

[24]"Ie suppose que le Corps n'est autre chose qu'vno statuë ou machine de terre, que Dieu forme tout exprés, pour la rendre la plus semblable à nous qu'il est possible: en sorte que, non seulement ie luy donne au dehors la couleur et la figure de tous nos membres, mais aussi qu'il met au dedans toutes les pieces qui sont requises pour faire qu'elle marche, qu'elle mange, qu'elle respire, et enfin qu'elle imite

toutes celles de nos fonctions qui peuuent estre imaginées proceder de la matiere, et ne dependre que de la disposition des organes." Descartes, *Oeuvres*, XI (1909), 120 (*Traité de l'Homme*, 1633).

[25]Cf. Descartes, *Oeuvres*, VI, 46-53; XI, 123, 127; XI, 228-245. Rothschuh, Karl Eduard, "René Descartes und die Theorie der Lebenserscheinungen," Sudhoff's *Archiv* 50 (1966) 25-42.

[26]ie me contentay de supposer que Dieu formast le corps d'vn homme...aucune ame raisonnable, ny aucune autre chose pour y seruir d'ame vegetante ou sensitiue, sinon qu'il excitast en son coeur vn de ces feux sans lumiere, que i'auois desia explicez, et que ie ne concenois point d'autre nature que celuy qui échaufe le foin, lorsqu'on l'a renfermé auant qu'il fust sec, ou qui fait bouillir les vins nouueaux, lorsqu'on les laisse cuuer sur la rape." Descartes, *Oeuvres*, VI (1902), 46 (*Discours*, 1637).

[27]"Motus et pulsus cordis," " cor principium vitae et sol microcosmi," Harvey, *De motu*, 165.

[28]Descartes to Plempius, 23 March 1638: "Nam cum, vt explices quo pacto cor in hominis cadauere ab animâ absente mouere possit, confugis ad calorem et spiritum viuificum, tanquam animae instrumenta, quae in virtute eius hoc agant, quid, quaeso, aliud est quam extrema velle experiri?" Descartes, *Oeuvres*, II, (1898), 65.

[29]"Or en supposant que le coeur se meut en la façon qu' Heruaeus le décrit, non seulement il faut imaginer quelque faculté qui cause ce mouuement, la nature de laquelle est beaucoup plus difficile à conceuoir, que tout ce qu'il pretent expliquer par elle; mais il faudroit supposer, outre cela, d'autres facultez qui changeassent les qualitez du sang, pendant qu'il est dans le coeur." Descartes, *Oeuvres*, XI (1909), 243-244 (*De la formation de l'animal*, 1647-1648).

[30]Et neantmoins il importe si fort de connoistre la vraye cause du mouuement du coeur, que sans cela il est impossible de rien sçauoir touchant la Theorie de la Medecine, pource que toutes les autres fonctiones de l'animal en dépendant ainsi qu'on verra clairement de ce qui suit." *Ibid.*, 245.

[31]Descartes to Mersenne, 9 February 1639: "i'ay escrit le mesme qu'Herueus, a cause de la circulation du sang, qui leur donne seule dans la veue, i'explique toutefois tout ce qui appartient au mouuement du coeur d'vne façon entierement contraire a la siene...je veux bien qu'on pense que, si ce qui i'ay escrit de cela,... se trouue faux, tout le reste de ma Philosophie ne vaut rien." Descartes, *Oeuvres*, II (1898), 501.

[32]Praeterea memini me alias vidisse, cum ligna viridia vrerentur, vel poma coquerentur, vapores vi caloris ex eorum partibus interioribus emergentes non modo per angustas corticis rimas exeundo ventum imitari, quod nemo non aduertit, sed etiam interdum ita dispositam esse parte corticis, in qua tales rimae fiunt, vt aliquantum intumescat priusquam rima aperiatur; quae deindo rima aperta confestim detumescit, quia nempe omnis vapor illo tumore inclusus affatim tunc egreditur, nec nouus tam cito succedit. Sed paulo post, vapore alio succedente, pars eadem corticis rursum intumescit, et rima aperitur, et vapor exit, vt prius.

Atque hic modus saepius repetitus pulsationem cordis, non quidem viui, sed eius quod hic habeo ex anguilla excisum, perbelle imitatur." *Ibid.,* 67-68.

[33]"Et toutesfois cela ne proue autre chose, sinon les experiences mesme nous donnent souuent occasion de nous tromper, lors que nous n'examinons pas assez toutes les causes qu'elles peuuent auoir." Descartes, *Oeuvres,* XI (1909), 242 (*De la formation de l'animal,* 1647-1648).

[34]"Astronomiae exemplar non hic imitandum est;...Sed (sicut quis, eclipseos causam perquirens, supra lunam sisteretur, ubi sensu causam discerneret, non ratiocinio) sensibilium, quae sub sensum cadunt, nulla alia certior demonstratio ad fidem faciendam adduci poterit, quam sensus et autopsia." Harvey, *De circulatione,* 137-138.

[35]"Ad eos qui circulationem repudiant, quia neque efficientem, neque finalem causam vident, cui bono?...Prius in confesso esse debet, quod sit, antequam propter quid, inquirendum." *Ibid.,* 135-136.

# 27

## On the Stupidity of the Boeotians and the Batavians[1]

### PAUL F. CRANEFIELD

Voilà comme on écrit l'histoire! Depuis plus de trente siècles, les hommes s'adressent l'injure de Béotians, et nous sommes encore à chercher la valeur précise de ce mot.                          J. SAINT-LAGER, 1867[2]

THOMAS WILLIS, in a discussion of mental deficiency which was published in 1672,[3] speaks of the Boeotians as proverbially stupid: "ita, in Boeotia nasci, in Adagio idem est, ac fatuum esse." When Samuel Pordage translated this passage[4] in 1683 he made it read: "so, to be born in *Batavia,* is proverbially, as much as to say, a Fool."

This change of a single word by a translator brings to our attention the proverbial stupidity of the ancient Boeotians, the proverbial stupidity of the ancient Batavi, the supposed stupidity of the 17th century Batavians (i.e. the 17th century Dutch), the fairly common linking in 17th century texts of references to the Boeotians and to the Batavians, and the persistence in modern times of the word "Dutch" as a pejorative.[5]

Willis was probably echoing Horace, who said of Alexander the Great that he was competent to judge works of art but as a judge of poetry "you'ld swear that he'd been born in dank Boeotia's stagnant atmosphere..."[6] But Horace did not introduce the pejorative usage of Boeotia. That usage can be documented much earlier, in the odes of the (Boeotian) poet Pindar: "...The ancient words of shame, swine of Boeotia."[7]

A very probable source for Willis's use of the word Boeotian is found in Erasmus's extensive documentation of the term in his *Adagia,* where we find "Boeotian swine:...In the commentaries of the Greeks I found Boeotian mind meaning stupid and brutish."[8] Elsewhere Erasmus says

*Boeotian mind*: The Boeotians generally had a bad reputation for their doltishness, as was shown above. Hence anything that was insipid and foolish they would call Boeotian. Lucian in his 'Zeus the tragedian': 'What you have said is boorish and extremely Boeotian'. One also finds

Boeotian mind used to mean a stupid and doltish mind. Horatius 2. epist. I...[9]

These and many other ancient and modern slurs on the Boeotians were documented at great length by W. Rhys Roberts in 1895 in a monograph in which he defended the Boeotians from their detractors. Allowing that the Boeotians deserved some censure, especially for their role in the Persian wars, Roberts concludes that they were maligned chiefly because they were so unfortunate as to be neighbors of and thus to be compared with the Athenians. They would, he suggests, compare favorably with any other secondary Greek state, but in the Athenians "... Boeotia had, to her great detriment at the time and in future reputation, restless literary neighbors, who were as brilliant as they were troublesome."[10]

The reputation for stupidity of the Dutch and their ancestors is also ancient. We might note that in modern usage Batavia may refer to either part or all of the country known as Holland, the Dutch Republic or the Netherlands.[11] In the narrow sense of the word ancient Batavia was the home of the Batavi, the low land between the Waal and the Rhine which is now called Betuwe. The most famous aspersion on the Batavi is that of Martial: " 'You, you', says he 'are that Martial whose frivolity and jokes are known to all who do not have a Batavian ear' ".[12] Nor is there any shortage of derisory uses of the word Batavian or Dutch by Englishmen at the time of Willis. A famous example can be found in *Coryat's Crudities*:[13] "This country was heretofore called Batavia, and the inhabitants Batavi, which are mentioned by Caesar and Tacitus. They were in times past accounted a very sottish and foolish people, even as the Boeotians were amongst the ancient Graecians.".

The Oxford English Dictionary offers as an explanation for the derisive use of the word Dutch by the English the commercial rivalry between the two countries in the 17th century,[14] but this explanation was dismissed by Huizinga as follows:[15]

> It is well known that the word *Dutch*, used metaphorically, indicates in English just about everything that is ugly or unpleasant. In particular, it is used in connection with drunkenness....
>
> People would be inclined to hazard that "Dutch" had acquired its most unfavorable overtones in the period of the [17th century] naval wars with England, that it is the envy and enmity stemming from the days of van Tromp and De Ruyter that come out in the word. However, most of the relevant terms are older than this. The low opinion of the Dutch

was held by the English even in the time when they were our helpers and companions in arms; it is not possible to explain that scorn on the basis of hatred toward a hereditary enemy. For the traditional enemy of England had been France, and thereafter Spain; and Spain after all constituted our *common* enemy [by the 16th century]...

The difference in cultural *tone* between England and the [Batavian] Republic, the lack of a courtly and knightly element in Holland, accounts in part for the unfavorable valuation of our folk by the English, as revealed by the typification of the Dutchman in English literature. With the self-delusion that is inseparable from every aristocratic attitude towards life, the Englishman made himself perceive in us—who were actually his closest relations—all the traits that he would rather not perceive in himself. All the characteristics which his upbringing taught him to despise he named "Dutch". It was an example of the excessive criticism that we often see between brothers who usually reproach each other most bitterly for the faults they have themselves. It was the English Gentleman who passed judgment, and the multitude, who did not even lay claim to their way of life and attitudes, rejoiced in this judgment from the heart.

Whatever the reason for the use of the word Dutch as a pejorative, a number of linkings of Batavian and Boeotian are of interest as possible sources for Pordage's substitution (or perhaps, as evidence that such substitutions were so common-place as to need no explanation). The use of Dutch as a pejorative is documented by many 17th century phrase books,[16] but in Robertson's *Phraseologia generalis* we specifically find "As dull as a Dutchman; Ingenium Batavum, Boeoticum." Though hardly to be regarded as a source for Pordage's substitution since it dates from the 18th century, another parallel can be found in the Netherlands:[17] "...it was probably with the overzealous patriotism of an adopted citizen that Ruhnken would, in the passage from Martial, have changed *aurem ...Batavam* into aurem...Boeotam, 'Netherlandish ear' into 'Boeotian ear'." It is also amusing to note that Chapter 5 of Roberts book is entitled "The Boeotians as the Dutchmen of Greece."

Far and away the most likely passage to have influenced Pordage is found in the *Adagia* of Erasmus, where, under the heading *Batavian ear* we find[18] "As the Greeks say, Boeotian ear, meaning clumsy and coarse ear. Similarly Martial, in the sixth book of his Epigrams called an ear which is boorish, indelicate, and surly a Batavian ear: 'Tune es, tune, ...'" Thus Erasmus linked Boeotian and Batavian together and it is this explicit linking of the two in the widely read and influential *Adagia* which may very well account for Pordage's substitution of "Batavia" for Willis's "Boeotia," just as that *Adagia* may have led Willis to mention the Boeotians in the first place.

The proverbial stupidity of the Boeotians was cited in early writings on the history of mental deficiency. The proverb has frequently been taken as evidence that Boeotia was the center of endemic cretinism and as showing therefore that cretinism is a very ancient disease. Rudolf Virchow attributed the origin of this opinion to Foderé and took pains to refute it; Virchow took the matter up with philologists who assured him that the Boeotians might have been coarse or clumsy but that they were never regarded as mentally defective.[19] The conclusion that the Boeotians were cretins seems no more reasonable than would the conclusion that the Dutch were cretins in the 17th century. To be sure, a 17th century Dutch reader of Pordage, were there any such, coming across the substitution of Batavian for Boeotian, might well have comforted himself with a remark of Rabelais (*Gargantua,* Book I, Chapter 15) "Sou comme un Angloys.".

The late Dr. Walter Federn made important contributions to an early version of this article. Dr. Federn was so meticulously accurate and so cautious in drawing conclusions that I do not feel able to use his name as coauthor of this version, which may contain errors which he would have detected or conclusions with which he would not have agreed. I am indebted to Dr. F. Peter Woodford, The Rockefeller University, for translating the passage from Huizinga.

## References

[1]This study is based upon research in the history of mental deficiency which was supported by a grant from the National Institute for Child Health and Human Development (Grant HD-01198).

[2]Saint-Lager, J., *Études sur les causes du Crétinisme et du Goitre Endémique,* Paris, 1867.

[3]Willis, Thomas, *De Anima Brutorum,* Oxford, 1672, Chapter 13: Stupiditas sive Morosis. See Cranefield, P. F., "A Seventeenth Century View of Mental Deficiency and Schizophrenia: Thomas Willis on 'Stupidity or Foolishness' ", *Bull. Hist. Med.,* XXXV (1961), 291-316.,

[4]Willis, Thomas, *Two Discourses Concerning the Soul of Brutes...*Englished by S. Pordage, London, 1683.

[5]The term "dumb Dutchman" is in common use in the middlewest of the United States, where it often refers to Germans, "Dutch" standing in for "Deutsch". Yet

it is not documented in Mencken, H. L., *The American Language*, New York, 1937, nor in the supplements to that work, nor in Mathews, M. M., *A Dictionary of Americanisms*, Chicago, 1956. For documentation on the use of *Dutch* as a pejorative see Mencken, H. L., *The American Language, Supplement I*, New York, 1945, and Craigie, W. A., and Hallert, James R., *A Dictionary of American English on Historical Principles*, 1940, II, 843, 848, 850. See also n. 13 below.

[6]Horace, *Epistles*, II, 1, line 244: Boeotum in crasso jurares aere natum. The translation is that of Trevelyan, R. C., *Translations from Horace, Juvenal, and Montaigne*, Cambridge, 1941. The line also provides an early documentation of the theory that a "dank and stagnant" atmosphere could cause mental deficiency. This theory was particularly popular as an explanation for cretinism in the early 19th century.

[7]Pindar, *Olympia*, VI, line 90. The translation is from Lattimore, R., *The Odes of Pindar*, University of Chicago Press, 1959.

[8]*Adagiorum Des. Erasmi Roterodami chiliades quatuor cum sesquicenturia;...*, Coloniae Allobrogum., 1612. The passage cited is found in Chil. I, Cent. X, 6.

[9]*Ibid.*, Chil. II, Cent. III, 7. Erasmus's marginal note reads "in stolidum". Erasmus goes on to quote the passage in Horace which is discussed above (see note 6).

[10]Roberts, W. R., *The Ancient Boeotians: Their Character and Culture, and their Reputation*, Cambridge, 1895.

[11]The country under discussion is at present officially known as the Kingdom of the Netherlands. It has had many names and one is not always sure how to refer to it. This confusion of names stems in part from the perjorative quality of the words we are discussing. Indeed, H. L. Mencken remarks (in *The American Language, Supplement I*, 601) "The Netherlands Government, in 1934, tried to pull the teeth of the English pejoratives by ordering all its officials to drop *Dutch* and use Netherlands instead..."

[12]Martial, *Epistle* VI, 82, 4-6:

"Tune es, tune" ait "ille Martialis,
Cujus nequitias iocosque novit
Aurem qui modo non habet Batavam".

[13]*Coryat's Crudities* (1611), Cited from *Thomas Coryat, Coryat's Crudities*, MacLehose, Glasgow, 1905, II, 362.

[14]*The Oxford English Dictionary*, III, 729b: *Dutch*. 4. "Characteristic of or attributed to the Dutch; often with an opprobrious, or derisive application, largely due to the rivalry and enmity between the English and the Dutch in the 17th c." Compare also the following excerpts from *The Century Dictionary*, New York, 1914. *Dutch talent*, (naut.) any piece of nautical work which, while it may answer the purpose, and even show certain ingenuity, is not done in clever, shipshape style: defined by sailors as "main strength and stupidity." *Dutch courage*, artificial courage. *Dutch defense*, a sham defense.

[15]Huizinga, Johan, "Engelschen en Nederlanders in Shakespeare's Tijd," *De Gids,* (April-June 1924), 219-235, 367-383. Reprinted in *Tien Studiën,* (1926), 201-239.

[16]According to Tilley, Morris Palmer, *The Proverbs in England in the Sixteenth and Seventeenth Centuries* 1950, 177, the phrase "As dull as a Dutchman" can be found in:

Clarke, John, *Paroemiologia Anglo-Latina,* 1639, 296,
Howell, James, *Some Choice Proverbs...in French Toung,* 1659, 20;
Clarke, John, *Phraseologia Puerilis...or Selected Latine and English Phrases,* 4th ed., 1671, 104;
Robertson, William, *Phraseologia Generalis...A Full, Large, and General Phrase Book,* 1693, 510.

[17]Roberts, *op. cit.*

[18]Erasmus, *op. cit.,* Chil. III, Cent. VI, 35. Erasmus goes on to quote the epigram of Martial which is discussed above, (see note 12), and to defend his countrymen against this insult. Schrevel, in his edition of Martial which was published in 1661, says of this passage that three previous Dutch editors of Martial "...take it somewhat more lightly than did the great Erasmus and other compatriots [i.e., other Dutchmen]...they explain that Martial is congratulating himself on being read by everyone in Rome except the Batavians who, since they are accustomed to military service and a hard life as the body guard of the emperor, did not care much for these jokes."

[19]Virchow, Rudolf. *Gesammelte Abhandlungen zur Wissenschaftlichen Medicin.,* Frankfurt, 1856., 891-939: "Ueber den Cretinismus, namentlich in Franken, und über pathologische Schädelformen." The work by Foderé to which Virchow refers is *Traité du Goitre et du Crétinisme,* Paris, 1800.

# 28

# Francis Bacon and the Reform of Philosophy

## J. R. RAVETZ

## I. *Introduction*[1]

IN recent years, historians of science have come to see that the establishment of the new style of investigating Nature in the seventeenth century was different in many important respects from the tasks of consolidating and extending this work in later centuries. The greatest men were concerned with philosophical problems as much as with "scientific" ones, and indeed did not generally make any sharp separation between the two classes. The debates that took place were similarly a mixture of technical and metaphysical considerations. And engagement on the work was in many cases at least as much participation in a movement, as the following of a profession. With the new appreciation of this complexity of the work of the "scientific revolution", the old opposition between "internalist" and "externalist" approaches to the history of science can be correctly seen as the reflection of general philosophies of history imported into this special study. Each historian will naturally investigate those problems to which his interests and skills direct him; but no-one would now deny that the adoption of a "new philosophy" of Nature produced a qualitative difference between Galileo and earlier practitioners of the mathematical arts, nor that Boyle's and Newton's interests included the experimental philosophy of nature only as a special part.

This oecumenical approach brings many advantages, not least the freedom from choosing sides in a sterile debate. On the other hand, it has its characteristic dangers, in blurring the lines of definition of the subject-matter of the history of science. This is not so serious when it comes to distinguishing (for purposes of historical analysis) between particular studies in a natural science, from those in general philosophy, and from craftsmen's empirical investigations. It does raise the deepest problems for historical enquiry, at those points where the fields of enquiry involved have been subsequently excluded from the domain of genuine science. To argue, for instance, that magic and alchemy, or generally the "Hermetic" tradition, played an essential and positive role

97

in the establishment of modern science, is to contradict a tradition of the conception of "science" which goes back continuously to the earlier seventeenth century. To admit mystics and Rosicrucians into the respectable ancestry of our modern science may seem to involve a betrayal of the long struggle for the establishment of reason as the foundation of judgments in affairs concerning both Nature and man.[2] But we now know that we cannot simply exclude from the earlier history of science any man whose philosophy of nature would have been unacceptable to late-nineteenth-century German analytical chemists. Long ago Dr. Pagel exhibited the rich mixture of motifs involved in the work of van Helmont and his school; and more recently he has restored William Harvey as a philosopher rather than an hydraulic engineer.

Reason itself requires that we should not run away from established facts merely because they are uncomfortable to our inherited prejudices. Also, in this later twentieth century, the focus and emphasis of the ideological struggles involving science have changed suddenly from the versions that were current from the Enlightenment onwards. The completely natural powers provided to man by science are so great that "sorcery" has re-entered the vocabulary of discussions of science as a moral attribute.[3] And the Galilean style of applying "sense experience and necessary demonstrations" to simplified and abstracted aspects of the natural world has in technical applications led to the micro-rationality of devices which each perform their assigned functions superbly but which in aggregate threaten the survival of our species. In reaction to these new problems, the long-submerged current of mystical thinking has surfaced again, not merely in the "counter-culture" of rebellious students, but even in influential currents in the new ecological thought and propaganda.

With these new experiences of the present, we historians can and should have a new appreciative perception of the styles of thought that were suppressed in the seventeenth century. And as historians rather than propagandists, we can and should avoid a facile oversimplification of the complex and sometimes tragic interaction and conflict between styles of investigating nature which derived from opposed conceptions of that world and its relation to man and to God. In particular, the concept of "influence" (which more than any other carries the load of valuations) is a simple one only if we conceive intellectual history as a genealogy of ideas, hopping from book to book down through time. Rather, we should see the great philosophers as men grappling with the deepest and sometimes insoluble problems throughout their lives, adopting different provisional solutions, and thereby being open to different influences, at different times; and also struggling with the relics of their own earlier thoughts as they change and develop.

In this historical framework, the real influence of those currents of thought soon to be damned as "irrational" can be established, without necessarily pitching the historian into the very deepest questions of judgment on the whole process of the establishment of the new philosophy of Nature. We need only imagine that some at least of the great natural philosophers achieved commitment to their life's work in a period of youthful enthusiasm and dedication; and spent their subsequent years in a struggle to retain what could be retained, and to achieve what could be achieved, in the face of the contradictions thrown up by harsh experience. Although such a pattern is a commonplace in politics, it may seem entirely inappropriate to import it into the history of science. But the history with which we are concerned just now is of "science" in the largest sense; it concerns a movement for a Reformation in the philosophy of nature, in which the achievement of a particular sort of results by a particular style of research was only a part.

The career of each of the founders of the new philosophy of the seventeenth century can be studied in this way, and the differences in their achievements can be related to differences in their style and commitment. Thus, Galileo's Truth lay in a particular sort of realised mathematics, and his characteristic style can be seen in his very earliest production, the *Bilancetta*. On the deeper problems of metaphysics and ethics, he left very little evidence of concern; and even his theological excursions were in the nature of defensive polemics. For Descartes, the evidence of "enthusiasm" is there, but it is suggestive rather than conclusive for a direct personal involvement with Rosicrucianism.[4] However, the autobiographical accounts of medications and insights, and the "three visions", leave little doubt that Descartes was started on the road to his extension-and-motion ontology by problems of philosophy, and by experiences, which touched the roots of the problems of human existence. For Bacon, the case is easier to argue, and correspondingly less disturbing in its conclusions. For Bacon was neither a successful scientist, nor a consistent adherent of the new ontology of dead matter. A demonstration that his philosophy of science was influenced, and even shaped, by non-scientific considerations, may even offer ammunition to those historians of science who have all along wanted to throw him out of the list. But since the list of thoroughgoing professional scientists in the seventeenth century becomes shorter with each advance of historical scholarship, such prejudices may be allowed to wither away of their own accord.

## II. *Strategies for Reform*

There is no need to argue the case that Bacon saw himself not so much as a scientist, but as an agent of Reform, where the term is understood in its sixteenth-century rather than twentieth-century sense. By contrast, Descartes can be considered as trying to accomplish the sorts of task appropriate to both roles; and Galileo might be said to have become a reformer only when the unreformed state of his audience's minds became a nuisance and hindrance to him. We can therefore expect that Bacon's involvement in systematic philosophy, and in experimental science, would be casual and incidental; his achievements correspondingly less important; and the significance of his essays in these directions for an understanding of his basic philosophy, minimal. We have also got beyond the earlier tradition in British philosophy which constructed a Bacon who proclaimed the "inductive" philosophy of the later eighteenth and nineteenth centuries. Hence we are entitled to approach an understanding of Francis Bacon by an analysis of his strategy for reform in philosophy, and to use this as an interpretative framework for his many and varied pronouncements on the state of the world about him.

Any strategy for reform must include several distinct components if it is to serve as a coherent guide to action. Without arguing on the absolute correctness of any particular taxonomy, we may conveniently distinguish the following aspects. First, there must be a description of the present lamentable state, and an explanation for its occurrence. Second, there must be some characterization of the desired state, and also a guarantee for its possible existence. Third, there must be a plan for changing the bad present into the good future. And finally, there should also be some indication that the time is now ripe, so that recruits will come forward, and survive the inevitable temporary disappointments. To run this scheme on a familiar example, we may say that classical Marxism described the miseries of the proletariat and explained them in terms of the particular form of expropriation which defines capitalism; it was rather vague on Socialism and on its variety of Communism, but prided itself on its "scientific" as opposed to Utopian analysis of their inevitability; its plan rested on the conclusions of the earlier phases of analysis, and involved the activation of the industrial proletariat rather than of other classes who might be oppressed or rebellious (peasants and young intellectuals, for example); and the ripeness of time was established both by the intensified struggle of the proletariat and by Marx's optimistic aphorism, "Mankind sets only those problems which it can solve."

For Bacon, a plausible analysis of the strategy for reform can be achieved without difficulty. The present ills are described in many places, in a variety of ways. Starting with the dichotomy between "the Grecians and the alchemists",[5] we have the simile of the spider and the ant,[6] and the fine passage on the varieties of misguided endeavour in *Novum Organum* I, Aphorism.[7] For an explanation of present ills Bacon offers his "four idols", perhaps the most original part of his entire philosophy. The guarantee of the possibility of improvement in philosophy comes from the example of the mechanical arts, both in their progressive character[8] and in their previous achievements in the absence of any contact with philosophy.[9] For the advancement of learning itself, the institutional form is sketched as Salomon's House in the *New Atlantis;* there we see a fine division of labour,[10] and a fully autonomous community of research workers, gathering and processing facts in a disciplined style. The plan for the improvement of philosophy is based on achieving "colleges" where this sort of work can be done, and its correctness proved by its successes; and Bacon's own contribution is to provide the propaganda leading to the establishment of such an institution, on a Royal foundation. Finally, the ripeness of time is established by the numerous radical changes in the arts and in society over the few generations preceding Bacon's time; the frontispiece of the *Novum Organum,* with the Columbus of learning setting forth, symbolises the argument.

Such a strategy for reform fits in well with what a twentieth-century audience would expect, and as it is displayed in his writings it uses themes which must have been quite familiar to his own contemporaries. As evidence for Bacon's own views, it is not to be neglected; but it is evidence and not fact. For all Bacon's published writings were propaganda; their function was to convert his audience, and their relation to his own private views was purely incidental. Indeed, the essays which he suppressed as unsuitable for publication have a style and content which is strikingly different from those of his published writings; and it was these essays that provided Farrington with the clue to the deeper interpretation of Bacon that he achieved in his second study.

There is strong evidence, from the history of Bacon's life and work, to indicate that the publicly announced strategy of reform was only a part, and not the deeper part, of his personal vision of the task. In the first place, on the matter of the mechanical arts, he knew not whereof he spoke. The "three great inventions" of printing, gunpowder and the magnetic compass, were not first identified as such by him.[11] They were discussed by Cardano, and perhaps more significant, were dealt with in a popular French book, which was translated into English in 1594. The moral that Bacon drew from these inventions, that they were lighted upon by chance and owed nothing to "philosophy", is not merely incorrect but would have been recognised as such by anyone familiar with their recent history.[12]

Again, it is well known that Bacon's knowledge of the state of the sciences derived from his reading of books, and mostly general books at that. In retrospect, historians of science can discern fields in which great advances were being made in the period up to Bacon's life; in particular, anatomy, astronomy and mathematics. Bacon showed no recognition of these points of progress; but laid all of the sciences under his general condemnation. His conception of the ideal organisation of scientific research could not have come from any examples within philosophy or the mechanical arts; but it is a natural extrapolation from the type of research appropriate to a programme for the rationalisation of English law, one which was very dear to his heart. Indeed, his writings show an intellect trained in legal and literary skills, applied to this very different sort of work. His similes and rhetorical figures are nearly always taken from these fields and applied to natural philosophy and the arts; the cases where "nature" provides the insights for "man", are very few.

The conclusion of this line of argument could well be that Bacon was merely a literary showman, offering advice and instructions to people in a field of enquiry which he was too proud or too busy to learn properly. And, judging his published writings as propaganda exercises, such a conclusion would be hard to refute. But if we accept that with all the complexities and contradictions in his character, he was moved by a very deep commitment, this negative conclusion serves to throw up a new problem: what was he trying to do? If his programme for the sciences was not based on induction from personal experience of philosophy and the arts, wherein lay its driving force for him? Benjamin Farrington has provided the elements of an answer: that Bacon's deepest commitment was ethical and religious; and that the reform of natural philosophy was his choice of the strategic point for the achievement of the reform and redemption of mankind. To confirm and amplify this insight, I will show how a coherent and meaningful strategy for reform can be extracted from Bacon's affirmations in religion and ethics; and that this element is in fact essential for solving the problems raised by the technical and secular version of his strategy.

## III. *Bacon's Strategy for Reform*

We need not dwell on Bacon's numerous criticisms of the state of natural knowledge in his time. The causes of this evil condition are in three classes: ignorance of means, corruption of ends, and inherent infirmities in human reason. In the first class we have the analysis of the sterility of school logic, and of the one-sided endeavours, either purely empirical or purely theoretical; and then the positive suggestions towards a method of true induction that comprise the second book of the *Novum Organum*. On the ends of the endeavour, Bacon describes the narrow and distorted ends then governing the various sorts of work;[13] and offers several formulations of the true ends of natural philosophy, as "to establish and extend the power and dominion of the human race itself over the universe".[14] As an explanation of the corrupted state of philosophy, he provides the "four idols", which seem to be a deeper sceptical critique of human knowledge than the classical tradition provided, and indeed deeper than that which Descartes grappled. For we start with the defects of the mind itself, neither a *tabula rasa* of the empiricist tradition nor the true "mirror" of the rationalists.[15] These imperfections are magnified in each individual, according to the peculiarities of his constitution and temperament; he is then subjected to the brainwashing of school, where he reasons with words that do not correspond to real things; and finally comes to the theatre of higher education, where actors spout their lines devoid of all content.

At the naturalistic level, this explanation is self-sufficient, and indeed relevant to all times and places. But at the moral level, it has no meaning, except that of cynicism or despair. It certainly offers no clue in itself, to the possibility of reform; for any ordinary institutions would inevitably be corrupted by the prevailing tendencies to intellectual and moral decay. Bacon gave explicit recognition to the insolubility of the problem at this level, at the conclusion of his discussion of the Four Idols. There we read;

So much concerning the special classes of Idols, and their equipage: all of which must be renounced and put away with a fixed and solid determination, and the understanding thoroughly freed and cleansed; the entrance into the kingdom of man, founded the sciences, being not much other than the entrance into the kingdom of heaven, where into none may enter except as a little child.[16]

Is this comparison a mere figure of rhetoric? It seems unlikely to be so, for two reasons. First, this call for a moral reform (the cleansing as well as the freezing of the intellect), the requirement of the innocence of the child, is Bacon's only answer to the sceptical challenge of the Four Idols. Second, and more important, the conception of human history which was a commonplace for Bacon and for his successors through Newton, was that of a cosmic drama in which the successive acts were revealed in Scripture, and in which the Almighty is ever-present. The analogy between the two kingdoms was not one to be uttered lightly.

A stronger connection to the religious foundations of Bacon's vision is provided by a theme which is expressed in passages scattered through his published writings, and which dominates his unpublished essay, *On the Masculine Birth of Time.*[17] For the absence of the true ends of philosophy is not merely an intellectual deficiency; it is a moral defect as well. In that essay Bacon runs through the list of philosophers, ancient and modern, calling them to the bar of judgment. He speaks of the "sham philosophers" who "debauch our minds", and of those who are worse still, "the satellites and parasites of the great ones, the whole mob of professorial teachers". Lest there be any doubt on this point, he concludes:

But now I must recollect myself and do penance, for though my purpose was only to discredit it yet I have been handling what is unholy and unclean. What I have said against them is less than their monstrous guilt deserved.[18]

What is this "monstrous guilt"? It is composed of spiritual pride, showmanship, dishonesty, and lack of true humility before Nature or pity for mankind. To put it in a single word, we may say, "vanity". Bacon mentions "vanity" in an important place in his published work, in the prayer which concludes the Plan of the Work of the *Instauratio Magna*:

But man, when he turned to look upon the work which his hands had made, saw that all was vanity and vexation of spirit, and could find no rest therein.[19]

The same text is found in the *Meditationes Sacrae;*[20] and in the companion piece, *A Confession of Faith,* vanity comes into the cosmic drama:

> That upon the fall of Man, death and vanity entered by the justice of God, and the image of God in man was defaced, and heaven and earth which were made for man's use were subdued to corruption by his fall...[21]

A similar set of themes appears in a passage in the introduction to the *Historia Naturalis et Experimentalis*:

> For we copy the sin of our parents while we suffer for it. They wished to be like God, but their posterity wish to be even greater. For we create worlds, we direct and domineer over nature, we will have it that all things *are* as in our folly we think they should be, not as seems fittest to Divine wisdom, or as they are to be found in fact...[22]

The need for curing this vanity, as a prerequisite to any progress in philosophy, is expressed in the Preface to the *Instauratio Magna*:

> Wherein if I have made any progress, the way has been opened to me by no other means than the true and legitimate humiliation of the human spirit.[23]

Later in the same section, he concludes his prayer:

> Lastly, that knowledge now being discharged of that venom which the serpent infused into it, and which makes the mind to swell, we may not be wise above measure and sobriety, but cultivate truth in charity.[24]

If we wish, we can dismiss all this as rhetorical high-mindedness, supported by conventional piety. But to do so would require a wilful ignorance of the religious sensibility of English natural philosophers throughout the seventeenth century. It would also require us to imagine Francis Bacon, a man conscious of his talents from his earliest years, and determined to dedicate himself to the service of God and of man, spending so much of his life on a technocratic fantasy.

Taking this ethical and religious concern seriously, we note in the above passages that there is a Scriptural reference in the descriptions of the corrupted state. The "sin of our parents" is that of Adam and Eve, and the "serpent" is their tempter. Indeed Bacon sketched a history of the stages of the Fall of Man, relating the corruption of philosophy as he saw it to the Scriptural account. Concerning the Fall itself, Bacon is quite sure that this did not arise from man's desire for natural knowledge;[25] but just as the angels fell from lust of power, so man fell from lust of knowledge:[26] a knowledge of Good and Evil conceived as independent of God's will.[27] Bacon believed that the Fall of Adam was not complete and absolute (in agreement with those who traced the *prisca sapientia* to Noah, such as Newton and the Masonic tradition); for then,

> the law was first imprinted in that remnant of light of nature which was left after the fall, being sufficient to accuse...[28]

Later the manner of revelation changed, to the written law, the prophets, and finally Christ. However, even at that first Fall, there was

> the curse, which notwithstanding was no new creation, but a privation of part of the virtue of the first creation.[29]

Bacon does not hope for the original "virtue" of nature's workings to be restored; man must forever earn his rewards.

> In fact, there has been a second Fall; Wherefore our dominion over creatures is a second time forfeited, not undeservedly; and whereas after the fall of man some power over the resistance of creatures was still left to him—the power of subduing and managing them by true and solid arts—yet this too through our insolence, and because we desire to be like God and to follow the dictates of our own reason, we in great part lose.[30]

Bacon nowhere speaks explicitly of the time and character of this second Fall, but it is likely that he gave some support to a popular doctrine that it occurred with the building of the tower of Babel,[31] and also that traces of the true wisdom survived to the times of the development of Greek mythology.[32]

In the terms of this deeper analysis of the causes of the corrupted state of philosophy, the problem of providing a guarantee of successful reform is easily solved within the same framework. On this, Bacon is quite explicit. He made strong use of the injunction of Christ, "Ye err, not knowing the Scriptures, nor the power of God;"[33] from this distinction, he can interpret the former as revealing God's will, and the latter, His works as studied by natural philosophy. Moreover, Bacon provides an abundance of points to prove that God intended man to discover the nature of his Created world. First, He left his "seals and imprints"[34] on things, as well as his "footprints" or "vestiges". And these are the true Ideas of the divine, which are so different from the Idols of the human mind.[35] It is through God's grace that man will "write an apocalypse or true vision of the footsteps of the Creator imprinted on his creatures."[36] Moreover, these "vestiges", although not patent to the common view, were intended to be discovered. His hiding of the "characters and impressions of his providence",[37] as in the final causes of natural processes, makes His wisdom "shine forth more admirably", as that of the master politician "that can make other men the instruments of his ends and desires and yet never acquaint them with his purposes".[38] We are assured from Scripture that God did not wish to keep these evidences concealed, for as Solomon said, "The glory of God is to conceal a thing; the glory of the king is to search it out."[39] This concealment was not intended as a trial for man; rather,

> Even as though the divine nature took pleasure in the innocent and kindly sport of children playing at hide and seek, and vouchsafed of his kindness and goodness to admit the human spirit for his playfellow at that game.[40]

Thus we can be sure that the secrets of God's creation are meant for man to discover; and we can be equally sure that man's dominion over the natural world is a "divine bequest", as in the passage from Aphorism 129 that I quoted earlier.[41] This is supported by Bacon's references to man's partaking of the Sabbath with God, as in one of his famous prayers:

> Wherefore if we labor in thy works with the sweat of our brows thou wilt make us partakers of thy vision and thy sabbath.[42]

It also appears in the passage from the *Masculine Birth of Time* from which I quoted earlier; there Bacon promises his "son" that his "chaste wedlock" with things themselves will produce

> a blessed race of Heroes or Supermen who will overcome the immeasurable helplessness and poverty of the human race, which cause it more destruction than all giants, monsters or tyrants, and will make you peaceful, happy, prosperous and secure.[43]

We might also enquire whether Bacon offered some hint of the character of this promised knowledge; for here the theological conceptions may throw some light on the vexed question of what, if anything, Bacon meant by "form". First, we must not forget that Bacon's concern, as much as that of Descartes, was with a universal science, including all the arts of human and social behaviour.[44] Second, the knowledge desired was an un-mediated contact with "things themselves". For these are the creations of God; man should establish direct contact with them through contemplation of them; he considered himself as having "submitted my mind to things";[45] and that "commerce of the mind of man and things" is "more precious than anything on earth".[46] This union with things[47] is not merely an intellectual act, but is the key to the whole sacred endeavour of the material redemption of mankind. Thus in *The Masculine Birth of Time*, Bacon speaks from his "inmost heart", saying, "My dear, dear boy, what I propose is to unite you with *things themselves* in a chaste, holy and legal wedlock...", whose issue will be the redeeming Heroes of Supermen described above. Although in his writings on method, he promises only to take the human reason up to *"prima philosophia"* or *"sapientia"*, achieving the most fundamental and general axioms,[48] his conception of the reform extended further. Thus, in speaking of the ends of enquiry in the *On The Interpretation of Nature*, he dismisses the ignoble and vulgar purposes as elsewhere, and asserts:

> but it is a restitution and reinvesting (in great part) of man to the sovereignty and power (for whensoever he shall be able to call the creatures by their true names he shall again command them) which he had in his first state of creation...[49]

The completion of Bacon's programme for philosophy is then no less than the redemption of mankind, to the extent that is possible, from the consequences of the original Fall.[50]

It is clear that a goal of such cosmic significance could not be achieved merely by the establishment of a scientific research institution. The task of discovering God's works must proceed hand in hand with that of interpreting His will; otherwise it will surely be corrupted. Bacon nowhere says this; and indeed one optimistic passage indicates otherwise:

> Only let the human race recover that right over nature which belongs to it by divine bequest, and let power be given it; the exercise thereof will be governed by sound reason and true religion.[51]

However, we are justified in considering this as propaganda; for even in the Utopian *New Atlantis*, the sages of Salomon's House took no chances:

> And this we do also: we have consultations, which of the inventions and experiences which we have discovered shall be published, and which not; and all take an oath of secrecy, for the concealing of those which we think fit to keep secret: though some of those we do reveal sometime to the state, and some not.[52]

This caution, combined with Bacon's unflattering view of the intellectual and moral condition of the scholars of his own time, makes it certain that his was a task not to be accomplished by administrative means alone.

To carry out his programme, Bacon would need men whose wits were not only sharp, but also cleansed. These would necessarily be set off from the common, corrupted society of the time, either by their being already reformed, or by being ready to reform. How was Bacon to locate and recruit those few who were ready to embark on the great work in a spirit of humility, charity and innocence? On this, the evidence is that Bacon planned to operate on two levels, in a time-honoured fashion. For society at large, there was an exoteric doctrine, cast in the terms that could be generally appreciated, with hints of the deeper message. But there was also to be a brotherhood of "true sons of science".[53] Bacon publicly[53] invited membership in this; and so in a sense it was not esoteric. But it was for those few who had been able to reform, and on one important point Bacon's esoteric teaching would have been radically different from his public statements.

This relates to a problem where his assertions seem insincere or self-contradictory: the value, and future role, of the philosophy then dominant. Bacon is at pains to deny hostile intentions towards it:

> For I do not object to the use of this received philosophy, or others like it, for supplying matters for disputations or ornaments for discourse—for the professor's lecture and for the business of life.[54]

Later, he protests the sincerity of his professions of affection towards the "received sciences", citing his published writings, including the *Advancement of Learning*, as evidence.[55] But he protests a bit too much; for his disclaimers of general utility for his own philosophy turn into an affirmation of its innate superiority:

> It does not lie in the way. It cannot be caught up in passage. It does not flatter the understanding by conformity with preconceived notions. Now will it come down to the apprehension of the vulgar except by its utility and effects.[56]

For a long time I considered this to be an unresolved contradiction in Bacon's own thought, considering that his beloved studies of letters and the law fell within the class of inane works. But a reading of the unpublished *Refutation of Philosophies* gave the clue; there, the sage, "a man of peaceful and serene air, save that his face had become habituated to an expression of pity", spoke to his "sons", and advised:

Therefore keep your old philosophy. Use it when convenient. Keep one to deal with nature, and the other to deal with the populace. Every man of superior understanding in contact with inferiors wears a mask. If I may, as my habit is, speak freely among friends, then I advise you: Possess Lais but do not let her possess you.[57]

The reference is to a famous courtesan; the distinction was made in a reply by the philosopher Aristippus, to critics of his personal behaviour.

Through an appreciation of the essentially *moral* aspect of the reform proposed by Bacon, together with a text such as this one, we can resolve the question of the nature of his esoteric teaching. In his Note B to Ellis's reface to the *Novum Organum*,[58] Spedding reviewed the texts which seemed to call for an esoteric teaching. His conclusion was that Bacon proposed to withhold the publication of his Formula,

'not as a secret of too much value to be lightly revealed', but as a subject too abstruse to be handled successfully except by the fit and the few.

This is almost correct; but for "abstruse" one should substitute "holy". Bacon was sure that his method would "level men's wits", but those wits must *first have been purified, or* (at a later period) protected from the contamination of the false and impious philosophies.

We can now come to the final problem, that of establishing the ripeness of time, so that recruits will come forward in good heart. My interpretation of Bacon's solution to this problem might appear far-fetched or paradoxical, were it not for the support of his published texts, and the coherence of the religious framework of his strategy for reform as I have developed it up to this point. Bacon's discussion of this in the *Novum Organum* occupies the section from Aphorism 92 to Aphorism 114, giving the arguments for Hope, with some rambles *en route*. In Aphorism 92 he states that the greatest obstacle to progress has been despair; and by examples of his successes, he may with gentleness prepare men's minds with hope. The introduction to the section on Hope, Aphorism 93, provides a religious and theological foundation. It opens with:

The beginning is from God: for the business which is in hand, having the character of good so strongly impressed upon it, appears manifestly to proceed from God, who is the author of good, and the Father of Lights.[59]

Elsewhere Bacon makes a strong use of the term "light" as a synonym for knowledge. The passage continues with a Scriptural sanction for his programme for a gentle reform proceeding from small beginnings:

Now in divine operations even the smallest beginnings lead of a certainty to their end. And as it was said of spiritual things, 'The Kingdom of God cometh not with observation', so is it in all the greater works of Divine Providence; everything glides on smoothly and noiselessly, and the work is fairly going on before men are aware that it has begun.[60]

One might interpret this as an answer to the query by a sceptical reader, whether Bacon had succeeded in putting any of his fine words into practice. (In the previous Aphorism, he promised a set of particulars, admittedly the strongest means of inspiring hope, for later parts of the Instauration; and for the sake of gentleness, offered only the plan of the work at this stage).

So far the claims for hope in his programme are rather general; but he concludes the aphorism with material that puts the present age in its true setting:

Nor should the prophecy of Daniel be forgotten, touching the last ages of the world:—'Many shall go to and fro, and knowledge shall be increased:' clearly intimating that the thorough passage of the world (which now by so many distant voyages seems to be accomplished, or in the course of accomplishment), and the advancement of the sciences, are destined by fate, that is, by Divine Providence, to meet in the same age.[61]

In brief, Bacon believed that by his efforts he was helping to usher in the Millenium. One quotation from a large book is but slender evidence for such a dramatic thesis; but supporting evidence is found on the frontispiece of the *Instauratio Magna* as published. For there, under the well-known picture of the ship clearing the twin pillars on its way to the open sea, is the motto, *"multi pertransibunt et augebitur scientia."* Any reader familiar with Scripture would recognise the text, from the apocalyptic Daniel 12, verse 4 reads: "But thou, O Daniel, shut up the words, and seal the book, even to the end of time; many shall run to and fro, and knowledge shall be increased." Although the text itself has been questioned, and these connotations of Bacon's motto were doubtless lost on later generations (including those who chose the latter part for the motto of the University of Leeds), Bacon's readers would have been well aware of them. And in the context of thought of Bacon's time, a millenial belief supported by Scripture is not at all surprising. Any great reformer must have the touch of the saviour about him; and through the seventeenth century, the Holy Writ was an accepted source of clues to the meaning of the revolutions of times.

## Comments on Bacon's Strategy

It remains for me to deal with one outstanding problem in this interpretation of Bacon's strategy for reform; and then we can consider how
this throws light on other aspects of Bacon's endeavour. The problem is
that this interpretation apparently runs counter to Bacon's explicit statements of the separateness of theology and natural philosophy. The most
extended account of the damage done by theologians and divines is in
Aphorism 89x of the *Novum Organum,* Book I; there Bacon refers to
the "troublesome adversary and hard to deal with: namely, superstition,
and the blind and immoderate zeal of religion."[62] He then cites the story
of the Greeks who were found guilty of impiety for giving natural explanations for thunder and for storms, and mentions the Church Fathers
who denied the antipodes. He mentions also the defects of systematic
theology, and then the fears of natural philosophy resulting from "the
simpleness of certain divines". His defence of natural philosophy as the
"most faithful handmaid" of religion rests both on its power to dispel
superstition, and on the text "ye err in that ye know not the Scriptures
and the powers of God." None of this entails a secularisation of the
spirit of enquiry or of the conception of its ends; it is the sort of defence
of natural philosophy against incompetent zealots which was continued
in an apologetic tradition for science, at the hands of liberal Churchmen,
to the end of the nineteenth century.

There is one point where Bacon identifies a particular error in the
mixture of the natural and the divine, which might seem to argue
against the use of Scripture in any investigation of nature:

> In this vanity some of the moderns have with extreme levity indulged
> so far as to attempt to found a system of natural philosophy on the first
> chapter of Genesis, on the book of Job, and other parts of the sacred
> writings: seeking for the dead among the living: which also makes the
> inhibition and repression of it the more important, because from this
> unwholesome mixture of things human and divine there arises not only
> a fantastic philosophy but also an heretical religion. Very meet is it
> therefore that we be sober-minded and give to faith that only which
> is faith's.[63]

Fortunately, the mention of Job makes the identification of the culprits
easy, at least for those who know something of the history of alchemical
philosophy. Bacon's target here is the school of Paracelsus, and the
"heretical religion" would have been some variety of sectarianism,

radical both in religion and politics.[64] Hence Bacon would speak with unusual severity about its dangers, and advocate means of control out of keeping with his usual gentleness in political and religious affairs.

Indeed, any opposition between "natural philosophy" and "theology" in Bacon's thought is to some extent an artificial construct, since he deeply distrusted systematic theology itself. He considered that there were very strict limits on the powers and rights of the human mind to attempt to penetrate the divine mysteries. In the *de Augmentis* he discusses the proper use of natural theology to "refute and convince Atheism, but not to establish religion." For the world is the work of God and not His image; and from His works we can demonstrate that He exists and governs; in His works we can demonstrate the basic properties of God's presence, rule and benificence; and also "reasonably elicit" other "wonderful mysteries":

> But on the other side, out of the contemplation of nature and elements of human knowledge to induce any conclusion of reason or even any strong persuasion concerning the mysteries of faith, yea, or to inspect and sift them too curiously and search out the manner of the mystery, is in my opinion not safe.[65]

Bacon elsewhere gives hints that the corruption of theology has resulted from the same abuses of reason as the corruption of natural philosophy;[66] and also that the path towards true knowledge is the same in both cases: experience and aphorisms rather than argument and systems.[67]

We can safely conclude, then, that Bacon's conception of human knowledge of the divine did not entail a complete separation in spirit, methods, or ends, between enquiry into God's will and His works. In fact, if we look a bit more closely into Bacon's personal religion, we find the two endeavours brought into close relation. If we try to classify Bacon in respect to the problems of rational theology, we would probably call him a fideist. But this would be to apply a foreign and inappropriate scheme to Bacon's thought. His religion, like his philosophy of nature, was concerned primarily with practical works, and less with niceties of doctrine.[68] We express his view of the world very simply: man's corruption resulted from vanity; and man's redemption will be achieved by charity. For Bacon this was the message of Christ: he observed that all Christ's miracles were of mercy, not of judgment; each one was designed to help ordinary human beings with their ordinary problems. Similarly, in his meditation on Hypocrites, subtitled "I will have mercy and not sacrifice", he makes charity to be the touchstone of true religion. The meditation opens with:

> The ostenation of hyprocites is ever confined to the works of the first table of the law, which prescribes our duties to God. The reason is twofold: both because works of this class have a greater pomp of sanctity, and because they interfere less with their desires. The way to convict a hypocrite, therefore is to send him from the works of sacrifice to the works of mercy.

This penetrating observation is followed by one even more so:

> There are some however of a deeper and more inflated hypocrisy, who deceiving themselves, and fancying themselves worthy of a closer conversation with God, neglect the duties of charity towards their neighbour, as inferior matters.[69]

On charity itself, Bacon discussed the various circumstances in which it is ordinarily applied, to an enemy repentant or at least defeated.[70] None of these satisfied him; even the feeling that virtue is proceeding from one may be a form of pride. No, the "summit and exaltation" of charity comes only

> if evil overtake your enemy from elsewhere, and you in the inmost recesses of your heart are grieved and distressed, and feel no touch of joy, as thinking that the day of your revenge and redress has come...

Such a Christ-like conception of charity, encompassing a complete forgiveness and a complete love, should be kept in mind when we see the term in its frequent occurrence in exhortatory passages of Bacons. Pity for the sufferings of mankind comes out repeatedly in his various prayers, and his picture of a sage is of "a peaceful and serene air, save that his face had become habituated to the expression of pity."[71]

Far from imagining a "conflict between science and religion", Bacon saw the investigation of nature as a divine work. It not only served to reveal God's works, and to reform the intellect and soul of the enquirer, but also to imitate Christ in "the relief of man's estate". With this understanding of the connotations of his words, we may now see how Bacon's vision is encompassed in the final sentence of his prayer:

> Lastly, that knowledge being now discharged of the venom which the serpent infused into it, and which makes the mind of man to swell, we may not be wise above measure and sobriety, but cultivate truth in charity.[72]

With this interpretation of Bacon's conception of his task, we may be better equipped to approach the problem of his "sources" and of the development of his ideas. It is well known that many of his aphorisms and illustrations are derivative from published sources; and a thorough search of the relevant sets of literature might well reveal Bacon to have been a sort of philosophical magpie, picking up ideas from everywhere and then publishing them, rearranged and slightly polished, as his own. But to condemn him for this would be to misconceive his task, which was not to do original research, but to plead for a cause. Also, the roots of his commitment, and his informal synthesis of ideas, could not be assembled from a set of index-cards. We know that from an early age he was aware of this talents, and was determined to devote them to the service of man and God. It is possible that his earliest endeavours were in a literary-humanistic direction, culling the literature of aphorisms and apothegms, and from them distilling "axioms" on the nature of man. But this path was rejected, and by the age of thirty he had committed himself to finding the key in the study of nature. We simply do not know what person, or book, wrought this conversion. John Dee's departure from England probably came too early; and although Bruno was on hand during the crucial period,[73] he receives no mention whatever in Bacon's reflective writings, and his attack on institutional Christianity would be altogether too radical for Bacon's taste. Palissy the potter would probably have been only a self-educated workman for Bacon, not someone to provide him with his own particular version of the seventeenth-century commitment to approaching God through Nature. The most likely source of Bacon's conversion seems to be some current of pietistic Paracelsian philosophy; there one would find the mixture of the themes of Christian charity and a manual interaction with the things of Nature. The sentiments of scepticism of official learning, pity for the sufferings of mankind, and dedication to a pure and holy reform, that van Helmont shows in his autobiography,[74] are strikingly similar to those of Bacon. This is not to assert any link of influence between the two; but to indicate that their common form of commitment may well have derived from a common source.[75] Bacon's vehement condemnation of Paracelsian scriptural natural philosophy is not conclusive evidence against such an early influence; it is a commonplace in politics for a man to derive his permanent ideals from a radical source, and eventually comes to see the ongoing tradition of that source as the worst enemy of his programme.

Finally, we may consider whether this reinterpretation of Bacon has any significance for our understanding of the development of science from his time up to the present. Accepting the theological framework of his strategy for reform, we can add yet another criticism of his work to the already considerable stock. For in one respect he was wrong: not merely was the millenium not at hand in the early seventeenth century, but the growth of scientific knowledge and of the power of its applications neither required nor produced such a moral reform in society as he had considered essential. Even though ordinary life for ordinary people is more peaceful and humane by far in the advanced societies than it was in Bacon's time, the twentieth-century wars of ideology and empire have produced barbarities that match anything achieved during the wars of religion of the times before and after Bacon's career. Also, between Bacon's time and our own, his concern for the reform of the sciences could recede into past history as a curiosity of bygone times. Over the generations, natural science achieved appropriate methods of enquiry and viable social institutions for its work, so that it could progress to ever great triumphs.

But very recently, it has been impressed on us all that science lives not by Ph.D.'s alone. The political problems of the management of a large and complex scientific community, internally and in relation to its sources of financial support and recruitment, become ever more demanding; and the moral problems of responsibility for abhorrent applications of scientific results are likewise intensifying. This is not to say that the times are again ripe for a prophet with Bacon's particular message, or indeed for any prophet at all. But the moral commitment, and pity for mankind, that drove Bacon to make his contribution towards the advancement of learning, can no longer be dismissed as irrelevant or peripheral to the real business of science. Even if his scientific achievements are negligible, his elaborated methodology a bore, and his theological framework obsolete, yet in his aphorisms he may still speak to us.

## References

[1] A first draft of this paper was read to seminars at Leeds and at Cambridge in 1966. Its ideas have been developed in the course of teaching the *Novum Organum* at the Rijksuniversiteit te Utrecht. I am particularly grateful to Mr. van Drunen, then a student at Utrecht, and to Ir. H. Peters, of Boxtel, for their discussions of this aspect of Bacon and the materials which they made available to me.

[2] For a vigorous counter-attack on this tendency, see Hesse, Mary B. "Hermeticism and Historiography: An Apology for the Internal History of Science", *Minnesota Studies in the Philosophy of Science*. V (1971) (to appear).

[3] See Wiener, Norbert, *God & Golem, Inc.*, M.I.T. Press, 1964, 50-51.

[4]For a generally sceptical interpretation of the evidence for Descartes' involvement with the Rosicrucians, see Gouhier, H., *Les premières pensées de Descartes, contribution à l'histoire de l'anti-Renaissance*, Paris, 1958.

[5]See "Mr. Bacon in Praise of Knowledge", Bacon, *Works*, ed. Ellis, Spedding and Heath, London, VIII, 124.

[6]Bacon, *Novum Organum*, Book I, *Aphorism* 95, in *Works*, IV, 92-93.

[7]*Works*, IV, 79-80.

[8]*Novum Organum*, Bk. I, Aph. 74, in *Works*, IV, 74-75.

[9]*Ibid.*, Aph. 110, in *Works*, IV, 99-100.

[10]*Works*, III, 156-166.

[11]It is a commentary on the historiography of science that the immediate ancestry of Bacon's "Three Inventions" was discovered by Joseph Needham, in the course of tracing them back to China. A possible direct source for Bacon was le Roy, Louis, *Of the Interchangeable Course or Variety of Things in the Whole World*, English translation, 1594. I am indebted to Dr. P. Rattansi for the information on le Roy and on Needham's work.

[12]In his earlier writings, Bacon had no doubt that the discoveries were chance. Thus in the *Temporis Partus Masculus* he mentioned gunpowder as an example of a "lucky hit": "If gunpowder had been discovered, not by good luck but by good guidance, it would not have stood alone but been accompanied by a host of noble inventions of a kindred sort." (Translation from Farrington, B., *The Philosophy of Francis Bacon*, Liverpool University Press, 1964, 71). By the time of the writing of the *Novum Organum*, he was more cautious. In arguing for the possibility of new discoveries, he admitted that most of the standard examples "may seem to depend on certain properties of things themselves and nature, there is at any rate nothing in the art of printing which is not plain and obvious", *Novum Organum*, Bk. I, Aph. 110, in *Works*, IV, 100. His description of the process showed no acquaintance with the device of cast interchangeable type which distinguishes Western printing after Gutenberg from earlier methods of stamping an image in ink.

[13]*Ibid.*, Aph. 81, in *Works*, IV, 79.

[14]*Ibid.*, Aph. 129, in *Works*, IV, 144.

[15]See 'Plan of the Work', *Works*, IV, 26-27, for both points together.

[16]*Novum Organum*, Bk. I, Aph. 68, in *Works*, IV, 69.

[17]For an English translation, see Farrington, *op. cit.*, 59-72.

[18]*Ibid.*, 70.

[19]*Works*, IV, 33.

[20]tr., *ibid.*, VII, 243.

[21]*Works*, VII, 222.

[22]*Ibid.*, V, 132.

[23]*Ibid.*, IV, 19.

[24]*Ibid.*, IV, 20.

[25]Mag. Inst. Pref., *Ibid*, IV, 21.

[27]Conf. Faith, *Ibid.*, VII, 222.

[28]*Loc. cit.*

[29]*Works*, VII, 221.

[30]*Nat. and Exp. Hist.*, *Works*, V, 132.

[31]*Ibid.*, V, 133.

[32]For a full discussion, see Rossi, P., *Francis Bacon, From Magic to Science*, London, 1968, Ch. 3, 73-134.

[33]See the *Meditationes Sacrae*, tr. in *Works*, VII, 252; and *Novum Organum*, Bk. I, Aph. 89; *Works*, IV, 89.

[34]This figure is used many times; see *Plan of the Work*, *Works*, IV, 33; and the *Natural & Experimental History*, *Works*, V, 132.

[35]*Novum Organum*, Bk. I, Aph. 23; *Works*, IV, 51; and Aph. 124, *Works*, IV, 110.

[36]*Mag. Inst. Plan*, *Works*, IV, 33.

[37]*De Aug*, Bk. III, 5, *Works*, IV, 365.

[38]*Ibid.*, 364.

[39]*Novum Organum*, 129; *Works IV*, 114.

[40]*Mag. Inst. Pref.*, *Works*, IV, 20.

[41]*Works*, IV, 115.

[42]*Mag. Inst. Plan Works*, IV, 33.

[43]Farrington, *op. cit.*, 72.

[44]*De Aug*, Bk. III, Ch. 1; *Works*, IV, 336-340, and *Novum Organum*, Bk. I, 127; *Works*, IV, 112.

[45]*Novum Organum*, 129; *Works*, IV, 115.

[46]*Ibid.*, Aph. 113; *Works*, IV, 102.

[47]The importance of this contact with "Things" in Bacon's philosophy has perhaps been obscured by the translators' practice of using a variety of terms for "res", including "fact", "particulars" or "nature". Indeed, one may say that most of the times such terms appear in an English translation, the original is "res". It could be argued that the Latin term had extended connotations for Bacon, as it does in legal usage; but in every instance I have tested, the translation of "res" as "thing" improves the sense.

[48]*De Aug.*, Bk. III, 1; *Works*, IV, 337.

[49]*Works*, III, 222. See also *Novum Organum*, Preface, *Works*, IV, 20.

[50]This is hinted at in the Proem of the Great Instauration; I translate the third phrase as: "he (Bacon) thought that all trial should be made, whether that commerce between the Mind and Things (which is the most precious of anything on earth, or at least of earthly things), might be restored to its integrity, or at least brought to improvement." See *Works*, I, 121 and IV, 7, for original and translation.

[51]*Novum Organum*, Bk. 1, Aph. 129; Works, IV ,115.

[52]*Works*, III, 165.

[53]*Novum Organum, Pref., Works*, IV, 42.

[54]*Loc. cit.*

[55]*Novum Organum*, Bk. 1, Aph. 128; *Works*, IV, 113.

[56]*Novum Organum, Pref., Works*, IV, 42.

[57]Farrington, *op. cit.*, 108.

[58]*Works*, 107-113.

[59]*Works*, IV, 91.

[60]*Ibid.*, 91-92.

[61]*Ibid.*, 93.

[62]*Ibid.*, 87-89.

[63]*Novum Organum*, Bk. 1, Aph. 65; *Works*, IV, 66.

[64]I am indebted to Ir. H. Peters for this important identification.

[65]*De Aug.*, Bk. III, 2, *Works*, IV, 341-342.

[66]*Novum Organum*, Bk. I, Aph. 89; *Works*, IV, 88 and *De Aug.*, Bk. IX, 1, *Works*, V, 111-119.

[67]*Advancement of Learning, Works*, III, 487-488; and *De Aug.*, Bk. IX, 1; *Works*, V, 118.

[68]Farrington relates this emphasis to an English tradition, extending back through More and Colet. See Farrington, *op. cit.*, 17.

[69]*Meditationes Sacrae, Works*, VII, 249.

[70]*Ibid.*, 245-246.

[71]*The Refutation of Philosophies, Farrington*, op. cit., 104.

[72]*Novum Organum, Pref., Works*, IV, 20.

[73]Farrington, *op. cit.*, 27.

[74]See the opening pages of the *Oriatrike, or Physick Refined* (1662).

[75]One of the few "moderns" for whom Bacon shows any respect is Petrus Severinus, a moderate Paracelsian of Denmark.

# 29

## Francis Bacon and *Spiritus*

### D. P. WALKER

BACON nowhere gives a systematic exposition of his theory of spirits; but he discusses them so frequently that I think we can show two points clearly: first, that he believed in them firmly, and that they were an essential and fundamental part of his natural philosophy; secondly, that his theory of spirits was very close to that of the only two sources he mentions, Telesio and Donio.

In the *De Augmentis Scientiarum*[1] Bacon distinguishes two souls in man. The first is the rational soul, which is divine and infused directly by God; as we are told in the second account of man's creation: "the Lord God formed man of the dust of the ground, and breathed into his nostrils the breath of life; and man became a living soul."[2] The second is the irrational soul, also called the sensible or produced soul, which we have in common with the animals. This lower soul is derived from the elements; Bacon quotes from Genesis, I, 20, 24: "Let the waters bring forth.... Let the earth bring forth". It is the instrument of the rational soul. The first, higher, soul is outside the field of natural philosophy, and Bacon will leave it to the theologians. But the second, lower, soul has not yet been adequately investigated, and this lack must be made good.

Bacon begins his investigation by dismissing Aristotelian and scholastic theories of the soul:[3] "What use for the doctrine of the substance of the soul are the Actus Ultimus and Forma Corporis and suchlike logical trifles?" He then gives his own description of the lower soul:

Since the sensible or animals' soul must clearly be thought to be a corporeal substance, attenuated and made invisible by heat; a vapour (I say) conflated out of flamelike and airy natures, endowed with the softness of air for receiving impressions, and with the vigour of fire for launching actions; nourished partly by oily, partly by watery things; covered by the body, and in perfect animals located chiefly in the head, running through the nerves, and replenished and repaired by the spirituous blood of the arteries; as Bernardino Telesio, and his disciple

121

Agostino Donio, have in some measure not quite uselessly asserted....
This soul might better be called by the name Spiritus.

That is to say: Bacon's lower soul is very like the animal spirits of medical theory.[4] These are centered in the cavities of the brain, from which they flow through the nervous system to sense-organs and muscles. Their functions are motor-activity, sense-perception, and, usually, such lower psychological activities as appetite, *sensus communis,* and imagination. From now on, it will be simpler to call Bacon's lower soul *Spiritus,* as he suggests.

Bacon goes on to give an ordinary list of psychological faculties: intellect, reason, imagination, memory, appetite, will; but he does not distribute them between the two souls, i.e. between soul and *Spiritus.* It is however clear from what follows that imagination belongs to *Spiritus.* For he then gives the usual explanation of magical fascination, namely, that it is caused by the power of the imagination transmitted through the eyes from one man's Spiritus to another's.[5] *Spiritus,* then, encroaches on soul as far up the scale of faculties as imagination.

A little later Bacon complains that there has as yet been no proper investigation of motor-activity, because the lower soul has been considered as an entelechy or function, instead of as a corporeal substance.[6] What we must do is to inquire "How the compressions, dilations and agitations of the Spiritus (which without doubt is the fountainhead of motion) bend, excite, or drive the corporeal and gross mass of the parts of the body." We are not told how such an enquiry is to be carried out.

How we can put our knowledge of the *Spiritus* to practical use we learn in the *Historia Vitae et Mortis,* a treatise dealing with the prolongation of life and youth by a proper treatment of the *Spiritus.*[7] The way to postpone senility and death is to see to it that the *Spiritus* is dense and consequently has a gentle heat that will not dry up and eventually destroy the body. Ways of condensing the *Spiritus* are: to take opium, breathe cold air, smell fresh earth. Ways of keeping it gently warm are: to eat garlic, *Venus saepe excitata, raro peracta.* Violent emotions must be avoided, since they attentuate the *Spiritus;* moderate emotions, including sadness, are good because they strengthen and condense it.

This treatise also introduces a division of spirits into two kinds. Even inanimate things contain *Spiritus:*[8] "Let that which is most certain be posited as an assumption: in every tangible thing there is a spirit or pneumatic body, covered and inclosed by the tangible parts." Later we are told:[9] "In all living things are two kinds of spirit: dead spirits, such as are in inanimate things, and in addition a vital spirit." We can tabulate the specific differences between these two kinds of spirits as follows:[10]

| *Spiritus Mortuales* | *Spiritus Vitales* |
| --- | --- |
| are discontinuous, separated by parts of the body containing them. | are continuous, flowing through channels, which derive from a cavity or cavities, situated mainly in the brain. Lower animals, such as eels and birds, have very small cavities; hence most of their spirit is in the channels—as is shown by their bodies moving after decapitation. |
| are not hot. are like air. | are hot, like a combustible vapour before ignition. They are flamelike, but less hot than the gentlest flame, and are mostly mixed with air, *ut sit* (sc. *spiritus*) *et flammeae et aëreae naturae mysterium.* |
| appear mainly in an alchemical context. | appear mainly in a medical context; the *spiritus vitales* include the usual medical threefold spirits (natural, vital, animal). |

Since all bodies, including inanimate ones, contain *Spiritus,* all bodies perceive *(percipere);* only animals feel *(sentire).*[11] The difference between perceiving and feeling seems to be that the latter involves pleasure and pain. Nevertheless, the perceiving carried out by inanimate things is not merely an odd term for something like a chemical reaction, but is more like the reaction of a living body to a stimulus:[12]

> It is certain that all bodies whatsoever, though they have no sense, yet they have perception: for when one body is applied to another, there is a kind of election to embrace that which is agreeable, and to exclude or expel that which is ingrate: and whether the body be alterant or altered, evermore a perception precedeth operation; for else all bodies would be alike one to another.

For example, a weather-glass perceives hot and cold more subtly than do our senses.

Let us now look at Bacon's immediate sources: Telesio and Donio.

In Telesio's *De Rerum Natura juxta propria principia* (1587),[13] every physical event, and every kind of mental event, with one exception, is explained as a conflict between two principles, hot and cold, both of them endowed with sensation and a desire for self-preservation. These principles are themselves incorporeal, but they are present in all matter, so that everything in the world is both extended and sentient. Now the usual philosophical function of *Spiritus* is to be a bridge-concept between an immaterial, unextended mental world, and an extended, mindless physical world; *Spiritus* is matter so tenuous that it has nearly become soul and is sentient, or soul so gross that it has become matter and is extended. Telesio has no need of the term in this function, since for him everything is both extended and sentient. He uses *Spiritus* in order to account for centralized systems of activity. Every individual part of a man can feel, perceive, react appropriately, like all other matter; but man evidently performs these functions as an organized whole. Since for Telesio hot and subtle matter is especially sentient and active, medical spirits, which are warm, rarified and mobile, provide a convenient unifying agent.

There would seem to be no logical room in Telesio's system for an immaterial soul—indeed it seems specially designed to avoid it. But he does introduce one, and not merely because he wishes to remain an orthodox Christian, but because he sees that his system cannot account for all the activities of man. His two principles, hot and cold, and his spirit, tend always and only toward their self-preservation; the wholes built out of them, animals and men, must do this and no more. Thus all man's actions, thoughts and desires should be purely utilitarian. Telesio points out that in fact man persistently desires and seeks things that do not lead to his preservation or pleasure; that he is always anxiously, restlessly looking for what is far beyond these, for useless knowledge, for divine beings, for God Himself. The functions, then, of the immaterial, God-given soul in Telesio's philosophy are limited to non-utilitarian contemplation and feeling; the spirit by itself does all ordinary, practically orientated, feeling, perceiving, reasoning, acting.

The position of soul in this system is evidently precarious; give a little more to *Spiritus*, allow its reasoning or feeling to be more than utilitarian, and it will absorb the soul, make it unnecessary. This step was taken by Agostino Donio, a disciple of Telesio, in his *De Natura Hominis* (1581).[14] Unlike Telesio, Donio was a heretic, who had been five years in prison in Italy and who ended up at Cracow.[15] Throughout his book there is no mention of an incorporeal soul, but a psychology and physiology based solely on a Telesian *Spiritus*. Right at the end, however, Donio does tackle the relation of his psychology to Christian doctrine. In accordance with Telesian principles, the ideal situation of the *Spiritus* would be when surrounded entirely by substances like itself, hot, lucent and subtle, and not by cold, dark, gross flesh. At death the *Spiritus* will achieve this situation by leaving this body and uniting itself to the warm aether of the heavens. Donio concludes:[16]

> If indeed this spirit is the soul itself, to which God has promised (if it keeps His law) the enjoyment of celestial goods, and for whose salvation CHRIST JESUS GOD, KING AND OUR LORD, died, then we Christians must resolve, overcoming nature with God's help, to keep our spirit while in this body entirely uncorrupted by all adverse forces....

This identification of the soul with medical spirits had already appeared in Melanchthon's *De Anima* (1555) and in Servetus's *Christianismi Restitutio* (1553),[17] and, I think, in Antonio Persio's *Trattato dell' ingegno dell 'huomo* (1576)[18] and Vives's *De Anima et Vita* (1555).[19] It also appears a little later in Bodin's *Le Theatre de la Nature Universelle* (1597).[20] Now to identify the soul with medical spirits is to make the soul corporeal, i.e. extended, having parts, and capable of dissolution; and this is not only revolutionary philosophy, but also highly unorthodox theology. The few thinkers who took this step were most of them wildly heretical, Servetus, Donio, Bodin, but one of them was a Catholic, Vives, and one a Protestant, Melanchthon. The identification is carefully avoided by Telesio, Bacon and later Descartes, who all preserve an immaterial soul. Did they make this distinction between *Spiritus* and soul merely for the sake of religious orthodoxy?

For Telesio the answer is no. As we have seen, the non-utilitarian activities of man are a genuine reason for positing a soul as well as a Spiritus. For Descartes also the answer is no. In his whole system thought has absolute priority; the innate ideas are independent of all sense-impressions.[21] For Bacon I am not sure what the answer is, since he avoids discussing the functions of his higher soul.

As a scientific theory medical spirits have one obvious defect from a modern point of view: it would be very difficult to disprove them empirically, since they are invisible and are dissipated at death. But some attempts were made to provide positive empirical evidence for them. In a very comprehensive monograph on spirits by Domenico Bertacchi, *De*

*Spiritibus Libri Quatuor* (1584),[22] we find, for example, the following: the spurting forth of arterial blood and of semen shows that these heavy liquids must be mixed with something light and mobile; the fact that, if one eye is shut, the pupil of the other dilates, must be due to some kind of spirit being constantly transmitted to both; the instantaneous transmission of heat and cold which produces blushing and pallor from fear must be due to a subtle body, and so forth.

For Bacon and Descartes, who denied the possibility of a vacuum, the cerebral ventricles had to contain something, and, in spite of the latter's exclusion of all teleology, to serve some purpose.[23] Spirits enable Descartes, in the *Traité de l'Homme*,[24] to construct quite a good mechanical model of reflex-actions; this model is expressly compared to automata driven by water, that is to say, the spirits function like transmission in a car. But he nowhere suggests any experiment that could either confirm or refute the model. Where he goes beyond reflex-actions to explain sense-impressions, imagination and memory, his explanations only make sense if one assumes a rational soul in the little gland, the conarion, which, in this treatise, is not supposed to be there—and even then we are left with the ghost in the machine, a tiny little man in the conarion receiving and sending messages by means of the spirits. If, as for Bacon and other Telesians, spirits can themselves feel and perceive, such explanations are still more patently idle. There is no point in trying to explain the fact that I can see by positing a spirit in my eyes and brain which is able to see.

The acceptance of medical spirits was, I think, almost inevitable, and was in fact universal, until somebody could put forward an alternative explanation of sense-perception and motor-activity and of the connexion of these with the brain and nervous system. Nor did this acceptance do any harm when spirits were merely used as a stop-gap, and a scientist's attention was not concentrated on them. Vesalius, in the *De Humani corporis Fabrica* (1542),[25] is a good example of this. He accepts animal spirits, though not without suggesting that nervous transmission may be more of the nature of light, but wastes little time on them, and contemptuously dismisses the usual distribution of psychological faculties among the ventricles of the brain. The same cannot be said of Descartes, nor of Bacon and other Telesians, in whose works spirits play a major and essential part.

One of the very few 17th century writers to reject the whole system of medical spirits was William Harvey, in his *Exercitationes de generatione animalium* (1651);[26] but this rejection seems to have had very little effect. Moreover, Harvey transferred to the blood nearly all the traditional functions and qualities of spirit, including sensation.

The last aspect of the theory of *Spiritus* that I want to discuss is its close links with astrology and magic. These connexions are of two kinds.

First, man's *Spiritus* has a special affinity to the substance of the heavens, or is identical with it, and is therefore particularly subject to astral influences, usually thought to be conveyed by the *spiritus mundi*. This belief dates at least from the time of Aristotle, whose description of semen, in the *De Generatione Animalium*,[27] is constantly quoted by 16th and 17th century medical writers; what makes semen fertile is "the spirit which is contained in the foamy body of the semen, and the nature which is in the spirit, analogous to the element of the stars." From the time of Jean Fernel's *De Naurali parte Medicinae* (1542)[28] medical spirits were sometimes identified with the astral body or vehicle of the soul of the Neoplatonists.

Secondly, natural magic is centred on the power of the imagination (*vis imaginativa*), and imagining is done by the spirit, the higher faculties, reason and intellect, usually being given to the soul.[29]

Bacon believes in both these connexions. In his exposition of good astrology (*astrologia sana*) in the *De Augmentis*,[30] which retains the traditional planetary influences, his second rule is:[31] "the heavenly bodies do not act on all kinds of body, but only on rather soft ones, such as humours, air and spirits." A little later he plainly accepts the "influences which the heavenly bodies have on human spirits."[32] But in the *Slyva Sylvarum*[33] he rejects the *spiritus mundi* precisely because it leads to non-demonic magic. Having done so, however, he immediately goes on to suggest "experiments touching transmission of spirits and the force of the imagination," for example, the experiment of curing a sick gentleman by influencing the *Spiritus* of one of his servants who is naturally credulous. These co-called experiments show clearly that Bacon believed in the traditional doctrine of the magical power of imagination fortified by credulity.

The explicit reason Bacon gives for disliking magic is that it is too easy a way of reaching one's goal. In the *Advancement of Learning*,[34] when discussing the power of the imagination, he dismisses the claims of the Paracelsans and their "miracle-working faith," but accepts as "nearer to probability" "transmissions and operations from spirit to spirit without mediation of the senses," aided by the "force of confidence." But, he goes on,

If the imagination fortified have power, then it is material to know how to fortify and exalt it. And herein comes in crookedly and dangerously, a palliation of a great part of ceremonial magic. For it may be pretended, that ceremonies, characters, and charms, do work, not by any tacit or sacramental contract with evil spirits, but serve only to strengthen the imagination of him that useth it; as images are said by the Roman church to fix the cogitations, and raise the devotions of them that pray before them. But for mine own judgement, if it be admitted that imagination hath power, and that ceremonies fortify the imagination, and that they be used sincerely and intentionally for that purpose; yet I should hold them unlawful, as opposing to that first edict which God gave unto man, "In sudore vultûs comedes panem tuum." For they propound those noble effects, which God hath set forth unto man to be bought at the price of labour, to be attained by a few easy and slothful observances.

Earlier in the same work he had stated that it may be possible, by prolonged and arduous investigation, to achieve making gold or the rejuvenation of the old by operations on the Spiritus; but that false magicians wickedly try to do these things without sweat and toil.[35]

As Paolo Rossi has pointed out,[36] the doctrine of the Fall of Man is of cardinal importance for Bacon's view of the history of philosophy and science, and hence for his programme for present action. Adam lost his dominion over nature through a sin of disobedience and of pride, a sin committed in order to acquire the wrong kind of knowledge ("and ye shall be as Gods, knowing good and evil"). The only way back to this dominion was indicated by God's curse ("in the sweat of thy brow shalt thou eat bread"), that is, by patient, wearisome, humble work, directed at practically useful knowledge. Hence Bacon's attacks on all large-scale philosophical systems, and his belief that some pre-Socratics and still earlier workers had gone some way towards recovering this lost practical knowledge of nature, expressing it respectively in aphorisms and myths. Hence also his apparently emphatic rejections of natural magic. But here the situation is more complicated and puzzling. Aristotelian, Platonic, or scholastic systems, as well as being morally wrong because they are a repetition of Adam's sin of pride, are no good because they are sterile; they have not produced and cannot produce useful results. But, clearly, as we have seen, Bacon thought that magic, though equally sinful and presumptuous, probably had produced and could in the future produce useful effects, and even suggested detailed ways of investigating them. I think he must really have been in two minds. If the faith-healing experiments had had a 100% success, and if the supply of credulous servants did not give out, would we be justified in abandoning the patient investigation of the healing properties of herbs and drugs in favour of these magical techniques?

## References

[1]Bacon, Francis, *Works,* ed. Spedding, Ellis, etc., London 1857-1901, I 604 *seq.*

[2]Genesis, II, 7.

[3]Bacon, *op cit.,* I, 606. "Quid enim ad doctrinam de Substantia Animae faciunt Actus Ultimus et Forma Corporis, et hujusmodi nugae logicae? Anima siquidem Sensibilis sive Brutorum plane substantia corporea censenda est, a calore attenuata et facta invisibilis; aura (inquam) ex natura flammea et aërea conflata, aëris mollitie ad impressionem recipiendam, ignis vigore ad actionem vibrandam, dotata; partim ex oleosis partim ex aqueis nutrita; corpore obducta, atque in animalibus perfectis in capite praecipue locata, in nervis percurrens, et sanguine spirituoso arteriarum refecta et reparata; quemadmodum Bernardinus Telesius, et discipulus ejus Augustinus Donius, aliqua ex parte non omnino inutiliter asseruerunt."

[4]For spirits in general in antiquity, see Verbeke, G., *L'Evolution de la Doctrine du Pneuma du Stoïcisme à S. Augustin,* Paris, 1945. I know of no modern work on medical spirits, but cf. Walker, D. P., *Spiritual and Demonic Magic from Ficino to Campanella,* London, 1958, and "The Astral Body in Renaissance Medicine", *Journal of the Warburg and Courtauld Institutes,* XXI, 1958, 119-133. I have had to summarize or repeat parts of these works in this paper.

[5]Bacon, *op.cit.,* I, 607-8.

[6]*Ibid.,* I, 609-10 :"Quomodo vero compressiones et dilationes et agitationes spiritus (qui proculdubio motus fons est) corpoream et crassam partium molem flectat, excitet, aut pellat, adhuc diligenter inquisitum et tractatum non est. Neque mirum, cum Anima ipsa Sensibilis hactenus potius pro entelechia et functione quadam habita sit, quam pro substantia."

[7]*Ibid.,* II, 162 seq.

[8]*Ibid.,* II, 112 :"Loco *assumpti* ponatur, quod certissimum est; inesse omni tangibili spiritum sive corpus pneumaticum, partibus tangibilibus obtectum et inclusum."

[9]*Ibid.,* II, 214 :"In omnibus animatis duo sunt genera spirituum: spiritus mortuales, quales insunt inanimatis; et superadditus spiritus vitalis."

[10]*Ibid.,* II, 214 *seq.*

[11]*Ibid.,* I, 610-1.

[12]*Ibid.,* II, 602.

[13]Cf. Walker, *Spiritual & Demonic Magic,* 189-194.

[14]Cf. *ibid.*, 193-4.

[15]See Cantimori, Delio, *Italienische Haeretiker der Spätrenaissance*, Basel, 1949, 479.

[16]Donio, *De Natura Hominis*, Basel, 1581, 122 :"Qui quidem spiritus si est ea ipsa anima, cui á Deo (modo custodiat eius legem) fruitio coelestium bonorum promissa est: & pro cuius salute CHRISTUS IESUS DEUS, REX ET DOMINUS NOSTER, mortuus est: statuendum nobis christianis, eum, DEO sic providente, potentia naturam superante, sub hoc corpore ab omni vi impetentium servari omninò incorruptum..."

[17]See Walker, "The Atsral Body..." 121.

[18]See Walker, *Spiritual & Demonic Magic*, 195-8.

[19]Vives, Luis, *De Anima & Vita Libri tres*, Lugdun, 1555, 108, 131-2; Vives's apparent identification of *mens* and *spiritus* may be due only to a very loose use of the latter term.

[20]See Walker, *op. cit.*, 172.

[21]Cf. Descartes, René, *Oeuvres*, ed. Adam & Tannery, III, Paris, 1899, 418 (letter to Mersenne, 1641).

[22]See Walker, "The Astral Body..." 120 n.9.

[23]Cf. Descartes, *op. cit.*, III, 686-9 (letter to Vorstius, 1643).

[24]*Ibid.*, XI.,170 seq.

[25]Vesalius, Andreas, *De Humani corporis fabrica*, Basel, 1543, 623-4, 636.

[26]See Walker, *art. cit.* 130-3.

[27]Aristotle, *De Gen An.*, 736 B.

[28]See Walker, *art. cit.*, 119 seq.

[29]Cf. Walker, *Spiritual & Demonic Magic*, 75 seq. & *passim*.

[30]Bacon, *op. cit.*, I, 554-9.

[31]*Ibid.*, I, 555 :"Operatio coelestium in corpora omnigena non valet, sed tantum in teneriora, qualia sunt humores, aër, et spiritus."

[32]*Ibid.*, I, 558.

[33]*Ibid.*, II, 640-1, 652-660.

[34]*Ibid.*, III, 381; also in *De Augm.*, *ibid.*, I, 609.

[35]*Ibid.*, I, 574-5.

[36]Rossi, Paolo, *Francesco Bacone*, Bari, 1957, 104, 320 seq.

# 30

## Nobility of Man and Plurality of Worlds

### PAOLO ROSSI

*Translated by* ARTHUR BRICKMANN

### I

THE thesis of the non-centrality of the earth, the enlargement of the traditional boundaries of the universe, the affirmation of the plurality of worlds and the infinity of the cosmos—these opinions aroused in European culture not only a sense of exaltation and enthusiasm, but also, a feeling of astonishment and bewilderment, of beginning as well as ending. The seventeenth century seemed to Mersenne to mark the start of radical changes which went well beyond the confines of astronomy. In March of 1644, he asked Peiresc for an opinion of these upheavals. Did they not perhaps give one the feeling of the end of the world?

From Lovejoy to Tillyard, from Nicolson to Koyré many historians of ideas have analyzed on the characteristics, the dimensions, and the meaning of this crisis.[1] Their pages merit consideration in face of the numerous historiographical efforts, particularly those of the 1800's as well as more recent studies, to extend certain attitudes to all of seventeenth-century culture. Specifically, these efforts fixed on Bruno's enthusiasm for the idea of an infinity of worlds, his sense of joy at the crumbling of the walls which protected the image of a finite universe constructed in man's behalf.

The well-known verses of John Donne have been much quoted. But many shared the impression that the destruction of the old order of the world would be tantamount to the establishment of disorder, and that such disorder could spill over into the established moral and religious values. Gabriel Naudé, a lucid witness to his times, had clearly considered the revolutionary import of the new cosmology and its implicit perils:

> I fear that the old theological heresies are nothing compared to the new ones that the astronomers want to introduce with their worlds, or rather lunar and celestial earths. For the consequence of these latter heresies will be much more dangerous than that of the preceding ones and will introduce yet stranger revolutions.[2]

131

The idea of the order of the world, its harmony and proportion, was traditionally tied to the image of a finite universe. It was the cosmological conclusions that could be derived from this idea more than the affirmation of the mobility of the earth which seemed to threaten the very *form* of the universe; i.e., the very possibility of its continuing interpretation as a *system*. Francis Bacon was struck by precisely this threat in 1612. Could not belief in a plurality of worlds lead to denial of the very idea of a world-system? Could it not lead to a conception of the universe as a fragmented and disordered grouping of globes scattered in space, no longer possessing any form or system or common center?[3] Apart from the diversity of context and the profound difference of tone, Bacon's preoccupations were not greatly dissimilar in substance from those expressed one year earlier by John Donne, in the oft-quoted verses of *The Anatomy of the World*. Here the lament for the "new philosophy" (something much broader than the new astronomy), which "calls everything into doubt," coincided with the acknowledgment that the world had lost all "coherence," that it had been newly "crumbled into its atoms."[4]

Bacon's investigations, like Donne's bewilderment, certainly were not derived directly from the "geometrical" picture of the world that Copernicus had traced in *De Revolutionibus*. In that work the universe not only continued to be identified with the solar system, but it also retained a center about which solid and real spheres continued to rotate by virtue of their perfect spherical form. Nor did that universe definitely consist of globes scattered in infinite space, for it was enclosed by

the first and supreme sphere of all the fixed stars, which contains itself

and all things and which therefore is immobile and is the place of the universe to which motion and the position of all the other stars refer.[5]

Despite many reactions to Copernicus and many uncertainties about the new astronomy, it must never be forgotten that Bruno had placed the world of Copernicus and its innumerable worlds within an infinite and homogeneous space "which we may freely call the void." *"Omne movetur aut e vacuo, aut ad vacuum, aut in vacuo"* atoms and worlds move in the void or infinite space, as do atoms dispersed in the heavens. The infinite void of the Lucretian and atomistic vision of the world really seemed a kind of "natural location" for the Copernican solar system and for a plurality of such systems.[6] That reference to atomism present in Donne's verses was certainly not casual. The sun and the earth were "lost" in a crumbled universe.

Of course, in Copernicus' work there was no negation of the circularity and regularity of celestial motions, whereas Bruno had insisted at length upon this negation, interpreting spheres and epicycles as "poultices and prescriptions for doctoring nature...to the service of Master Aristotle." Certainly the text of *De Revolutionibus* could not make one think about the dissolution of any world—"system" nor of the shattering of the universe. It was Bruno, in the text of *Cena,* who had refuted the idea of every "continuous and regular" celestial motion "around the center"; who had affirmed the impossibility of perfect motions and perfect forms in the physical universe, given that every movement of natural bodies differs "from the simply circular and regular movement around a center." It was Bruno who saw in the laws of motion of the celestial bodies something characteristic of the individual stars and planets; who had entrusted the path which the heavenly bodies should take in the heavens to their "very soul" and their "intrinsic principle."[7] It was Bruno who had conceived of the heavenly bodies as animated beings in free movement and had insisted on the impossibility of constructing a harmonious picture of the universe within which one might make precise calculations:

> The motions characteristic of each of [the planets], beyond *(oltre)* this motion called worldly, and those characteristic of the so-called fixed [stars]—both of which must refer to the earth—are those which are seen. And such motions have as many variations as there are bodies; so that if motion is seen in all of the stars, which show no variation because of the great distance between them and us, the stars will never be seen coming together in one and the same order and measure of motion. Although they run their courses around the solar fire and they rotate around their own centers by their participation in the vital heat, we can never understand the differences in their approaches and withdrawals.[8]

Bruno had made a clear distinction between the universe and the worlds. To speak of a world-system does not mean, in his vision of the cosmos, to speak of a system of the universe. Astronomy, as the science of heavenly bodies, is legitimate insofar as it is the science of the worlds which fall into the range of our sensible perception. But beyond those worlds extends an infinite universe which contains an infinite plurality of worlds as well as all those "grand animals" which we call stars. It is a universe that has neither dimension nor measure, neither form nor figure. Both uniform and formless, it cannot yield a "system."[9]

In his passionate defense of Galileo, Tommaso Campanella is quite clearly aware of the profound difference between a) the thesis of an infinite plurality of worlds dispersed in an infinite space, and b) the maintenance of a *system*, of a form and therefore of an order in the universe.[10] Thanks to his wondrous instruments, Campanella says, Galileo showed us hitherto unknown fixed stars, taught us that the planets are similar to the moon in that they receive light from their sun and rotate about one another. From Galileo we learned that transmutations of elements occur in the sky, that clouds and vapors exist among the stars, that worlds are found in great numbers. The ninth of the eleven *Argumenta contra Galilaeum* asserts that it follows from such opinions that more worlds and earths and seas exist, as Mohammed said, and men that live in them. But, Campanella made clear, admitting more worlds is quite a different thing from maintaining, as Galileo did, that all systems are included in a unique system, enclosed in a unique space, and ordered in a greater unity.[11] Galileos assertions are not to be confused with those of Democritus or Epicurus:

> To admit more uncoordinated worlds in order to constitute of them a single one *(absque ordine ad unum)*, as Democritus and Epicurus did, is an error of faith: because it follows that the worlds are formed by chance without the ordering intervention of God. To the contrary, to conceive numerous minor systems within a highest one *(plura systemata parva intra unum maximum)*, ordered according to the divine mind, is not at all contrary to Scripture but only to Aristotle.[12]

Galileo, as Campanella says a little later, discovered not many worlds, but many systems in this one world, ordered toward a unity *(non plures mundos, sed plura systemata in hoc mundo detegit, ordinata ad unum)*.

## II

Copernicus, Kepler, and Galileo, beyond the differences, the affinities, and the divergences, maintain the firm image of a universe as a unitary system. They see in the world the expression of a divine order, the manifestation of principles or mathematical-geometrical archetypes. From this point of view, their "geometric" astronomy contrasts, on the whole, with that which has been not inappropriately called Bruno's "astrobiology." Galileo avoids Bruno's perspectives, notwithstanding their common enthusiasm for Copernicus and their common negation of the interpretation of the Copernican doctrine as a hypothesis. He repeatedly insists on the world as a "perfect body," a well-ordered composition of parts arranged according to the best possible order. And, like Copernicus, he places at the foundation of his consideration of the cosmos two premisses of a general nature: the order of the universe and the pre-eminence of circular motion.

> I say that I agree with the things that he [Aristotle] said up to here and I admit that the world is a body endowed with all dimensions, and therefore perfect. And I add that as such it is necessarily highly ordered, that is to say composed of parts arranged with paramount and perfect order among themselves....I therefore conclude that only circular motion can naturally befit the natural bodies, when they are integrating the universe and constituted in the optimal arrangement; and linear motion, as far as one can say, is assigned by nature to its bodies and their parts whenever they are out of place, set up in a perverse arrangement, and therefore needing to bring themselves back to the state as quickly as possible. From this it seems to me that one may conclude reasonably enough that to maintain the perfect order between the parts of the world, it is necessary to say that movable things can have only circular motions, and if there are some things which do not move circularly, these are necessarily immobile, there being nothing else except quiet and circular motion suited to the conservation of order.[13]

That singular mixture of Lucretian, Copernican, Neoplatonic, and Hermetic themes was characteristic of many authors—among them Cusa, Palingenius, and Bruno—who were far from the rigor and co-herence of the Galileo's scientific thought. And yet, in this mixture one may discern those five innovative ideas or "revolutionary cosmographical theses" which Lovejoy delineated, more than thirty years ago, as characteristic of a changed world view:

1) the assertion that other planets of our solar system are inhabited by sentient and rational beings;

2) the destruction of the external walls of the medieval universe, whether they be identified with the extreme crystalline sphere or with a definite region of the fixed stars, and the dispersion of these stars within vast and irregular spaces:

3) the idea of the fixed stars as suns similar to ours, all or nearly all surrounded by their own systems of planets;

4) the hypothesis that also the planets of these other worlds are inhabited by rational beings; and

5) the assertion of the actual infinity of the physical universe in space and of the number of solar systems contained therein.[14]

Lovejoy tended to draw too sharp a distinction between the philosophical and cultural aspects of the scientific revolution and those aspects which were more properly technical and astronomical. But he was undoubtedly right in singling out Bruno as the principal representative of the doctrine of a decentralized, infinite, and infinitely populated universe.[15] And Lovejoy was equally correct in affirming that none of the five theses was advanced by Copernicus, and that both the doctrine of infinity and that of the plurality of worlds were rejected, in various ways, by the three great astronomers of Bruno's time and the succeeding generation: Brahe, Kepler, and Galileo.[16]

## III

In 1638, four years after the publication of Kepler's *Somnium seu opus posthumum de astronomia lunari,* John Wilkins published one of the most important popular-science books of the seventeenth century: *The Discovery of a New World, or a Discourse tending to prove that it is probable there may be another Habitable World in the Moon.*[17] In defending his hypothesis, Wilkins recalls the incredulity that surrounded Columbus' project, the derision which throughout history has always accompanied the discovery of new truths, the dogmatism of popular opinions, and the blindness of academics and scholars who for centuries obstinately denied the existence of forms of life at the Antipodes. The author resolutely adopts Bacon's theses concerning antiquity and the relations between tradition and progress in the sciences:

> This is a false conceit for us to thinke that amongst the ancient variety and search of opinions, the best hath still prevailed. Time (saith the learned Verulam) seems to be of the nature of a river or streame, which carrieth downe to us that which is light or blowne up, but sinketh that which is weighty and solid....It must needes be a great impediment unto the growth of sciences for men still so to plod on upon beaten principles, as to be afraid of entertaining any things that may seem to contradict them. An unwillingness to take such things into examination, is one of those errours of learning in these times observed by the judicious Verulam.[18]

Wilkins thoroughly understood the theological difficulties present in the hypothesis of infinite inhabited worlds. Such an assertion had been considered heretical since the most ancient times; it contrasted with Moses' account and the words of John, both of whom had referred to a single world. It implied *improvidence* on the part of God if the worlds were of the same kind, since none would be more nearly perfect than the others; whereas, if the worlds were conceived of as diverse in kind, none of them might be called "a world" or "universe," since any one would lack in universal perfection. But it is particularly significant that, among the arguments most widely used against the hypothesis of a plurality of worlds and against the Copernican system, he remembered the argument deduced

> from the vileness of our earth, because it consists of a more sordid and base matter than any other part of the world; and therefore must be situated in the centre, which is the worst place, and at the greatest distance from those purer incorruptible bodies, the heavens.[19]

Galileo had referred to precisely this kind of argument in the *Dialogue*, when he had Salviati say:

> We seek to ennoble and perfect the Earth, when we try to make it similar to the heavenly bodies and in a certain way to put it almost in heaven, from which your philosophers have banished it.[20]

It is often useless to cite the texts, and many true statements seem destined to fall into the void when they contrast with the more diffused *idola theatri*. To read the digressions of novelists, essayists, journalists, and intellectuals of various kinds after the space projects and the landing on the moon, and to read the pages of many historians and philosophers, it would seem that geocentrism and anthropocentrism have always been indissolubly welded together. The acceptance of the astronomical doctrines of Copernicus' hereby seems to have implied the renunciation of an anthropocentric world-view as such. Lovejoy unsuccessfully devoted many pages of his major historical work to demonstrating the falsity of these associations. In so doing he called attention to the "diabolicentric" character of medieval cosmology, to the fact that the geocentric cosmology served more to humiliate man than to exalt him, to the fact that Copernicanism was opposed partly because it assigned man a too-lofty abode and transported him into a place not unlike that which is characteristic of the immutable and immortal fixed heavens:

> It was not the position of our planet in space, but the fact that it alone was supposed to have an indigenous population of rational beings whose final destiny was not yet settled, that gave it its unique status in the world and a unique share in the attention of Heaven. If it was the only region of corruption it was also the only region of generation; here alone new souls were born, immortal destinies still hung in the balance, and, in some sense, the fulfillment of the design of the Creator himself was at stake. If, then, this dim and squalid cellar of the universe was (with one exception) the last respectable place in which any beings could have their abode, it was also the place in which all that was really dramatic and stirring was going on....So that a single natural folly of an unsophisticated pair in Mesopotamia could, by its consequences, constrain one of the persons of the Godhead to take on human flesh and live and die upon this globe for man's salvation.[21]

If there are more worlds, as was to be asked at the end of the seventeenth century, did Christ redeem all those worlds? And is this not in contrast to the Scripture which calls him the Savior of the world? And if he was the Savior of a single world, how can we know that ours, specifically was so favored and not some other one of which we know nothing?[22]

Dreyer and Koyré,[23] among others, gave attention to the "exceptional" position which Copernicus attributed to the earth, with the planets rotating around the center of the earth's orbit. But it is actually in the work of Kepler, who first transported the sun to the center of planetary motions and the universe, that we find the vivid consciousness of a radical contrast: the theses of the infinity of the universe and the plurality of worlds are irreconcilable with the affirmation of the centrality of man in the universe. If Bruno is right, Kepler suggests, if the universe no longer has a center and is no longer enclosed within external limits; if there is no longer a limit consisting of that "skin or shirt of the universe" (*mundi cutis sive tunica,* in which Kepler firmly believed) which is similar to a lantern protecting the flame of the sun from the winds and reflecting the light everywhere like an opaque and illuminated wall; if it is true that every point could be the center, if there are as many worlds as there are fixed stars;[24] if the solar system could appear to a hypothetical inhabitant of the constellation Canis just as the fixed stars appear to us; if the sun is only one of the infinite stars dispersed in an infinite space; and if other planets rotate around those suns, then the biological and moral status of earth and the solar system is no longer unique, and the image of a universe constructed for man has really been destroyed. The privileged position of the solar system, situated equidistant from the fixed stars, thereby falls; the image of man as master and dominator of creation must be abandoned.

Kepler, as is well known, resolutely opposed the Brunian infinitization of the universe, decisively rejecting the assimilation of the sun to the fixed stars. He firmly maintained the uniqueness of the sun and of the solar system, contrasting it to the immobile profusion of fixed stars.[25] Kepler's *Dissertatio* has often been used to narrow the gap between the positions of Galileo and Bruno, while disregarding Kepler's principal preoccupation in that text: he seeks to distinguish clearly between precisely these two positions, showing that Galileo's astronomical discoveries do not in any way constitute a proof of the validity of Bruno's infinitist cosmology. When referring to Kepler one must bear in mind, as Koyré pointed out, that Kepler subdivided the visible world in a completely different way from his predecessors:

> In effect, he neither opposes the earth to the skies, nor, in spite of his veneration of the sun, opposes it to the planets, but he opposes the immobile world as a whole (the sun, space, the fixed stars) to the mobile world, which includes the planets and the earth and which, for the same reason, acquires in his thought a unity and a similarity of nature and structure which subject it to the same physical laws.[26]

On the basis of this fundamental contrast, Kepler could not have been unfavorably impressed by the discovery of new satellites or new moons which rotate around the planets of the solar system. But the discovery of new planets rotating around one of the fixed stars[27] or around the sun would pose grave difficulties for his vision of the world, proving correct the theses of Bruno and Wackher von Wackhenfels, Bruno's enthusiastic follower. In the same way, and for the same reasons, it was perfectly possible for Kepler to conceive of the existence of inhabited planets inside the solar system; but the idea of a plurality of worlds or of systems in which life would be present had to be firmly rejected. Our world, the solar system, constitutes a *unicum* in the universe. It was created for man—to serve his needs, his requirements, and his hopes.

## IV

The beginning of the *Dissertatio cum Nuncio Sidereo*[28] gives the precise meaning of a discussion whose foundations are riddled with a series of doubts and uncertainties which Kepler saw in dramatic fashion. Kepler begins his account at the time when he had withdrawn to his home for a brief vacation. Around the middle of March the news reached Germany that Galileo, *usu perspicilli duplicati,* had discovered four previously unknown planets. Wackher, from his carriage in front of the house, brought Kepler the incredible news.

> In considering it I was struck with such amazement and my soul was so moved (the old quarrel which had divided us was suddenly resolved) that, he for joy and I for blushing, both for laughter and disoriented by the news, he could hardly speak and I could hardly listen.[29]

Waiting to see the text of *Sidereus Nuncius,* "with extraordinary greed to read its contents," Kepler and van Wackhenfels gave it two differing interpretations. According to Kepler, just as the earth has its moon which rotates around it, so might Galileo have seen four other tiny moons rotating in very narrow paths around the small masses of Saturn, Mars, Jupiter, or Venus (excluding Mercury, too immersed in rays of the sun).

> To Wackher on the other hand it seemed certain that these new planets spun around some fixed star (something similar to that which he had foreseen for some time, deducing from the speculations of the Cardinal of Cusa and Giordano Bruno). If four planets had remained hidden up until now, what was to keep us from believing that innumerable others might be subsequently discovered? And that therefore this world is itself infinite, as was suggested by Melissus and by the Englishman William Gilbert, author of magnetic philosophy? And that there are infinitely many other worlds similar to ours (or, as Bruno says, infinitely many other earths), as was held by Democritus and Leucippus and, among more recent philosophers, Bruno and Edmund Bruce, your friend, Galileo, and mine?[30]

The reading of the Galilean text proved Kepler correct, and he emerged encouraged. Bruno's exile into the infinite opening, (*exilium in illo infinito*) seemed averted:

> If you had discovered planets rotating around one of the fixed stars, the stock and prison were already ready for me by way of Bruno's innumera-

bility, or rather exile into that infinity. For the moment *(in praesens)* you have therefore freed me from the great fear which had welled in me at the first news of your book (because of my opponent's cry of triumph), given that you affirm that these four planets do not rotate around one of the fixed stars but around the planet Jupiter.[31]

Galileo's discoveries, Kepler makes clear, serve rather to show the invalidity of Bruno's and Edmund Bruce's theses:

> You reform the doctrine of our Bruce, which he borrowed from Bruno, in such a way that you put it partially in doubt. They believed that other bodies would also have their moons around them, as does our earth. You show that, in general, they spoke the truth. They held however that it was the fixed stars which were thus surrounded, and Bruno also spoke about the reason for which this necessarily had to come about: that is, that the fixed stars are of the same nature as the sun and as fire, and the planets are as water, and, according to an inviolable law of nature, it happens that these different things combine, and neither can the sun do without the planets, that is fire without its water, nor vice-versa. But your observations show that his reasoning on this point is not valid *(hanc igitur illius rationem infirmam esse tua detegunt experimenta)*.[32]

Even admitting that the fixed stars are suns, no moon has been seen turning around them. According to the opinions of some people, Galileo's discoveries raise the possibility that this phenomenon may be observed in the future. It is a possibility that threatens us *(nobis minatur)*, Kepler suggests, and, anyhow, Jupiter is one of the planets which Bruno identified with earths

> and here around it four other planets; and Bruno's reasoning did not predict that this would happen for earths, but for suns.[33]

Galileo's discoveries cannot be used, then, as arguments in support of the Brunian thesis. Moreover they do not endanger the *doctrina de aspectibus* which constitutes the prime foundation of astrology. What must be underscored here is not, however, the defense of astrology,[34] which remains in its place *(manet suo loco)* even after the discovery of the four Medici planets. The important point is Kepler's will to oppose Bruno and the possible Brunian interpretations of Galileo's discoveries, by firmly maintaining the anthropocentric point of view. This perspective sees the earth as the highest place in the universe and the only one suitable for the nobility of man, master of the world. The impossibility of any nature's subsisting and acting autonomously—i.e., independent of anyone capable of contemplating and understanding it— is the basis for Kepler's discussion of the possibility of other inhabitants within the solar system.

> If in fact there are four planets that rotate around Jupiter at different distances and rates of speed, and if on the surface of Jupiter there isn't anyone who observes this marvelous phenomenon with his own eyes, then to whose benefit do these planets exist? In fact, as concerns us who find ourselves on this earth, I do not know what argument could persuade me to believe that above all they serve us, who never see them. Nor is it is necessary to wait until all of us, having been furnished with your lenses, Galileo, are able to observe them ordinarily....It is clear that these four planets have not been prepared principally for us who live on the earth, but for the Jupiterian creatures who live all around the globe of Jupiter....Our moon does not represent to all other globes what it represents to us, and those four little moons do not represent to us what they represent to Jupiter; thus the respective satellites serve the individual globes of the planets and their inhabitants.[35]

But, with the hypothesis about the inhabitants of Jupiter or Mars, the anthropocentric preoccupation immediately re-emerges. The possibility that other planets of the solar system are inhabited raises a grave question:

> If there are globes in the sky similar to our earth, are we perhaps headed toward competition with them, in order to know who holds the best place in the world *(meliorem mundi plagam)?* If in fact the globes of these planets are more noble, then we are not the most noble of all rational creatures. How then can everything be for man? And how can we be the masters of God's works?[36]

Kepler has one principal preoccupation. He seeks to demonstrate not only

> that this system of planets, in one of which we men find ourselves, is found in the principal spot in the universe, around the heart of the universe which is the sun; but also, in particular, that we men find ourselves on the globe which is most suited to the most important and most noble rational creature among all physical bodies.[73]

The other worlds that Bruno talks about are either similar to or different from ours. If they are similar, would they be infinite if every one of them encompassed every perfection within itself? And didn't Bruno talk about diversity in the types of movement? Doesn't varying the distances, which determine the period of the movements, also change the order and perfection of the configurations from which the distances are inferred? And, still with the hypothesis of a total similarity, what would be the reason for multiplication of the creatures and the Galileos, (who observe new stars in the new worlds) to a number as great as there are worlds? But, on the other hand, given the hypothesis of diversity, those worlds would be arranged in configurations different from the five perfect ones according to which God arranged our world, and they would therefore be less noble than ours. From this argument it follows that our world, which is the solar system, is the most important of all, even in the case that there were more than one.[38]

Within the solar system, then, the earth is more important than the globe of Jupiter and is the most worthy location for the dominant creature (*dominantis creaturae*) that is man. The sun is at the center of the universe; it is the heart of the world, the source of heat and the origin of life. Man properly should keep away from that regal throne, acknowledging his wretchedness and the grandeur of God from the uniqueness of his own abode. God, not man, is the root of beauty and order in the world. But for this very reason of contemplation, for which purpose man has been gifted with sight, he could not have resided in the center. For the purpose of contemplation it is necessary that his gaze be capable of ranging around and that he be transported by annual motion on this ship that is the earth (*sed oportet ut navigio hoc telluris annuo motu circumspacietur lustrandi causa*). The earth, moreover, occupies the central position among the primary globes (outside: Mars, Jupiter, Saturn; inside: Venus, Mercury, the sun). Its orbit is inserted between the two orders of a) the three primary bodies—cube, tetrahedron, dodechahedron— and b) the two secondary bodies—icosahedron, octagon. On earth, finally, one can still distinguish Mercury, last of the primary planets, which, though difficult to see from earth, would be far less visible from Jupiter or Saturn. Thus, the earth has been assigned to man, as the highest intelligence, in order that he might contemplate all the planets

> and we, earth-bound men, might glory with some justification at the gorgeous residence of our bodies and we should be thankful to the creator.[39]

For Kepler, then, the earth occupies a unique place in the structure of the solar system and the universe. On the earth lives the "contemplative creature," created in the image and likeness of God. This creature is in a position to reconstruct rationally that perfect architecture in which the grandeur of God is expressed; he is even in a position to reconstruct those "archetypal laws" which, through God, presided over the creation of the world. The universe was created to serve this contemplative creature and the laws of the Divine Mathematician were enacted for him. For Kepler, man and his home remained at the center of the cosmic drama of creation and redemption.

The propositions expressed in the *Dissertatio* certainly were not momentary or isolated positions. One need only open Kepler's *Epitome astronomiae copernicanae,* published at Linz and Frankfort between 1618 and 1621, to find the earth's exceptional position in the universe confirmed with unequivocal emphasis, although in a more strictly technical argument:

> *Where do you feel the investigation on the proportions of heavenly bodies should begin?*—From the earth, because it is the home of the contemplating creature that was made in the image of God the Creator... because the earthly orb is the figurative middle among the planets...and the proportional middle between the limits of the superior and the inferior planets. The order of these proportions, finally, proclaims that the Creator...began from the earth as his first measure....The earth in fact had to be the home of the contemplative creature, whom the universe was created to grace....Since the earth was destined to become the home of a measuring creature, it is clear that it had to become the measure of the heavenly bodies with its body, and the measure of lines or distances with its radius, insofar as it is linear.[40]

The sense of secret, hidden horror that Kepler had manifested in 1606 for Bruno's vision would never be relieved:

> That thought bears with it I know not what secret, hidden horror: we feel lost in that immensity to which limits and the center are denied, to which every determinate place is consequently denied.[41]

## V

In another area, historically very complicated but nonetheless different from that within which the major astronomers of the seventeenth century had been moving, several notions had to be reinforced and developed to full maturity. These ideas included the negation of anthropomorphism; the image of a nature infinitely vaster and more powerful than man; and the representation of a God to whose infinite power and majesty an infinite place is suitable (as Digges stated), whose infinite capacity (as Bruno put it) cannot be "frustrated," and whose efficacy cannot remain "idle," just as "the possibility of infinite worlds which might exist" cannot be "defrauded." Within this perspective, reference to the Democritean and Lucretian tradition operated with predominant force. And at its hands that "terrestrial" vision of the cosmos which had persisted even in the new astronomy was destined to topple.

The dispute concerning the habitability and plurality of worlds[42] had had a rather ancient tradition, whose fundamental elements had been accurately summarized in the great encyclopedia published by Giorgio Valla early in the sixteenth century. This tradition is by now well-known —its essential terms were brought into prominence throughout Europe by Nicholas of Cusa, Palingenius Stellatus, Giordano Bruno, Giovan Battista Benedetti, Digges, Lower, Harriot, Burton, and Gilbert. In 1567, Melanchthon had formulated a series of physical and theological objections to the thesis of the habitability of worlds, objections which were to be repeated innumerable times and to reappear with greater or lesser polemical force in Protestant and Catholic circles. The pages on the plurality of inhabited worlds in Tommaso Campanella's *Apologia pro Galilaeo* (1622) would often be cited and remembered as the authoritative source for John Wilkins, Robert Burton, and Pierre Borel. In 1634, Kepler's *Somnium* appeared, in 1647, Henry More's *Democritus platonissans*. In the *Almagestum Novum* (1651) one of the two great texts of selenography, Giovan Battista Riccioli referred to Aristotle, Ficino, and Kepler in opposing the doctrine of inhabited worlds. Five years later Athanasius Kircher re-examined the same problem. He was well aware of the real terms of the dispute, though he maintained a fairly ambiguous perspective based upon concessions to the modern thinkers and contemporary reaffirmations of Aristotelianism.

The books and tracts dedicated to extraterrestrial voyages and to descriptions of the lunar world and its inhabitants exerted an appreciable weight on the argument. Between 1638 and 1666, a series of fundamental texts saw the light: Francis Godwin's *The Man in the Moone,* Johann Hevelius' *Selenographia,* Peter Heylyn's *Cosmographia,* Cyrano de Bergerac's *Les Etats et Empires de la Lune,* and Margaret Cavendish's

*Description of a new world.* The celebrated writings of Fontenelle and Huygens, published at the end of the century, actually constituted (although many, particularly Fontenelle, did not realize it) the end and outcome of a discussion which had already been articulated for more than two centuries, joining themes and cultural experiences of widely disparate natures.

To appreciate this eclecticism it will suffice to consider briefly a little-known but nonetheless significant text, the *Discours nouveau prouvant la pluralité des mondes, que les astres sont des terres habitées et la terre une estoile,* published in Geneva in 1657 by Pierre Borel and translated into English the following year by Daniel Sashott.[43] Presented by the author as a fragment of a much larger work on the life and philosophy of Democritus, the book begins with a dedication to Sir Kenelm Digby and closes with a lengthy citation from the *Zodiacus Vitae* of Palingenius. The most-frequently repeated names are those of Montaigne, Copernicus, Kepler, and Campanella. Bruno, though never mentioned, is ever-present; and the world-view of Lucretius (the book is permeated with quotations from *De rerum natura*) constitutes the framework on which Borel's reflections are articulated. To Borel, the great Galilean discoveries appear to be definitive proof of the truth of the Copernican system, as well as proof of the validity of those hypotheses about inhabited worlds which had been formulated by Xenophanes, Melissus, Pythagoras, Democritus, Epicurus, and Plutarch, and which had subsequently been fancifully renewed by Lucan and Ariosto:

> That grand Galileo, who seems to have been born to clarify the doubts of astronomy, has discovered new things in the stars with his marvelous invention, the telescope, and is the first to turn his telescope toward the stars. By means of that instrument he has seen that the Milky Way is composed of little stars...and has seen the lunar surface to be not smooth but full of mountains and cavities....His discovery of four new planets has obliged many to believe that Jupiter is another world or another sun around which other plants spin....Some Stoics believed that there were inhabitants not only on the moon, but on the body of the sun, and Campanella affirmed that these living and shining abodes may have their inhabitants, perhaps wiser than we....But it is Galileo who, in our time, has seen the moon clearly and has noted that it could be inhabited.[44]

The moon has lost its status as a perfect body; it has been revealed as similar to the earth and the latter, seen from the moon, would be nothing but a bigger moon. If the earth, as Copernicus taught, is no longer at the center of the universe, and if the moon is similar to an earth, as Galileo saw, then even the other globes far from the center may be considered "earths similar to that which we inhabit." The centrality of the earth in the universe guaranteed it an exceptional position, and justified the presence of living and thinking beings on it alone.

> But if the earth moves in the heavens *(dans les airs)* and, like the other stars, runs its course far from the center of the world, what is to prevent us from considering it a star and considering the stars as so many other earths?[45]

Borel believes in the infinity of (or absence of limits to) a universe populated by infinitely many stars; and yet, referring to Copernicus, he does not abandon the image of the sun as a great lamp of the cosmos, which constitutes the center of the universe:

> The blue sky which we see is not something solid and real, but is the limit of our sight in a certain spot of the infinite spaces of the heavens, which are the common location where an infinity of large globes of various natures are placed, inhabited by various animals which the sun, placed at the center, enlightens equally, illuminating everything just as a big lamp in the middle of a room illuminates all the corners.[46]

The limitless and infinitely populated universe is a large rational animal which God generated out of himself *(sortit comme hors de lui)*, pouring himself completely into the creatures *(s'escoula comme tout en les creatures)*. It is not by accident that Borel cites the *Asclepius* and Mercurius Trismegistus; for the Hermetic and Brunian thesis of a living universe seems to him capable of reinforcing the Copernican hypothesis of the earth's motion as well as the doctrine of inhabited worlds.

> If the world is a rational animal...it will not be strange to believe that the earth is in movement, nor consequently that it is an errant star or an inhabited planet and that therefore, other stars may also be inhabited.[47]

Standing before the disbelievers in the plurality of worlds, who lack solid arguments, one might imitate Democritus and laugh at their ignorance. They actually accuse God of impotence and idleness. In opposition to them Borel calls attention to two metaphysical presuppositions: that of the non-uniformity or infinite variability of Nature, and that of the infinity of the Divine Cause which must necessarily manifest itself in the infinity of the cosmos:

> Nature is so diverse in all its operations, and God has invested such variety in all his works, that we find nothing uniform in this world. Everything is different, and this grand diversity causes us to admire the creator of the universe all the more....
>
> One objects...that, there being only a single principle and first mover, a single God or first cause, the world should correspond to his Archetype —there should be but a single world. But we have above demonstrated the contrary: in that God exists infinitely, worlds must be infinite....If there could not be diverse worlds in the universe, God would not be able to act with all his power and freedom, but only out of some necessity. It would be a great impiety even to think this, because God certainly not only could have made other worlds, but could have made them far more perfect than ours....If God, having been able to create more worlds, had not done so, his power could be said to be in some way idle, useless, and limited....God seeks everything that does not imply contradiction, and a plurality of worlds does not imply contradiction either on the part of God or on the part of the things created.[48]

Noting the arguments developed by Campanella in the *Apologia pro Galilaeo*, Borel constrains himself to show at length that his thesis is not in conflict with the text of the Holy Scriptures. He understands full well that a positive solution to the problem of a plurality of inhabited worlds is not devoid of dangerous theological implications: the account in *Galilaeo*, Borel constrains himself to show at length that his thesis is not in inhabit, resolving itself into a discourse more mystical than scientific, directed toward evoking admiration more than communicating real knowledge:

> This doctrine of several inhabited worlds or globes does not conflict with the Holy Scriptures, which speak to us solely of the creation of that world which we inhabit. The doctrine even admits to leaving us in a discussion more mystical than clear *(plus en discours mystique que clairement)*, merely touching lightly on the other creatures of the universe, with the purpose of giving to the weak spirits of men a subject more for admiration than for edification.[49]

Montaigne is the best-loved of Borel's masters, the man who taught us to deny a world of guaranteed certainties, to doubt everything, to admit like Socrates that we know nothing. About the middle of the century, in an era of great transformations and radical changes, these teachings appeared particularly valid and current to Borel:

> We know of nothing that could not or might not be discussed—theology itself is not exempt...astrology, medicine, jurisprudence, and physics vary every day and see their foundations crumble. Ramus has inverted the philosophy of Aristotle; Copernicus, the astronomy of Ptolemy; Paracelsus, the medicine of Galen—in such fashion that, each one having his own followers, everything seems plausible and we don't know whom to believe; and we are forced to admit that what we know is considerably less than what we don't know.[50]

This universal "plausibility" may cause skepticism to reverse into its opposite, transforming itself in the hopes of great innovations and enterprises.[51] If (repeats Borel, with Bacon) someone had described beforehand the results of the art of printing, which offers man a kind of immortality, of lenses, which help us to approach distant objects, of artillery, which destroys fortifications, men would have noted these descriptions with indifference or scorn in much the same way that for centuries the supporters of the Antipodes had been scorned and Columbus' plans were long rejected. Borel forced himself, however, to impose precise limits on the continued use of analogies, on his very imagination itself, with results that today might seem disconcerting.

> Some have imagined that man will be able to discover the art of flying, just as he has imitated the fish in swimming....But, even when he could fly, it would hardly be useful to our purpose, because man could not raise himself very high, owing to his weight; he could not remain still to contemplate the sky; nor could he use visual aids; but he would have his mind wholly occupied with driving his machine.[52]

## VI

Nothwithstanding quotations from the *Asclepius* and fleeting mention of the doctrine of man the microcosm, nor the fundamental uncertainties expressed in the assertion of a center in an infinite universe, Borel is aware of a fundamental antithesis. The thesis of a plurality of inhabited worlds is in radical antithesis to that other thesis which sees in the earth an exceptional spot of the universe, conceiving the cosmos and nature as existing for man and serving man:

Those who think that the infinite number of heavenly bodies was created for the terrestrial globe and for the utility of its inhabitants are greatly mistaken; for natural reason dissuades us from believing that greater things serve the lesser, that the more noble serve the more base. Consequently it is more probable that every globe constitutes an earth or a particular world.... If there were more worlds, they would have been created in vain because one cannot demonstrate that they have any usefulness: this reasoning is so weak that this alone suffices to refute it— that of which we know not the use was not created in vain. Otherwise the Indies, whose usefulness we have ignored, and the southern lands, which are still unknown to us, would have been created in vain, for this very reason.[53]

Borel's text is important not because it contains original doctrines or hypotheses, but because it presents in a unified way the terms of a discussion whose intertwined complex of arguments was drawn from diverse traditions and different fields of culture. Even in his rejection of the singularity of the terrestrial point of view (i.e., a universe built for man and working for man), he resumes and repeats a theme present in diverse positions and diffused in philosophical, scientific, and literary works. It is a theme that is variously tied to the renewal of Democritean and Lucretian themes, to Cartesian physics, and to materialistic and libertarian currents—a theme which would express itself with singular force in Spinozism and, later, in the positions of Diderot and the materialists of eighteenth-century France.

Montaigne had already asked, in the *Apologie de Raymond Sebond,* how man could assume that the wondrous movement of the heavenly vault, the eternal light of the flames which turn at its peak, and the awesome movements of the sea, all could have been formed and then could have continued to exist for his utility and his advantage. Was it not ridiculous that a miserable creature, riveted to the worst and most putrid part of the universe, incapable of dominating even himself, would call himself owner or master of the world and presume to set himself up as the only being in a position to recognize the architecture of the cosmos?[54] In the *Dialogo sui massimi sistemi,* Galileo had had Simplicius qualify as "either fabulous or impious thought" the hypothesis of men on the moon, a hypothesis which Galileo rejected decisively in the same pages. Yet he still had attributed to Simplicius the doctrine according to which "we should not admit that anything in the universe was created in vain and to be idle." For whose benefit, Simplicius asked, would a vast space without stars have been placed between Saturn and the sphere of stars? Does it not appear vain and superfluous in view of this beautiful ordering of planets, arranged around the earth "in distances proportioned to produce its effects thereon for our benefit?" Salviati answered:

> It seems to me that we arrogate too much to ourselves, Mister Simplicius, in that we desire that taking care of us would be the whole task and the end beyond which nothing else is done or dispensed by divine wisdom and power.
>
> But I would not want us to constrict his hand so much; rather we should content ourselves with being certain that God and Nature are so much concerned with the governance of human things that they could not be more so, even if they are taking care of nothing else but mankind....
>
> I am sure that Divine Providence overlooks nothing of what is expected in the governance of human affairs. But as for myself, insofar as I follow my own argument, I could not comfortably make myself believe that there could not be other things in the universe which are dependent on his infinite wisdom...and I say that it is temerity to want to make our puny discussion judge the works of God, and to call vain and superfluous everything in the universe which is not useful to us.[55]

The Galilean presentation is extremely cautious, almost fleeting, so much that Sagredo, in his intercessions, immediately feels the need to correct Salviati's position by trimming it down still further. And he transforms "is not useful to us" into a more ambiguous "that we do not know to be useful to us."

At mid-century, and far removed from this diminution, stands Cyrano de Bergerac, disciple of the doctrine of an organic universe comparable to a gigantic living being. Bergerac, linked to the thought of Campanella, Gassendi, and La Mothe Le Vayer, mixes themes from Hermetic Platonism, Cabala, Democritean and Epicurean atomism, the Averroistic tradition, and the new cosmology of Copernicus, Galileo, and Kepler. In a quite beautiful passage he protests "the insufferable pride of humans," "the insolence of these brutes" who conceive of the universe as serving the needs of man.

> Like a man whose boat sails near dry land, who has the impression of standing still while the coast is moving, so men, spinning around the

sky with the earth, held that the sky itself was turning around them. Add to this the insufferable pride of humans, who persuade themselves that Nature was created expressly for them, as if it were probable that the sun...was lit to make their medlar-trees mature and to till their cabbages. As for myself, far from subscribing to the impudence of these brutes, I believe that the planets are worlds around the sun, and that the fixed stars are also suns with planets around them, i.e., worlds which we cannot see from here....For how can one imagine in good faith that these immense globes are only great deserted earths, while ours, precisely because we crawl about there, a dozen arrogant rogues, would have been created to command everyone? What! Because the sun measures our days and our years, does this mean that it was made to keep us from banging our heads against walls? No! No! This visible god illuminates man purely by accident, just as the flame of the king accidentally illuminates the teamster who passes in the street.[56]

To man's view-point, Montaigne had opposed that of the duckling and the crane; Cyrano had spoken of medlars and cabbages. With less broad-mindedness but with much greater theoretical force, Descartes had also rejected the legitimacy of making use of an anthropocentric point of view, at least in physics. In the *Principia* of 1644, he said:

We should not presume too much unto ourselves, as it seems that we would be doing...if we were persuaded that it is only for our use that God created everything, or if we would merely pretend to be able to know, with the force of our spirit, what are the ends for which he created everything....It is in no way probable that all things were created for us in such way that God had no other reason for creating them. And it seems to me that it would be ridiculous to want to use this opinion as a basis for physical reasonings, since we could not doubt that there would be an infinity of things which are now in the world or which once were there and have now completely ceased to exist, without any man having seen them or known them, and without their ever having been of any use.[57]

In a letter written in 1641, Descartes had already said that since we cannot know God's purpose, it would be absurd to hold, first, that he had no other end in creating the universe than the praising of men, and further, that the sun was created with the sole purpose of furnishing man with light.[58] The earth, as he would affirm in the *Principia*, is no more than a point when compared to the sky; its extreme tininess and the enormous distance of the fixed stars might seem incredible to those whose spirits are not used to considering the marvels of God, and who think that the earth is the principal part of the universe because it is the home of man, for whose benefit they are convinced, without any reason, that all things have been made.[59]

One year after the publication of the *Principia,* in writing to Elisabeth, Descartes threw light on the "moral" kinds of consequences implicit in the position that all the heavens were created only to serve earth, and that the earth was created solely for man. In this case, one comes to think that the earth is our principal home and this life our best life. One attributes to other creatures imperfections which they do not have. And, with impertinent presumption, one seeks to assume the role of "counselor of God."[60] Christina of Sweden's objection to these theses, as reported by Chanut, raise, among other issues, the problem of inhabited worlds:

> If we conceive the world in the vast extension that you attribute to it, it is impossible that man retains an honorable rank there. On the contrary, he will consider himself as if in a small recess with all the land which he inhabits, out of proportion to the immeasurable size of the rest. He will most probably hold that all these stars have inhabitants, or, still better, that they have earths around them, full of creatures more intelligent and better than he. Undoubtedly he will at least lose the opinion that the infinite size of the world was constructed for him, or that he can somehow make use of it.[61]

In reply, Descartes said we are not obliged to believe that man is the end of creation. It is true that in *Genesis* man seems to be the main subject of creation. But it must be kept in mind that the story was written principally for man, and that the Holy Spirit specified in it those things which concern man and refer to him. The conviction that God created everything for us derives principally from the work of the preachers who want to inflame us with love for God and to show us how other creatures are useful to us, without having us consider as well the other ends for which God created them.

> It seems to me that the mystery of the incarnation and all the other advantages which God bestowed on man do not preclude the possibility that he might have granted infinitely many others, very great, to an infinity of other creatures. And, not even inferring from this that there may be intelligent creatures on the stars or elsewhere, I still do not see

that there would be any reason by which to prove that there are not;
but I always leave these questions, once posed, suspended, preferring
not to deny and not to affirm anything.[62]

To leave the question in suspension, neither affirming nor denying—
Yet, at the end of his life, in the colloquium with Burman, Descartes
again put forward the hypothesis of a plurality of inhabited worlds, in
a polemic against anthropocentrism:

> This is the common habit of men, to believe themselves very dear to
> God and to suppose therefore that everything was made for them, that
> the earth, their home, comes first above all else, that here everything is
> found and that everything has been done in his behalf. But do we
> know whether God produced anything outside of this earth, these stars,
> etc.? Do we know whether he gathered other creatures of various
> species in it, other lives and so to speak other men, or at least beings
> analogous to men? ...Do we know whether God produced infinite
> species of creatures, virtually lavishing all his power on creation? ...We
> ought not to presume too much, as if everything were in our power
> and working for us, when perhaps elsewhere there exist innumerable
> other creatures of higher quality than ourselves.[63]

These questions and hypotheses did not exert a direct influence on the
discussion of the inhabitability of worlds. But the mechanistic cosmology of Descartes lent himself to wide use in affirming the thesis of an
infinitely populated universe—one may simply think of Fontenelle. In
any case, the theme of the insufficiency and sterility of the traditional
anthropocentric vision pervades all of European culture. It certainly
is not necessary to cite the well-known texts of Hobbes, Spinoza, or
Pascal; and it is obviously worth noting that the expression man is not
the reason for which all things happen (*non omnia hominum causa
fieri*), which was positively underscored even by Leibniz,[64] was destined
to assume rather diverse meanings in various contexts.

In the *Experimenta nova* of 1659, Otto von Guericke once again
took up the theme of the Infinite God (*infinitus dominus*) who rules
infinitely the infinite multitude of creatures (*infinite imperat infinitam
creaturaeum multitudinem*) from whom divine power issues forth
deducing from this idea the consequence that

> it is repugnant to believe that the immensity of the universe exists only
> for the earth and for its inhabitants.[66]

All things were created for man: but this cannot mean, Huygens would affirm, that the huge bodies of stars, which we see only partially and which, in great part, we would never have seen without the help of the telescope, were created for our use and contemplation.[66]

Von Guericke's argument is echoed by Thomas Burnet in the *Telluris theoria sacra* of 1681. Here also there is no longer space for the celebration of an ordered and perfect cosmos built for the master of the world, in which divine wisdom reveals itself as acting·always in man's service. The Neoplatonics of Cambridge and Henry More had held that a vital or "plastic" principal of nature is stressed in the perfect hierarchies—in Burnet, supporter of a pessimistic and tragically baroque image of the world, these perfect hierarchies have disappeared.

Burnet saw clearly that the familiar and "popular" image of the universe, described in the Sacred Texts and subsequently "translated" into the Aristotelian and Ptolemaic language, had been replaced at the hands of the new physics. The new image was that of an immense universe which was no longer constructed in man's image, which could no longer in any way be conceived as a kind of "appendix" to earth, nor could it be seen as serving earth. Bruno's "relativistic" position, for which the moon is a sky for us just as we are a sky for the moon and a star or sky for the other stars,[67] was resolved into a vision of a universe in ruins—a universe destined for consumption and death, within which the earth is a rejection of Nature, an obscure and sordid particle suspended in the depths without further limits to the heavens. The accusation of impiety, traditionally brought against the supporters of the Copernican and Brunian doctrines, was turned back upon those asserting the earth's centrality, precedence, and uniqueness in the universe:

> The result is that the fixed stars are igneous bodies and that they do not all adhere to a single surface. Some are more remote than others from earth and more deeply immersed in the sky, and therefore no center *(umbilicum)* exists common to all. To think that our earth, this obscure and sordid particle of the universe, lesser than the individual fixed stars as much in mass as in dignity, is the heart of the immense body of the world, to think that it is the noblest and most vital part of the world, is contrary to reason and to the nature of things. And I re-affirm, haughtily, that one cannot think, without offending either the work or its Maker, that this earth, discard and dregs of Nature, is the principal one among all things and virtually the primogenitor among all creatures.[68]

The Brunian image of a universe devoid of an "umbilical" and a center was joined in these pages with doubts concerning the possibility of encompassing the entire history of the world in the too-brief space allowed by religious orthodoxy. In fact, the hypothesis of a slow formation of the universe turned the earth, long since dethroned from its central position and no longer primogenitor or origin, into the product of a slow and tiring temporal process which was interrupted by catastrophies and ruinations of worlds. Moses' "popular" account was threatened—it did not contain descriptions of real events and was not translatable into a scientific discourse, but rather was dictated by observations of a "political" nature. The earth was formed as the result of a natural process, and nature and the cosmos could no longer continue to be conceived as a sort of "appendix" to earth:

> Granting the security of the laws of nature, these and other similar celestial phenomena can be limited only with great difficulty, over a period of six millenia. It rather behooves us to admit that the origin of our earth and that of all the universe, be it intellectual or material, were neither identical nor contemporaneous. There is no reason to be astonished at the fact that Moses did not distinguish these things and did not treat the origin of the universe separately from that of our sublunar world. The people, in fact, do not distinguish these things nor consider them separately. The great majority of men in fact consider the rest of Nature and of the universe as a sort of appendix to our world and the earth (*pro quadam habet orbis nostri aut telluri appendice*), as something that has no value in itself, but that is adapted to the uses of mankind because it can serve his requirements.[69]

Five years later, in 1686, the limpid, brilliant argument of Fontenelle would come forth:

> Our own particular folly also consists of the belief that all of nature, without exception, is intended for our uses. And when our philosophers are asked the use of that prodigious number of fixed stars, a part of which would be sufficient to do that which all of them do, they respond coldly: they serve to enliven the view.[70]

You are not, exclaimed Borel nearly half a century earlier, like those farmers who, never having seen the big cities, do not understand throughout their lives that there may be cities bigger and more beautiful than their villages.[71] The whole earth is an object which, according to ancient tradition but also from various perspectives and with highly diverse intentions, had been considered *"le plus vil e abiect de tous."* It had now taken form as a lost village and a province, as had happened at the beginning of the century to the Mediterranean and the whole Western world, in the face of geographical discoveries, voyages to unknown lands and distant peoples, and in the face of *Terra australis incognita*:

What are we doubting? What are we terrified of? Of shadows? Of ourselves? In that place there is a sky, there is an earth, no doubt there are men, perhaps much more civilized than ourselves. Who would ever have suspected such intelligence and such good judgment in the Chinese? Such a great number of arts? Such a vast and various science of all things? While we continue to believe that all the Muses reside in that humble dwelling which is our Western world *(in hoc occidentali gurgustiolo)*, they smile. And not without reason.[72]

## VII

Plurality of worlds did not always mean affirmation of the infinity of the universe. This belief did not always imply the conviction that forms of life or other thinking beings exist in the infinity of the cosmos. One could speak of infinitely many globes and earths which populate a cosmos, immense and yet still enclosed by the sky of the fixed stars (as did Lower and Harriot); one could distinguish (as did Descartes) between infinity and limitlessness; one could even speak (as did Borel) of an infinite universe which nonetheless had the sun as its center. The still unwritten history of the long dispute on the existence of inhabited worlds does, it is true, variously intermingle with and attach itself to certain historical accounts. But it does not coincide with the history of the long chain of being or "the principle of plenitude," nor with that of the passage "from the closed world to the infinite universe," nor with that of the imaginary voyages and the discovery of "bon sauvage." That dispute concerning populated worlds and the conclusions linked with it contribute, at any rate, to pose a profound threat to a "terrestrial" and anthropocentric conception of the universe, removing all meaning from the traditional discourse of the Humanists concerning the nobility and dignity of man. To acquire more than a merely literary and rhetorical meaning, it now had to be formulated differently, inserted into a different context, and consequently to assume a new meaning. Laboriously, a new image of Nature and of the place of man in Nature had been born, an image which would have highly diverse outlets and would be variously utilized.

It is, however, certain that the protagonists of this story—from Bruno to Wilkins, from Borel to Burnet, from Huygens to Fontenelle—sought to support their vision of the world by variously and freely adapting the most important and disturbing results which had arisen from the work of the great astronomers of the seventeenth century. In so doing, they achieved what we might today call not invariably legitimate or cautious extrapolations, instituting hurried analogies. But their "fantasie" and their analogical procedures also contributed not a little toward changing the course of ideas. First Copernicus; later Kepler, so strongly conditioned by metaphysical presuppositions; then Galileo himself, always so lucid and rigorous—all voluntarily abandoned to the "philosophers" these arguments and inquiries, these questions which were then unresolvable and which remain unresolved.

## References

[1]Lovejoy, A. O., *The Great Chain of Being*, Cambridge, Mass., 1936; Tillyard, E. M., *The Elizabethan World Picture*, London, 1943; Harris, V., *All coherence gone*, Chicago, 1949; Nicolson, M. H., *The breaking of the Circle*, Evanston, 1950; Koyré, A., *From the closed World to the infinite Universe*, Baltimore, 1957. For Mersenne's sentence, cf. Lenoble, R., *Mersenne our la naissance du mécanisme*, Paris, 1943, 342.

[2]Naudé, G., letter to Ismäel Boulliau on August 15, 1640, published in Pintard, R., *Le libertinage erudit*, Paris, 1943, 472.

[3]*Descriptio Globi Intellectualis*, in *The World of Francis Bacon*, ed. Ellis, R. L., Spedding, J. and Heath, D. D., London, 1887-1892, III, 741.

[4]Cf. Nicholson, M. H., *Science and Imagination*, Ithaca, 1962, 30.

[5]Copernicus, N., *De revolutionibus*, ed. Koyré, A., Paris, 1934, 115.

[6]Cf. Kuhn, Th., *The Copernican Revolution*, Cambridge, Mass., 1957, 237.

[7]Bruno, G., *La Cena de le ceneri*, ed. Aquilecchia, G., Torino, 1955, 165. Cf. *De Immenso*, in *Opera*, I, 1, 369: "Mathematice...circularis motus non est in materia;" *Cena, op. cit.*, 208: "Muovensi dunque la terra e gli altri pianeti secondo le proprie differenze locali dal principio instrinseco, che è l'anima propria....Questi corridori hanno il principio di moti intrinseco la propria natura, la propria anima, la propria intelligenza."

[8]Bruno, G., *De l'infinito, universo e mondi*, in *Opere*, I, 340.

[9]On the irrelevance of the term *system* to the Brunian vocabulary, on the counterposition of an astrobiology to a cosmic geometry, cf. Michel, P. H., *La cosmologie de G. Bruno*, Paris, 1962, 194, 232-33.

[10]For the attitudes assumed by Campanella in facing these problems and for the indication of numerous texts, cf. Badaloni, N., *Tommaso Campanella*, Milan, 1965, 230-36. The failure to adhere to the Copernican system, which Firpo points out, is documented among other places in the precise expression contained in the *Apologia*, according to which the earth "pensilis apparet in medio mundi." Cf. Campanella, T., *Apologia di Galileo*, ed. Firpo, L., Torino, 1968, 80. The quotations and the page of the text of the Frankfort edition of 1622, reproduced in the appendix, are drawn from this edition.

[11]*Ibid.*, pp. 50, 118: "Non enim plures mundos ponit Galilaeus, sed omnia systemata sub uno et intra unum aethera fere immensum."

[12]*Ibid.*, pp. 51, 119. The quotation which follows is on 52, 121.

[13]Galilei, G., *Opere*, VII, pp. 55-56. Cf. Copernicus, N., *op. cit.*, 56, 57: "Principio advertendum nobis est globosum esse mundum, sive quod ipsa forma perfectissima sit omnium...sive quod ipsa capacissima sit figurarum, quae comprehensurum omnia et conservaturum maxime decet...Post haec memorabimus corporum caelestium motum esse circularem. Mobilitas enim sphaerae est in circulum volvi, ipso actu formam suam exprimentis."

[14]Lovejoy, A. O., *The Great Chain of Being*, Cambridge, Mass., 1957, 108.

[15]*Ibid.*, p. 116: "He not only preached it throughout Western Europe with the fervor of an evangelist, but also first gave a thorough statement of the grounds on which it was to gain acceptance from the general public." This passage was underscored by Koyré, A., *op. cit.*, 39.

[16]*Ibid.*, 121-122.

[17]The quotations which follow are drawn from the text of the first edition, London, 1638, printed by E. G. for Michael Sparke and Edward Forrest (copy used: British Museum 19098).

[18]*Ibid., To the Reader* (unnumbered pages). For how much precedes it in the text, cf. 3, 12, 54.

[19]*Ibid.*, 68.

[20]Galilei, G., *Opere*, VII, 62.

[21]Lovejoy, A. O., *op. cit.*, 102-103.

[22]Cf. *Athenian Mercury*, London, 1691, Suppl. 2, 13.

[23]Koyré, A., *La révolution astronomique*, Paris, 1961, 69, 113. Dreyer, J. L., *A History of Astronomy from Thales to Kepler*, New York 1953, 343.

[24]Cf. Kepler, *De stella nova in pede sepentarii*, in *Opera*, II, 688, and for the previously quoted expression, *Epitome*, in *Werke*, 259.

[25]Cf. Koyré, A., *From the closed World*, 73 ff.

[26]Koyré, A., *La révolution astronomique*, 122-122.

[27]Cf. Koyré, A., *From the closed World*, 74. On the interpretation of Galileo's discovery as it relates to the fixed stars, which Kepler held to be invisible to the naked eye not because they were too far away, but because they were too small, on the smallness and lesser brightness of the fixed stars in comparison with the sun, and on the uniqueness of the latter, see *ibid.*, 75.

[28]The text of the *Dissertatio* is contained in vol. III of the *Opere* of Galileo, as well as in editions of the works of Kepler (*Gesammelte Werke*, München, 1938-1959, IV, 281-311). Recent translations include those of Franz Hammer (Gräfelfing, 1964) and E. Rosen (New York and London, 1965).

[29]Kepler, *Dissertatio*, in *Werke*, IV, 288.

[30]*Ibid.*, 289.

[31]*Ibid.*, 304.

[32]*Ibid.*, 305.

[33]*Ibid.*

[34]*Ibid.*, 306.

[35]*Ibid.*

[36]*Ibid.*, 307.

[37]*Ibid.*, 307-308.

[38]*Ibid.*, 307-309.

[39]*Ibid.*, 309.

[40]Kepler, *Epitome*, in *Werke*, VII, 276-279.

[41]*De stella nova*, in *Johannis Kepleri Opera Omnia*, ed. Frisch, Ch., Francofurti et Erlangae, 1858-1871, II, 688.

[42]On these themes: McColley, G., "The seventeenth-century doctrine of a plurality of worlds," in *Annals of Science*, 1936, 385-430 (but see also the specifications concerning Copernicus in Koyré, A., *From the closed World*, 36); Munitz, M. K., "One Universe or Many?" in the volume *Roots of Scientific Thought*, New York, 1958, 593-617. Barely usable are the works of Flammarion, C., *La pluralité des mondes habités*, Paris, 1862, and Wallace, A. R., *Man's Place in the Universe*, New York, 1903. McColley's work, or that part of it concerning the classical world, is integrated into the study by Cornford, F. M., "Innumerable Worlds in the Pre-Socratic Philosophy," in *Classical Quarterly*, 1934, 1-16. A large number of textual references may be found in Nicolson, M., *Voyages to the Moon*, New York, 1960.

[43]The following quotations are taken from the pages of the first edition (copy used: British Museum 531.e.44). The English edition of 1658 (London, printed by John Streater) does not include the translation of the verses of

Palingenius Stellatus, which occupy Chapter 48 in the French text. Among the reasons for the translation "the worthinesse and great esteem and acuity of spirit of the Person of honour Sir Kenelm Digby, to whom it was offered by the Author." Among the other works of this singular personality, to whom Thorndike gives very little attention (Thorndike, L., *History of magic and experimental science,* New York, 1958, VII, 153-54), the following are particularly noteworthy: *Les antiquités de la ville et comté de Castres d'Albigeois,* Castres, 1649; *Bibliotheca Chimica, seu catalogus librorum philosophicorum hermeticorum,* Parisiis, 1654 (an exemplary copy of this edition is to be found at the Bodleian Library—Ms. Ashm. 1374—with handwritten marginal notes by Elias Ashmole); *De vero telescopii inventore, cum brevi omnium conspiciliorum historia,* Hagae Comitum, 1655; *Historiarum et observationum medico-physicarum centuriae IV,* Parisiis, 1656; *Vitae R. Cartesii summi philosophi compendium,* Parisiis, 1656 (with an *Elenchus manuscriptorum Cartesii Stocholmi repertorum post eius* obitum, pp. 16-19); *Tresor de recherches et antiquités Galouises et Françoises en ordre alphabetique,* Paris, 1655; *Hortus seu armamentarium simplicium, minaralium, plantarum et animalium ad artem medicam utilium,* Castris, 1666.

44Borel, *Discours nouveau,* 29, 30, 43.

45*Ibid.,* 17; cf. 9-10, 16.

46*Ibid.,* 12. On the centrality of the sun, see 14-15.

47*Ibid.,* 26. For the preceding quotations, cf. 14, 23.

48*Ibid.,* 19, 46, 37, 58. For the last part of the quotation, cf. Bruno, G. *De Immenso,* in *Opera* I, 1, 242ff.; Spinoza, B., *Ethica,* I, prop. 16.

49*Borel,* op. cit., 14-15.

50*Ibid.,* p. 3. On Montaigne, see 24, 26.

51The first edition of the *De vero telescopii inventore,* bears portraits of Zacharian Iansen "primus conspiciliorum inventor" and Hans Lipperhy "secundus conspiciliorum inventor," but Borel enthusiastically underlines the newness of the Galilean enterprise: "Sileant igitur Athenae antiquae cum fabuloso suo Lynceo, sileant fabulae quae viros terrae penetralia oculis penetrantes extare afferunt, quibus thesauros et fontes fodinasque percipiant: extant hodie lyncei veri ac praestantiores quorum visum nihil effugere potest" (3, copy used: British Museum 48.a.17).

52Borel, *Discours nouveau,* 66.

53*Ibid.,* 12-13, 48.

54Montaigne, M. de, *Essais,* II, 12.

55Galileo, G., *Opere,* VII, 394-96.

56*Les états et Empires de la lune,* written in 1649, was published in Paris in 1656. On the relationships among Cyrano and Descartes and Gassendi, cf. Chapter 3 in

Spink, J. S., *French free-thought from Gassendi to Voltaire*, London, 1960, 48-66. An attentive examination of the philosophical-cultural basis for Cyrano's work may be found in the essay by Erba, L., *L'incidenza della magia nell 'opera di Cyrano de Bergerac*, Milan, 1960.

[57]*Oeuvres de Descartes*, ed. Adam, Ch., and Tannery, P., Paris, 1897-1913, VIII, 1, 180-181.

[58]To Endergeest August, 1641, in *Correspondence*, ed. Adam and Milhaud, V, 54.

[59]Oeuvres de Descartes, VIII, 1, 197-98. For the comparison between the earth and a grain of sand, *Correspondence*, VII, 349.

[60]To Elisabeth, September 15, 1645, in *Correspondence*, VI, 301.

[61]P. Chanut to Descartes, May 11, 1647, in *Correspondence*, VII, 313-314.

[62]To Chanut, June 6, 1647, in *Correspondence*, VII, 347-349.

[63]*Oeuvres, de Descartes*, V, 168.

[64]*Philos. Schrift*, I, 150.

[65]Guericke, O. von, *Experimenta nova*, Amstelodami, 1672, 216, 243.

[66]Huygens, Ch., *Cosmoteoros sive de terris coelestibus oerumque ornatu conjecturae*, Hagae Comitum, 1968, 8, and cf. *Oeuvres*, The Hague, 1888-1950, XXI, 669.

[67]Bruno, G., *La cena delle ceneri*, ed. Aquilecchia, 100: "Atteso che non più la luna è cielo a noi che noi alla luna." *Acrotisumus*, in *Opera*, I, 69: "Non etenim nos minus lunae et cuicumque astro, astrum coelumque sumus quam universa ipsa nobis esse possunt."

[68]Burnet, Th., *Archeologia Philosophica*, London, 1733, 405-06, 415. The first edition is dated 1692. The affirmation of the infinity of the universe as proof of divine power reappears in Ray, J., *The Wisdom of God manifested in the Work of Creation*, London, 1720, 20 (the first edition dates from 1680).

[69]*Ibid.*, 415.

[70]Fontenelle, B. de, *Entretiens sur la pluralité des mondes*, Amsterdam, 1719, 23. The first edition dates from 1686.

[71]Borel, P., *Discours nouveau*, 14, 32.

[72]Mercurius, Britannicus (Hall, Joseph), *Mundus alter et idem sive Terra Australis ante hac semper incognita longis itineribus peregrini Academici nuperrime lustrata*, Hanoviae, 1607. The edition used here is the Frankfort edition, s.d. in the copy of the British Museum 684.d.5. The passage is on page 9. In the edition of 1643 (in the British Museum 1080.d.14), the texts of Campanella's *Città del Sole* and Bacon's *New Atlantis* were added. A modern edition of the English translation of 1620 (which has the title *The Discovery of a New World or a Description of the South Indies*) was edited by H. Brown, Cambridge, Mass, 1937.

# 31

## On Symbolic Thought in Cartesianism

### WALTHER RIESE[1]

T HE essential message which Descartes was called upon to transmit to his century is not to be found in the solution of those concrete problems which at his time occupied the scholars; it is rather in the building of a *complete system,* which he intended to substitute totally for the doctrine of the "schools", and in which all substantial qualities and forms were replaced by a universal mechanism interpreting all phenomena of the visible world with the help of no more than the three concepts of extension, figure and movement. In this sentence is laid down Descartes' system of the world. Here are also the reasons for Descartes' dominant position in the history of science and medicine for 300 years. It is not too well known that in those passages in which he dealt with the nature and the criterion of a living organism, Descartes was very far from confounding man with his intellect.

Repeatedly, but particularly in his *Dioptrics,* he warned his readers not to conceive the images transmitted by the nerves to the brain as faithful copies of the objects. Nothing can come from external objects to our mind by the medium of the senses, he said, *except certain corporeal movements; but neither these movements themselves, nor the figures arising from them, are conceived by us such as they are in the organs of sense.* There are many things besides images, he also said, that can excite our thought; as, for example, words and signs, which in no way resemble the things they signify...

> On the same paper, with the same pen and ink, by merely moving the point of the pen over the paper in a particular way, we can trace letters that will raise in the minds of our readers the thoughts of combats, tempests, or the furies, and the passions of indignation and sorrow; in place of which, if the pen be moved in another way hardly different from the former, this slight change will cause thoughts widely different from the above, such as those of repose, peace, pleasantness, and the quite opposite passions of love and joy...

Descartes here reached the *symbolic* nature of human thought and its expression in spoken and written language—an interpretation which,

163

in our time, proved to promise greater insight into the dynamics of speech defects resulting from brain lesions than their description in merely physiological terms, those of purely motor or sensory type. The symbolic nature of human language has been traced back by this writer to Aristotle. In our time it has become the essential component in Henry Head's interpretation of aphasia, i.e. speech defects resulting from brain lesions.

One of Descartes' tests to demonstrate that machines were not really men, is

> that although such machines might execute many things with equal or perhaps greater perfection than any of us, they would, without doubt, fail in certain others from which it could be discovered that they did not act from knowledge, but solely from the disposition of their organs: for while Reason is an universal instrument that is alike available on every occasion, these organs, on the contrary, need a particular arrangement for each particular action; whence it must be morally impossible that there should exist in any machine a diversity of organs sufficient to enable it to act in all the occurrences, of life, in the way in which our reason enables us to act.

From these quotations I derived the conclusion that Descartes was very far from confounding man with his intellect;[2] he held the view that man's rational soul or reason sets the *limit* to the machine and its usefulness to serve as a model for man's truly human endowment.[3] It would appear that heavy demands are made on the twentieth-century reader who learns that the rational soul "could by no means be educated from the power of the matter and that it is 'of a nature wholly independent of the body.' " More than two centuries later, another French philosopher, Henri Bergson, trying to refute psychophysical parallelism, reached the conclusion that man's thought transcends his brain. The reason for Descartes' unwillingness to grant boundless powers to body and brain are to be found in the fact that he was anxious to assign to man his proper and unique place in the whole of living creatures, to distinguish his from the "brutes," and to save man's moral nature or, above all, in Cartesian terms, to save the indestructibility of his soul.

## References

[1]This investigation was supported by Public Health Service Research Grant RO1 MH 12875 from the U.S. Department of Health, Education, and Welfare Public Health Service, Bethesda, Maryland.

[2]He replied to one of his opponents: "One thing is certain: I know myself as a thought, and I positively do not know myself as a brain."

[3]Riese, W., "Descartes' Ideas of Brain Function." Lecture delivered on July 15, 1957, in London, to the Anglo-American Symposium on the History and Philosophy of Knowledge of the Brain and its Functions. In *The History and Philosophy of Knowledge of the Brain and its Functions,* (ed.), F. N. I. Poynter, Oxford, 1958, 115-134. The last two paragraphs have been borrowed from my London lecture.

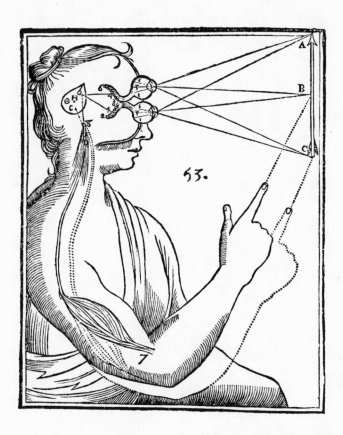

# 32

## Newton's Alchemical Studies

### P. M. RATTANSI

N EWTON'S alchemical studies first came to public notice when
Brewster published his magisterial biography of Newton in 1855.
Brewster was troubled by Newton's obsessive interest in the sub-
ject, and confessed that:

> we cannot understand how a mind of such power, and nobly occupied
> with the abstractions of geometry, and the study of the material world,
> could stoop to be even the copyist of the most contemptible alchemical
> poetry, and the annotator of a work, the obvious product of a fool and
> a knave.[1]

But the full extent of Newton's interest in the subject became clear only
when the Cambridge University committee which examined the Portsmouth Manuscripts published their report in 1888, and even more fully
when the alchemical manuscripts were described in detail in the catalogue
of the Sotheby sale of 1936 which was to scatter them all over the world.[2]
It was now revealed that, besides the 1,300,000 words on the theological
and Biblical topics, there were extant about 650,000 words on alchemy,
almost wholly in Newton's own hand.[3]

It seems fair to say that historians who have discussed Newton's
alchemical studies since Brewster have tended to adopt diametrically
opposed views about their significance. L. T. More, in his 1934 biography
of Newton, claimed:

> The fact of the matter is, Newton was an alchemist, and his major inter-
> est in chemistry, in his earlier years, centered on the possibility of trans-
> muting metals.

Lord Keynes, who helped to save a great many of the alchemical manuscripts from dispersion at the 1936 sale, commented in 1947 (in what
has been called "an unfortunately memorable phrase")[5] that Newton, who
had left behind him an enormous mass of alchemical material that was
"wholly magical and wholly devoid of scientific value," was to be seen

as "not the first of the age of reason," but "the last of the magicians."[6] After a more searching and careful survey, the historian of alchemy and early chemistry, F. Sherwood Taylor, reaffirmed More's judgement in 1956:

> He conducted alchemical experiments, he read widely and universally in alchemical treatises of all types, and he wrote alchemy, not like Newton, but like an alchemist.

There are obvious difficulties in accepting such a verdict. Not only does it radically challenge our image of Newton as the greatest of the early modern scientists who broke the spell both of scholasticism and of the Renaissance pseudo-sciences in the study of nature. It also raises in an acute form the problem of reconciling his supposedly alchemical commitments with his published views on chemical topics. However strange Newton's views on Biblical prophecy may now appear, they presumably have little relevance for understanding his scientific work; but it seems inconceivable that there should be no connection between his alchemical studies and the reasonably coherent chemical philosophy which can be reconstructed from his printed works. The historians who have described Newton as an "alchemist" have done little to link that belief with his "official" science. L. T. More suggested that Newton was searching for some unifying principle that would connect all chemical actions. Sherwood Taylor pointed to Newton's attempts to explain gravitation, electrical and magnetic actions, and animal motion in terms of an aethereal medium, and saw here a connection with alchemy, since "a great part of alchemy is concerned with that universal medium, the philosopher's mercury."

Such suggestions have seemed to others to raise more problems than they set out to solve. Professor and Mrs. Rupert Hall have commented that to identify the aether of the "General Scholium" with the "Philosophical Mercury" of the alchemists, instead of making Newton's thinking more comprehensible, makes it less so.[8] Since that view prefaces their own valuable and pioneering study (1958) of the neglected notebook of Newton in which he had actually recorded many of his chemical (or alchemical?) experiments, it is surprising that their conclusions do not, at first sight, seem to conflict with L. T. More's and Sherwood Taylor's assessment. They state that most of Newton's experiments on metals aimed at discovering ways in which metals could be made more volatile, as well as at preparing alloys of low melting and boiling points. Sal

Ammoniac was a key ingredient in both sorts of experiments. The Halls admit that the alchemists of the time shared these aims. The art of changing volatile to fixed had "an alchemical significance." Though Newton never explained his interest in alloys of a low melting point, it was probably connected with the alchemical search for the "philosopher's mercury." Again, Newton's preference for using indeterminate ores rather than smelted metal was perhaps connected with the alchemical idea that the metallic mineral was alive and fertile, while smelted metal was dead and inert.

But the Halls insist that these striking similarities must not be taken to mean that Newton aimed at the same results—the Stone and the Elixir—as the alchemists. They point to his careful techniques, keen attention to measurement, and "rational" interpretation of alchemical terms and symbols as proof of Newton's "rational" approach to alchemy. Newton's work on *speculum* metals for his reflecting telescope perhaps provoked questions in his mind about the structure of metals and alloys. Besides this accidental stimulus, he may have found metals extremely suitable subjects for the study of structural composition. And when one studied metallurgical chemistry in the seventeenth century, where else would one turn to than the alchemist. The notebook itself provides no clues about Newton's purpose. But (the Halls contend) except as a repository of certain valuable facts, alchemy had nothing to offer Newton: it was not a variant natural philosophy, but merely a theory of metals plus the operations necessary for its realisation, with a lump of gold as the end-product.[9]

However much such a view of Newton's alchemical studies may seem to fit the Newton we know from the *Principia* and the *Opticks,* it is not free from many difficulties. First of all, the alchemical excerpts, considered both in respect to the choice of authors and of topics, do not really support the idea that Newton was merely looking for chemical and metallurgical information. A large number of extracts are descriptions of alchemical processes; others relate to such alchemical topics as the different sorts of stones created by the alchemists and the fantastic powers they conferred on the possessor; and a whole class of extracts (mostly from the alchemist Michael Maier) is an elaborate discussion of the alchemical significance of pagan mythology. Moreover, in a number of his own manuscript compositions, Newton employs alchemical beliefs in a matter of fact way in his discussion of the problem of generation in the animal, vegetable, and mineral kingdoms: for example, in a manuscript now in the Burndy Library, which discusses the properties of the "two Elixirs" and of the Alkahest.[10]

Secondly, Newton himself, to judge from an early indication of his opinion, did not regard alchemy merely as an *Goldmachenkunst*. A rare occasion, when (to use his own words) he "shot his bolt" about alchemy, was in a letter to Henry Oldenberg (then Secretary of the Royal Society) on 26th April 1676, commenting on a paper by Robert Boyle in the *Philosophical Transactions* on the "incalescence" of gold and mercury. Boyle had offered a corpuscular explanation of the process, and Newton offered an alternative one, in terms of the size and mechanical actions of the particles. But he went on to commend Boyle for concealing some parts of the process, since it was

> possibly an inlet to something more noble, and not to be communicated without immense dammage to ye world if there be any verity in ye Hermetick writers...[11]

To discover its true significance, Boyle should hold his "high silence" and reflect on his true experiment or consult someone who really understood what Boyle had talked about,

> that is, of a true Hermetic Philosopher, whose judgmt (if there be any such) would be more to be regarded in this point then that of all ye world beside to ye contrary, there being other things beside ye transmutation of metalls (if those great pretenders bragg not) wch none but they understand.

The letter is laced with caution about the claims of the alchemists, but the hint that Boyle did not really comprehend what manner of things he was meddling with, recurs in Newton's later correspondence. These remarks, together with the evidence of the manuscripts, reinforce a feeling that it is far easier to attribute Boyle's interest in alchemical authors to a search for valuable information than Newton's.

Newton's comment that the wide dissemination of alchemical secrets could result in "immense dammage to ye world" may refer merely to the monetary and social consequences of easy transmutation; but he hinted that more was involved than transmutation. In the alchemical works he himself studied, success in alchemy was said to open the gates to knowledge of all the secrets of the universe. His contemporary, Elias Ashmole, introducting the collection which Newton constantly studied, said that making gold was

> scarce any intent of the ancient Philosophers, and lowest use the Adepti made of the Materia. For they being lovers of Wisdom more than worldly Wealth, drove at higher and more Excellent Operations: And certainly He to whom the whole Course of Nature lyes open, rejoyceth not so much that he can make Gold and Silver, or the Divells to become subject to him, as that he sees the Heavens open, the Angells of God Ascending and Descending, and that his own Name is fairely written in the Book of Life...
>
> In briefe, by the true and various uses of the Philosopher's Prima Materia...the perfection of Liberall Sciences are made known, the whole Wisdome of Nature may be grasped: And...There are yet hid greater things than these, for we have seen but few of his Workes.[12]

In pointing out the difficulties of what its expositors see as a more rational interpretation of Newton's alchemical studies, I may seem to have slid back to viewing him as a convinced alchemist. But it is to be noted that even in the letter to Oldenburg in which he extols the knowledge of the Hermetic philosophers, Newton couches his explanation of Boyle's process in strictly corpuscular and mechanical terms. We seem to be impaled here on the horns of a dilemma: how could the rational and scientific Newton, who obviously interpreted alchemical processes not in mystical or traditional alchemical terms, but within a mechanical framework, have placed any credence in their larger and wilder claims?

I should like to suggest that the relation between Newton's alchemical studies and his "official" science becomes clearer if we examine the assumptions guiding two other sorts of studies which absorbed a great deal of his attention. These are, first, his Biblical studies,[13] especially of the prophetic books of the Bible; and second, his studies of ancient natural philosophy, undertaken in the 1690's in connection with the revised second edition of the *Principia*. Underlying both sorts of studies, for Newton, was the assumption that truth—whether about the unfolding course of history or the true system of the world—was anciently given, but in a veiled and enigmatic form to conceal it from the vulgar. The prefiguring of future events in Scripture would become clear only when those events had come to pass, for their sole function was to *demonstrate* the Providence which guided the course of history; that was the task which Newton attempted in his study of ancient history. Similarly, the fact that the ancients had possessed knowledge of the true physical system of the world could only be seen when that system had been recovered, on the basis of a rigorous inductive and experimental method. So convinced was Newton that this was so, that he intended at the time to add classical annotations in the second edition to show that the key propositions of the *Principia* were well known to some of the ancients; indeed, he argues in elaborate detail that Pythagoras must have known the law of universal gravitation. What Newton was employing was a characteristic Renaissance tactic, the idea of a *prisca sapientia* which had served to legitimize the concern of the Florentine Platonists with the Hermetic magical works, and later, from the end of the sixteenth century, to remove the tinge of atheism from atomic doctrines by attributing them to a certain Moschus, who, many classical scholars held, was none other than Moses himself; and Newton's contemporaries at Cambridge, the Platonists Henry More and Ralph Cudworth, used the same tactic to present the Mechanical Philosophy as no more than the restoration of an ancient Mosaic theology-cum-natural philosophy which had become separated after Pythagoras.

Now the idea of a pristine knowledge of nature, delivered in a mysterious text—the "Tabula Smaragdina"—and to be unravelled by the practical "work of the fire", aided by the works of the succession of masters through the ages who had penetrated the secret, is central to alchemy. Expanding earlier hints and influenced by a Renaissance mythographic tradition, the 17th century German alchemist, Michael Maier, had greatly extended the range of alchemically "relevant" materials by arguing that the whole of Greek and Roman mythology was a veiled representation of alchemical secrets.

In view of his later attitude, it is probably significant that even during his last year at school at Grantham, Newton owned and annotated a work expounding the ethical, historical, and scientific significance of the fables narrated by Ovid in his *Metamorphoses*.[14] When he came to Cambridge he imbibed the mechanical philosophy during his undergraduate years, not only from the works of Descartes and other continental masters, but also from those of Henry More, where it was presented as the rediscovery of a most ancient philosophy. The earliest known indication of Newton's alchemical interest is the letter he wrote to his friend Francis Aston in 1669, and the manuscript evidence makes it certain that the transmutations he asked Aston to investigate during his travels are derived from the works of Michael Maier. Newton's continuous fascination with Maier's works is evident from the long extracts he made from them, and from the many citations in the various alchemical indices which Newton compiled. Newton's own chemical experiments began probably at this time, and continued at least until 1696.[15]

As his letter to Oldenburg in 1676 hinted, Newton did not regard alchemy merely as the search for transmutation; much deeper things were involved in it. The symbolic and enigmatic form in which alchemists had expressed themselves was essential to the nature of the art. His views on alchemy have, in fact, a much less modern ring than those of Robert Boyle. Boyle probably influenced Newton profoundly in his belief that the mechanical philosophers should concern themselves much more closely with chemical phenomena, in part by studying the experiments reported by the best of the chemical authors. Boyle did not wish to dismiss the possibility that some alchemical "adepts" may have been in possession of the secret of transmutation, for the corpuscular philosophy implied the transmutability of matter.[16] But he was emphatic in asserting that these valuable results were only an accidental byproduct of the fact that the alchemists had sought the Stone and the Elixir by practical laboratory operations. Certainly, their confused and false theories had nothing to offer to the mechanical philosopher, and were based on competing element-theories which had all now been refuted. Most of the authors whom Boyle himself discussed in this connection were those who had renounced the search for transmutation in favour of the search for *arcana* and "Quintessences" useful in medicine: Paracelsus and followers of his *tria prima* like Duchesne and Beguin; Sala; Sennert; Libavius; and especially Helmont.

None of these particular authors appear in the lists of the best chemical authors compiled at various times by Newton. His interest was in the great masters of the alchemical succession, from the Hermes Trismegistus whom he took to have lived in the time of the Patriarchs down to contemporaries like the Theodorus Mundanus, whose alchemical views were published by Edmund Dickinson in 1686.[17] More than half of the authors he most frequently consulted were then believed to have lived between the time of Moses and the thirteenth century. Those in whom Boyle was especially interested do not appear in Newton's lists, presumably because they did not concern themselves primarily with the "Great Work" (although Helmont is studied for his "Alkahest"). The extant Newtonian alchemical manuscripts consist almost wholly of extracts from alchemical works, and there can be no doubt that most of them deal with the processes involved in making the Stone. However, these works insisted at the same time that the Stone was valued by the true *adepti* not because it would transmute metals and cure all diseases, but because it would make it possible to understand the greatest secret of nature: the subtle spirit or the "Philosopher's Mercury" which was the source of all activity in the universe. To quote Ashmole again:

> ...the Power and Vertue is not in Plants, Stones, Minerals &c. (though we sensibly perceive the Effects from them) but 'tis that universal and All-piercing Spirit, the One operative vertue and immortall Seede of Worldly things, that God in the beginning infused into the Chaos, which is every where Active and still flows through the world in all kindes of things by universall extension, and manifests itself by the aforesaid Productions. Which Spirit a true Artist knowes how-so to handle (though its activity be as it were dul'd and streightly bound up, in the close Prison of Grosse and Earthie bodies) as to take it from Corporeity, free it from Captivity, and let it loose that it may freely worke as it doth in the AEtheriall Bodies.[18]

The Hermetic Tablet, the basic text of alchemy, described the operations of this Spirit, and many of Newton's extracts deal with the numerous different forms of activity in the universe in which it was involved.[19] It is difficult to understand how, without a conviction that deep truths were concealed in alchemy, Newton should have attached much significance to such ideas, or to have believed (as the Halls contend) that

> the profoundly esoteric terminology of alchemy was only an extension of the superficially esoteric language of ordinary chemistry; and similarly that the more recondite experimentation of the former was but an extension of the better-known and clearer experimentation of the latter.[20]

Boyle, in various places, referred to "the Universal spirit, asserted by some Chymists", as a substitute for or in combination with the *tria prima* of elements, but implied that it was superfluous, since it would have to be understood in corpuscular terms before it could satisfactorily explain any thing in nature.[21] Newton's assumptions, on the other hand, imply some sort of dialectic between new inductively- and experimentally- based scientific knowledge and the ancient texts: the rise of the mechanical philosophy made a deeper penetration into the meaning of those texts possible, but did not invalidate the truths they embodied.[22] The Aristotelian element-theory was employed, in most part, in the alchemical texts to characterise the various phases of matter, and Newton took over that phraseology in many of his own works; and he characteristically read a deeper meaning into the sulphur-mercury theory, arguing in an early draft of his "De natura acidorum":

> Note that what is said by chemists, that everything is made from sulphur and mercury is true, because by sulphur they mean acid, and by mercury they mean earth.[23]

If the interpretation that has been offered of the enormous amount of time and labour devoted by Newton to the study of an astonishing variety of alchemical writings and to experiments over several decades is correct, then we must seriously re-examine Sherwood Taylor's suggestion that there is some connection between Newton's various aethereal speculations and the "philosopher's mercury" sought by the alchemists. The alchemical flavour of the aethereal hypotheses presented by Newton in his 1675 letter to Oldenburg and 1679 letter to Boyle has been noted by a number of authors.[24] The letter to Oldenburg is primarily concerned with describing an optical hypothesis, but is prefaced by a long section outlining a wide range of phenomena (including electrical and magnetic actions, chemical phenomena, animal motion, and gravitation) which are explained in terms of an aethereal medium. There can be no doubt that Newton's account offers variations on the Cartesian vortical aether and is strongly influenced by Boyle's model of the "ocean of air".[25] But at least three of the themes of these speculations bear a striking resemblance to those he was studying at that time in the alchemical authors. These are: firstly, the creation of all things from aether by condensation, and the idea of a particular spirit within that aether which is contained within the pores of matter as a principle of activity "for the continual uses of nature"; secondly, the continual condensation of that particular spirit by the earth, while the exchange of 'as much matter" sent out in an aerial form from the bowels of the earth sets up a circulation; thirdly, the existence of "sociability" and "unsociability" between various substances through "a secret principle" and action of intermediaries in resolving it.

The first two themes are directly related to the *Tabula* and its interpretation by alchemical authors. A manuscript commentary on the *Tabula* in Newton's hand describes how all things were generated from the alchemical chaos or aether, and how that aether ascends into the heavens by sublimations and in time by reiterated sublimations descends to earth— a process which the alchemist must emulate in his own operations. The third theme, that of the secret sympathies and antipathies between various chemical substances, was a basic one in alchemical discussions.[26]

Newton sought to explain a much wider range of phenomena by his "Spirit" than was usual in alchemical discussions;[27] and, of course, there is no analogue in the alchemical writings for his explanation of many of these phenomena in terms of the "mechanical" properties of the aether. But that he was equating the alchemical *spiritus* with a quasi-Cartesian ether can now be shown much more convincingly by recourse to the Burndy Library manuscript already cited. In that document Newton considered a favourite alchemical theme, the analogy between generation and maturation in each of the three kingdoms of nature, for the light it cast upon the "vegetation of metals", and, presumably, upon the processes by which the Great Work might be accomplished.

Newton sharply distinguished nature's "vegetable" actions from the "purely mechanical" ones. The former included generation and corruption, the latter gravitation, the tides, "meteors" and "vulgar Chymistry". The reactions of ordinary chemistry may at times seem to human senses "as strange transmutations as those of nature", but they really involved merely the "mechanical coalitions or separations of particles". If vegetation involved something more, then "this difference is vast and fundamental because nothing could ever yet be made without vegetation which nature useth to produce by it", and he significantly included the supposed transmutation of iron into copper as an example.[28] What distinguished vegetation from mechanism was the fact that it consisted of an interaction between the aether as an activating principle and the "rudements" or seeds of things, that is "that substance in them that is attained to the fullest degree of maturity that is in that thing". The descent of the aether from the heavens could itself be explained mechanically. Enormous quantities of vapours and airs ascended continually from the earth by "mineral dissolutions and fermentation" and they compressed the aether and finally forced it to descend, illustrating once more that it was "very agreeable to nature's proceedings to make a circulation of all things": "Thus this earth resembles a great animal or rather inanimate vegetable, and draws in aethereal breath for its daily refreshment & vital ferment & transpires again with gross exhalations"... And thus a great pt if not all the moles of sensible matter is nothing but AEther congealed & interwoven into various textures whose life depends on that pt of it wch is in a middle state, not wholly distinct & loose from it like ye AEther in wch it swims as in a fluid nor wholly joined & compacted together with it under one form but in some degree condensed [&] united to it & yet remaining of a much more rare texture & subtle disposition & so this seems to be the principle of its acting."

On further reflection Newton concluded that "'tis more probable ye aether is but a vehicle to some more active spt & $y^e$ bodies may be concreted of both together, they may imbibe aether well as air in generation & in $y^e$ aether $y^e$ spt is entangled. This spt is $y^e$ body of light because both have a prodigious active principle, both are prodigious workers..."

These remarks do much to clarify Newton's view of alchemy at the time. In the course of developing his thoughts on the "vegetation of metals," he cited the Elixir and the Alkahest, the initially green colour of the Stone and the generation of much air in the Stone's "first solution" as part of his evidence. His identification of the most active part of the aether with light is particularly interesting. The *spiritus* was regarded by the alchemists as present in all bodies, constituting the principle of their activity. When extracted from substances and concentrated within the Stone, it was often described as being most like light. The *spiritus* must necessarily be a substance of the finest subtlety since it entered the smallest parts of gross matter and separated them in the processes of generation and maturation, but (in Newton's own words) "not after $y^e$ way of common menstruums by rending them violently asunder &c.", but by "a more subtle sweet & noble way of working..." Newton's reflections seem, then, to indicate that Newton may, at least at that time, have conceived the goal of the alchemical quest as the recovery of the body of light itself through practical laboratory operations. Newton had not ceased to speculate on these lines even when he published his *Opticks* in its second English edition of 1717, and in Query 30 he asked: "Are not gross Bodies and Light convertible into one another, and may not Bodies receive much of their Activity from Particles of Light which enter their Composition?...The changing of Bodies into Light, and Light into Bodies, is very comfortable to the Course of Nature, which seems delighted with Transmutations."[29]

Newton's thoughts on the aether and the *spiritus* are made more intelligible when they are viewed against the vicissitudes of the idea of *spiritus* through the 16th and 17th centuries, and its place in one particular variant of the mechanical philosophy in England. The alchemical *spiritus* was invoked in natural-philosophical discussions by authors of very different philosophical allegiances. It provided a *rationale* for non-demonic "natural magic" to the Florentine Platonists and their successors;[30] furnished an explanation of the Aristotelian "occult" qualities for Jean Fernel;[31] and served as an explanatory principle in the works of such innovators as Telesio, Basso, Campanella, and Francis Bacon.[32] The "Spagyrick" authors who wished to turn chemical studies away from traditional alchemy and towards medicine often identified the *spiritus* with particular substances; for example Glauber and the Paracelsians equated it with the "nitro-aerial spirit," unintentionally aiding its identification with familiar substances.[33] So various were the functions assigned to the *spiritus*, which was itself increasingly regarded as a material fluid, that William Harvey condemned it as the *deus ex machina* of inferior writers.[34]

More immediately relevant for studying Newton's ideas is the tactic adopted in 1657 by Henry More, the Cambridge Platonist, in his amalgam of Cartesianism and Neo-Platonism. He identified the First and Second Matters of Descartes with the *spiritus* of the Renaissance Platonists—the *spiritus* which Ficino had said was the same as the alchemical Fifth Element or Quintessence—in order to avoid the Cartesian dualism of mind and matter.[35] A simple identification of the alchemical *spiritus* and the Cartesian ether will be found, again, with citations to Henry More, in the professedly Cartesian work, *Experimental Philosophy*, published by Newton's contemporary, Henry Power in 1664. Power called it "the main (though invisible) Agent in all Natures three Kingdoms Mineral, Vegetal, and Animal."[36] They were responsible for fermentation in minerals, vegetation and maturation in plants, and life, sense, and motion in animals; they explained the conjunction of soul and body in man through the mediation of the animal spirits.

Henry More's view of the mechanical philosophy as the restoration of the lost "Mosaic" system of the world seems to have generally influenced Newton, and it is likely that he was equally impressed by More's pointing to the basic similarities between the Neo-Platonic *spiritus* and the Cartesian aether. Given these assumptions, the alchemical texts would enormously extend the range of materials in which that aether had been discussed and described, and even open the possibility of being able to recover that extremely active substance through laboratory operations. That was not incompatible with devising "mechanically" intelligible explanations of the myriad phenomena which ultimately depended on the action of the aether.

This paper has attempted to outline an approach to Newton's alchemical studies that would avoid the opposing dangers of either isolating them from his total scientific and intellectual labours, or of splitting Newton into irreconcilable "scientific" and "mystical" selves. The changes in Newton's attitude to alchemy, and their bearing on, say, the "cometary spirit" of the *Principia,* and the "Active Principles" of the *Opticks,* are problems for future research to clarify. But we cannot even begin to grapple with them unless we take account of a legacy of Renaissance ideas which had not lost their force during Newton's lifetime.

What is particularly impressive, and perhaps vital for understanding the complexities of Newton's own world-view, is the influence of the Renaissance "pristine" concept in Newton's attempts to unify some of the major ideas enshrined in the very different sorts of literature he studied intensively at various periods of his life: the vast labyrinth of alchemy; the theology of the early Church Fathers, especially the Alexandrian Fathers; and the scientific views of the ancients. Historians of ideas have recently begun to explore the recurrence and transformation of such ideas as those of the *pneuma,* or the teachings of the mysterious Hermes Trismegistus, in these different sorts of works.[37] The Newtonian manuscripts show that Newton was well aware of these resemblances, and regarded them as proof of the consonance between the truths he had discovered by rigorous scientific procedures and the clues scattered in enigmatic form in very disparate realms of ancient and late-antique thought.

It is true that the approach advocated here demands a significant modification of the conventional view of Newton. Certainly, the labels of "Rationalist," "empiricist," or "mystic" which have been variously applied in this context fail to do justice to the complexities of Newton's thought. In common with the other great natural philosophers of his age, like Descartes, or even more, like Leibniz, Newton strove for a unified solution that would encompass not only the mysteries of celestial and terrestrial physics, but also the perennial religious problems of the relation between the Creator and his universe. These wider endeavours of Newton may appear naively fundamentalist and philosophically unsophisticated when compared, say, with the coherence and majesty of the system of Leibniz. But any total account of Newton's thought must fully consider them. Otherwise, we shall remain wedded to a simplistic view of the rich, strange, complex world of Newton's thought, and harried by problems of interpretation which have usually been met by desperate expedients which recent achievements in the historiography of science, particularly the outstanding work of Walter Pagel,[37] should make us extremely wary of adopting.

The "strange seas of thought" over which Isaac Newton voyaged may now seem even stranger than we had suspected. Charting their extent and plumbing their depths will demand a sensitivity and a breadth of contextual knowledge for which Pagel's work has set up almost impossibly high standards.

## References

[1]Brewster, Sir David, *"Memoirs of the Life, Writings, & Discoveries of Sir Isaac Newton"*, Edinburg & London, 1855, II, 374-5.

[2]*"A Catalogue of the Portsmouth Collection of Books and Papers Written by or belonging to Sir Isaac Newton...Drawn up by the Syndicate appointed the 6th November 1872"*, Cambridge, 1888. *Catalogue of the Newton Papers*, Sotheby's, London, 1936.

[3]Estimate by F. Sherwood Taylor, "An Alchemical Work of Sir Isaac Newton", *Ambix*, V (1956), 60.

[4]More, L. T., *Isaac Newton, A Biography*, New York & London, 1934, 158 and 52.

[5]Boas, Marie, and Hall, A. Rupert, "Newton's Chemical Experiments," *Archives internationales d'Histoire des sciences, XI* (1958), 113.

[6]The Royal Society, *Newton Tercentenary Celebrations* (15-19 July 1946), Cambridge, 1947, J. M. Keynes, "Newton, the Man," 32 & 27.

[7]Taylor, *op. cit.*, 63.

[8]Halls, 118.

[9]*Ibid.*, 133-152.

[10]The item was listed in the Sotheby Sale Catalogue as No. 516, and begins: "Of natures obvious laws & processes in vegetation."

[11]Turnbull, H. W., (ed.), *The Correspondence of Isaac Newton*, II, Cambridge, 1960, 1-3; Boyle's paper appeared in *Phil. Trans.*, X (1675/6), 515-33.

[12]*Theatrum Chemicum Britannicum*, London, 1652, Prolegomena, [A4ᵛ] & B2ʳ.

[13]Discussed in McGuire, J. E. & Rattansi, P. M., "Newton and the 'Pipes of Pan,'" *Notes & Records of the Royal Society of London, XXI* (1966), 108-143. Cf. Newton on *Daniel and the Apocalypse*, (ed.) White, W., London, 1922, 305-6.

[14]*A Descriptive Catalogue of the Grace K. Babson Collection of the Works of Sir Isaac Newton*, New York, 1950, 187-6, records: "Sabinus, Georgius... Ovidii / Metamorphoses, / sev Fabvlae Poeticae: / Earemque Interpretatio / Ethica, Physica et Historica / ...ultima editio, 1593, Frankfurt," and on the flyleaf: "Isaci Newtoni / Liber / Octobris 15 / 1659. / praetium -o-1-6," and various marginal notes.

[15]On Newton's interest in alchemy, consult Brewster, More, the Halls, Sherwood Taylor, in works cited *supra.;* also Forbes, R. J., "Was Newton an alchemist?," *Chymia, II* (1949), 27-36, and Geoghegan, D., "Some Indications of Newton's

attitude towards Alchemy," *Ambix, VI* (1957), 102-106. Keynes Manuscript 32 at King's College, Cambridge, contains 88 pages of notes in Newton's hands from four works by Maier, totalling about 50,000 words; Maier continued to be cited in the indices Newton compiled in the late 17th century.

[16]See e.g. Boyle, *Works,* (ed.) Birch, T., 1744, III, 621; cf. the appendix on "the Producibleness of Chymicall Principles" added to the 1680 ed. of the *Sceptical Chymist,* where Boyle affirms his strong belief in adepts with "among other rare things some *Alkahestical* or other extraordinarily potent Menstruum," p. [ *7[rv] ].

[17]The shortest list among the Keynes MSS. reads: "Best authors: Hermes, Turba, Morien, Artephius, Abraham the Jew and Flammel, Scala, Ripley, Maier, the great Rosary, Charnock, Trevisan, Philalethea, D'espagnet." The longest list, among those grouped in Keynes, M. S. 13, contains 63 works, including Edmund Dickinson's of 1684.

[18]Ashmole, *op. cit.,* 446-7.

[19]An English translation of the *Tabula* in Newton's hand, as well the Latin text with a commentary, are in Keynes, M. S. 28; cf. in the Burndy Library MS.: "That vegetation is y$^e$ sole effect of a latent spt & that this spt is y$^e$ same in all things only discriminated by degrees of maturity..."

[20]Halls, *op. cit.,* 151-2.

[21]Boyle, *Works,* III, 453.

[22]McGuire & Rattansi, *op. cit.;* in the manuscript discussed there, Newton said that by the fiction of a lion falling out of the moon and stones out of the sun Anaxagoras indicated the gravity of the sun and moon towards the earth, and the force of rotation against gravity, respectively, for "the mystical philosophers by this kind of fiction were wont to adumbrate the doctrines in mystical language." Cf. Newton's note in Keynes MS. 32: "Pythagoras fuit adeptus, (fit ejus metampsychosis cum tinctura lapidis in imperfecta metalla transfertur. fflata (i.e. lapis Philos) non est conedena.)"

[23]Newton, *Correspondence,* III, 206 and 210.

[24]E.G. Löhne, J., in *Archive for the History of Exact Sciences, I* (1961), 401.

[25]Guerlac, Henry, *Newton et Epicure,* Paris, 1963, 9.

[26]Festugière, P., *La revelation d'Hermès Trismégiste,* Paris, 1944, I, 233-237.

[27]Cf. (ed.) Turnbull, H. W., *The Correspondence of Isaac Newton,* I, Cambridge, 1959, 11 and note 6, 13.

[28]Cited from the Dover ed., New York, 1952, 374. In *ibid.,* 405, Newton said that in the observations and queries of the Third Book, he had "only begun the Analysis of what remains to be discovere'd about Light and its Effects upon the Frame of Nature, hinting several things about it, and leaving the Hints to be examin'd and improv'd by the further Experiments and Observations of such as are inquisitive."

[29]Walker, D. P., *Spiritual and demonic Magic from Ficino to Campanella,* London, 1958.

[30]Walker, "The Astral Body in Renaissance Medicine," *Journal of the Warburg & Courtauld Institutes, XXI* (1958).

[31]Siebeck, H., "Neue beiträge zur entwicklungsgeschichte des Geist-Begriffs," *Archiv für Geschichte der Philosophie, XX* (1914), 1-16.

[32]Sherwood Taylor, F., "The Idea of the Quintessence," in (ed.) Underwood, E. Ashworth, *Science, Medicine and History,* London, 1953, I, 247-265.

[33]In the "Excert. alt. ad J. Riolan," 1649, and again in the *De generatione* (1651), Harvey rejected any attempt to explain vital phenomena by a material cause, and aduced empirical evidence against the presence of the *spiritus* in physiological cavities. On the sun, the spirit, and the aerial niter in the seventeenth century chemical literature see Allen G. Debus, "The Sun in the Universe of Robert Fludd," *Le Soleil à la Renaissance—Sciences et Mythes,* Travaux de l'Institut pour l'étude de la Renaissance et de l'Humanisme, Brussels, 1965, 259-278; "The Paracelsian Aerial Niter," *Isis, LV* (1964), 43-61.

[34]More, Henry, *The Immortality of the Soul* (1659), B. 2, ch. iv.

[35]Power, Henry, *Experimental Philosophy in Three Books,* London, 1664, "A Digression on Animal Spirits," 61-71; also C. Webster, "Henry Power's Experimental Philosophy," *Ambix XIV* (1967), 150-78 and Rattansi, *Ambix XVI* (1969), 173-5.

[36]Verbeke, G., *L'Evolution de la doctrine du pneuma,* Paris & Louvain, 1945; Festugière, *op. cit.* (note 26).

[37]See Pagel's remarks in *Das Medizinische Weltbild des Paracelsus, seine zussamenhänge mit Neuplatonismus und Gnosis,* Wiesbaden, 1962, 14-16.

# 33

# Newton and the Hermetic Tradition

## RICHARD S. WESTFALL

ONE lively and active facet of the lively and active enterprise that is Newtonian scholarship today is the continuing revelation of the presence in Newton's mind of modes of thought long deemed antithetical to the modern scientific enterprise. Rumored in the 18th century, these aspects of Newton's thought were grouped together under the heading of mysticism and associated with the alleged influence of Jacob Boehme. In religious and literary circles, the stories have continued to be repeated into the 20th century, while scientists and historians of science have generally rejected them, usually with some asperity.[1] The investigation of Newton's papers has now substantiated a factual foundation to the stories that cannot be ignored or denied. Lord Keyne's examination of the alchemical manuscripts he purchased at auction suggested that Newton's interest in alchemy extended much farther than anyone had been ready to believe. Careful studies of the manuscripts that contain his speculations on nature indicate that an outlook at least somewhat related to alchemy pervaded them.[2] In their details, the earlier stories undoubtedly need correction. In its present usage, the word 'mysticism' lacks any precise meaning, and I am convinced that characterizing Newton as a mystic does little or nothing to serve the cause of historical understanding. The influence of Boehme has not been confirmed. On the other hand, a profoundly religious dimension of Newton's philosophy of nature, whether or not we call it mystical, cannot be mistaken, and if Boehme did not influence him, others similar in outlook unquestionably did. One thing that the study of Newton's papers has established beyond any doubt, in my opinion, is the role of the Hermetic tradition in shaping his concept of nature.

As I use it in this paper, I intend the phrase 'Hermetic tradition' to have a general meaning rather than a specific one. I am not referring to the philosophy of any single man. I do not insist that individual ideas I call Hermetic were original or unique with that system of philosophy. Although the Hermetic influence had religious connotations in Newton's mind, I do not wish to contend that the affective dimension of the Hermetic philosophy flamed up in Newton in its pristine intensity; even in his tortured psyche I do not find anything approaching the demonic quality of a Bruno.[3] As I use it here, the 'Hermetic tradition' refers primarily to three closely related aspects of a conception of nature shared, I believe, by every Hermetic philosopher. First, nature was seen as active. Far from passive and inert, dominated by forces external to them, individual bodies have their own sources of activity, active principles, whereby they set themselves in operation and perform their specific acts. Second, nature was seen as animate. The Hermetic tradition expressed an organic view of nature in which no meaningful distinction of animate from inanimate existed. As it perceived the whole of nature in organic terms, so also it understood processes that we regard as entirely physical in terms of organic analogies. It held that metals grow in the earth. The non-precious metals are in some sense aborted remnants of a natural process which, carried to its conclusion, yields gold as its mature product. In undertaking to complete and accelerate the process of nature, the alchemist was in effect seeking to grow gold. Third, nature was seen as psychic. Projecting the mind onto nature, the Hermetic tradition understood the characteristic actions of bodies in similar terms. Bodies exercise influences on each other, sympathies and antipathies. As Francis Bacon asserted, though bodies "have no sense, yet they have perception..." whereby they recognize which ones to embrace and which to reject. Such a concept of natural action entailed the consequence that agents are specific rather than general in their operation. Bacon went on to conclude that "evermore a perception precedeth operation; for else all bodies would be alike one to another."[4] The attraction of like for like, however it was expressed, was one of the characteristic ideas of the Hermetic tradition. All three aspects of the Hermetic conception of nature were associated with the notion of spirit, the locus and carrier of activity, life, and perception. In the Hermetic tradition, the spiritual and the physical thoroughly penetrated each other and did not stand in sharp distinction.

The mechanical philosophy of nature, which played such a central role in 17th century science, appears to stand starkly in contrast to the Hermetic. Where the latter posited active principles, the mechanical philosophy asserted the inert inactivity of a matter dominated in its motion by forces and laws external to it. Instead of interpreting physical phenomena in organic terms, it explained organic processes by mechanisms and banished life itself from the universe. Although it did not also banish thought from existence, it did separate it utterly from matter, so that physical action had nothing in common with psychic processes. I believe I am correct in saying that the history of science has been virtually unanimous in seeing these two philosophies of nature as mutual antitheses. Scholarship has been instructed in this interpretation by 17th century science itself, to which the word 'occult', evoking Hermetic ideas, was the ultimate pejorative term which admitted no appeal. Early in the century, Galileo expressed his amazement that Kepler, in explaining the tides, had given his assent to the "moon's dominion over the waters, to occult properties, and to such puerilities."[5] At the end of the century, Newton, himself suspected of the same crime by continental Cartesians, forgot himself enough to abandon the bludgeon momentarily for the rapier by turning the charge against his accusers. Some philosophers, he said, in a reference too obvious to be missed, explain the cohesion of bodies by the quiescence of their particles relative to each other, "that is, by an occult Quality..."[6] 'Occult qualities' could refer to many things, but above all the phrase referred to the modes of explanation prevalent in the Hermetic tradition. Where the 17th century rushed in, modern scholarship has not been slow to follow, and one central feature of the scientific revolution has appeared to be the replacement of the Hermetic conception of nature by the mechanical.

I wish to propose that the logical antithesis, as it appears to us, of the two conceptions of nature was not an operative historical antithesis. I do not refer to the considerable chronological overlap of the two philosophies. No one has been silly enough to suggest that the mechanical philosophy seized the throne and slew the pretender all on a day. Rather I refer primarily to the content of the mechanical tradition itself. The more I have studied it, the more it has seemed to be pervaded with conceptions, disguised by mechanistic veneers, that can only be explained as descendants from the Hermetic tradition. In the 17th century, the two schools of natural philosophy assumed a far more subtle relationship than the idea of blunt antagonism admits. The capacity of the mechanical philosophy to transpose any theory or conception into the idiom of material particles in motion allowed Hermetic ideas to operate within an overtly mechanistic framework. The interpenetration of the two philosophies took different forms in the works of different men according to their philosophical rigor. In Newton, peculiarly Hermetic notions fostered the crucial development of his scientific thought, and in the concept of force became a central element both in the enduring science of mechanics and in the accepted idea of nature. The fundamental question for Newtonian scholarship, as it appears to me, is not the presence of Hermetic elements in his philosophy of nature; their presence has been demonstrated beyond reasonable doubt. The fundamental question is the mutual interaction of the two traditions in the development of Newton's scientific thought.

Already in Descartes, who more than any other one man was the fountainhead of the mechanistic school, the complex inter-relation of the two philosophies of nature manifested itself. Descartes intended to purge natural philosophy of the Hermetic infection by his rigorous dualism of mind and body. By confining psychic processes entirely to *res cogitans,* he reduced physical nature to a passive *res extensa* to which active principles are unknown. Physical nature consists solely of inert matter in motion, its particles able to act on each other only by impact. A more thorough rejection of the Hermetic outlook is hard to imagine. Nevertheless, by itself, Descartes' *res extensa* offered a mere ontology of physical nature, and his mechanical philosophy only an idiom in which to discuss phenomena. The content of the discussion had to come from somewhere, and occasionally at least it came from Hermetic sources. Thus the 20th century reader is somewhat disconcerted to find Descartes explaining how the pressure of clouds moulds exhalations so that blood or even small animals can rain occasionally from the heavens, and describing an effluvial device that causes the blood of a murdered man to flow when the murderer approaches.[7] Undoubtedly the asserted phenomena in these cases derived from popular superstitions long repeated and were not invented by Hermetic writers, although Hermetic philosophy did tend to relish similar prodigies. For its part, the mechanical philosophy contained no criteria that defined the limits of possible phenomena. Its program was to explain phenomena in mechanistic terms, and Descartes' explanations were unexceptionably mechanistic. On the level of insignificant detail, the examples suggest how Hermetic elements could penetrate the structure of a mechanical philosophy of nature.

Far more important was Descartes' treatment of matter. In the *Principles of Philosophy,* he explained how mechanical necessity divides the plenum into three forms of matter. Probably Descartes himself did not realize how faithfully the three forms repeated the characteristics of the Paracelsian *tria prima,* and in the case of his subtle matter, the most vehemently agitated particles, he cast the active principles of Hermetic philosophy into mechanistic form. The concept of 'spirit' always contained an element of ambiguity, and mechanical philosophers found no difficulty in translating 'spirit' as extremely fine, aethereal matter. Descartes showed the way in this respect, as he did in ascribing a higher intensity of motion—the very word *'action'* and several cognates, usually signifying degree of motion, appear throughout his writings—to the now mechanized spirit. In the discussion of many phenomena, of fire, for example, he summoned the subtle matter onto the stage, like a *deus ex machina,* to play the role of an active principle. Of course, Descartes always implied that its 'agitation' resulted from mechanical necessity. In fact, he never analysed in detail how it was caused—his mechanics could not have carried the analysis through in any case—but rather dragged it in by brute force whenever a phenomenon appeared to reveal a level of activity not present before. In such passages, his subtle matter can only be seen as a mechanistic rendition of an Hermetic active principle.

I do not wish to argue in any sense that Descartes' philosophy as a whole should be seen as a translation of Hermetic philosophy into the language of matter in motion. A rigorous philosopher, he understood the intent of his own reformulation of natural philosophy very well, and he generally carried through the program of replacing the inherent activity of bodies with the passivity of a matter dominated by external mechanical necessity—especially when discussion did not focus on particular phenomena. Much the same can be said of Robert Boyle, whose inability to bring a sentence to a successful conclusion should not be allowed to conceal his considerable understanding of the mechanical philosophy's implications. Again in Boyle's case, however, it is instructive to read him in conjunction with van Helmont, and difficult to resist the conclusion that his chemistry was largely a statement of van Helmont's in terms of particles in motion. How readily the Helmontian element of water accommodated itself to the mechanical idea of a uniform matter from which all bodies are composed. Van Helmont argued that all things are made from water and performed the famous experiment with the tree. Boyle asserted that "almost of any thing, may at length be made any thing,"[8] and to prove it repeated van Helmont's experiment with the tree at least twice. If on one level the Hermetic tradition stood in contrast to the mechanical philosophy of nature, on other levels they communicated without difficulty.

And if such were the case with men like Descartes and Boyle, philosophers who thoroughly explored the implications of the new philosophy of nature, how much more was it so with others to whom the mechanical philosophy was little more than a popular idiom of scientific discourse. Sir Kenneth Digby's pamphlet on *The Cure of Wounds by the Powder of Sympathy* merely plastered a thin veneer of effluvial jargon onto an Hermetic concept.[9] Nicholas Lemery did much the same with van Helmont's realization that an alkali neutralizes an acid, a reaction that became the central feature of Lemery's chemistry. All was expressed in overtly mechanistic terms. Acids became sharp, pointed particles—pins, in effect. The very shape embodied a good part of the activity associated with acid 'spirits'. "I hope no body will offer to dispute whether an *acid* has points or no, seeing every ones experience does demonstrate it," Lemery remarked with untroubled confidence; "they need but taste an *acid* to be satisfied of it, for it pricks the tongue like any thing keen, and finely cut."[10] Alkalis in turn become porous particles —pin cushions, in effect. The basic reaction of Lemery's chemistry, the neutralization of an acid by an alkali, exhibited itself as a pin thrust into a pin cushion. His descriptions of the process suggest that a good part of the Hermetic perception of it survived despite the mechanistic image. When an acid is poured on an alkali salt, it "enters into the pores, and violently divides the parts, whence follows the *Effervescency*. For the points of the *acid,* which are in continual motion, entering into the pores of this *salt,* where there is not space enough for them to move in, therefore they disperse themselves, and break the parts with violence."[11] The mere adoption of mechanistic language had reshaped Lemery's understanding of the reaction less than one might have expected.

Perhaps no example illustrates the survival of Hermetic modes of thought in mechanistic costumes better than John Mayow's nitro-aerial spirit. In keeping with the intellectual temper of the age, Mayow tricked out his nitro-aerial spirit, the very name of which derived from the Paracelsian tradition, in particulate dress, and his essays on it abound in mechanistic figures. No amount of disguise, however, made his nitro-aerial particles cease to be Hermetic active principles. Mayow's argument that combustion and animal life are sustained by nitro-aerial spirit is well-known. Equally interesting is his interpretation of the air's decrease in volume in the experiments he recounted. He saw it, not as the consumption of one component of the air, but as the destruction of its force of elasticity consequent on removal of nitro-aerial particles. The same 'spirit' that supports animal life and combustion also causes air to have a force of elasticity. Mayow contended that it is responsible for vegetable life as well. Not only does it maintain animal heat by fermenting with saline-sulfurous particles in the blood; but by effervescing with other saline-sulfurous particles distributed through the nerves, it also enables animals to contract their muscles and move. An extension of its role in combustion explains how the nitro-aerial spirit in saltpetre causes the explosion of gunpowder, and its connection with saltpetre equally associates it with the activity of spirit of nitre.[12] Mayow did not explore the apparent contradiction of an active principle in the context of a mechanical philosophy of nature, but the mere translation of the nitro-aerial spirit into mechanistic language clearly changed very little in the concept itself.

With the example of Mayow in mind, consider one of Newton's early speculations on the system of nature, "An Hypothesis Explaining the Properties of Light," which he sent to the Royal Society in 1675. The "Hypothesis" posited the existence of an aether diffused through the entire universe. Like air which it resembles, though it is more subtle and more elastic, the aether can condense; and in its condensed form it provides the substance of all the bodies in the world. "Perhaps the whole frame of Nature may be nothing but aether condensed by a fermental principle..."[13] What can condense can also vaporize, of course, and aether from bodies that continually decompose is carried up from earth to replenish the celestial supply, whence an equal quantity is as constantly borne down to be condensed anew. "For nature is a perpetual circulatory worker, generating fluids out of solids, and solids out of fluids, fixed things out of volatile, & volatile out of fixed, subtle out of gross, & gross out of subtle, Some things to ascend & make the upper terrestrial juices, Rivers and the Atmosphere; & by consequence others to descend for a Requital to the former."[14]

The "Hypothesis of Light" has recently been called an alchemical cosmogeny,[15] and certainly this description is hard to deny. The paper pictures the earth as a vast alembic, perpetually distilling its contents into an aetherial spirit which precipitates only to be distilled again. The "vast body of the Earth," he speculated suggestively "...may be every where to the very center in perpetual working..."[16] The hint of vital activity in the references to fermentation repeated itself in the idea that condensed aether was shaped into various forms initially by the Creator, "and ever since by the power of Nature, w[ch] by virtue of the command Increase & Multiply, became a complete Imitation of the copies sett her by the Protoplast." [17] Moreover, the nature he described comes replete with active principles of one sort and another. The corpuscles of light contain a "Principle of Motion," and "the maine flegmatic body of aether" has diffused through it divers "aethereall Spirits" that cause sundry phenomena, much as "the vitall aereall Spirit requisite for the conservation of flame & vitall motions" is diffused through the air.[18] Newton called on the aether, and the aetherial spirits diffused through it, to explain a range of active phenomena not wholly unlike those which Mayow traced to his nitro-aerial particles—gravity, magnetism, static electric phenomena, the cohesion of bodies, elasticity, heat, sense perception, muscular motion, vegetable growth.

If one can describe the "Hypothesis" as an alchemical cosmogeny, however, one can describe it with equal justice as a mechanical system of nature. It shares all the characteristics of standard mechanical philosophies. The aether, which appears so alchemical from one perspective, reveals itself from another as the uniform matter basic to every mechanical system. If the aether causes such actions as electrical and gravitational attractions, it does so by accepted mechanical means, effluvial and particulate mechanisms effecting all the motions. Above all, the explanations of optical phenomena, to which the "Hypothesis" primarily addressed itself, are mechanistic; Newton traced all the changes of direction that a ray of light can undergo, reflections, refractions, diffractions, to pressures arising from the aether's variation in density. In every respect, the "Hypothesis of Light" repeats the pattern I have been suggesting as common in the 17th century, the perpetuation of Hermetic modes of thought within the framework of an overtly mechanistic system.

The "Hypothesis of Light" presented the first organized exposition of Newton's speculations on natural philosophy. It was not their last exposition. Such speculations formed a continuous web that extended throughout his scientific career, offering to the historian the critical key to the understanding of Newton's thought. Sometime in the decade following the "Hypothesis," his conception of nature underwent a fundamental revision which involved the rejection of the aether and its invisible mechanisms, and the substitution for them of forces of attraction and repulsion between material particles. We can best interpret his change of direction by examining it from the perspective offered by the Hermetic and mechanical philosophies. A degree of tension between the two was always present. The animism and the active principles of the Hermetic tradition might be disguised; they could not be wholly assimilated into a mechanical system as the 17th century understood it. It appears to me that the unassimilated Hermetic elements shaped the reformulation of Newton's conception of nature, leading him in the end to an expanded view of a mechanical universe through which concepts of Hermetic origin were permanently built into the structure of modern science.

The phrase 'active principles' continued to appear prominently in Newton's mature system. For the most part, it referred to forces of attraction and repulsion between bodies and between particles of matter. In Query 31, for example, he argued for the necessity of active principles to maintain the quantity of motion in the universe. *Vis inertiae* is wholly passive; it cannot generate motion but can only maintain it. Because of factors such as friction, however, motion constantly tends to run down, and "there is a necessity of conserving and recruiting it by active Principles, such as are the cause of Gravity...and the cause of Fermentation...For we meet with very little Motion in the World, besides what is owing to these active Principles."[19] In some contexts, Newton's use of 'active principles' retains more of the concept's original Hermetic connotations. Attractive powers are not evenly distributed among substances in his view. They are associated especially with acids. "For whatever doth strongly attract, and is strongly attracted, may be call'd an Acid."[20] The vigor with which acids dissolve bodies derives directly from their special strength. An acid that lies hidden in divers substances, such as sulfur, may initiate putrefactions and fermentations, and sulfurous bodies act more strongly on light because of their acidic content. Whereas the refractive power of bodies is generally proportional to their specific gravities, "sulphurous bodies caeteris paribus are most strongly refractive & therefore tis probablie $y^t$ $y^e$ refractory power lies in $y^e$ sulfur & is proportional not to $y^e$ specific weight or density of $y^e$ whole body but to that of $y^e$ sulphur alone."[21] Newton also speculated that corpuscles of light themselves are the ultimate source of active powers in the world.

> Do not bodies & light mutually change into one another? And may not bodies receive their most active powers from the particles of light $w^{ch}$ enter their composition? ...Now since light is the most active of all bodies known to us, & enters the composition of all natural bodies, why may it not be the chief principle of activity in them?[22]

By arguing that attractions are always strongest in proportion to bulk in smaller bodies, Newton went on ostensibly to reduce the active principles to his ordinary concept of force. Nevertheless it is impossible not to recognize other factors in such passages and to feel again something of the earlier tension between Hermetic ideas and the mechanical system in which they were embedded.

It is worthy of note that the animistic suggestions of the "Hypothesis" also survived in Newton's speculations, although he confined his most explicit statements to private papers that he did not publish. Whereas he was content to speak of forces of attraction and repulsion on the scientific level of discourse, he did not believe in the metaphysical reality of such action at a distance. Attractions are apparent only. Every body is immediately present to God, whose infinite presence constitutes infinite space; and God moves bodies about as though they attract each other. Despite his denials, Newton conceived of God virtually as the soul of the world, moving bodies even as the human will moves the body with which it is associated. Matter is passive, receiving motion in proportion to the forces impressed upon it. Such laws of motion are passive also, but active laws exist as well.

> Life & will are active Principles by w^ch we move our bodies, & thence arise other laws of motion unknown to us. And since all matter duly formed is attended with signes of life & all things are framed w^th perfect art & wisdom & Nature does nothing in vain: if there be an universal life & all space be the sensorium of a thinking being who by immediate presence perceives their pictures in the brain, the laws of motion arising from life or will may be on universal extent.[23]

Although such passages are invaluable for the understanding of Newton, they have left little or no imprint on the structure of modern science. The same can hardly be said of the Newtonian concept of force, which became the cornerstone of his mature idea of nature. Throughout his speculations, from his undergraduate notebook to the final revision of the Queries, Newton focused on a set of crucial phenomena that seemed to offer the key to understanding nature. The cohesion of bodies, the expansion of air, capillary action, surface tension in fluids—all appear in association with aetherial mechanisms in the "Hypothesis"; all later found their explication through forces of attraction and repulsion between particles of matter. In addition to these four, a number of chemical phenomena began to hold his attention soon after the "Hypothesis"; and in Query 31, his classic exposition of the forces between bodies, chemical evidence carried the major burden of the argument. In some reactions, heat is generated. Newton believed that heat is the motion of material particles, and he referred its generation to the forces of attraction and repulsion between particles. Most revealing of all was the evidence of what we would call today elective affinities. Already in the "Hypothesis," Newton referred in passing to a "secret principle of unsociableness..." whereby some substances refuse to mix with each other.[24] From the later examples with which he illustrated it, his conception appears to have been influenced by the principles of "congruity" and "incongruity" that Robert Hooke had proposed.[25] Of all the Hermetic elements in the "Hypothesis" none stood in more uneasy relation to the mechanical system. Newton insisted that liquids are disposed to penetrate bodies "on other accounts than their Subtility...," and he repeated the same notion in his letter on chemistry sent to Oldenburg early in 1676.[26] In the manuscript preface and conclusion that he drafted for the first edition of the *Principia,* and in Query 31, Newton referred chemical affinities to forces between particles—forces which are specific to certain substances. The secret principles of sociableness and unsociableness and the later forces were renditions of the attraction of like for like and the rejection of unlike, the occult sympathies and antipathies of the Hermetic tradition.

The development of Newton's conception of Nature followed the fluctuating tension between the Hermetic and the mechanical elements within his thought. The mechanical philosophy provided his access to the world of science; and whatever else he saw in nature at different times, he never ceased to see in it the play of material particles in motion. By the early 1680's, however, the Hermetic influence bade fair to dominate his picture of nature at the expense of the mechanical. Not only was the idea of attractions and repulsions anathema to mechanical philosophers of strict persuasion, but the specificity of the forces he admitted was perhaps more damning. Twenty years later, in Query 31, Newton rejected the charge that attractions are occult qualities and spoke of reducing phenomena to a few general principles. He was deluding himself. His "Hypothesis of Light" had expressed the program of the mechanical philosophy by reducing the composition of all bodies to one matter common to the entire universe and affinities had appeared to be mysterious secret principles in this context. In contrast his specific forces, reflecting the radical nominalism of the Hermetic tradition and implying a multiplicity of irreducible substances, threatened constantly to shatter the unity of natural processes into a myriad of particular agents.

Newton's concept of forces between particles derived initially from the world of terrestrial phenomena, especially chemical reactions. In

1679-80, when he first began seriously to work on the dynamics of orbital motion, he applied his chemical idea of attraction to the cosmos. His solution of the elliptical orbit in 1679-80 did not contain the concept of universal gravitation.[27] Kepler and others had already extended the attraction of like for like to the idea of a gravitational attraction specific to each planet, and Roberval and Hooke had stretched the idea still further to consider the sun and planets as a system of related bodies. There are strong reasons to believe that Newton's celestial dynamics started from such a position. In a correspondence with Flamsteed in 1681 on comets, he refused the suggestion that the two comets of 1680-81 were in fact one comet which reversed its course in the vicinity of the sun. The nearly unanimous judgment of the ages had held that comets are phenomena foreign to the planetary system, and Newton did not consider that the dynamics of planetary motion worked out in the previous year might apply to such alien intruders. Even in 1684, when he wrote the tract *De motu,* effectively the first draft of the *Principia,* he had not yet arrived at the concept of universal gravitation. *De motu* confined itself primarily to the mechanics of orbital motion, and the few additional problems it included worked toward a generalized mechanics but not toward the idea of universal gravitation. Only in revising *De motu* did he finally conclude that weight is uniformly proportional to mass, an essential element in the concept of universal gravitation.[28] Meanwhile other evidence was rolling in. In contrast to his letters of 1681, the first draft of *De motu* had treated comets as planets. Newton soon realized that Kepler's third law implies the uniform attraction of all planetary matter to the sun, so that weight is proportional to mass in planets as it is in terrestrial bodies, while the applicability of the third law to the satellites of Jupiter implies both the uniformity of their attraction to Jupiter and the uniform attraction of the entire Jovian system to the sun. Finally, the proposition at which he arrived in 1685 about the attraction of homogeneous spheres can be valid only if every particle of matter attracts every other particle uniformly. Here was a concept of attraction radically different from the one with which he had started. Although it utilized the idea of force, it rejected the specificity of force and found a new bond of union with the mechanical tradition by returning to the notion of the uniformity of matter.[29]

The cry of occult qualities greeted the publication of the *Principia.* In more than one sense, the mechanists who raised the cry were justified. Not only did the concept of attraction violate their sense of philosophic propriety, but the origin of the concept was the very Hermetic tradition they suspected. Imagine their outrage had Newton also published his speculations on specific forces in the *Principia* as he originally planned. The champions of mechanical orthodoxy failed to realize what benefit the Hermetic idea could bestow on the mechanical philosophy of nature. Like them, Newton believed in a mechanical universe populated by particles of matter in motion. By adding force to their bleak ontology, however, he enabled science to transcend the level of verbal mechanisms, in the emptiness of which 17th century science nearly stifled itself, and to reach the level of quantitative rational mechanics. Nowhere was the possibility more evident than in the *Principia's* concept of universal gravitation, but in principle it was true of his specific attractions as well. Newton saw them all in quantitative terms. Experiments with capillary action attempted to measure the attraction between glass and the ascending liquid.[30] Comparisons of optical paths with the trajectories of projectiles allowed the attractive force of a corpuscle of light to be measured in terms of gravitational force.[31] Whereas dynamical thought in the 17th century had generally associated force with a moving body, Newton defined force as an external action that effects a proportional change in the inertial motion of a body. The attractions and repulsions with which his philosophy of nature dealt synchronized harmoniously with the pattern of his quantified dynamics. In such terms the active principles of the Hermetic tradition could lead the relatively crude mechanical philosophy of 17th century science to a higher plane of sophistication. The Hermetic elements in Newton's thought were not in the end antithetical to the scientific enterprise. Quite the contrary, by wedding the two traditions, the Hermetic and the mechanical, to each other, he established the family line that claims as its direct descendant the very science that sneers today uncomprehendingly at the occult ideas associated with Hermetic philosophy.

## References

[1] Let us have no pretences. My article, "Isaac Newton: Religious Rationalist of Mystic?" *Review of Religion*, XXII (1957-8), 155-70, is not last on the scale of asperity in its rejection of such claims. This present article revises at least some of the assertions made in the earlier one. Whatever other merits it may have, the earlier article does mention much of the literature in which Newton's asserted mysticism and its relation to his natural philosophy is discussed.

[2] Lord Keynes, "Newton, the Man," *Newton Tercentenary Celebrations*, published by the Royal Society, Cambridge, 1947, 27-34; McGuire, J.E., and Rattansi,

P.M., "Newton and the 'Pipes of Pan'," *Notes and Records of the Royal Society of London,* XXI (1966), 108-43; McGuire, J. E., "Body and Void in Newton's De Mundi Systemate: Some New Sources," *Archive for History of Exact Sciences,* III (1966), 206-48; McGuire, J. E., "Force, Active Principles, and Newton's Invisible Realm," *Ambix,* XV (1968), 154-208. *Cf.* also an article based on published sources rather than manuscripts: Kubrin, David, "Newton and the Cyclical Cosmos: Providence and the Mechanical Philosophy," *Journal of the History of Ideas,* XXVIII (1967), 325-46.

[3]In an article not yet published, "Hermeticism and Historiography: An Apology for the Internal History of Science," Mary Hesse argues against the importance of the Hermetic tradition by contending that it became increasingly sterile during the 17th century. My present article implies that such a judgment, even if true, does not negate the influence of Hermetic ideas.

[4]*The Works of Francis Bacon,* ed. James Spedding, Robert Leslie Ellis, and Douglas Denon Heath, 15 vols, Boston, 1870-82, V, 63.

[5]Galileo, *Dialogue Concerning the Two Chief World Systems,* trans. Stillman Drake, Berkeley, 1953, 462.

[6]Newton, *Opticks,* New York, 1952, 388.

[7]*Météores; Oeuvres de Descartes,* ed. Charles Adam and Paul Tannery, 12 vols., Paris, 1897-1910, VI, 321. *Principles of Philosophy,* IV, 187; *Ibid.,* IX, 309.

[8]*The Works of the Honourable Robert Boyle,* ed. Thomas Birch, 5 vols., London, 1744, II, 474. On the relationship of van Helmont and Boyle see Debus, Allen G., "Fire Analysis and the Elements in the Sixteenth and the Seventeenth Centuries", *Annals of Science,* XXIII (1967), 127-47.

[9]Digby, Sir Kenneth, *A Late Discourse Made in a Solemn Assembly of Nobles and Learned Men at Montpellier in France, Touching the Cure of Wounds by the Powder of Sympathy,* 3rd ed., London, 1660.

[10]Lemery, Nicholas, *A Course of Chymistry,* trans. from the French, 3rd. ed., London, 1698, 24-5.

[11]*Ibid.,* 22.

[12]Mayow, John, *Medico-physical Works,* trans. A. Crum Brown and Leonard Dobbin, Edinburgh, 1907. See especially the first treatise, *On Sal Nitrum and Nitro-aërial spirit,* the second treatise, *On Respiration,* and the fourth treatise, *On Muscular Motion.* For the background to the concept see Debus, Allen G., "The Paracelsian Aerial Niter," *Isis,* LV (1964), 43-61.

[13]*The Correspondence of Isaac Newton,* ed. H. W. Turnbull and J. F. Scott, 4 vols., continuing, Cambridge, 1959, I, 364.

[14]*Ibid.,* I, 366.

[15]McGuire, J. E., "Transmutation and Immutability: Newton's Doctrine of Physical Qualities," *Ambix,* XIV (1967), 84-6.

[16]Newton, *Correspondence,* I, 365-6.

[17]*Ibid.*, I, 364.

[18]*Ibid.*, I, 370, 364-5.

[19]Newton, *Opticks*, 399.

[20]*De natura acidorum; Isaac Newton's Papers & Letters on Natural Philosophy,* ed. I. Bernard Cohen, Cambridge, Mass., 1958, 258.

[21]From a MS. connected with the first edition of the *Opticks;* University Library Cambridge, *Add. MS. 3970.3,* f 337.

[22]From a MS. connected with the Latin edition of the *Opticks* (1706); *Ibid.,* f. 292.

[23]*Ibid.,* 3970.9, f. 619.

[24]Newton, *Correspondence,* I, 368.

[25]Hooke, Robert, *An Attempt for the Explication of the Phaenomena, Observable in an Experiment Published by the Honourable Robert Boyle, Esq; in the XXXV. Experiment of his Epistolical Discourse Touching the Aire,* London, 1661. Virtually the entire pamphlet, with some additional material, was included in the *Micrographia,* London, 1665, 11-31.

[26]Newton, *Correspondence,* I, 368, and II, 1.

[27]Herivel, J. W., *The Background to Newton's Principia,* Oxford, 1965, 246-54.

[28]In a paper of revisions to the third version of *De motu* that probably derives from the early months of 1685, Newton said that the quantity of matter in a body is usually proportional to its weight. He proposed an experiment with pendulums to measure the quantity of matter; when two equal pendulums with bobs of equal weight are set swinging, the quantities of matter in the two bobs will be inversely proportional to the number of swings in equal times. Apparently he carried out his own proposed experiment, and in a blank space opposite the original passage he recorded that "the heaviness of gravitating bodies is proportional to their quantity of matter...The oscillations of two equal pendulums of the same weight are counted and the bulk of matter in each case will be inversely as the number of oscillations made in the same time. But careful experiments made on gold, silver, lead, glass, sand, common salt, wood, and wheat always led to the same number of oscillations." *Ibid,* 319.

[29]As the later publication of Query 31 attests, Newton never reconciled the two contradictory ideas of matter involved in the concepts of specific forces on the one hand and universal gravitation on the other. In greater or lesser prominence, the contradiction continued as a dichotomy between chemical and physical conceptions of matter until the twentieth century, when the understanding of atomic structure resolved both into the heterogenity of ultimate particles.

[30]Using two sheets of glass that meet at a very small angle, Newton measured the attraction exerted on a drop of orange juice by inclining the entire apparatus until the capillary attraction that urged the drop toward the concourse of the two sheets held the weight of the drop in equilibrium. He concluded that the

attraction varies inversely as the distances between the sheets of glass for constant areas of attracting surface. At very short distances the attraction could become immense. At the distance that Newton believed, on the basis of his optical work, to be the diameter of the smallest particles in bodies, the capillary attraction exerted over a circular surface one inch in diameter would be great enough to support a column of water two or three furlongs in length. *Opticks,* 392-4.

[31]He concluded that the attractive force of a corpuscle of light is $10^{15}$ times as powerful in proportion to its quantity of matter as the gravity of a projectile. *Ibid.,* 320-1.

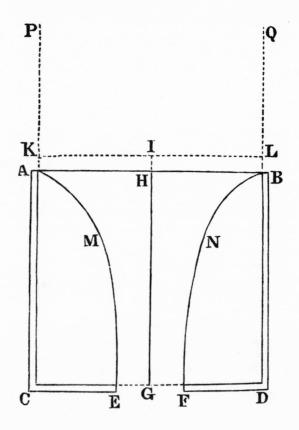

# 34

# Newton and Keplerian Inertia:
# an Echo of Newton's Controversy with Leibniz

## I. BERNARD COHEN

NEWTON'S *Principia* shows the reader, almost from the very start, the author's unbounded admiration for Galileo and his reserve in giving credit to Kepler for his major discoveries. Thus Galileo is alleged to have known at least the first two of the three *Axiomata sive Leges Motus*[1] on which the *Principia* is based, whereas Kepler is not even mentioned when Newton introduces the first two of the three Keplerian laws of planetary motion[2] (elliptical orbits, and equal areas in equal times).[3] Kepler appears in the *Principia* only in two limited rôles: as the discoverer of the third or harmonic law, and as an observer of comets. He is not even given credit for having recognized the generality of his law: that it applies to the system of Jupiter's satellites as well as to the circulation of the planets about the Sun.[4]

It is, therefore, of great interest to observe that in his own copy of the second edition of the *Principia*, published in Cambridge in 1713, Newton inserted a slip of paper containing a note about Kepler and dynamics, an addition intended for a future edition or reprint, if one were called for. With a minor variation, he then copied out onto the text page the contents of this note. An addition was to be made to the discussion of Definition III, of *materiae vis insita*, of which Newton had said, in the *Principia*:

> Haec semper proportionalis est suo corpori, neque differt quicquam ab inertia Massae, nisi in modo concipiendi....Unde etiam vis insita nomine significantissimo vis inertiae dici possit.
>
> ["This force is ever proportional to the body whose force it is; and differs nothing from the inactivity of the Mass, but in our manner of conceiving it....Upon which account, this *Vis Insita*, may, by a most significant name, be called *Vis Inertiae* or Force of Inactivity."[5]]

This *materiae vis insita* was the *potentia* by which every body, of and by itself, insofar as it can,[6] *perseverat in statu suo vel quiescendi vel movendi uniformiter in directum* (perseveres in its state of rest [resting] or of moving uniformly in a right line). It was to this attribute of *materiae vis insita* that Newton wished to make an addition. He wrote, on that slip of paper which is still in his copy of the second edition,

> Ad pag. 2 lin. 9 Adde;
> Non intelligo vim inertiae Kepleri qua corpora ad quietem tendunt, sed vim manendi in eodem seu quiescendi seu movendi statu.
>
> ["I do not mean the Keplerian force of inertia by which bodies incline to rest, but a force maintaining (them) in the same state of rest or of motion."][7]

This note makes it evident that, at least after 1713 (when the second edition of the *Principia* was published), Newton was acquainted with Kepler's concept of inertia, and understood the sense in which it differed from his own.[8]

Newton, however, did not introduce this comment about Kepler into the third and final edition of the *Principia,* published in London in 1726. And so we are led to ask why. Possibly Newton may have had a change of heart, and so decided to cancel this proposed addition, notable for the fact that it occurs twice in his annotated copy—once on a slip of paper and once on the text page. I have found one other occurrence of this same statement among the Newton MSS relating to the *Principia* in the Portsmouth Collection, on a fragment of a letter (or possibly an envelope).[9] Here Newton begins the sentence exactly as he has done in the one quoted above, "Non intelligo vim inertiae Kepleri..." and continues in identical fashion almost to the very end. But now he has written "...in eodem quiescendi [statu *del.*] vel movendi statu"—which is exactly equivalent in meaning to the other version. What is interesting, however, is that after having written out this alternative version, Newton proceeded to strike out "Kepleri" and to substitute in its place the word "aliquorum": thus he would now make a contrast between his own concept of "vis inertiae" and that of "some men" who are not specified. Presumably "aliquorum" would have been intended to include both Leibniz and Kepler.

In addition to wondering why Newton suppressed this proposed emendation (he did not cancel it!), we are also led to ask why he had introduced it in the first place. There is no certain evidence that enables us to specify Newton's motivation for either of these acts, but I believe it very probable or likely that they were both related specifically to the quarrel with Leibniz. It may be pointed out that not only is Newton's statement about Kepler interesting to us for its double appearance in Newton to have been more favorable to Kepler than to himself. Cer-projected alteration by Newton in any known copy of the *Principia* to either the text of Definition III or the paragraph discussing it.[10]

Newton's comment suggests that he was led to compare and contrast his own concept of inertia and Kepler's after reading a provocative re-mark, perhaps a criticism of his own definition of inertia as it appeared in the *Principia,* or a comment attributing the inertial concept to Kepler rather than Newton, or even a comparison that might have seemed to Newton to have been more favorable to Kepler than to himself. Cer-tainly Newton was noted for his over-sensitivity to any form of direct or indirect criticism, and it would have been in line with his customary behaviour so to react at once. It is not possible, however, that the criti-cism or comment that Newton had encountered would have provided his first acquaintance with Kepler's concept of "natural inertia", although we do not know for certain how and when Newton first may have learned the fundamentals of Kepler's dynamics.[10] So far as is known, Newton never owned any of Kepler's books; there is none listed in the catalogue of books belonging to Newton's library.[12] Nor have I found any manu-script annotations made by Newton which would show that he had been studying or reading any book of Kepler's, in the way that the notes in a commonplace book suggest he had been reading Salusbury's English translation of Galileo's *Dialogo.*[13] Presumably, therefore, Newton's isolated statement concerning Kepler and inertia was not merely the result of Newton's study of the writings of his illustrious German pre-decessor. Newton's general ignorance of Kepler's dynamics is not only displayed in the first edition of the *Principia;* the situation is in fact unaltered in the later ones. But for the MS note that I found in Newton's copy of the *Principia,* it might have been believed that Newton had never learned anything about Keplerian dynamics.

The question, then, is why for a short time around 1713 Newton held it to be important to criticize Kepler for his concept of inertia by showing how inadequate or limited that concept is. The answer, I believe, is to be found in a discussion of inertia by Leibniz, in which Kepler and Descartes are mentioned by name while Newton is ignored—although Newton is referred to elsewhere in the same book, and in fact is cited rather prominently for his advocacy of a doctrine which Leibniz condemns on philosophical grounds.

The book in question is Leibniz's *Theodicy,* or—to give it its full title—*Essais de Théodicée sur la bonté de dieu, la liberté de l'homme et l'origine du mal,* published in Amsterdam by Isaac Troyel in 1710. In the preliminary essay, "Discours de la conformité de la foy avec la raison," Leibniz criticizes Newton for basing his physics on the concept of forces acting "at a distance." "Il est vray," Leibniz declares (§19), "que, depuis quelque temps, les philosophes modernes ont rejetté l'operation naturelle immediate d'un corps sur un autre corps éloigné," and he affirms, "j'avoue que je suis de leur sentiment." Everyone, however, Leibniz was forced to admit, did not reject this concept: "Cependant l'operation en distance vient d'être rehabilitée en Angleterre par l'excellent M. Newton, qui soutient qu'il est de la nature des corps de s'attirer et de se peser les uns sur les autres, à proportion de la masse d'un chacun et des rayons d'attraction qu'il reçoit."

The above statement of Leibniz's disagreement with Newton's position occurs on page 27. A little later on,[13] Leibniz treats of inertia as a concept figuring in the physics of Kepler and of Descartes, without either mentioning Newton or referring to his *Principia.* Leibniz writes:

> 30. Le celebre Kepler et apres luy M. Descartes (dans ses Lettres) ont parlé de *l'inertie naturelle des corps;* et c'est quelque chose qu'on peut considerer comme un parfaite image et même comme un échantillon de la limitation originale des creatures, pour faire voir que la privation fait le formel des imperfections et des inconveniens qui se trouvent dans la substance aussi bien que dans ses actions. Posons que le courant d'une même riviere emporte avec soy plusieurs bateaux, qui ne different entre eux que dans la charge, les uns étant chargés de bois, les autres de pierre, et les uns plus, les autres moins. Cela étant, il arrivera que les bateaux les plus chargés iront plus lentement que les autres, pourvu qu'on suppose que le vent, ou la rame, ou quelque autre moyen semblable ne les aide point. Ce n'est pas proprement la pesanteur qui est la cause de ce retardement, puisque les bateaux descendent au lieu de monter, mais c'est la même cause qui augmente aussi la pesanteur dans les corps qui ont plus de densité, c'est à dire qui sont moins spongieux et plus chargés de matiere qui leur est propre; car celle qui passe à travers des pores, ne recevant pas le même mouvement, ne doit pas entrer en ligne de compte. [Part I, §30]

This paragraph exhibits a monument of confusion, chiefly because of a bad example, with indefinite conditions. Certainly, if the barges or ships were moored side-by-side and then the hawsers holding them in place were to be cut, we would expect to find the lighter ones initially moving forward ahead of the heavier ones. The reason is, according to Newton's dynamics, that the same force (the current of the river) will—*caeteris paribus* (the ships having the same size and shape,[14] and there being no aid to motion from wind or oars)—produce different accelerations. The more heavily laden ships (greater mass) will thus, in any given short time, have a smaller acceleration than the others (according to Newton's Second Law) and will acquire a smaller speed. In a time depending on a variety of circumstances, all vessels will attain a maximum speed, the speed of the current itself.[15] Hence, as a general statement, Leibniz's conclusion (that the more heavily laden boats "iront plus lentement que les autres") is wrong. It is true only at the start of the motion, or for some limited time after the ships begin to move. Our Newtonian explanation of the Leibnizian example invokes the concept of "mass" or "inertia" as a measure of resistance to acceleration, not to motion. Hence it is necessary to add to this example two major conditions: the start of motion from a state of rest,[15] and a specification of the time during which the acceleration takes place.

Leibniz appears to be saying that force produces motion, and not that force produces acceleration; and that motion (speed) is proportional to a motive force (the river current), and in some inverse proportion to the resistance.[16] This is rather pre-Newtonian physics, a neo-Aristotelian law of motion, modified only by Kepler's concept of inertia and his identification of inertia with resistance. That is, Leibniz is using inertia in the Keplerian sense of a laziness in matter, an "inert-ness," a propensity of bodies to be at rest and to stay at rest (anywhere in the universe) unless a motive force acts upon them.[17] Newton was quite correct in thus distinguishing his concept from this one, since his "force" of inertia did not oppose motion and thus tend to keep bodies at rest; rather he posited inertia (or the "force of inertia") as one that maintains bodies in whatever state they may happen to be—whether of rest or of moving in a straight line at constant speed.[18]

Furthermore, according to Leibniz, the difference in motion of the two boats is due not so much to their weights, properly speaking, as to that same cause which also increases the weight of bodies with greater density. Presumably Leibniz has reference here to bodies of identical bulk or volume, but different densities. But he then goes on to discuss the receipt of movement in relation to porosity, which appears as a digression from the original subject of inertia under discussion. Rather than explore here the vagaries of this particular explanation of Leibniz, let us turn to a later statement in the *Theodicy,* in which there is yet another reference to inertia and to Kepler, one which states expressly and unambiguously the concept of inertia as resistance to motion which Newton attributes to Kepler in his manuscript note:

> 380....Kepler, Mathematicien moderne des plus excellens, a reconnu une espece d'imperfection dans la matiere, lors même qu'il n'y a point de mouvement dereglé: c'est ce qu'il appele son *inertie naturelle,* qui luy donne une resistance au mouvement, par laquelle une plus grande masse reçoit moins de vitesse d'une même force. Il y a de la solidité dans cette remarque, & je m'en suis servi utilement cy dessus pour avoir une comparaison qui montrât comment l'imperfection originale des creatures donne des bornes à l'action du créateur, qui tend au bien. Mais comme la matiere est elle même un effect de Dieu, elle ne fournit qu'une comparaison et un exemple, et ne sauroit être la source même du mal, et de l'imperfection.[19]

Once again there can be no doubt that "natural inertia," as conceived by Kepler, is said by Leibniz to be a resistance to movement (hence a tendency to be at rest or to come to rest) and is not the Newtonian tendency to maintain a given state whether of rest or of movement, so long as the latter is uniform and rectilinear. Furthermore, in line with Aristotelian dynamics, applied to the Keplerian concept of inertia, Leibniz asserts without qualification that the speed given to a body by a force is less the greater its inertia, or its resistance to motion. We may well be astonished to see Leibniz in 1710 still advocating such a basic principle of neo-Aristotelian or neo-Scholastic physics (that, to express it in a simple equation, speed $= \dfrac{\text{motive force}}{\text{resistance}}$); and to find that he should do so while mentioning Descartes, from whose law of inertia in his *Principia philosophiae* Newton without doubt derived his own law of inertia for his own *Principia philosophiae*.[20]

The example given by Leibniz of ships being moved by a stream of water takes on a special significance when related to the Leibnizian celestial mechanics, as expounded for example in his *Tentamen,* or "Essay on the Causes of the Motions of the Heavenly Bodies."[21] This work was composed and published by Leibniz in haste after reading the review of the *Principia* in the *Acta Eruditorum* and before he had seen Newton's book; he wished to establish his priority for certain demonstrations which he said he had conceived independently some time earlier.[22] This essay is largely Keplerian and Cartesian. Newton was angered by this "Essay," which he found to have no merit and to contain many errors. Even if Leibniz had not seen the *Principia,* but only the "epitome of it...printed in the Leipzig *Acta,*" Newton said, "he ought nevertheless to have seen it [the book] before he published his own thoughts concerning these same matters, and this so that he might not err through haste in a new and difficult subject, or by stealing unjustly from Newton what he had discovered, or by annoyingly repeating what Newton had already said before...."[23]

Leibniz's "Essay" opens with an expression of undisguised admiration for a single scientist: Johannes Kepler, "that incomparable man, whom the fates had watched over that he might be the first among mortals to publish the laws of the heavens, the truth of things, and the principles of the gods."[24] Kepler had found the three laws of planetary motion, fundamental to any discussion of the mechanism of the universe. But even Kepler, said Leibniz:

> ...was not yet able to assign the causes to so many and so uniform truths, either because his mind was hampered by belief in Intelligences or inexplicable sympathetic radiations, or because a more profound geometry and science of motions were not yet as advanced in his time as they are now. Nevertheless, he revealed the way of inquiring for the reasons. For it is to him that we owe the first proof of the true cause of gravity and of the law of nature on which gravity depends, that rotating bodies tend to recede from their centers along the tangent, and thus if stems or bits of straw swim in water, and if the water, by the rotation of the vessel, moves in a vortex, the water, being denser than the stems, and therefore being forced away from the center more strongly than the stems, will push the stems toward the center...[25]

Of course, Kepler did not have the whole key to the mechanism of the universe, and "he was still somewhat in doubt, and ignorant of his own riches, and insufficiently aware of how many things follow therefrom, both in physics and especially in astronomy." Leibniz stated unequivocally that "Descartes later used [Kepler's results] brilliantly, although, as is his custom, he concealed their author." Leibniz meant that Descartes had taken over the Keplerian concept of the vortex, not that Descartes had used Kepler's laws of planetary motion.

In the *Tentamen* (or "Essay"), Leibniz used a set of primary postulates of celestial mechanics based on the Keplerian-Cartesian concept of fluid vortex: a planet "must be driven along by the motion of an ambient fluid." Another example used by Leibniz was "Torricelli's opinion…that the entire aether, together with the planets, is driven around the sun by the motion of the sun around its own centre, as water is moved by a stick rotated about its own axis in the middle of a vessel at rest; and like bits of straw or stems swimming in water, stars nearer the centre revolve more quickly."[26]

Hence we may see that when, in the *Theodicy*, Leibniz gave an example of ships being driven along by a fluid, he was invoking an example similar to the motion of planets being carried along in their orbits by a fluid vortex—and this must surely have served to remind Newton of the *Tentamen*. Newton, who knew the *Tentamen* thoroughly, could not have helped but associate Leibniz with what he considered the erroneous scientific (vortical) principles of Kepler as well as of Descartes. When he read the statements about Kepler in the *Theodicy*, at the time when he was in full tilt against Leibniz, it would have been a very natural reaction for him to have contrasted Kepler's inertia and his own, and to have disassociated himself from Kepler's concepts.

Newton owned a copy of Leibniz's *Theodicy*, which may be found today in the library of Trinity College, Cambridge, in that portion of Newton's personal library presented to Trinity College some twenty-five years ago. Newton's copy of the *Theodicy* was distributed in England by an English publisher, although the text is in French and the book itself was published in Amsterdam. This copy bears both the Huggins and Barnsley ("Philosophemur") bookplates.[27] Three works by Leibniz have been bound together, apparently by the bookseller, since there is bound in (at the end of the volume) a fourth item of 16 pages in length: *A CATALOGUE of some Books sold by* WILLIAM INNYS, *at the Prince's-Arms in St. Paul's Church-Yard*. William Innys was the publisher of the second edition (1717) of Newton's *Opticks;* William and John Innys, publishers to the Royal Society, issued the second Latin edition (1719) and the third and fourth English editions (1721, 1730) of the *Opticks* and also the third and final edition (1726) of Newton's *Principia*.

I have found no evidence as to when Newton may have obtained his copy of Leibniz's *Theodicy*. But in 1710, when that book was published, Newton was certainly very much interested in anything and everything that Leibniz had written. The Newton-Leibniz controversy was then going full tilt. The controversy between these two men was not confined to the question of priority in the invention of the calculus, but was also extended to proper principles of dynamics and the bases of true religion. In 1712, in the course of preparing the second edition of the *Principia*, Roger Cotes and Newton corresponded about the criticism of Newtonian dynamics in some letters of Leibniz and the Dutch scientist Nicolas Hartsoeker; published twice before in French, these letters had just been printed for the third time, now in English translation.[28] This publication drew from Newton's pen a letter to the editor, which was not printed, but a partial reply is to be found in Cotes' Preface to the second edition of the *Principia* and in the General Scholium Newton then wrote as a conclusion to the treatise. Before long Leibniz had denounced the Newtonian philosophy to the Princess of Wales and this produced yet another controversy, this one carried on between Leibniz and Samuel Clarke as principals.[29] In 1714, one year after the publication of both the *Commercium Epistolicum* (the Newtonian statement of charges against Leibniz[30]) and the second edition of the *Principia*, Newton wrote and published an anonymous *Recensio libri*, describing the *Commercium Epistolicum* and referring to Leibniz's criticism of Newton in both the *Theodicy* and the letters to Hartsoeker. The *Recensio* also dealt with Leibniz's *Tentamen*.

Newton was fully aware that in the *Tentamen* Leibniz had adopted a position contrary to his own about gravitation. In his personal copy of the *Theodicy*, he called attention to this passage on page 27, by folding a corner of the page so that the tip of the triangular fold pointed to the offensive sentence. This was one of Newton's ways of indicating passages of signficance in the books he owned. So we are not surprised to find that he similarly folded down the page where Leibniz referred to Kepler's concept of inertia and invoked the example of the ships moved by a river current.

In 1714, when Newton published the *Recensio Libri*, his last major fulmination against Leibniz, he might very well have entered the note into his copy of the second edition of the *Principia* to dissociate the Newtonian *vis inertiae* (or *vis insita materiae*) as completely as possible from the "natural inertia" postulated by Kepler and so conspicuously lauded by Leibniz. Thus he would make plain in his *Principia* the degree to which he was as far removed from the physics of Kepler as he was from the physics of Descartes. We have no way of knowing why, once having decided to add to any new edition of the *Principia* a contrast between Keplerian and Newtonian inertia, Newton did not do so. Unlike other

emendations once proposed and later withdrawn, this one is not can-
celled. In 1725-1726, when the third edition was being prepared for
the press, Leibniz had been dead for about a decade; presumably his
endorsement of a Keplerian physical concept was no longer of any consequence for Newton. Happily, Newton did not then alter his *Principia*
by adding an explicit disparagement of Kepler's physics to the implicit
denial of Kepler's primary discovery of the elliptical orbits of planets and
the law of areas.

## References

[1] In the Scholium to the Laws of Motion, at the beginning of the *Principia*, Newton
says: "By the two first Laws and the first two Corollaries, Galileo discover'd that
the descent of bodies observ'd the duplicate ratio of the time, and that the motion
of projectiles was in the curve of a Parabola...." All quotations from the *Principia*
are taken from Andrew Motte's translation, *The mathematical principles of natural
philosophy by Sir Isaac Newton,* translated into English by Andrew Motte, 1729,
with an introduction by I. Bernard Cohen, London, 1968.

[2] The area law and the elliptical shape of the orbits are both discussed extensively
in Book I, where Kepler's name does not appear. In Book III (on "The system
of the world"), the area law appears again in Phaenomenon I, Phaen. II, Phaen.
V, and Phaen. VI. The harmonic law for Jupiter's satellites appears in Phaen. I,
for those of Saturn in Phaen. II. Phaen. IV is devoted to the harmonic law for
the "five primary Planets"; Newton says, "This proportion, first observ'd by Kepler,
is now receiv'd by all astronomers." In the first edition (1687), these "Phaenomena" were included among the "Hypotheses" at the beginning of Book III,
and did not include the harmonic law for the satellites of Saturn, since Newton
referred then only to the single satellite discovered by Huygens and not to the
others discovered by Cassini (first mentioned in the second edition of 1713).

[3] In a tract *De motu...*, written just before Newton began to write the *Principia,*
he did give explicit credit to Kepler when he mentioned the elliptical orbits of
planets and the area law. A scholium to Prob. 2 reads: "Therefore the major
planets revolve in ellipses having a focus in the centre of the Sun; and the
radius-vectors to the Sun describe areas proportional to the times, exactly as
Kepler supposed." Quoted from the translation by A. R. Hall and Marie Boas
Hall, *Unpublished scientific papers of Isaac Newton,* Cambridge, 1962, (253),
277.

[4] The extension of the harmonic law to the system of Jupiter's satellites occurs
in the *Epitome astronomiae Copernicanae.*

[5] Motte's translation; see note 1 *supra.* "Inertia" was introduced into the exact
sciences as a technical expression by Johannes Kepler. See further, note 17 *infra.*

[6] On the sense of "quantum in se est," as used here by Newton (and translated
by me, not by "as much as in it lies," but by "of and by itself, insofar as it can"),
see my article, " 'Quantum in se est': Newton's concept of inertia in relation to

Descartes and Lucretius," *Notes & Records of the Royal Society of London, XIX* (1964), 131-155.

[7]The copy of the second edition (1713) of the *Principia* in which Newton entered this remark is at present in the Library of Trinity College, Cambridge. All of the corrections, emendations, and additions which Newton made in his personal copies of the first and second editions of the *Principia* (there are two of each, one annotated, the other interleaved and annotated, so making four in all) are included among the variant readings in (ed.) Koyré, Alexandre, Cohen, I. B., and Whitman, Anne, *Isaac Newton's Philosophiae naturalis principia mathematica, the third edition (1726) with variant readings,* 2 vols., Cambridge and Cambridge, 1972.

[8]See Cohen, I.B., *Introduction to Newton's 'Principia',* Cambridge and Cambridge, 1971, Ch. II, §4. This topic is explored further in Chapter II of my *Transformations of scientific ideas,* based on the Wiles Lectures, delivered at Queen's University, Belfast, 1966, to be published by Cambridge University Press in 1973.

[9]University Library, Cambridge, MS Add. 3965, f. 423.

[10]See the edition referred to in note 7 *supra* 40-41.

[11]On Newton's knowledge of Kepler's Laws of planetary motion, see Whiteside, D. T., "Newton's early thoughts on planetary motion: a fresh look," *British Journal for the History of Science, II* (1964), 117-37.

I have found that Newton encountered Kepler's concept of "natural intertia" (and the expression "natural inertia") in an edition of Descartes's correspondence, which he read during his student days; the evidence for this statement may be found in Chapter II of my *Transformations of scientific ideas,* cited in note 8 *supra.*

[12]For the books in Newton's library, see the "Inventory" made by the executors of his estate, published in De Villamil, R., *Newton: the man,* London, (1931). Newton did own a copy of Jeremiah Horrox's *Opera posthuma,* which he had received as a gift in 1672 from John Collins.

On the date of this edition, and some bibliographical aspects of it, see Rigaud, S. P., *Correspondence of scientific men of the seventeenth century,* Oxford, 1851, II, 149-50; on the gift to Newton, see *ibid.,* 320-321.

[13]See Herivel, John, *The background to Newton's Principia,* Oxford, 1965, 183 sqq., 189. Herivel says he is "indebted to the late H. W. Turnbull for pointing out that almost all of the original data for Newton's calculations…must have come from Galileo's *Dialogue,* most probably from Salusbury's translation."

[14]So as to eliminate any effects of friction between the ships and the moving water.

[15]Or from some initial speed less than the final speed.

[16]If Leibniz had been using a concept current in the late 17th and early 18th centuries, in which the force acts impulsively, then he would have been correct in assuming that "force" is proportional to the momentum it produces ("F" $\alpha$ MV). That is, if the time in which the "force" acts is infinitesimally small, so that the "force" acts "instantaneously," as when a blow is given to a ball by a tennis

racquet, then—if there is *no* external resistance whatever—the velocity V produced in each of several bodies by any given such impulsive "force" F will be inversely proportional to its mass M. This is, in fact, the form in which Newton stated the Second Law of Motion in the *Principia;* he assumed that a succession of such blows or impulsive force-action would become, in the limit (as the time between them approached zero), a continuous force, and he constantly used and even stated explicitly a "derived" form of the Second Law stating that the magnitude and direction of the change in momentum per unit time is proportional to the force acting.

It is possible that Leibniz had been thinking of an impulsive force, in which case his illustration of "natural inertia" would almost have made sense. But the action of a river-current on a boat is not impulsive; certainly no one could conceive this action to be single and instantaneous and not continuous. Even if the river-current were to exert a single blow, and then (by a miracle) the current were to cease, the result would be a momentary motion resisted by the friction between boat and water; the motion would cease almost at once.

[17]I have discussed Kepler's concept of inertia in the Wiles Lectures (see note 8 *supra*). See, further, Koyré, Alexandre, *La révolution astronomique*, Paris, 1961, Kepler, ch. 5; also Rosen, Edward, "Kepler's *Harmonics* and his concept of inertia,"*American Journal of Physics, XXXIV* (1966), 610-613; also Appendix I ("Kepler's concept of inertia") to Rosen's translation, *Kepler's Somnium, the dream, or posthumous work on lunar astronomy*, Madison, 1967.

[18]Newton's use of the word "force" in relation to inertia ("vis inertiae") is confusing to a modern reader. But, as Newton himself explained (*Opticks*, Query 31; Dover, edition, 397), this *"Vis inertiae* is a passive Principle by which Bodies persist in their Motion or Rest" and it thus cannot ever act by "putting Bodies into Motion," or changing their state of motion or of rest. The *vis inertiae* differs in this feature from what Newton called "active"forces, which may produce or alter a body's "quantity of motion" (or momentum) according to the Second Law of Motion.

[19]This quotation, and the above quotations from Leibniz's *Theodicy*, are taken from (ed.) Gerhardt, C. J.: *Die philosophischen Schriften von Gottfried Wilhelm Leibniz*, Zweite Abtheilung, Sechster Band, Hildesheim, 1965—photo-reprint.

[20]For evidence concerning this point, see my article, " 'Quantum in se est,' " cited in note 6 *supra*.

[21]"Tentamen de motuum coelestium causis," *Acta Eruditorum*, Febr. 1689, 82-96 (reprinted in Leibniz's *Math. Schriften*, XI, 135-144).

[22]See the Royal Society's edition of *The correspondence of Isaac Newton*, III, (ed.) Turnbull, H. W., Cambridge, 1961, 3, 5.

[23]Printed in Latin in (ed.) Edleston, J., *The correspondence of Sir Isaac Newton and Professor Cotes*, London and Cambridge, 1850, 308-309; quoted from a translation made by E. J. Collins.

[24]Quoted from a translation of Leibniz's *Tentamen* made by E. J. Collins.

[25]*Ibid.*

[26]*Ibid.* On Leibniz's dynamics, see Aiton, E. J., "The celestial mechanics of Leibniz," *Annals of Science, XVI* (1960), 65-82; "The celestial mechanics of Leibniz in the light of Newtonian criticism," *ibid., XVIII* (1962), 31-41; "The celestial mechanics of Leibniz: a new interpretation," *ibid., XX* (1964), 111-123; An imaginary error in the celestial mechanics of Leibniz, *ibid., XXI* (1965), 169-173.

[27]Trinity College Library, pressmark No. 8.82. See De Villamil's essay, cited in note 12 *supra.*

[28]See Cotes's letter to Newton of 18 March 1712/13 (wrongly dated 18 Feb.), printed by Edleston, *op. cit.* (n. 23 *supra*), 153. Cotes refers to the "Weekly Paper called Memoires of Literature," no. 18, vol. 2, 5 May 1712.

[29]The texts of the "Leibniz-Clarke correspondence" have been often reprinted, not only in the original French and English, but in German and in Russian translation. On the extent of Newton's involvement in Cotes' replies to Leibniz, see Koyré, Alexandre, and Cohen, I. B., "Newton & the Leibniz-Clarke correspondence, with Conti, & Des Maizeaux," *Archives Internationales d'Histoire des Science, XV* (1962), 63-126.

[30]The most recent scholarly edition of this work is *Commercium epistolicum J. Collins et aliorum de analysi promota, etc., ou Correspondence de J. Collins et d'autres savants célèbres du XVIIe siècle, relative á l'analyse supérieure, réimprimée sur l'édition originale de 1712, complétée par une collection de justificatives et de documents,* publiée par J. B. Biot et F. Lefort, Paris, 1856. Concerning Newton's authorship of the account of the *Commercium epistolicum,* published anonymously in the *Philosophical Transactions,* see De Morgan, Augustus, "On the authorship...," *Philosophical Magazine, III* (1852), 440-444.

The writer gratefully acknowledges the support given by the National Science Foundation to the research on which this article is based.

# 35

# The Constitution of Saltpeter, According to Becher and Stahl

## ROBERT P. MULTHAUF

SALTPETER (potassium nitrate, $KNO_3$). A white crystalline salt; diamorphous; anhydrous. Specific gravity 2.1. Melting point 339°F. Water soluble, with marked increase in solubility with temperature. Solution tastes cool and bitter. Decomposed at red heat, and by sulphuric acid, yielding oxygen, nitrogen, and acids and oxides of nitrogen. Deflagrates when heated with combustible bodies, which it oxidizes. Occurs in nature as an efflorescence in the soil especially in populous tropical regions.

THE substance was apparently a Chinese discovery, as was its property of crystallization and the increase in its water solubility with heat, for these properties were made use of in its production. Its property of deflagration, which was made use of in "black" gunpowder, was also known in China before saltpeter was known at all in Europe. The history of the scientific analysis of the substance, however, falls largely between ca. 1600, when the fabulous "Basil Valentine"[1], observed its deflagration with charcoal, and 1776, when Lavoisier discovered the elemental composition of nitric acid, although it was not completely resolved until 1807, when Davy demonstrated the composite nature of potash.

During most of this period it remained uncertain which was "simpler", saltpeter, potash, or nitric acid, and only towards the end of the 17th century was a serious attempt made to determine the mutual relationships of these three substances. The attempt was made by J. J. Becher and G. E. Stahl, whose success it is the purpose of this paper to explore.

Saltpeter was unknown in Europe prior to the 13th century, but was known thereafter in two very important connections, as an ingredient of gunpowder and of the mixture which yielded the most familiar mineral acid, nitric (aqua fortis). Despite this, the chemist does not seem to have been very curious about the constitution of saltpeter, prior to the end of the 16th century, perhaps because it had little use in medicine.

Paracelsus, although he made regular use of saltpeter in his practice, largely ignored it in his chemical theories. Nor did Libavius or Beguin, respectively the leading theorist and textbook writer of the end of the 16th century, make significant observations on the subject. But their approximate contemporary, the pseudonymous "Basil Valentine," took a fling at the analysis of saltpeter, and pronounced it to be predominantly fire and air, plus a "subtile spirit." This subtile spirit was discovered by Basil in the spectacular reaction in which molten saltpeter is "detonated" by the addition of charcoal. That this rediscovery made a profound impression is symptomatic of the chemists' previous indifference to gunpowder. "I am internally hot and externally cold," Basil wrote, personifying saltpeter, "my cooling is more powerful than that of saturn, but my spirit is hotter than anything." Thus we see the chemist, once inspired, fitting together the cooling effect of saltpeter on the tongue, which Basil could hardly have been the first to notice, with the heating effect of the substance in reaction, to form an aphorism, if not a theory. By the time of J. R. Glauber,[2] a little over a half-century later, saltpeter was "the essential salt, or salt of nature," and consequently the base of other salts.

Glauber was apparently the first to succeed in decomposing a substance and in synthesizing it from the products of its analysis, and he accomplished it with saltpeter. Dividing a sample into two parts, he distilled one with clay to yield an "acid spirit of nitre" and ignited the other with charcoal to give a "liquor of fixed nitre." He then combined the two and reported the product to be "common saltpeter," a conclusion he clinched by the identity of its crystal form.

Glauber reacted to his discovery with an enthusiasm reminiscent of that of Basil Valentine. He thought that he had discovered the long sought universal solvent, for the acid spirit of saltpeter was already regarded as a variety of the universal acid, and he claimed that his "liquor of fixed nitre" (which would have been partially causticized potash) would dissolve all materials which were impervious to acid. More than ever convinced that saltpeter is the elementary salt, he claimed that the other salts can be transmuted into saltpeter, and gives a process for converting common salt into saltpeter, "in some hours."

In writing on saltpeter in his book, *Prosperity of Germany,* Glauber refers to a whole series of other books in which he has discussed it, "for saltpeter is such a subject as you can never have too much of."[3] Judging from the profusion of the literature on saltpeter from this time, many others thought so too. We will, however, pass over the other numerous "discoveries" of sensational properties of saltpeter, to consider the attempt to integrate the substance into a general theory of chemistry.

In the first half of the 17th century, chemistry was not only a subject without a tenable scientific foundation, as Robert Boyle was to point out, but it scarcely had any foundation at all. The extension of interest to the analysis of substances, like saltpeter, which the chemist had not previously worried about, tended to dissolve whatever agreement had existed about elements, principles, and the like. Into this teeming wilderness stepped Becher, and after him Stahl, to wrestle with the problem of a scientific foundation for chemistry.

J. J. Becher (1635-82) received the M.D. degree at Mainz in 1661, at the age of 26, having published his first book, *Metallurgia,* the previous year. In 1664 he published *Oepidus chymicus,* a traditional book occupied with primal material, "principles" form, etc., and dealing largely with generalities. Five years later he produced his most substantial book, *Physica subterranea,* which was intended as a two part discussion of the genesis of the earth and of the analysis of its constituent parts, but of which the second part never appeared. He mentions, in passing, his "special treatise on saltpeter,"[4] which, unless it is lost, must refer to the *Centrum mundi concatenatum....*"or the texture and anatomy of saltpeter and salt, the two great products of the world." It was to be published posthumously in 1689. During the remainder of his lifetime, Becher endowed the *Physica subterranea* with three supplements, between 1671 in 1680, reportedly published an *Epistolae chemicae* in Amsterdam in 1673, and issued two compilations in 1682, the year of his death. One of these is *Narrische Weisheit and weise Narrheit,* "a hundred political, physical, mechanical and mercantile concepts and propositions"—a kind of book of inventions and discoveries. The other is a collection of 1500 chemical processes, collected from "the best manuscripts and laboratories" (which he lists), published under the name *Chymischer Glucks-Hafen.*

Becher's posthumous publications, *Tripus Hermeticus fatidicus* (1689), *Chymische Rosengarten* (1717), and *Opuscula chymica rariora* (1719), are scarcely less miscellaneous; and finally there is the *Specimen Beccherianum* (1702), assembled by Stahl from Becher's writings, and augmented. About all one can say of these works is that they were composed during the two decades (1662-1682), which Becher himself describes as his period of preoccupation with chemistry.[5]

In accordance with tradition, Becher constructed his chemistry around a system of elements—which he, liked Paracelsus, called "principles." His system was empirical, it was more adaptable to the realities of chemical analysis, and it was more-or-less original. Its principal defect was perhaps inconsistency. Becher was unable to decide just how many elements there are. Stahl decided this for him, namely that there are five; air, water, and three earths, vitrifying, inflammable, and fluid; but a residue of inconsistency remained, in Stahl's inability to decide what to do about the element, air, of which he made virtually no use.

In *Oedipus chymicus* Becher gives instructions for the analysis of "any animal," by distilling it. The products, he tells us, will be spirits, oil, volatile salt and fixed salt, all of which he calls essential principles of "substances," and phlegm and earth (the caput mortum), which are "accidental principles."[6] It is the same with vegetables, but slightly different with minerals, which yield sulphur and salt as essential principle and mineral acid and a mineral earth as accidental. He does not mention saltpeter, and is vague enough about "salt," which comprises on one level all "non-oily humidities, either liquid or congealed," but is on another the ubiquitous salt "principle" which had been a fixture of literary chemistry since Paracelsus.

In his treatise on "the two great products of the world," saltpeter and common salt, he gives us a kind of analysis, declaring that the former contains an exceedingly simple sulphurous eartth, differentiating it from common salt, where the earth is mercurial. The context is alchemical, for the mercurial salt earth generates silver, the sulphurous saltpeter earth gold. On the other hand, salt and saltpeter are related through an affinity (magnetism), which is more occult than that between iron and the loadstone (magnetum), or between mercury and gold.[7] And yet again, he says that there are masculine and feminine sulphurous properties, a burning red which is in saltpeter and a non-inflammable white which is in common salt. Bringing "common sulphur" into the picture, he says that they are joined in that substance.[8] These passages emphasize Becher's preoccupation with metal ennoblement, which is perhaps sufficiently demonstrated by his decision to augment the *Physica subterranea* with three successive alchemical appendices, instead of completing the second part, which, in 1669, he had promised "shortly."[9]

So far as saltpeter is concerned, however, references to it are almost

too incidental to be evaluated, and his view of the substance seemes determined by the point of view he occupies at the moment. On occasion we
find him simply including it among the salts, in a conventional classifi-
cation of materials which goes back to Avicenna.[10] In *Alphabetum minerale* he compares it with alkali, as well as salt, in containing a "subtile
red mud," against a "clear vitrifiable earth" in alkali and an "incombustible
arsenical earth" in salt. This leads him to associate saltpeter with the
atmosphere, alkali with the earth, and salt with the sea.[11] In *Chymischer
Glucks-Hafen*[12] it is saltpeter, sal ammoniac, and alkali, which have particular importance for "our work," and here again saltpeter acts as a
"magnet," this time for air. He says that saltpeter is like calcined tartar,
which through its dryness attracts air, but the context is that of a
macrocosm-microcosm theory that there is within the earth a "central
sun," which corresponds to the "heavenly sun." Prepared with dung,
preferably sheep dung, saltpeter exhibits its magnet-like property in
attracting, in this case, "heavenly water." Or, again, rain receives the
power of life from the air and joins with the saltpeter in the earth.

His observations on the mineral acids are in the same vein. In *Alphabetum minerale* the solvent effects of nitric and hydrochloric acids lead
him to declare that the spirit of saltpeter is a liquid sulphur, and the spirit
of sal a liquid salt (sal aquem liquidum).[13] But in a supplementary commentary to the "Centrum mundi concatenatum," he says that "the spirit
of common saltpeter is nothing else than saltpeter elevated in its whole
substance, its normal form taken away and through rarefaction made
corrosive, in the same way that common ice, its whole substance dissolved
by heat, becomes water." "Thus saltpeter in the form of a solid salt is
converted in its whole substance by fire to a fluid body, which is improp-
erly called spirit of saltpeter because it has the nature of saltpeter and is
by an easy manipulation converted back into solid saltpeter. It is thought
to be the same with common salt and its spirit."[14]

It may be noted that in all this Becher was not indifferent to his
predecessors. Glauber and Kesler are supposed to be in agreement with
his ideas about the alchemical significance of saltpeter and salt, and
Sendovogius and Ortelius are liberally cited on the theory of a "central
sun" within the earth.[15]Nor was he antagonistic to the theory, which
was the most prominent notion about saltpeter in his time, that it derived
its essential substance from a "subtle spirit" in the air. In *Physia subterranea* he describes putrefaction in the earth as "nitrosum," and indicates that saltpeter is commonly made in quantity this way. He speaks

vaguely there of its constitution as a rearrangement of saline and oily particles, and goes on to say that saltpeter is not the end of putrefaction, for when its igneous parts are separated the remainder is converted into earth (he notes that van Helmont had claimed to be able to convert saltpeter into earth), but an earth having a singular attraction for "aereal spirit," which causes it again to become saltpeter.[16] In *Narrische Weisheit,* on the other hand, he speaks of its extraction from the soil as a sowing of the earth with saltpeter, as of other salts (vitriol, common salt) and metals, "to make them grow and augment." They take an increment from the air, others from water and from earth, a statement which is illustrated by his observation of the "Dettfort" (Deptford, London) vitriol works, where air is "drawn under the earth," and the earth then leached with water, producing vitriol. He says that several artificial saltpeter works are operating successfully in Germany, after the plan described by Martin Schmuck in his *Thesauriolo.*[17] But perhaps a more exciting idea, for his successors, was his observation, in "Alphabetum minerale," that saltpeter is easily changed into alcali, common salt into saltpeter, and alcali into common salt.[18]

It does not appear that we can credit Becher with a positive contribution to the science of saltpeter, for which he is perhaps not to be reproached, since this was clearly not one of his major objectives. His principal objective appears to have been metal-ennoblement, for this is the most recurrent theme in his writings. The work for which he is most famous, the initiation of the "phlogiston system" of chemistry seems not to have been involved in his consideration of saltpeter. Yet Becher did consider saltpeter not in isolation, but as part of a natural system. For the further development of this we must turn to Stahl.

Georg Ernst Stahl (1660-1734) received the MD degree at Jena in 1683, and published his first (medical) book in that year. He was already interested in chemistry, having read, he tells us, manuscripts of Jacob Barner (1641-1686) when he was 15. At Jena he studied under another chemist, G. W. Wedel (1645-1721) but he had already developed preference for Becher, an affinity which may have originated in a reaction against other authorities of the time, for Stahl objected to the mechanism of Descartes, the theorizing of van Helmont, and to Sylvius de la Boe and Willis on both counts.[19] Barner was a follower of van Helmont and Wedel followed Sylvius.

Stahl leaped into the chemical fray with a pair of books in 1697-98, *Zymotechnia fundamentalis,* a book about "fermentation" considered in a very broad sense, and a collection of *Observationes chemica-physica-medica curiosae.* The use of such titles, which was characteristics of Stahl, contributed greatly to confuse the seeker after his literary remains to a degree exceeding even the case of Becher.

In 1702 Stahl published *Specimen Beccherianum,* which he says is collected from Becher's works, plus some additions of his own, and the next year he fathered a new edition of *Physica subterranea.* Between 1715 and 1723 he published three books with such characteristically Stahlian titles as *Detailed reflections...*and *Incidental thoughts"*[20] dealing with salts, with "the so-called sulphur," and with a miscellany of other subjects, including "certain fragments on the natural history of saltpeter." Beginning in 1723 Stahl's name appeared on a series of works of general chemistry, resembling the *Physica subterranea* in scope, but involving an incredible confusion of titles. Poggendorf lists them as *Chymia rationalis et experimentalis* (1720), *Fundamenta chymicae dogmaticae et rationalis* (1723), and *Fundamenta chymiae dogmaticae, rationalis et experimentalis* (1732), and says that none of them are really by Stahl. Peter Shaw, who translated part of the second into English, says that it represents lecture notes which "got abroad in several manuscript copies" from Stahl's Jena lectures, "but at length a more authentic Latin edition was published, with the Author's connivance" in 1723.[21]

Stahl's interest in Becher, in phlogiston, and in saltpeter, seem to have emerged contemporaneously in 1697-98. On saltpeter, "Certain fragments" were written in 1698, published in Latin in 1715, in a much enlarged German version in 1734 (republished in 1748), and finally summarized in the famous Paris Academy collection of writings on saltpeter in 1776.[22] The work is subdivided into three chapters, on the natural history of saltpeter, on its chemical history, and on the physical and chemical theory of the substance. In the first part he classifies it as a "mineral salt," along with vitriol, alum, halonitrum, sal gemme and commune, says it is born from oily putrifying things, with the concurrance of the acid in the earth, and that it is remarkable as a substance containing air, which he thinks however extraneous and not bound as a "principle."[23] In the second part he describes its production in nature, in the promotion of which technologists had been interested for three centuries, in behalf of the gunpowder supply. Turning to theory in the third part, he speaks of a "salino-sulphureous substance," which has very similar properties to Becher's "sulphureous earth," and which somehow produces a new "acido-sulphurous salt" which is saltpeter. The explanation which follows, in which the universal acid plays a great role, does not noticeably elucidate this, and we find him subsequently, in his treatise on the sulphur principle, declaring that the true nature of saltpeter is to be found only in its spirit, and wondering inconclusively about the origin of "the inflammable nature" and how it retains its acidity.[24] His most decisive statement on saltpeter is a "proof" that it contains phlogiston, since it is "the only salt which burns in a closed space."[25]

Stahl frequently calls attention to the involvement of "fixed alkali" in the formation of saltpeter, but its involvement seems not to be that of an ingredient. Like air, it is accidental; it makes the saltpeter spirit solid, or disposes it to crystallization. In the work on salts we find Stahl deciding that saltpeter is a kind of common salt.[26] He notes that urine and excrements which give rise to saltpeter are in fact salty, and decides that in the process of the decay the salt is first transformed into a volatile salt and then into a nitrous salt. A little later he tells of an experiment in which the common salt is placed in an unglazed clay tube and the ends stoppered. The tube is then moistened with urine, hung in a dark place, and in the course of time saltpeter appears on the outside. He maintains that it is composed of a part of the salt, a part of the clay tube, and part of the urine.[27]

In Stahl's "textbook" saltpeter is discussed more-or-less systematically, although inconsistently enough to lend credence to the view that that work was compiled from the notes of students. Salts are defined as mixed bodies consisting of earth and water, "of a fluid consistence," mean degree of volatility, corrosive, and soluble in "earths." Their species differ as the difference between "terrestrial concretes" with which they come into contact and corrode. Thus they differ in their "grosser substance."[28]

A great role in Stahl's chemistry was played by the "universal acid," which is composed, he says, of water and the first (vitrifying) earth. He also says that "the spirit of sulphur is as it were the one pure and universal salt…as genius to species."[29] The idea of regarding sulphuric acid as a "universal" acid—the parent of the other acids—predated both Stahl and Becher, as did that of equating a universal acid and universal salt. In the 1720 version of his book he says that saltpeter is formed when the universal acid combines with the "second (inflammable) earth" ("die andere Terra"-phlogiston) in just the right proportions. It is "neither dense and solid nor fire resistant, but altogether volatile;" however it can be made heavy and fire resistant by being combined with certain earths.[30] But in a special section on saltpeter, he calls it a combination of "an oily and volatile saline mixt" and "a very, very subtile alkaline earth."

The evidence for the presence of "an oily and volatile mixt" in saltpeter is given, in a later version of the book, as "the place wherein (natural) saltpeter is generated," that is, soil impregnated with animal waste. But Stahl now recognizes that saltpeter is neither inflammable nor extremely volatile, both typical qualities of substances which are oily and volatile, so he decides that he is concerned not (with) "the substance itself," but with "the principle of this substance;" or, to put it another way, with only "some essential part" of the substance.[31]

He has similar difficulties with the "subtile alkaline earth," which is apparently not to be confused with the "certain earths" which make saltpeter heavy and fire resistant (probably calcium carbonate) nor with potash, which contributes to saltpeter a "principle of crystallization." He appears to be seeking this subtile alkaline earth through a series of experiments designed to "divide" it from the more volatile part by distillation and sulphuric acid, calcined vitriol, or "dusty earth" (all of which would have driven off the oxides and acids of nitrogen), but in each case the alkaline earth of saltpeter remains mixed with "still more immovable earthy particles," and he doesn't arrive at any significant identification of the desired constituent of saltpeter.[32]

In his final word, Stahl again takes a stand against the theory that saltpeter comes from air, which he says "can be taken with a grain of salt."[33]

What did Stahl's followers make of this? His followers were legion, to the degree that most authorities find it easier to mention the exceptions, who are usually named as Hermann Boerhaave and Friedrich Hoffmann (who was Stahl's colleague at Jena). The opinions of the following three followers may perhaps suffice to clarify and answer the query.

Johann Juncker (1676-1735) wrote a chemical text avowedly on the principles of Becher and Stahl, and faithfully relates that the vitrifying earth principle, when united to water, produces the universal acid, which is also called the universal salt ,"since it constitutes most of the different kinds of salt." When the universal acid/salt further unites with the phlogistic earth principle "aided by a movement of putrefaction"—"but not too strongly"—nitric acid results. Combined with an alkali this acid yields saltpeter, but when it comes to alkalis we find Juncker arguing that the mineral acids can "pass from the mineral to the vegetable kingdom," producing a vegetable acid, which "fused with a very little phlogiston on a vitrifiable earth" forms a fixed alkali.[34]

Caspar Neumann (1683-1737) held that saltpeter may best be called a mineral, and its chief ingredient a mineral acid; but beyond that he gets into similar difficulties. Is it natural or artificial, he asks, and answers that it is natural in its first form, but artificial in its final, crystallized, form. The addition of fixed alkali salt which brings about the latter he attributes to "art." Neumann finds that the composition of saltpeter varies with one's point of view. Nature's "ingredients" are a salty-oily-urinous substance, an earth which attracts this salt, and the acid salt of the air. But from the point of view of "physical mixtion" the components are an acid salt, something inflammable, something watery, something of a friable terrestrial nature, and something urino-saline. The latter, however, is destroyed in the refining process, leaving only the first four. The crucial ingredient is the acid, which he decides, after some consideration, is probably the universal, or sulphuric, acid of the air.[35]

Stahl's star had not dimmed much on the eve of the chemical revolution associated with Lavoisier, for it continues to shine in the famous chemical dictionary of Pierre Macquer. To be sure, Macquer betrays some doubt. After defining saltpeter, a little more precisely than Stahl had done, as a neutral salt composed of nitric acid saturated with a fixed vegetable alkali, he questions the Becher-Stahl analysis of nitric acid. But it is the only one he mentions, and he limits his own contribution to a long list of the properties of the substance. As to alkali, Macquer says more confidently that it is composed of acid, of earth, and of a little phlogiston, and he confounds the several alkalis to the degree that he classifies the "fixed alkali of nitre" as a peculiar and discrete member of the species.[36] It was, in fact, potassium carbonate obtained by deflagrating saltpeter with charcoal, the product of the experiment with which "Basil Valentine" had begun the scientific history of saltpeter.

Stahl differs from Becher in removing his discussion of saltpeter from the context of alchemy. This is no small difference, and yet without the focal point of metal-ennoblement Stahl is clearly hard-put to find a focus for chemical theory. He is no more able to adhere rigorously to his system of elements than had been such predecessors as Aristotle and Paracelsus. Like them, he constantly redefines his elements in terms of their properties, in a variety of ways which go far to nullify their function as elements. The universal acid, which was not an element, seems to play a more primary role in his theory.

Moreover the idea of the universal acid seems to have inhibited Stahl from attempting a serious elucidation of the character of nitric acid, especially in view of what can only be called his prejudice against the involvement of air in chemical phenomena. In both of these respects, Stahl's doctrine of saltpeter can only be called a regression from the position taken by Becher.

They agree, however, and both agree with Glauber, on the close relationship between saltpeter and common salt. Between them they accumulate a substantial body of argument and experiment which un-doubtedly encouraged the idea of producing saltpeter "for national de-fense" through synthetic processes, of which there were numerous examples, especially in German lands, in the later 18th century.

As far as the elucidation of saltpeter is concerned, Stahl moved far away, in the wrong direction, from numerous more tenable explanations, involving air, made in the previous generation. But the authors of these explanations, such as Glauber, John Mayow, and Robert Boyle, did not even attempt to consider the substance as part of a general system of chemistry. Stahl at least made the attempt. Perhaps what he needed above all was a stable terminology, for nothing is more obvious than the difficulty of his successors, from his immediate followers down to the contemporary historian of chemistry, in defining Stahl's views with any precision. About a half century after his death, the French chemists brought forth a stable terminology. That they simultaneously brought for the modern elucidation of the constitution of saltpeter is probably no coincidence.

## References

[1]Basil Valentine, "Bericht vom Quecksilber...Saltpeter..." Anhang to *Von den Grossen Stein der Uralter,* Strassburg, 1651, 92-3. It may be noted here that I have consistently rendered such variant names of the substance (nitre, salnitre, etc.) as "saltpeter."

[2]Glauber, J. R., "A treatise on the importance of salts, metals and plants," *Works,* London, 1689, Pt. 1, 275; "Spagyrica pharmaceutica," *ibid.* 1, 99-100.

[3]*Ibid,* Pt. 1, 335-6.

[4]Becher, J. J., *Actorum laboratorii chymici Monacensis, seu physicae subterraneae,* Frankfort, 1669, Bk. 1, V, Ch. 1, n. 51. In later editions this book was simply called *Physica subterranea.*

[5]Becher, *Chymischer Glucks-Hafen, Frankfurt, 1682.* I have used all the works mentioned above except for the *Epistola chemica* of 1673. My list does not accord

very well, however, with the list of eighteen mentioned in Roth-Scholtze's biography (in Becher's *Chymischer Rosengarten*, Nurnberg, 1717, 25-6). Becher's confusing bibliography is discussed in Hassinger, H., *Johann Joachim Becher*, Wien, 1951, 254ff, and Partington, J. R., *A history of chemistry*, II, London, 1961, 640ff.

[6]Becher, *Oedipus chymicus*, Amsterdam, 1664, 45-6 (also in Manget, J. J., *Bibliotheca chemica curiosa*, Geneva, 1702. 1, 313b). This system of analysis by destructive distillation had appeared in the works of other chemists a half century earlier.

[7]Becher, "Centrum mundi concatenatum," *Opuscula chymica rariori*, Nurnberg and Altdorf, 1719, 69, 82.

[8]Becher, "Alphabetum minerale", *Opuscula...*, 122.

[9]Becher, *Actorum laboratorii chymicii...*, Dedicatio.

[10]Becher, *Specimen Beccherianum*, Leipzig, 1738, Pt. 1, Sec. 2, 103.

[11]Becher, "Alphabetum minerale," *Opuscula...*, 119.

[12]Becher, *Chymischer Glucks-Hafen*, 140, 146, 171.

[13]Becher, "Alphabetum minerale," *Opuscula...*, 142.

[14]Becher, "Centrum mundi concatenatum," Commentary, *Opuscula...*, 80.

[15]Michael Sendovogius (1566-1646) was a celebrated alchemist, Abraham Ortelius (1527-98) the famous geographer. Kesler may refer to Andreas Kesler (1595-1643) a theologian.

[16]Becher, *Physica subterranea*, Leipzig, 1738, 144-5.

[17]Schmuck, Martin, *Thesauriolo*, Frankfort, 1682. 60-62. Schmuck's *Secretorum naturalium chymicorum et medicorum thesauriolus*, Nurnberg, 1649, gives a conventional account of saltpeter production in Pt. 2, 10-12.

[18]Becher, "Alphabetum minerale," *Opuscula...*, 116.

[19]Becher, *Physica subterranea*, Leipzig, 1703, Prefatio, (by Stahl).

[20]Stahl, Georg Ernst, *Ausführliche Betrachtung...von den Salzen*, Halle, 1723, and *Zufällige Gedanken...über den Streit von dem sogennanten Sulphure*, Halle, 1718 (French translations, published, respectively, in 1771 and 1776, were simply called *Traité de sels*, and *Traité du soufre*). The third work was his *Opusculum chymicophysico-medicum*, Halle, 1715.

[21]Shaw, Peter, *Philosophical principles of universal chemistry*, London, 1730, vii (Advertisement). These all seem to be variants of the same text (cf. Partington, *op. cit.*, 661-2).

[22]Académie des Sciences (Paris), *Recueil des Memoires et d'observations sur la formation et sur la fabrication du salpetre*, Paris, 1776, 43-65.

[23]Stahl, "Fragmenta quaedam ad historiam naturalem nitri pertinenta," *Opusculum chymico-physico-medicum*, Halle, 1715, 534, 542. The "Fragmenta" is dated 1698. See also Becker, *Specimen Beccherianum*, 21.

[24]Stahl, *Zufällige Gedanken*..., 223, 227 (p. 14 in *Traité du soufre*).

[25]Stahl, "Fragmenta," *Opusculum chymico-physico-medium*, 58.

[26]Stahl, *Ausführliche Betrachtung*..., 130.

[29]Stahl, *Chymia rationalis*..., 19, Shaw, *op. cit.*, 79, Stahl *Fundamenta chymiae*... Pt. 1, (1746), 50.

[30]Stahl, *Chymia rationalis*..., 19-20.

[31]Shaw, *op. cit.*, 89, Stahl, *Fundamenta chymiae*...(1746), 56.

[32]Shaw, *op. cit.*, 29-24, Stahl *Fundamenta chymiae*...(1746), 58-60.

[33]Stahl, *Fundamenta chymiae*..., Pt. 3 (1747), 146.

[34]Juncker, Johann, *Elemens de chymie suivant les principes de M. Juncker*, Paris, 1757, 1, 57 (French trans. by Dmachy).

[35]Newman, Caspar, *Lectiones publicae von vier subjectis chemicis*, Berlin, 1732, 5, 24-28.

[36]Pierre Macquer, *Dictionnaire de chymie*, Paris, 1778, articles on nitre, acide nitreux, alkali fixe.

# 36

## The Sieur de la Rivière,
## Paracelsian Physician of Henri IV

### HUGH TREVOR-ROPER

THE sieur de la Rivière, *premier médicin* of Henry IV from 1594 to 1605, is mentioned by several contemporary writers, but not with much detail or even by an exact name. The historian Jacques Auguste de Thou, who mentions him as one of the doctors consulted in the famous case of Marthe Brossier, the pretended demoniac, in 1599, calls him "N. Riverius," which, in the 18th century French translation of de Thou's work appears as Nicolas de Rivière.[1] On the other hand Theodore de Mayerne, who knew him well, refers to him as "D. Ian. Riverius" ("Ian." being presumably a misprint for "Joan.")[2] Sully, Agrippa d'Aubigné, Pierre de l'Estoile and other writers of his time simply refer to him as Rivière, de la Rivière or in Latin, Riverius or Riparius. These writers do not tell us much about him. More modern writers have added darkness rather than light by confusing such little identity as he has with that of another and very different doctor who happened to assume the same territorial title. The purpose of this essay is to rescue the *premier médecin* from this confusion and provide, for the first time, some account of his true character and significance.

First let us see him, as far as possible, through the eyes of his contemporaries. What they tell us can be started very briefly. They inform us that he was a Huguenot and a Paracelsian, though not, apparently, a bigot either in religious or in medical doctrine; and that he was greatly valued by Henri IV, who genuinely lamented his death. Sully, a fellow Huguenot, though not himself the most religious of men, says that la Rivière had not much religion, but inclined more to Protestantism than to Catholicism; and he adds that he was good at casting nativities, and he quotes, as a particular example of his skill, his horoscope of Louis XIII.[3] Agrippa d'Aubigné is more explicit. Writing somewhat satirically, in the name of the apostate Hugenot grandee Nicholas Harlay de Sancy, he describes la Rivière (who was de Sancy's doctor) as "bon Galéniste et très-bon Paracelsiste. It dit que la doctrine de Galien est honorable et non méprisable pour la pathologie et profitable pour les boutiques. L'autre, pourvu que ce soit de vrais préceptes de Paracelse, est bonne à suivre pour la vérité, pour la subtilité, pour l'épargne, en somme pour la thérapeutique. Partant ít fait de son âme comme de son corps: étant Romain pour le profit et Huguenot pour la guérison de son âme."[4] This somewhat sardonic view is confirmed by d'Aubigné's own letters to la Rivière, to which we shall refer later: there d'Aubigné implicitly though politely reproves the physician for indifference in religion, disbelief in witchcraft and demoniac possession, and a general scepticism about the supernatural. La Rivière's orthodox medical colleagues evidently looked upon him with distrust. Some of them even regarded him as little better than a quack.[5]

These views must be respected. On the other hand we must remember that the reign of Henri IV was a period of fierce doctrinal controversy, in matters of medicine as in matters of religion, and la Rivière was clearly the representative, indeed the leader, of a party. This party was the party of the "chemical doctors" who were violently attacked by the established Galenists of the university of Paris. The two best known members of this party, and those who, by their writings, became most deeply involved in controversy with the medical establishment, were Joseph du Chesne, who wrote in Latin under the name of Quercetanus, and Theodore de Mayerne, who afterwards became famous as court-doctor of James I and Charles I of England. Both du Chesne and Mayerne were *médecins ordinaires* of Henri IV under la Rivière; both, like him, were Huguenots and 'iatrochemists'; both worked in partnership with him in private practice. Both acknowledged la Rivière as their patron. Mayerne sang his praises as the greatest doctor of the time, 'whatever the dirty crowd of ignorant men may mouth against him' *quicquid obganniat imperitorum coenosa turba*). Du Chesne dedicated to him his treatise on the gout and the stone, and tells us incidentally something about la Rivière's travels: how, "not content with vulgar medicine," he travelled in Germany under the auspices of the duc de Bouillon and was greatly admired by that "star of French genius," Philippe Canaye de Fresne, who was then acting as French ambassador in Germany.[6]

Such is the sum, as far as I know, of contemporary published evidence concerning the *premier médecin*. But later writers, thanks to a plausible speculation, have added considerably to it. For the last two centuries every writer who has sought to give any account of la Rivière has assumed without question that he was identical with Roch le Baillif, sieur de la

Rivière, generally characterized as "le fameux empirique." *Prima facie,*
this identification seems probable enough. Roch le Baillif, like the *premier
médecin,* was a Huguenot and a Paracelsian. Like him, he fell foul of the
orthodox Galenist establishment of Paris: indeed, in 1578-9, he was
was chased out of Paris by it. Like him, he nevertheless penetrated court
circles, and could describe himself, from 1579 to 1592, as *médecin ordinaire du roi.* Like him, he was suspected of inconstancy in religion. Moreover, the careers of the two men seem neatly to fit into a common frame.
By 1592 Roch le Baillif, sieur de la Rivière, had published several works
of somewhat crude Paracelsian propaganda. Thereafter we lose trace of
that name, but in 1594 we picked up the trail of a Paracelsian Huguenot
sieur de la *Rivière* who in that year is appointed *premier médecin du roi.*
Such a happy coincidence of name, time and character seems irresistible,
and it is natural to suppose that the persecuted Huguenot Paracelsian
*médecin ordinaire* of 1579-1592 is the humble caterpillar of which the
established, but still unpopular Huguenot Paracelsian *premier médecin*
of 1594-1605 is the airborne butterfly. Admittedly, after 1592, the name
of Roch le Baillif is heard no more, but the territorial title "sieur de la
Rivière" provides the continuity.

The assumption is certainly plausible. However, I am now persuaded
that it is false, and that two quite distinct persons have been confused
under one name, with consequent injustice to the reputation of the
*premier médecin.* I was first driven to this conclusion by the evidence
of the letters and papers of the *premier médecin* which his disciple
Théodore de Mayerne brought with him to England in 1611 and which
are now incorporated in Mayerne's papers in the Sloane MSS in the
British Museum.[7] A reading of these papers has caused me to re-examine
the evidence on which the identity of the *médecin ordinaire* and the
*premier médecin* has been assumed, and I have found this evidence
inadequate. Further study of the positive evidence has convinced me that
the conclusion is anyway untenable: that Roch le Baillif and the *premier
médecin* are distinct and incompatible persons. I had already reached
this conclusion when the archivist at Rennes, whom I had consulated
on the subject of Roch le Baillif, drew my attention to the thesis of
Emmanuel Philipot on the Breton writer Noël du Fail.[8] Reading this
work, I realized that Philipot, starting from a different position, had come
to the same conclusion. He had shown that Roch le Baillif could hardly
have become the *premier médecin,* just as I had convinced myself that the
*premier médecin* could hardly have been Roch le Baillif. However, since

Philipot's work seems unknown to the historians of medecine. I shall not take it for granted but will subsume his evidence in my own.

In order to disentangle the confusion, it is convenient to begin with the entanglement. The identification of Roch le Baillif with the *premier médecin* was first made, as far as I can discover, in 1693, by the Huguenot scholar Jacob le Duchat, in his commentary on Agrippa d'Aubigné's *Confession de Sancy*. Le Duchat there gives a note on the *premier médecin* la Rivière, "que je suppose avoir été pareillement connu sous le nom de Roche le Bailly, seigneur de la Rivière."[9] Le Duchat was a learned and accurate historical scholar, and his opinions carry weight; but since he admits that his identification is a mere supposition, it is clear that he knew of no concrete evidence to support it; nor have I been able to discover any such evidence in the material which has become available since his time. However, his admitted supposition was soon adopted by the scholars of the 18th century and became the unquestioned assumption of later writers.

The man who effected the change was the learned and prolific Jansenist writer the abbé Claude-Pierre Goujet. Goujet accepted the identification made by le Duchat and in 1735, in his Supplement to the *Grand Dictionnaire Historique* of Moréri, he added such details as he knew concerning the *premier médecin* to the existing account of Roch le Baillif. These details, like all the abbé's additions, were incorporated into the text of the next edition of the dictionary (1759). From this source all latter works of reference repeated the confusion, and if new biographical details were discovered, whether of Roch le Baillif or of the *premier médecin,* they were immediately credited to the synthetic personality thus established. Thus Roch le Baillif, sieur de la Rivière, Huguenot and Paracelsian, born in Normandy, educated in Geneva, practising in Brittany, driven from Paris by the Faculty, brought back in triumph by the King, and dying there as *premier médecin* in 1605 appears in J.-F. Carrère's *Bibliothèque historique et critique de la médicine* (1776), in N.F.J. Eloy's *Dictionnaire historique de la médicine* (1778), in Michaud's *Biographie Generale* (1862), in the great Huguenot biographical dictionary, *la France Protestante* of the brothers Haag (1846-59), and in such bibliographical works as Edouard Frère's *Manuel du Bibliographe Normand* (1860) and Antoine de la Borderie's *Archives du Bibliophile Breton* (1885). Philipot's doubts, published in 1914, passed unnoticed, and the old identification repeated from source to source and consecrated by such repetition, is included in the current third edition of August Hirsch's *Biographisches Lexikon der Hervor-ragenden Artzten* (ed. E. Gurlt and N. Wernich, 1962). Thus all standard works of reference declare without hesitation (but also without evidence) that the *premier médecin* was the author of the works, and suffered the misfortunes, of the "famous empiric" Roch le Baillif.

If we are to test so inveterate an hypothesis we must ignore all these later compilations, which assume its truth, and begin again from the unquestioned evidence. We must separate the evidence which demonstrably refers to Roch le Baillif from that which refers, no less demonstrably, to the *premier médecin*. Only when we have built up the personalities and biographies of the two persons on the basis of such exclusive material can we decide whether, in the end, they must remain distinct or can be merged in one individual. We shall begin with the earlier of the two persons, or of the two stages in the life of one person.

The life of Roch le Baillif, sieur de la Rivière, is documented by his own published works and by the records of his trial before the Parlement of Paris in 1579. To this printed evidence Emmanuel Philipot has added some further archival evidence, mainly from local sources. From these documents it emerges clearly that le Baillif was a native of Falaise in Normandy; that he claimed to have been awarded a doctorate by the local university of Caen (a claim which the doctors of Caen, when consulted by Madame de Rohan, denied); and that he was twice married. His first wife was Françoise Poret, presumably a relation of his apothecary in Paris, who bore that surname; his second was Julienne Riou, a Breton woman. The contract for the second marriage is dated 13 January 1573, before a Breton notary employed by the family of Rohan. It is thus clear that already, by this date, le Baillif was settled in Brittany as a dependent of that great Breton family.[10]

Le Baillif's first known patron was Henri de Rohan, Prince de Guemené, known as "le Goutteux," who lived at the château de Blain. After Henri de Rohan's death in 1576, he was maintained by his younger brother Louis de Rohan, known as "L'Aveugle," of whom he declared himself, in 1578, "très humble subject et vassal." Le Baillif treated Henri de Rohan for his gout; no doubt he also treated Louis for his blindness. He also treated a Madame de Rohan, and his enemies declared that he had caused the death, in childbirth, of another lady of the family. Perhaps it was on this last occasion that Madame de Rohan's suspicions were aroused and she wrote to the doctors of Caen to check le Baillif's claim to a doctorate. In 1577 he published an account of the antiquities and singularities of Brittany, which he dedicated to the nobility of Brittany. In this he gave particular prominence to the family of Rohan, which was descended (he said) from the learned astrologer Ruhan, the son of Armoreus, the founder of Brittany. Armoreus, in turn, was the son of Aeneas and carried the lineage of the Rohan family back before Abra-ham.[11] Le Baillif seems, at this time at least, to have been a Huguenot. His known friends were Huguenots; so were his printers; and the Rohan family were the leaders and protectors of Huguenotism in Brittany.[12]

He was also a committed, indeed a fanatical Paracelsist. His treatise on Brittany is Paracelsian in its emphasis on natural phenomena, mineral deposits, medicinal baths, etc. In 1578 he published his *Demosterion,* in which he claimed to reduce the science of Paracelsus into a series of 300 aphorisms. He there described himself as "sectateur, à mon pouvoir, du divin Paracelse." His enemies described him as "le singe de Paracelse," which was not unfair, for his Paracelsianism is of a primitive, funda-mentalist, even vulgar kind. They also said that he piqued himself, above all, on astrology; and this is compatible with the title of one of his works.[13] He also practised cheiromancy and other forms of divination, and de-scribed himself as a "spagyrist," or Paracelsian alchemical physician, and "edelphe," or Paracelsian seer.[14]

We do not know when, or where, or in what circumstances Roch le Baillif received the Paracelsian revelation. Paracelsianism was largely a Protestant heresy and most of the early French Paracelsians discovered it in Protestant countries—Germany or Switzerland—or through Prot-estant teachers who had studied there. Le Baillif himself cites Para-celsus' German disciples Winter von Andernach, Adam von Bodenstein, Gerard Dorn, Peter Hassereus. It is tempting to suppose that he must, at some time, have travelled abroad. However, we have no evidence of such travel, and possibly he received his ideas at second-band. If Roch le Baillif had studied abroad, he would probably have claimed a foreign doctorate rather than risk exposure by claiming one from the local college of Caen. This fact alone suggests that his youth was spent in his native province. The statements—which even Philipot repeats—that he emigrated to Geneva with his father and studied there rest on no authority but seem to spring from confusion with the other la Rivière.

Some time before the beginning of 1578, le Baillif's relations with the Rohan family were interrupted by a violent episode. It seems that certain servants of M. de Rohan, "esmeus d'une vengeance mal reglée," had plotted to kill him; that le Baillif turned the tables on them, denounced them to the officers of the Law, and secured their execution; and that this episode was the cause, or at least the occasion, of his departure from Brittany to Paris and his attempt to practise medicine there. At all events, he now ceased to cite the Rohan family as his patrons and described himself as "conseiller et médecin ordinaire" of the king and the duc de Mercoeur. The duc de Mercoeur was the leader of the Catholic party in Brittany and as such the natural rival and enemy of the family of Rohan. It seems, therefore, that le Baillif had found it necessary to change his allegiance. His appointment as *médecin ordinaire* to Henry III was no doubt titular and acquired for him by Mercoeur, who was brother-in-law to the king. However, even this protection did not secure him against a series of persecutions in Paris. He was accused of coining false money. He was thrown into prison. Finally his medical activities aroused the professional jealousy of the doctors of Paris.

It seems that the Medical Faculty of Paris, the guardian alike of orthodoxy and monopoly, was looking for an opportunity to strike a blow at this dangerous new heresy of Paracelsianism and that le Baillif pre-sented himself as a convenient victim. On 17 June 1578 the first blow was struck: the Faculty forbade him to practice or lecture in Paris, not being a doctor of the university. Le Baillif ignored the ban and on 30 April 1579, at the instance of the Dean of the Faculty, who described him as "this plague," he was haled before the Parlement of Paris. The trial was a notable show of strength. The university employed three well-known advocates, one of whom, Barnabé Brisson, *advocat du roi,* spoke so elo-quently in defence of Hippocrates and ancient medicine that the Faculty, overcome by emotion, solemnly undertook to give him and his family free, non-Paracelsian medical attention for three generations.[15] Le Baillif had an even môre distinguished counsel, the famous lawyer-historian Etienne Pasquier, who had made his name defending the claims of the University against the Jesuits in 1564. Pasquier would long remember this "case of the Paracelsists" which he had pleaded "for three Thursdays, before a vast crowd of people":[16] it caused him to speak tolerantly of Paracel-sianism afterwards, though he did not himself accept its claims. But all his forensic eloquence on behalf of le Baillif proved vain. On 2 June 1579 the Parlement issued an *arrêt* forbidding le Baillif to practise "etiam inter volentes" and ordering him to leave the city under pain of corporal punishment. The dean of the Faculty, Henri de Monanteuil, was so pleased with his achievement in ridding the city of this charlatan that he afterwards caused it to be recorded on his own tomb.[17]

Le Baillif now returned to Brittany and to the protection of his noble patrons there. By 1580 he was established at Rennes and was again describing himself as *médecin ordinaire* of the king and of the duc de Mercoeur. As such he published more works of vulgar Paracelsianism, dedicated to Mercoeur. In the political struggle in Brittany he was apparently an active supporter of Mercoeur. In May 1584, when the *bourgeois* of Rennes were preparing to welcome Mercoeur to their town, it was le Baillif whom they proposed to commission as their poet. No doubt it was through Mercoeur's patronage that he was appointed, in 1588, as medical adviser to the Parlement of Rennes. When war broke out between Henri III and the ultra-catholic *Sainté Ligue,* the forces of the *Ligue* in Brittany were led by Mercoeur. Le Baillif thereupon supported his local aristocratic, not his distant royal patron. Whether he was still a Huguenot or not we do not know, but his behavior was certainly that of a Ligueur. In the testimony given to the royal officers after the murder of the Guise brothers, in the spring and summer of 1589, we are told that le Baillif, being now very rich from his practice, fitted out his son, the sieur de St. Martin, with 1000 *écus,* to command a company in the service of Mercoeur; and the young man, in command of forty or fifty men, horse and foot, with a trumpeter, ravaged the countryside, ransacked, pillaged and burnt the houses of the royalists, seized and sold their movable property, and held their persons to ransom.[18]

However the father was evidently more circumspect than the son in his political loyalty. Though he frequented ultra-Catholic families le Baillif did not over-expose himself, and when the tide turned we find him back in favour with the Huguenot party and his old patrons, the Rohan. In 1591, he dedicated a work to the new head of the family, the young Henri, vicomte de Rohan, as his "très-humble et affectionné serviteur et vassal."

Henri de Rohan was the nephew of Henri le Goutteux and Louis l'Aveugle and would become the great Huguenot leader of the next century. Le Baillif now claimed to have been saved by Rohan's authority from "la dent vènéneuse des envieux."[19] Since Henri de Rohan was only born in 1579 this can hardly refer to the Parisian prosecution of that year when le Baillif was anyway out of favour with the Rohan family and was protected by their rivals. Presumably after the defeat of the Ligue, he felt in danger from the Huguenot revenge and sought refuge with the young Rohan's widowed mother. We may note that after 1589 le Baillif no longer appears as doctor of the duc de Mercoeur: he now signs his works as *conseiller et médecin ordinaire du roy et de la cour de Parlement de Bretagne.* The king was now Henri IV. The agility with which le Baillif switched from side to side in politics (and perhaps also in religion) is remarkable. The most favourable construction that we can put on it is that he was not—or not necessarily—a timeserver but could have been a *politique.* After all, even the greatest thinker of the *politiques,* Jean Bodin, had once been a Huguenot and became, for a time, a *Ligueur.* But Bodin, was not able, like le Baillif, to reverse the somersault.

Roch le Baillif's last known work was published in 1592. It was dedicated to Henri IV. The dedication implies that he relies on the protection of the king. The book itself is a literary dialogue or symposium designed to show that Paracelsus, in his medical philosophy, had never departed from the teaching of Hippocrates.[20] This had always been le Baillif's thesis, although even his defenders had found it implausible.[21] In July of the same year, 1592, we find le Baillif, who is described as a physician of Rennes, employed by a Breton gentleman, Gilles Satin, sieur de la Teillaye, to make a steel or copper corset to correct the shoulder of his hunchbacked child.[22] That is the last glimpse that we have of Roch le Baillif, sieur de la Rivière, as distinct from his alleged reincarnation the sieur de la Rivière, *premier médecin* of Henri IV.

From this account it is obvious that le Baillif was a man of limited horizons, both intellectual and local. Though he acquired powerful patrons and eloquent advertisers of his works, these works show very little medical knowledge as distinct from popular Paracelsian philosophy. As the 18th century medical historian Eloy wrote of le Baillif's *Traité de l'homme et de son essentielle anatomie* (1580), "on y trouve peu d'anatomie mais beaucoup de verbiage inintelligible." His general education was also poor. No person of intellectual stature seems to have respected him. Noël de Fail, the Breton writer, who defended him in his difficulties and wrote a laudatory preface to his *Demosterion,* soon saw through his pretensions and dismissed him as a charlatan.[23] It is questionable whether he knew Latin. All his books were written in French (although the aphorisms of the *Demosterion* were presented in Latin too). His critics in the Faculty of Medicine in Paris declared that he knew no Latin and that he justified his admitted ignorance by saying "que les maladies ne se guérissent ny en latin ny en grec: que c'est assez que la chose soit entendue et les remèdes cogneus." Hippocrates and Galen, he said, wrote in Greek because it was their native tongue. For the same reason the "Arabs" wrote in Arabic and he himself wrote in French. His critics would not accept this specious argument: to them Latin was by now the essential language of medicine, whose technicalities could not be discussed except with the aid of its specialised vocabulary. They therefore insisted on examining le Baillif in that language, and they took visible pleasure in recording the knots in which they tied him and the solecisms which he committed. Michel Marescot, a distinguished physician, afterwards one of Henri's IV's *médecins ordinaires* and, as such, a friend and colleague of the *premier médicin* la Rivière,[24] protested before the Parlement that he would gladly argue with a learned Paracelsian but that he could do nothing "cum hoc homine plane ignaro."

Indeed, the whole trial of Roch le Baillif seems to have been something of a disappointment to the Paris doctors. They had intended to strike a spectacular blow at the Paracelsian doctrines which, at that time, had newly invaded France. The solemnity of the occasion, the importance of the counsel employed on both sides, the lasting memories of the affair retained by Etienne Pasquier, all suggest this. But le Baillif could not sustain his part. As Emmanuel Philipot wrote "on avait préparé une grande machine de guerre contre le Paracelsisme et l'on fut déçu de se trouver en présence d'un médecin surtout empirique dont le bagage doctrinal était assez léger."[25]

Locally, le Baillif was equally limited. All such evidence as clearly refers to him indicates a career confined to Normandy and Brittany except for his brief and unsuccessful incursion into Paris in 1578-80. All his works, except during the year in Paris, were printed in Rennes. His known friends, his patients, his patrons, are all inhabitants of Normandy or Brittany. His writings also have a provincial quality. The Paracelsianism which they express is crude and repetitive and he seldom breaks out of his narrow repertoire of ritual phrases. As the Parisian doctors put it, le Baillif, "a toute question proposée, tousjour chantoit l'une de ses trois chansons ... à sçavoir, de ses trois principes, Sel, Soufre et Mercure; de la séparation du pur et de l'impur; et du microcosme." In short, he appears, on all the available evidence, to have been a monoglot, provincial crank.

What happened to him after 1592? If we have no later record of his life, at least we have a record of his death. The register of burials in the parish of Saint Sauveur, Rennes, tells us that Roch le Baillif, sieur de la Rivière, was buried there on 8 January 1598. This fact alone would seem conclusive proof that he was not identical with the *premier médecin* of Henri IV. Attempts have been made to save the old theory by supposing that this entry refers to the burial of an otherwise unrecorded son of le Baillif. These attempts are not very plausible, and Emmanuel Philipot has effectively refuted them by discovering further documentary evidence of le Baillif's death at that time.[26] But Philipot thought it prudent to add that "le probleme sera definitivement élucidé lorsqu'un chercheur aura pris la peine d'étudier la biographie du médecin de Henri IV, mort en 1605." To him, therefore, we now turn.

The first question concerns his true name. Vincenzo Minutoli, the accurate Swiss scholar who, at the end of the 17th century, supplied information to Pierre Bayle, refers to him as "M. Ribbit de la Rivière"[27] and it can be stated confidently that his original name was Jean Ribit: he normally signs his own letters, and is addressed by his correspondents, as Joannes Riverius, and at least on one occasion he signs as "Jo. Ribbittus."[28] According to le Duchat—who on this occasion writes confidently, as one stating a fact, not merely a supposition—he was the son of one Jean Ribit who professed theology at Geneva. This statement has been denied by the brothers Haag, who say roundly that "rien ne justifie cette assertion du savant critique."[29] But the only ground which the brothers Haag give for rejecting the statement is that no professor of theology called Ribit is recorded at the university of Geneva. This ground is insufficient, for there was a well-known professor of theology called Jean Ribit at the academy of Lausanne, and clearly it was of him that le Duchat was thinking.

This Jean Ribit, the professor, was a Huguenot who had fled to Switzerland from Savoy. He had been born at Sales in the district of Faucigny, Savoy,[30] and had studied Greek at the collège de la Roche in Faucigny, under Hubert Louis, and afterwards at the university of Paris. In 1538 he was in Zurich, where he married Agnes Rosin of Zurich. In 1540 he succeeded his close friend Conrad Gesner as professor of Greek at Lausanne.[31] He published editions of Xenophon, Lucian and other Greek writers. In 1547, though primarily a Hellenist, he became professor of theology at Lausanne. Resigning in 1559, he bcame regent of the college of Geneva and then professor of biblical exegesis at Orléans, where he died in 1564.[32] There were other Ribits in Geneva at this time, no doubt of the same family. Helenus Ribit, who seems to have been a brother of Jean Ribit, practised there as a lawyer and Hippolyte Ribit worked as a goldsmith.[33] That Jean Ribit, the future *premier médecin*, came from this family of Savoyard Huguenots settled on Lake Leman is very probable, for he was born in or near Geneva and studied in Savoy, and we find him, in later life, revisiting Lausanne.[34] He was most probably, as le Duchat states, the son of Jean Ribit the Hellenist who, as we know from his letters, had a son called Jean.[35]

That Jean Ribit, the future *premier médecin* was born in or near Geneva is clear from a letter sent to him long afterwards by Agrippa d'Aubigné.[36] This letter is undated, but it deals with the subject of demoniac possession: it may well have been occasioned by the case of Marthe Brossier in 1599. In it d'Aubigné reminds la Rivière of the case of "la démoniaque de Cartigny, au pays de vostre naissance et de vos études de vous et de moy." This demoniac had appeared in the village of Cartigny, near Geneva, and had created great excitement by answering questions in numerous languages. The professor of Hebrew at Geneva, Antoine Chevalier, had questioned her in Hebrew; three Orientals visiting the West and then in Geneva had been called in to converse with her in the eighteen different Eastern languages which they commanded and d'Aubigné himself had put to her "deux petites questions greques." D'Aubigné remarks that he hardly needs to remind la Rivière of this episode since "vous estiez lors à Genève et say bien que vous la visitiez." This episode can be dated to the years 1565-7, when the young d'Aubigné was in Geneva and Antoine Chevalier was still professor of Hebrew there. The year of la Rivière's birth can be deduced from a letter which he wrote, on 20 June 1591, to Joachim Camerarius II, the famous Nuremberg physician and humanist, and in which he implies that we was then 45 years old. [37] From these two documents we may therefore conclude that he was born in or about 1546, in or near Geneva. This fact alone effectively distinguishes him from Roch de Baillif, who clearly describes himself, on the title-page of his work on the antiquities of Brittany, "as natif de Fallaize."

The same letter of Agrippa d'Aubigné also shows that Jean Ribit had at least part of his education at Geneva. He is not recorded as a student of Calvin's Academy: probably he studied at the collège de Genève of which his father was regent, and where Agrippa d'Aubigné also studied.[38] Under his father (assuming that Jean Ribit was his father), he would be sure of a good humanist education in "philosophy"—i.e. in Latin and Greek,—and his letters show that he was fluent and elegant in both languages. Unlike Roch le Baillif, who wrote even his medical works in French, Jean Ribit wrote even his private letters to Frenchmen in Latin. Of his later education we know nothing except what he casually reveals in another letter to Camerarius, of 30 June 1591. Writing about the medical use of white antimony (*flores antimonii*), he there states it was first so used "in Turin twenty years ago, when I attended the lectures of Argenterius there."[39] Argenterius—Giovanni Argenterio—was a native of Piedmont whom Emmanuel Philibert, duke of Savoy, had lured back from Naples to be professor of medicine at his university at Mondovì, and then, from 1566 to 1571, when the university had been restored to Turin, at Turin. He was a humanist doctor, an advocate of novelty in medicine, and interested in chemical innovations.[40] From this evidence it is clear that Ribit studied medicine at Turin in or before 1571.

The connexion between Geneva and Turin is natural enough. Many Piedmontese had settled in Geneva, especially physicians and apothecaries: indeed, the medical profession in Geneva, at this time, was almost cornered by the Piedmontese.[41] But of course these Piedmontese immigrants were Protestants. Like Jean Ribit senior, they had fled from the dominions of the duke of Savoy to avoid religious persecution. In these circumstances, it is a little odd that Jean Ribit junior should move in the opposite direction. Why, we may ask, did he not rather go, if he were to study medicine, to the Protestant university of Basel, the best medical school in Europe, where Conrad Gesner himself, his father's closest friend, was professor? In this connexion we may notice a remark by le Duchat that the young Ribit was converted to Catholicism. Le Duchat gives no source for this statement, but it may well be true. If true, it would explain the somewhat censorious attitude of his old friend, the unyielding Calvinist Agrippa d'Aubigné. D'Aubigné did not approve of religious inconstancy. In any case, Ribit's conversion, if it took place, does not seem to have had a lasting effect. Perhaps, as Duchat suggests, it was the effect of temporary worldly ambition. Perhaps it was only a brief phase, like the Catholicism through which Bayle and Gibbon would pass on their way to a mature scepticism.

Jean Ribit was at Turin in or before 1571. Of the next 18 years of his life we know almost nothing. Only one document even refers to them. In a letter to Caspar Peucer, of 15 February 1591, Ribit states that, "having laid the foundations of medical theory by attendance in the schools of France and Italy," he had travelled over "almost all Europe"—except apparently Germany—in order to confirm theory by practice. The reason which he gave for avoiding Germany in his travels is interesting. We shall come to it shortly. Where in fact he went we cannot even guess. Some of the most enterprising 16th century doctors, like Ambroise Paré and Joseph du Chesne, attached themselves to warring armies and improved their art by practice in camps or military hospitals. Others found employment in the courts of princes. Doctors from the schools of Italy were employed in the courts of Poland and Hungary. Doctors from Piedmont seem to have been particularly energetic. Apart from the Piedmontese in Geneva, we know of a Piedmontese doctor called Botal who made a career in France,[42] and a doctor from a noble Piedmontese family, Giovanni Giorgio Biandrata introduced medical and religious heresy into Calvinist Transylvania. Ribit's implied distinction between "almost all Europe" on one hand and France, Italy and Germany on the other suggests that his travels may have been in Eastern Europe. But this is mere speculation. We know nothing positive until the late 1580s, when we find Ribit equipped with the territorial title of sieur de la Rivière—presumably he had acquired a property of that name—and established in or close to the court of Henri de Navarre. In the early months of 1589 he was apparently in Genoa.[43] He then returned to the court of Navarre at Nérac. He was evidently patronised by Henri's only sister, Catherine de Navarre, afterwards Duchess of Lorraine and Bar and a stronger Protestant than her brother; for it was she who recommended him to the famous Huguenot nobleman, the stormy petrel of Huguenot politics, Henri de la Tour d'Auvergne, vicomte de Turenne, afterwards duc de Bouillon. Turenne had fought as a volunteer in the Netherlands, had spent 18 months as a prisoner of the Duke of Parma, and now, on his return to freedom, had been shot in the buttock by an arquebus during a private affray on the river Garonne. He had suffered long and seriously from these and older injuries when he was told about la Rivière and called him in. On 1st October 1589, by his own account, la Rivière arrived at Turenne's house at Mont-de-Marsan and was put in sole charge of his health.[44]

For the next five years, la Rivière was Turenne's physician. Late in 1590, when Turenne was sent by Henri IV, now king of France, on a special embassy to Queen Elizabeth, in order to seek English support against Spain and the Ligue, la Rivière accompanied him. He was evidently seriously ill in England—indeed, by his own account, nearly died there.[45] Early next year, Turenne went on from England to Germany in order to raise continetal allies for Henri IV, and la Rivière accompanied him on this journey too. For him the journey had a double purpose: he went not only as Turenne's medical attendant but also, as his friend Joseph du Chesne tells us, to study chemical medicine in its native home.[46]

Turenne's travels in Germany are well documented. He sailed from Colchester to Flushing, travelled through the Netherlands, visited the courts of Dresden, Berlin, Heidelberg, Cassel, Württemberg, and the city of Frankfurt, and returned to France at the head of a German army in the autumn of 1591. In October 1591 he married, at Sedan, Charlotte, sister and heiress of Guillaume-Robert de la Marck, and thus became duc de Bouillon and prince of Sedan. Rivière was certainly with him in Dresden and Frankfurt, for some of his letters were written from those cities. Turenné was accompanied, for much of his journey, by Queen Elizabeth's special ambassador, the Genoese *émigré* Sir Horatio Pallavicino, who had sailed with him from England.[47] Pallavicino also became a patient of la Rivière, who treated him—as he treated the resident French ambassador Philippe Canaye de Fresne—for gout. Pallavicino (like Canaye) evidently thought highly of la Rivière and obtained from him *consilia* or prescriptions for his old mother in Genoa.[48]

While in Dresden with Turenne, la Rivière wrote a very interesting letter which we have already quoted. This is the letter in which he described his earlier travels. The letter was addressed to Caspar Peucer, the humanist historian and reformer who was also physician first to August, Elector of Saxony, and then to Joachim Ernst, Prince of Anhalt. After describing his travels over "almost all Europe," la Rivière admits that he had hitherto avoided Germany, a land (he allows) fertile of learned and religious men, and he attempts to explain this omission. He had been deterred, he says by the swarms of "spagyrists who proclaim Paracelsus as the leader of their sect." These "spagyrists," he explains, having first sprung up in Germany, have now invaded France too. They insinuate themselves into noble households, even into the royal court, offering quick and easy cures for all diseases, refusing rational discussion, and trumpeting their exaggerated claims with insolent rhetoric. La Rivière is careful to explain that he is not a bigot in the matter: he does not accept the arguments of the most famous critic of Paracelsus, Thomas Erastus of Heidelberg. He merely wishes to judge Paracelsians claims objectively. But this, he complains, is precisely what the Paracelsians themselves will not allow. They will not submit their method to objective tests. In fact, explains la Rivière, "I have never yet met a Paracelsian who was a sound, learned man: everywhere I have found them garrulous imposters..." This long attack on the Paracelsian "sectaries" almost reads like a description, by an enemy, of Roch le Baillif, *sectateur du divin Paracelse,* physician to the king and to the nobility of Brittany.

However, la Rivière makes it clear that if he attacks the Paracelsian fanatics, it is only in order to discover it, if he can, the element of true science which may be contained in Paracelsianism. His experience of these quacks, he says, has forced him to ask certain questions. First, are the marvelous cures which are ascribed to Paracelsus true? Secondly, if true, are they accidental or scientific? Thirdly, among all the German disciples of Paracelsus is there any one who can rival his master? Finally, what is the considered opinion of the best German doctors about that whole tribe? After all, Paracelsus lived in Germany, wrote in German, and it was from Germany that his followers had spilled out over Europe, for like the Jesuits, they creep into every country, wherever money is to be made or found... La Rivière is very anxious to be fair. He realises that the active Paracelsians may be wrongly attacked by supercilious armchair physicians: "in medical consultations those who are trained only in academic medicine often reject remedies which are proved valid by use, simply because they cannot rationally explain them;" and he gives as an example the famous weapon-salve which, if applied to the weapon which inflicted the wound, cures the victim "even if the patient and the medicine are many miles apart, as I have often witnessed..." To us, the illustration may not seem very cogent, but at least the general proposition is unexceptionable.

This objective, critical attitude towards Paracelsian medicine is further shown by another letter which la Rivière wrote almost at the same time. It is his letter of 30 June 1591 to Joachim Camerarius—the same letter in which he describes his attendance at the lectures of Argenterius in Turin. Here he discusses the chemical process whereby "white antimony" was prepared for medical use. The method of Argenterius, he says was by mere sublimation; but this left a poisonous residue. La Rivière had seen a second method used in France, for the cure of venereal disease. This, he said, was "a secret remedy devised by an accomplished 'dogmatic' (i.e. Galenist) physician of my acquaintance...I have never used it, as I only follow safe courses, publicly known and tested." The use of antimony in medicine was of course a badge of Paracelsianism, and all those who employed chemical remedies were accused by the orthodox of killing their patients with "this demon of antimony." La Rivère's caution, and his Baconian rejection of secret remedies, distinguishes him clearly from the more fundamentalist disciples of Paracelsus.

La Rivière presumably returned to France with Turenne in the autumn of 1591. He was still with Turenne (now duc de Bouillon) in 1594.

Then, on the death of d'Ailleboust, the reigning *premier médecin,* Henri
IV applied for his services and Bouillon released him to serve, for the
next eleven years, as *premier médecin du roi.*[49] One of la Rivière's first
acts, after his appointment, was to write to Joachim Camerarius in Nuremberg in order to learn from him the most up-to-date antidote to the
poison upon which the king's baffled enemies were now relying to destroy
him. We have the letter in which Camerarius replied. After congratulating la Rivière on his appointment, and expressing horror at the infa-
mous designs of regicide, he offered some useful hints. There was the
"Saxon powder" which Camerarius himself had first communicated to his
friends. It would work well in dry bodies like that of Henri IV. There was
the liquid extract of gentian used by the late king of Sweden. But best of
all was quince-juice mixed with orange. Other doctors believed in prophy-
lactic gems, but these were not recommended by Camerarius.[50]

The character of Jean Ribit, sieur de la Rivière, which emerges from
this admittedly scanty evidence is very different from that of his contemporary Roch le Baillif, sieur de la Rivière, and the confusion between
them, based on little more than a very common territorial title, has
injured the reputation of the *premier médecin.* In fact the characters and
careers of the two men are quite incompatible. Their physical courses
probably never crossed. One was born in Normandy, the other in Switzerland. One based his life in Brittany, the other in Navarre. The surviving
writings of one are all in French, of the other in Latin. One was a provincial autodidact, the other an educated and travelled humanist. And
in medicine, although both were Paracelsian, their Paracelsianism was
very different. One was a bigot, a fundamentalist, the other a critical adherent of Paracelsianism.

Ribit de la Rivière was a Paracelsian indeed, but a Paracelsian of the
second or third generation, who had rejected the mumbo-jumbo of the
master and converted the original Paracelsian impulse into a critical
interest in chemical remedies. Although he published nothing to be
remembered by, even the few documents which survive show that he
was a man of learning who moved among the intellectual *élite* of his
time. He was a friend or correspondent of Agrippa d'Aubigné, Philippe
Canaye de Fresne, Joachim Camerarius, Casper Peucer. It is unfortunate
that Agrippa d'Aubigné, who was so careful to preserve the letters
written by himself, did not keep those which he received, so that we do
not know, at first hand, the views expressed by la Rivière in their "disputes" about Nature and the supernatural; but it seems clear that la

Rivière was a good deal more "modern," in some ways, than his protesting correspondent. The severe d'Aubigné rebuked him for "vos libertez et gayetez ordinaires," for his infection by the "vanities of the court", and for his scepticism. He was particularly shocked by la Rivière's insistence that he had never seen anything supernatural in the case of demoniac possession. To correct such "libertine" views, d'Aubigné sent him authentic and detailed narratives of possession, sorcery, witchcraft and magic, including a graphic account of a witches' sabbat at Pau in Navarre. D'Aubigné himself had attended the trial, together with the king and the Huguenot *élite*. The evidence had convinced them that the sabbat were real, had led to 34 executions, and had corrected the mistaken scepticism of certain other physicians "who had learned in Paris to change the crime of sorcery into mere illness." However, even the censorious d'Aubigné respected la Rivière as a doctor: he addressed him as "le plus grand médecin que l'Europe connoisse."[51] Mayerne similarly described him as "medentium omnium hodie viventium facile coryphaeus ac princeps"; and the same opinion was expressed by the English diplomatist Sir Dudley Carleton. When la Rivière and Marescot died, almost at the same time, of an epidemic then raging in Paris, Carleton deplored the loss of "the two greatest physicians of this town, and for one of them it may be said, of this time."[52]

La Rivière died in Paris on 5 November 1605. Jean-Baptiste le Grain, the chronicler of the reign of Henri IV, who was one of his friends and patients, tells a story of his death. When the doctor felt that his end was near (says le Grain), he sent for his servants and distributed among them his money, plate and other movable possessions. Having done so, he ordered them to leave the house and not to return. When all had gone and nothing was left in his house but the bed on which he lay, he was visited by his medical friends, who came to enquire after his health and attend his sickness. La Rivière asked them to summon his servants, to which they replied that no servant was at hand: on their arrival they had found the doors open and the house empty. La Rivière then said, "Adieu Messieurs, il est donc tems que je m'en aille aussi, puisque mon bagage est parti," and died. The story has been doubted because it was applied, when first printed, 150 years after the event, to the synthetic la Rivière who had by then become established in the historical record; and it was known that Roch le Baillif left heirs of his body. But le Grain clearly told it of the *premier médecin,* and as we have no record that the *premier médecin* was married or had heirs, we may reasonably suppose it to be true. It is certainly compatible with those "libertez et gayetez ordinaires" which d'Aubigné deplored in him and with the roguish character, implicit in the epitaph pronounced upon him by Pierre de l'Estoile: "le bon larron que Dieu a regardé pour luy faire misericorde."[53]

After his death, one of la Rivière's friends, unlike d'Aubigné, took some care of his papers. This was his most famous and successful disciple, Theodore de Mayerne. Mayerne came to Paris some time after taking his medical degree at Montpellier in 1597. From 1599 to 1601 he was away from Paris accompanying the young Henri de Rohan—the same Henri de Rohan to whom Roch le Baillif had dedicated his penultimate book—on his grand tour of Europe. He returned to Paris before the end of 1601, and from then until la Rivière's death in 1605 he assisted him regularly in his practice. La Rivière secured Mayerne's appointment as *médecin ordinaire* to the king and Mayerne's papers record numerous private consultations with la Rivière and several *consilia,* or letters of medical advice, from him.

In 1602 Mayerne began a list of the cures achieved by la Rivière and himself "in certain great and desperate illnesses," and he afterwards recorded the patients who, "having been abandoned by the doctors of Paris, were cured by us and recovered their health."[54] One of these was Roger de St. Lary, duc de Bellegarde, Grand Ecuyer de France, the former *mignon* of Henri III, who had organised the assassination in 1589 of the two brothers the duc de Guise and the cardinal de Guise, and then, on the assassination of his master, had become the confidant of Henri IV. He was a sufferer, like so many of their patients, from venereal disease; but he recovered, Mayerne noted, adding piously *"soli Deo laus et gloria";* and twenty years later he recorded in the margin of the page, "he is alive and well and has never, from the time of that cure, felt the slightest trace of that disease."[55] Others included some very distinguished names. There was Antoine Séguier, *président à mortier;* Madame de Retz; "la Concini", the wife of the *premier écuyer* of Marie de Médicis, afterwards notorious as Maréchal d'Ancre; and Renée Burlamachi, widow of Cesare Balbani, afterwards wife of Agrippa d'Aubigné. She too, Mayerne observed, lived happily ever after, not dying till 1641.[56] Another famous patient was Armand du Plessis, bishop of Luçon, the future cardinal de Richelieu. He too suffered severely from venereal disease,[57] and his case prompted Mayerne to write a treatise on the subject of his complaint.[58]

Mayerne ultimately inherited most of la Rivière's Parisian patients, including his old patron the duc de Bouillon,[59] the apostate de Sancy, the

Huguenot duc de Thouars, and indeed almost the whole *haute société protestante*. He would have inherited Henri IV too, if he had been willing to become a Roman Catholic. Instead, after the assassination of the king, he emigrated to England and made a great career there. But the personal notes which he took with him to England contain more remedies derived from la Rivière than from any other source, and the manuscript books which he treasured consisted predominantly of the medical papers of la Rivière and of la Rivière's master Fernel.[60] It seems, in fact, that Mayerne's extraordinary success as a physician, both in the Paris of Henri IV and in the London of James I, Charles I, and Cromwell, was based largely on the practice of his medical patron la Rivière.

It is unlikely that la Rivière will ever receive the full study suggested by Emmanuel Philipot. He published no book and left, so far as we know, no personal papers; and without such aids it is difficult to trace even a royal doctor in the 16th century. But at least his name should be rescued from the taint which has clung to it for the last two centuries in consequence of the casual conjecture of Jacob le Duchat and the consequent general assumption that his quality as a doctor is to be deduced from the primitive and fanatical Paracelsianism of the provincial empiric Roch le Baillif, sieur de la Rivière.

## References

[1] J. A. de Thou, *Historiae sui temporis*, lib cxxiii.

[2] Theodore de Mayerne, *Apologia* (la Rochelle, 1603), 13.

[3] *Memoires du duc de Sully*, ed. L. R. Lefèvre, 1942, 249. Rivière's prediction concerning Louis XIII, quoted by Sully, is recorded, in the hand of J. Dupuy, in B.N., MS Dupuy 588 fo. 205.

[4] Agrippa d'Aubigné, "Confession de Sancy," printed in Pierre L'Estoile, *Journal de Henri III* (Hague, 1744) V. 384.

[5] e.g. Joannes Renodaeus (Jean de Renoud), *Institutionum Pharmaceuticarum...* (Paris, 1608), *de Materia Medica...* lib III cap. xxxiv.

[6] Mayerne, *Apologia*, l.c.; Jos. Quercetanus [du Chesne] *de Priscorum Philosophorum Vera Medicinae Materia* (1603), 213.

[7] The two most important documents for la Rivière are MS Sloane 2089, which contains several letters to and from la Rivière, and MS Sloane 2111, which is anonymous, but which is proved by internal evidence and by the evidence of MS Sloane 2089 to be by la Rivière. MS Sloane 1996 consists largely of material from la Rivière. Other MSS in the Sloane collection containing incidental evidence from

or about la Rivière will be cited as they are relevant. It may be remarked that the confusion concerning la Rivière is still further confounded by the printed index to the Sloane MSS, in which the *premier médecin* is consistently confused with the 17th century French physician Lazare Rivière.

[8]Emmanuel Philipot, *La Vie et l'Oeuvre Littéraire de Noël du Fail, gentilhomme breton* (Paris, 1914).

[9]L'Estoile, *Journal de Henri III* (Hague, 1744) V. 394.

[10]See the document concerning his marriage cited by Philipot, *op. cit.* p. 349. In 1579 le Baillif's critics declared to the Parlement of Paris that "en toute la Bretagne ...la Rivière n'en a pas peu guarir un seul en cinq ans", which implies that he had been practising in Brittany for at least five years.

[11]*Petit Traicté de l'antiquité et de la singularité de la Bretagne armorique* (Rennes, 1578).

[12]He was evidently a close friend of the Huguenot Noël du Fail. His printers at Rennes, Julien du Clos and Pierre le Bret, were both Huguenots. In the course of his trial in 1579, frequent references were made to le Baillif's religious unorthodoxy, and the Dean of tht Faculty described him as "a Luther."

[13]*Discours sur la signification de la comète apparue en Occident au signe du Sagittaire le 10 Nov* (Rennes, 1577). I have not been able to trace a copy of this work.

[14]'Edelphus', le Baillif explained, "est qui iuxta naturam elementi pronosticat" (*Demosterion*, p. 131). Cf. Martin Ruland, *Lexicon Alchemiae*...(Frankfurt, 1612) 193: "Edelphus, qui ex elementorum natura prognosticat."

[15]Registres MSS de la Faculté VIII. 128 foll., quoted by F. Brunot, *Historie de la Langue Francaise II* (1906) 10-11.

[16]Philipot, *op. cit.; Les Lettres d'Etienne Pasquier*...(Paris, 1619) I., 455; II., 752, 787.

[17]C-P Goujet, *Histoire du Collège de France.*

[18]See the depositions against the Ligueurs made before the Sénéchal de Rennes in 1589 and published by F. Joüon de Longrais in *Bulletin et Memoires de la Société Archéologique du Départment d'Ille-et-Vilaine,* tom. XLI (Rennes, 1911), 154-7, 163, 178.

[19]*Traicté de la Cause de la Briefve Vie de plusieurs Princes et Grands*... (Rennes, 1591).

[20]*La Conformité de l'ancienne et moderne médicine d'Hippocrate à Paracelse*... (Rennes, 1592).

[21]Le Baillif had already put forward this thesis in his *Demosterion* (1578). Etienne Pasquier, who defended him in court, and his cause in correspondence, could not swallow this part of his argument: to him the medical system of Paracelsus was

"de tout contraire en principes à celle d'Hippocrate et Galien" (*Lettres d'Etienne Pasquier*, II, 546).

[22]"Livre de Raison de Gilles Satin, sieur de la Teillaye 1591-1597" in *Bulletin Archéologique de l'Association Bretonne*, tom. XVI (St. Brieuc, 1898), 454.

[23]Philipot, *op. cit.*, 354 foll.

[24]See, for example, MS Sloane 2089, fo. 78 v.

[25]Philipot, *op. cit.*, 358.

[26]Philipot, *op. cit.*, 348-9. The document cited is an authorisation signed on 25 January 1598 by Jacques le Baillif, son of Roch le Baillif, allowing his brother-in-law Olivier le Bel to deal with the inheritance of "déffunt noble homme Roch le Baillif, sieur de la Rivière, son beau-père."

[27]Pierre Bayle, *Dictionnaire*, s.v. 'Mayerne'.

[28]MS Sloane 2089, fo. 78 v.

[29]Haag, *La France Protestante*, s.v. Ribit.

[30]N. Weiss, in *Biographie Universelle*, *s.v.* "Ribit", denies that Ribit was a Savoyard: "on ne sait sur quel fondement Fabricius, *Bibliotheca Graeca* [Hamburg 1717] t. VIII, 822, dit que Ribit était Savoisien: rien de l'indique dans les titres et dans les préfaces de ses ouvrages..." In fact Ribit explicitly names himself as "Joannes Ribittus, Sabaudus" in the table of contents of his Latin translation of Maximus, Theophilus and Tatian, *Sententiarum sive capitum theologorum ...tomi tres* (Zurich, 1546).

[31]Gesner records the fact in his *Bibliotheca Universalis* (Zurich, 1545) fo. 450 v., where he calls Ribit "summus amicus meus."

[32]On Jean Ribit the Hellenist see A.-L. Herminjard, *Correspondance des Réformateurs dans les pays de langue française* (Geneva, 1866-97) IV, 288 etc.; Henri Vuilleumier, *Histoire de l'Eglise Réformée du Pays de Vaud* (Lausanne, 1927-33) I, 398, 407, 667, 734, 748, etc.

[33]Helenus Ribit, *Vita Aemylii Ferretti*, Lyon, 1553, preface; Herminjard, *op. cit.*, viii, 133, ix. 16, 485. I deduce that Helenus Ribit was the brother of Jean Ribit from the letters of Jean Ribit in B.N. MS Latin 8641 (see below, note 35).

[34]In MS Sloane 2059 there are several letters between la Rivière and another doctor, Gerald Boyssonade, originally from Agen. In two letters, Boyssonade and Rivière regret their failure to meet in Lausanne. Rivière writes from Caumont, near Avignon, presumably on his way from Lausanne to Navarre. It seems that Boyssonade then followed Rivière, whom he regarded as his patron ("nam a maecenatis latere ne latum quidem unguem discedam") to Navarre, for we find him established in Condom, in close and regular contact with la Rivière at Nérac. Unfortunately these letters are imperfectly dated.

[35]B.N. MS Latin 8641. This is a notebook of Jean Ribit the Hellenist, containing drafts of his letters, sermons, etc.

[36]*Oeuvres Complètes d'Agrippa d'Aubigné* ed. Reaume et Caussade (1873-1892) I., 423. Emmanuel Philipot, *op. cit.* p. 348, by an extraordinary misinterpretation (and misquotation) of this letter, uses it to argue that la Rivière, like Roch le Baillif, was born in Normandy, where there is apparently a village called Cartigny near Isigny. In fact the letter, with its explicit references to Geneva and Chevalier, is perfectly clear. Since Agrippa d'Aubigné was not Norman either, it is difficult to see how even Philipot's misquotation could lead to such a conclusion.

[37]MS Sloane 2089 fo. 74.

[38]The brothers Haag, *La France Protestante,* s.v. 'le Baillif', say of the synthetic la Rivière that he was "né à Falaise mais èlevé à Genevè par son perè, qui y avait cherché un asyle contre la persecution et qui y professait, dit-on, la théologie". Jean Ribit is recognisable in all but the birthplace and Haag may have had authority for the education of Ribit by his father. If Ribit studied at the Collège de Genève, d'Aubigné's phrase "de vos études de vous et de moy" becomes more definite.

[39]MS Sloane 2089 fo. 74 v.

[40]See Pier Giacosa, "La medicina in Piemonte nel secolo XVI," in *Studi pubblicati dalla Regia Università di Torino nel IV centenario della nascita di Emmanuele Filberto* (Turin, 1928).

[41]See Arturo Pascal, "La Colonia piemontese a Ginevra nel secolo XVI," in D. Cantimori et al. (ed.) *Ginevra e l'Italia* (Florence, 1959), 114-5.

[42]*Lettres d'Etienne Pasquier, II,* 537. This is no doubt the Boutal who is claimed as a precursor by Joseph du Chesne in his *Sclopetarius* (1575)

[43]FS Sloane 2089 fos. 75v-77. This is a letter from la Rivière to a Genoese doctor Ottavio Boerio or Boere, dated 8 cal. Jun. 1591 (26 May 1591). Rivière there says that the tumults of France were reported to him as he was leaving Genoa for France and that these had prevented him from writing to Boerio earlier to thank him for his hospitality in Genoa. I presume that these "tumults" were the events of the summer of 1589.

[44]MS Sloane 2111.

[45]MS Sloane 2089 fo. 77.

[46]Quercetanus (Joseph du Chesne), *de Priscorum Philosophorum...*, *loc. cit.*

[47]For an account of the journey from England see Historical MSS Commission, *MSS of Marquess of Salisbury,* IV 102.

[48]Quercetanus, *loc. cit.* MS Sloane 2111 fo. 9; 2089 fo. 75 v.-77.

[49]L'Estoile, *Journal de Henri IV* (ed. Paul Bonnefon, Paris 1888-96), vi. 219.

[50]MS Sloane 2089 fo. 73 v.

[51] Agrippa d'Aubigné, *Oeuvres*, I, 428-433.

[52] HMC *Marquess of Salisbury*, XVII, 454.

[53] The story was first printed by the abbé Goujet in his article in the Paris supplement to Moreri's *Le Grand Dictionnaire* (1735), incorporated in the text of the edition of 1759. (s.v. "Bailli"). Goujet there ascribed it to a manuscript journal of le Grain which he had seen, and which he describes more fully in his article on le Grain in the same work (s.v. "Grain"). The diary is evidently still unpublished. The story is repeated, without evidence of its source, by J. F. Carrère, *Bibliothèque historique de la médecine* (Paris 1776), s.v. 'Baillif'. J. N. F. Eloy, who rejected it on the above grounds (*Dictionnaire historique de la médecine*, Mons, 1778, I. 248-9.), took it from Carrère and was evidently unaware that it had good contemporary authority. The remark of l'Estoile is in his *Journal de Henri IV*, VIII 194.

[54] MS Sloane 2089 fo. 23, 27 v.

[55] MS Sloane 1996 fo. 55 v.

[56] MS Sloane 2089 fo. 35.

[57] *Ibid.*, fo. 27 v. Richelieu appears in the list as "Mr le Cardinal"; but the list (like the other entries in this MS) has clearly been copied later, as the other titles show. That the reference is to Richelieu is clear from the reference in Mayerne's 'Ephemerides' where the patient is described as "Mr. de Lusson, Maij 1605, Gonorrhoea inveterata a vj. mensibus cum caruncula circa collum vesicae dura", and Mayerne has afterwards written in the margin "Cardinal de Richel." (MS Sloane 2059 fo. 45).

[58] The title of Mayerne's work *de gonorrhoeae inveteratae et carunculae et ulceris in meatu urinario curatione* almost exactly repeats his description of Richelieu's complaint. Though not published till 1619, in the correspondence of Fabricius Hildanus (Oppenheim 1619), this treatise was written before May 1607—i.e. about the time of Richelieu's treatment (MS Sloane 2105 A fo. 17).

[59] MS Sloane 2062 fo. 1. This was on 1 October 1609—i.e. after the death of Joseph du Chesne (Quercetanus) who had worked in partnership with la Rivière and Mayerne.

[60] MS Sloane 2046 fo. 42: "Catalogus librorum quos mecum sumpsi in Angliam." Of 15 titles, six are by la Rivière, two by Fernel, and one by Fernel's disciple le Paulmier.

# 37

## A Chinese Puzzle:
## Eighth or Eighteenth?

### JOSEPH NEEDHAM

As is well known, the Jesuit Mission of the seventeenth century played a great role in transmitting to China the newly developed modern sciences of mathematics, astronomy and physics. In the eighteenth century, however, for various reasons, they did almost nothing to pass on the new chemistry. Yet there is a strange story to tell about one possible attempt to put the discovery of oxygen into Chinese. At the same time it confronts us with one of the most singular literary puzzles which has presented itself in the whole course of our studies on the history of science in China.

In 1810 Julius Klaproth published in the *Mémoires* of the Academy of Sciences of St. Petersburg a short paper "On the chemical knowledge of the Chinese in the 8th century." Introducing this, he said that "as we have so few exact notions about the state of chemistry among the Ancients, and especially among the asiatick peoples, it seems to me that the following extracts, taken from a Chinese book treating of this science, might offer some interest, for they demonstrate that the people already had, several centuries ago, certain ideas, inexact though they might be, on the effects of oxygen." He went on to relate that in 1802 he had copied and translated some passages from a Chinese manuscript of 68 pages, one among those which had been brought back from China by the late Mons. Bournon, and (presumably) deposited in one of the libraries of the Russian capital. The title of this "small collection of chemical and metallurgical experiments" was *Phing Lung Jen,*[a] a phrase which Klaproth translated as "Confessions of the Peaceful Dragon."[1] It had been written, he said, according to the MS. itself, by one Maò hhóa[2] in a *ping-shen* year, the first of the Chih-Tê[b] reign-period, i.e., +756. He failed to give the characters for the author's name, but said that he had searched for him in the *Wan Hsing Thung Phu*[c] and the *Wên Hsien Thung Khao* without success. Klaproth then went on to give his partial translation of chapter 3 and chapter 9, the first on the oxygen of the air and its significance for the calces of metals, the second on the metals themselves and some of their derivative compounds, prefacing these by a discussion of the leading ideas in the work.

Klaproth thought he could recognize them as Taoist.

It is easy to see [he wrote] that his [the author's] system is similar to that of the Dáo-chè *(Tao shih*[d])...In his first chapter the author says: 'All that man can perceive and observe by the senses, and all that he can conceive with his mind and imagination, is composed of two fundamental principles, the Yänn (Yang) and the Ῡne (Yin), which designate the perfect and the imperfect.' This system is represented in the Eight Goúa *(kua)* of Foǔ-hhῩ (Fu Hsi). The Yang is the powerful and the perfected, the Yin is the diametrically opposite. Our author, however, often diverges from this definition in the course of his work, and one can clearly see that he assumes infinite modifications of these two principles, which manifest themselves in the forms of the world. In this he differs from the system of the *Tao shih,* which explains the differences in forms of visible objects by continual changes in the proportions of Yang and Yin.

Then he plunges in to the supposedly Thang account of oxygen.

Ch. 3. The Atmosphere. The *Hhiá-chênn-ki (hsia shêng chhi*[e])[3] is the *chhi* which rests on the surface of the earth and which rises up to the clouds. When the proportion of Yin, which forms part of its composition, is too great, it is not so perfect (or full) as the *chhi* beyond the clouds. We can feel the *hsia shêng chhi* by the sense of touch, but the elemental fire with which it is mixed makes it invisible to our eyes. There are several methods which purify it and rob it of a part of its Yin. This is done first by things which are modifications of the Yang, such as the metals, sulphur *(lieôu-hhouânn, liu huang*[hh]) and charcoal *(táne, than*[r]). When these substances burn they amalgamate with the Yin[4] of the air, and give new combinations of the two fundamental principles.

The Yin of the air *(Kῐ-ῐne, chhi Yin*[g]) is never pure, but by the aid of fire one can extract it from *Tchine-chĕ*[5], from saltpetre *(Hhò-siaǭ, huo hsiao*[h]) and from the stone called *Hhé-tánn-chĕ*.[6] It enters also into the composition of water, where it is so closely bound with the Yang that (its) decomposition becomes very difficult. The elemental fire hides the Yin of the air from our eyes, and we recognise it only by its effects.

For Klaproth this was important, since it showed that the Chinese of the +8th century "had rather clear ideas about oxygen, which they called chhi Yin,[j] or the imperfect (part) of the air." What else could combine with heated metals, sulphur and carbon, forming new compounds with them? He added that it was "very interesting that they thought water to be a composite (body), since in Europe it was so long regarded as an element."

Klaproth's excerpt from chapter 9 was less sensational.

Ch. 9. The Metals. There are five principal metals apart from gold; silver, copper, iron, tin and lead.

Gold is the most perfect (Yang), and in general the symbol of the perfection of matter because it contains no Yin whatever; this is why it dominates the four quarters of the world. Silver contains already a little, copper more, and finally lead is the most impure of all the metals. Gold never amalgamates with the Yin of the air, and is always found native. The greatest heat does not change it.

If one purges the silver of its Yin it becomes gold, but as it is always bound to its sulphur, this operation becomes very difficult. Only the silver of Ssī lôunn-chane (mountain) in Tiēne-dschoŭ (Thien-chu,[k] India)[7] lends itself to this change. Lao Tzu knew how to change any kind of silver into gold, but did not do it as he himself possessed the golden mountain.[8]

Copper is found native in mountains, or mineralised with the Yin of the air, or with sulphur.[9] When repeatedly melted it loses much of its redness.[10] It is too tightly bound to the Yin to be detached from it. It also readily attracts the Yin of the air, of water, and of alum *(Be-fâne, pai fan¹)*, the resulting composition being (a kind of) verdigris *(Toúnn-sieóu, thung hsiu,*[m,n] basic copper carbonate).[11]

To get a fine green pigment from copper one must calcine the rust of this metal,[12] and then boil it with white alum in a sufficient amount of water. After it has cooled it will be green, and one must add some natron solution *(Guiēne-choùy, chien shui*°)[13] which will precipitate the green colour called *Siaò-lou-chĕ (hsiao lü sê*ᵖ).[14] This is used in painting for the colour of plant and bamboo leaves.

To get a blue pigment from copper one must mix three tçán[15] of the rust of red copper with 17 tçán of sal ammoniac *(Naó chŭ, nao sha*ᵗᵗ) and boil this mixture with pure water. Hhiéne-pânn,[16] who lived in the Han dynasty, was the inventor of this pigment.[17]

If one melts copper with the stone Yánn-chĕ[18] it takes a greenish colour and becomes harder.[19] The utensils made from this copper in the Sung dynasty are much esteemed.[20] It is said that the Eight Kua of Taí-hháo-foú-hhȳ̄ᵘᵘ were engraved on a plate of this kind of copper.

Klaproth, who found some difficulty in identifying the substances mentioned in this passage, had less to say about it than about the other. But it merits a word or two. The opening seems to betray a knowledge or half-knowledge of the sulphur-mercury theory of metals, though in the light of what went before a reader might have understood them to be all composed of nitrogen and oxygen; as for "perfection," it also has a European flavour, though not quite excluded from the classical *Huai Nan Tzu* tradition. The explanation of the corrosion of copper is interesting and not ill-phrased, while the making of green and blue pigments from copper salts indicates some practical knowledge. Finally there seems to be a clear mention of brass manufacture.

What is one to make of this curious text? No notice was taken of it for close on eighty years after Klaproth's first presentation in 1807, but then it was disinterred by Duckworth who put the oxygen part into English and taking the date at its face value called for further information. Naturally no one had anything to say. Klaproth was translated into Italian by Guareschi in 1904, and after that wider interest was aroused. Passing mentions were accorded by Moissan[21] and Mellor,[22] while von Lippmann dismissed the whole matter as a late forgery.[23] The most serious discussion was that of Muccioli, who concluded that the MS. text was of the +18th rather than the 8th century, Chhing not Thang in date, regarding it as an effort to put into Chinese the ideas of the new chemistry, after Priestley and after +1774; the work therefore of one or other of the Jesuits or of their scholarly Chinese friends. This is why the problem is such an intriguing one. The idea of a late date, in this case the Ming, was also proposed by Chinese chemists and historians of chemistry, notably Huang Su-Fêng[cc] (with Fu Wei-Phing[s] and Su Chi-Chhing[y]), in his preface to the 1936 Chinese translation of Weeks' book on the discovery of the chemical elements;[24] but Yuan Han-Chhing was reluctant to accept this, pointing to the general decay of alchemy and chemistry in the Ming period.[25] Yuan Han-Chhing himself inclines to believe in a Thang dating for the document. Some of Muccioli's reasons why "Mao Hua" could not be pre-Priestley were rather unconvincing, such as the vagueness and sexuality of the Yin-Yang theory, but he was certainly justified in pointing out that the discoveries of Priestley's time would not have been possible without good apparatus of glass, high-temperature equipment, the electric current,[26] and all the other inventions which permitted pneumatic chemistry such as the collection of gases over mercury. But does the "Mao Hua" MS. pretend to be a document of this kind? The real problem is that its obscurity and naïveté could arise either from its speculative (though penetrating) nature,

based on only very rough experiments, if it is Thang, or from the difficulties of Jesuits and Chinese scholars in the Chhing attempting to render
some idea of the new chemistry into the traditional idiom of that language.

Yuan Han-Chhing, who has considered the matter at length,[27] reviews
what "Mao Hua's" ideas comprised. He was sure that some change
occurred in atmospheric air after the combustion of charcoal or sulphur,
and that other substances such as saltpetre would give off some "air" to
the air; since it was natural to regard everything as composed of Yin and
Yang, it would not have been unnatural to consider atmospheric air as
also so composed. Nor would a similar composition of water have been
unthinkable; we must beware of reading too much factual background
knowledge into the words of the document. Combustion, then, dimin-
ished the Yin chhi of the air, heating of certain minerals increased it.
Here one must bear in mind that even in the +8th century the Chinese
had been making the oxides or calces of metals for hundreds of years
by heating them in air. Datable about +640, the *Tan Ching Yao Chüeh*[t]
(Essentials of the Elixir Manuals), probably by Sun Ssu-Mo,[u] contains
a clear process for the making of red mercuric oxide ($HgO$) by long-
continued heating of mercury under conditions of limited admission of
air.[28]Similarly the oxides of lead (minium, litharge and massicot) had
been made industrially ever since the Warring States period.[29] The fact
that nothing at all is said about weighings, such as those which proved
the combination of a part of the air with the metal during oxidation, as
in the pioneer work of Jean Rey (+1630),[30] may be an argument for
the earlier date, since at the end of the eighteenth century the Jesuits or
their friends would have been very conscious of this.

The second passage may seem almost more indigenously Chinese than
the first, for the alchemical motif is present, and there is no mention of
processes which we know the people of mediaeval China did not use.
As for the explanation of the "rusting" of copper, it might again be
interpreted much too cleverly by seeing in the reference to the alum, a
sulphate, some hint of modern knowledge that the corrosion is generally
a basic sulphate. Thus provided one takes the "Mao Hua" tractate as
essentially speculative, inspired guesswork rather than a record of precise
experiments, it is impossible so far to exclude it as a text of the Thang.[31]

Yet there remain many curious, not to say suspicious, circumstances.
First, no one has seen the work since Klaproth described it, and until
someone can discover it again in one of the great Russian libraries, so
that its paper and script can be examined, judgment can only be sus-

pended. Secondly, Thang MSS, apart from the famous buried library of the Tunhuang caves, are extremely rare, though this could of course have been a much later copy, one of a succession handed down through the ages, the kind of thing in fact which Chhü Thai-Su sent to his Jesuit friends to be burnt.[32] Supposing that one of them had plucked it from the burning? On the other hand the most exhaustive searches, carried on in the Chinese collections and bibliographies of Europe as well as in China, have completely failed to unearth any reference either to Mao Hua or a *Phing Lung Jen*.[33] This in itself is odd because most of the mediaeval alchemists and iatro-chemists can usually be picked up in two or three collateral references, even if only in the hagiography. As for the title, we have long surmised that *Jen* could have been a mis-reading of *Chih*,[w] which would make the title much more natural. In this case we could take *Phing* as a verb instead of Klaproth's adjective, and translate: "Records of the Pacification (i.e., Subduing) of the Dragon," that is to say, the formation of the calces of metals (cf. p. 255), an interpretation closely in line with the thinking of alchemists in all the old civilisations. An alternative suggestion is due to Yuan Han-Chhing,[34] who draws attention to a well-known aphorism in *fêng-shui*[x] geomancy;[35] *Shan lung i hsün, phing lung nan jen*,[y] which means: "The dragon of the mountains (i.e., the lay of the land, or configuration of the earth) is easy to detect and measure; the dragon of the plains is difficult to recognise." In this case the title would have been right as Klaproth had it, and metaphorical, signifying that the hidden processes in chemical reactions were as difficult to understand as the "veins of the earth" in flat country. So that *Phing* would be a noun, and the translation would be: "Recognition of the Dragon (i.e., the processes) in the Plains (i.e., the baffling chemical phenomena)." Both these possibilities would consort with a date either Thang or Chhing.

Provisionally, for our placing, we have chosen the latter alternative, assuming that the text was the work of one of the Jesuits such as Cibot or Collas, or, even more probably, one of their Chinese friends who had been talking with them about the discovery of oxygen in Europe. But then how can one explain the Thang date on the MS.? Someone could have added it spuriously before the text left China; someone, for that matter, could have insinuated crucial sentences into what was genuinely Thang writing. But against this it must be said that in all the work reported in our volumes we have come across exceedingly few, if any, false datings or claims to antiquity supported by false interpolated passages—where scientific matters were concerned no one in that Confucian culture would have thought it worth while, at least before the very end of the nineteenth century.[36] Spurious ascriptions and attributions of whole books are an entirely different matter, of those there were many, just as in European culture mediaeval authors liked to father their works on names already venerated,[37] but this kind of thing can almost always be put right by philological and bibliographical criticism, a humanistic technique in which the Chinese themselves excelled earlier than anyone else.[38]

Alternatively Klaproth could have made some elementary sinological mistake. But it is difficult to see what it could have been. It is true that he was young at the time. Born in Berlin [39] in +1783, he began the study of Chinese at the age of 14. A voracious polymath in oriental languages (Arabic, Persian, Turkish, Hebrew), he began to publish from 1800 onwards, and in 1804 at the age of 21 was called to the St. Petersburg Academy of Sciences as "Adjunctus f.d. orientalischen Sprachen u. Literatur." In the following year he went east with the embassy of Count Golovkin to China, and although this never got beyond the frontier on account of a disagreement about ceremonial, the journey was not unsuccessful for Klaproth since it enabled him to learn Manchu and Mongol by the way, and to collect a great number of books. By 1807 he was a member of the Academy, and then undertook adventurous travels in the south, the Caucasus, Persia and Afghanistan, travels which led before long to his downfall and departure from Russia because his reports were considered to show too clearly the weakness of Russian power in those regions. There is no immediate need to follow his further career in France, his relations with Napoleon, etc., but only to remind ourselves that in the penultimate year of his life, 1834, he published a monograph on the history of the magnetic compass so good that it is still usable at the present day, and greatly helped us in writing the relevant section in our work. Young as he was at the time (1802), it is hard to believe either that Klaproth misinterpreted his text, or that he was guilty (as might conceivably be thought possible) of a scholarly hoax designed to attract interest and further his career. But we should be happier if we could find out something definite about the Mons. Bournon who brought the MS. back from China—so far all searches in the French and the sinological literature have proved unavailing. The solution of the puzzle is more likely to come from the Soviet sinologists than anyone else, for they may be able to trace the MS. itself, and they may succeed in finding out who

Bournon was and what (from his connections) he is likely to have brought home with him. Perhaps this intriguing document will have the honour of being transferred, in later editions of our book, from its present place back to the great days of the Thang.

Of one thing we can be reasonably sure; there were Jesuits towards the end of the +18th century who were very enamoured of the Yin-Yang theory as a general natural philosophy. On 26 June 1789, J. J. M. Amiot, in the course of a letter (probably thinking of the new discoveries in electricity), wrote in these terms:

> Here, as in our France, men construct [philosophical] systems, but they fall into desuetude and are soon forgotten when they are not founded on the two great principles Yang and Yin. Yang and Yin, Yin and Yang, when well conceived and well understood, are alone capable of introducing man into the sanctuary of Nature, and unveiling for him even the most secret of her mysteries. Everything happens by the varying combinations of the Yin and Yang, it is by them that all Beings reproduce themselves, and that everything maintains itself in the living state. If the Yang and the Yin were to cease to combine with each other, the whole world would return to chaos. These, you will tell me, are the dreams of the Chinese; we are not necessitated yet to adopt them in preference to those of our European savants. All right, but one day you will adopt them—judging by the productions of your modern Physicists!

## References

[1] More probable interpretations are suggested below.

[2] Judging from Klaproth's other romanisations, this could hardly be anything else than Mao Hua, since Hs- would be inadmissable here. One could however think of Mao Kua or Mao Khua. Chang Tzu-Kung,[z] in his 1952 translation of Weeks, very naturally presumed Mao Hua,[aa] though in earlier translations Huang Su-Fêng[cc] and Yü Jen-Chün[bb] (1936) had adopted Ma Ho,[dd] much less likely though retained by Yuan Han-Chhing; and Chu Jen-Hung[ee] (1937) had suggested Mao[ff] as the surname. The Japanese translation (1941) chose Mêng Kao,[gg] very improbable; and as Yuan points out, Mao-Hua could be a *hao* or literary name, giving no clue to the family name at all. I should like to take this opportunity of thanking Dr. Chang Tzu-Kung again most warmly for much help and many talks during my time in China during the war years, as also Dr. Yuan Han-Chhing, whom I knew at Lanchow.

[3] Literally "underneath rising-up vapour or *pneuma*," i.e., air. This interpretation is a conjecture of Muccioli, for Klaproth gave no characters. Huang Su-Fêng and Yü Jen-Chün supposed *han chen chhi*,[ii] impossible on Klaproth's romanisation.

[4]The original has Yang, but this must have been a slip of Klaproth's pen, as Muccioli also saw.

[5]This has puzzled everyone. Klaproth gave no characters, but thought it was a mineral having something to do with grindstones. So perhaps it was (*hsi*) *chen shih*[ij] or (*fan*) *ching shih*[kk] (RP/76, 100), both meaning magnetite or black iron oxide. It could also have been zinc carbonate, *kan shih*[ll] (RP/59), wrongly read as *chhien shih*. And *chün shih*[mm] (RP/87) is a synonym for copper sulphate. Yuan Han-Chhing wrote *chhing shih*,[i] lapis lazuli, a complex aluminum-sodium sulphate-silicate, which would not make sense here; cf. Partington, *General and Inorganic Chemistry*, 2nd ed., London, 1951, 426. But he took it to mean some form of calcium carbonate, with what authority we do not know.

[6]*Hei tan*,[nn] *hei than*,[oo] is coal, but no remotely likely oxygen-containing substance has been found to fill this bill. Klaproth gave no characters for any of his substances, but commented upon this one as "a black stone found in marshes," conceivably *hei tan shih*.[pp] But no such term, or anything like it, appears in even the greatest Chinese encyclopaedias. Yuan Han-Chhing supposes *hei than shih*,[qq] equally meaningless, unless coal, which won't do.

[7]This reference is obscure, through it may be an allusion to Ceylon.

[8]Of spiritual perfection, no doubt. But of course the Logos of Taoism was always regarded in later times as an alchemist.

[9]Ores of copper certainly do include oxides and sulphides. But could this really have been said by anyone in the +8th century?

[10]Perhaps a reference to the making of high-tin bronzes.

[11]The patina and corrosion product of copper is at least as likely to be the basic sulphate (and in sea air the chloride) as the basic carbonate (Partington, *op. cit.*, 330, 333; Mellor, *Modern Inorganic Chemistry*, London, 1916, 378). The term verdigris ("Greek green") also means the acetate, prepared as a pigment and for medicinal use by exposing copper to the fumes of warm vinegar *(Pên Tshao Kang Mu*, ch. 8, p. 11); *Thien Kung Khai Wu; Chinese Technology in the Seventeenth Century*, by Sung Ying-Hsing, trans. by Sun Jen I-Tu and Sun Hsüeh-Chuan, University Park and London, Penn., 1966, suppl. to ch. 16, 287; cf. Yü Fei-An, *Chung-Kuo Hua Yen-sê-ti Yen-Chiu* (A Study of the Pigments used by Chinese Painters), Chao-Hua Mei-Shu, Peking, 1955, 1957, 5. This was called *thung lü*,[rr] or better *thung chhing*.[ss] Ko Hung already knew (in *Pên Tshao Kang Mu*, ch. 8) that applying it to wood prevents rotting.

[12]Presumably this means heating to obtain oxides. Sulphates would be formed in the next step.

[13]A mixture of the carbonate, sulphate and chloride of sodium. Naturally occurring. Klaproth recognized this.

[14]This must be the carbonate, verditer, the same as *thung lü*,[rr] properly so called, or *shih lü*.[q]

[15]Presumably *chhien*,[WW] mace, or tenths of an ounce.

[16]Neither Klaproth nor anyone since has been able to pin down this individual.

[17]Perhaps this was the preparation of cupric chloride, unless it was a conversion of the basic to the regular sulphate.

[18]Not certainly identifiable, but one suspects some zinc ore.

[19]This is surely a reference to the making of brass.

[20]How was a Thang writer referring to the Sung? Huang Su-Fêng and Yü Jen-Chün were so upset by this that they transliterated Shang,[V] which was absurd, for brass does not go back that far. Yuan Han-Chhing corrected them but did not offer the obvious escape route that he might have been speaking of the Liu-Sung (+420 to +477). For early brass-making this is not implausible, but one would like some supporting evidence.

[21]*Traité de Chimie Minerale*, 5 vols., Paris, 1904, Vol. I, 191, 238.

[22]*Comprehensive Treatise on Inorganic and Theoretical Chemistry*, 15 vols., London, 1923, I, 347. He said merely that there could have been no connection between Mao Hua and the definitive later discoveries in Europe.

[23]*Enstehung und Ausbreitung der Alchemie, mit einem Anhang, Zur älteren Geschichte der Metalle; ein Beitrag zur Kulturgeschichte*, 3 vols., Berlin, 1919 and 1931, and Weinheim, 1954, 460. But von Lippmann was so intemperate and so wrong in his general estimate of Chinese alchemy and protochemistry that the force of his remarks is now long spent.

[24]Cf. the Engl. ed., Weeks, M.E. *The Discovery of the Elements*, Pa., U.S.A., 1933, 35 ff.

[25]Yuan Han-Chhing, *Chung-Kuo Hua-Hsüeh Shih Lun Wên Chi* (Collected Papers on the History of Chemistry in China), Peking, 1956, 229. Also if "Mao Hua" was a pseudonym, why should not the late writer have taken the much more usual course of fathering his book on Ko Hung, Sun Ssu-Mo or Lü Tung-Pin, one or other of the great proto-chemical names of antiquity? Also if the Ming would have been too late for genuineness it would have been too early for Priestley.

[26]The electrolytic decomposition of water was accomplished in preliminary experiments by G. Beccaria (+1758), P. van Troostwijk & J. R. Deiman (+1789) and G. Pearson (+1797); then definitively with full recognition of the gases by Carlisle & Nicholson in 1800.

[27]Yuan Han-Chhing, *op. cit.*, 27, 221 ff.

[28]*Yün Chi Chhi Chhien*, ch. 71; p. 12a; tr. Sivin, N., "Preliminary Studies in Chinese Alchemy" ch. 1, *Jap. Studies in the History of Science*, 6 (1967), 19 I.

[29]Cf. Needham, Joseph *et al. Science and Civilisation in China*, 7 vols. in 12 or more parts, Cambridge, 1954-, V, pts. 3, 4.

[30]See Partington, J. R., *A History of Chemistry*, London, 1961-, II (+1500

to +1700), 631 ff. Before Lavoisier's definitive solution of the problem in +1777 there had been many demonstrations of the increase of weight on calcination, as by Bayen in +1774 and N. Lemery in +1690 (cf. Partington, *op. cit.*, III (+1700 to 1800), 38, 395, 421 ff.)

[31]The expression *chhi Yin,* however, "the Yin of the air," has a very un-Chinese feel about it, and one would rather expect *Yin chhi.* In modern Chinese chemical terminology, oxygen is of course oppositely named *yang.*[xx]

[32]Needham *et al., op. cit.,* IV, pt. 1, 244.

[33]What Chhen Kuo-Fu could not find (Yuan, *Collected Papers,* p. 228), it is hardly likely that anyone else will.

[34]*Ibid.,* 225.

[35]See Needham *et al., op. cit.,* IV, pt. 1, 239 ff.

[36]*Ibid.,* I, 43, fn. It is quite inconceivable that any of the Jesuits or their Chinese friends would have put a Thang date—or for that matter an assumed name—on anything which they themselves had written.

[37]Think, apart from anything else, of the Geberian books and the Lullian Corpus. Or in the earlier Arabic world, the Jābirian Corpus.

[38]Needham, *et al., op. cit.,* II, 390 ff.

[39]He was the son of Martin H. Klaproth (+1743 to 1817) the celebrated chemist, on whom see Partington, *op. cit.,* III, 654 ff. It was a parallel to the Biots, the chemist-astronomer father J. B. Biot, and the orientalist son E. Biot; cf. Needham *et al., op. cit.,* III, 183.

a 平龍認    h 火硝

b 至德    i 青石

c 萬姓統譜    j 氣陰

d 道士    k 天竺

e 下升氣    l 白礬

f 炭    m 銅銹

g 氣陰    n 銅鏽

o 鹻水

p 小綠色

q 石綠

r 商

s 傅緯平

t 丹經要訣

u 孫思邈

v 蘇繼廎

w 志

x 風水

y 山龍易尋平龍難認

z 張資琪

aa 毛華

bb 俞人駿

cc 黃素封

dd 馬和

ee 朱任宏

ff 芳

gg 盂詧

hh 硫黃

ii 含真氣

jj 吸針石

kk 反經石

ll 乾石

mm 君石

nn 黑丹

oo 黑炭

pp 黑澶石

qq 黑炭石

rr 銅綠

ss 銅青

tt 硇砂

uu 太昊伏羲

vv 銅綠

ww 錢

xx 氣

## Bibliography

Amiot, J. J. M., "Extrait d'une Lettre...". *Mém. concernant l'Histoire, les Sciences les Arts, les Moeurs et les Usages des Chinois*, 1791, *15*, v.

Duckworth, C. W., "The Discovery of Oxygen." *Chemical News*, 1886, *53*, 250.

Guareschi, S. Tr. of Klaproth, *Suppl. Ann. all' Enciclopedia di Chimica*, 1904, *20*, 449.

Klaproth, J., "Sur les Connaissances Chimiques des Chinois dans le 8ème Siècle." *Mém de l'Acad. Imp. Sci. St. Petersburg*, 1810, *2*, 476.

von Lippmann, E. O., *Enstehung und Ausbreitung der Alchemie, mit einem Anhang, Zur älteren Geschichte der Metalle; ein Beitrag zur Kulturgeschichte*, 3 vols. Vol. 1, Springer, Berlin, 1919. Vol. 2, Springer, Berlin, 1931. Vol. 3 (posthumous, finished in 1940, ed. R. von Lippmann), Verlag Chemie, Weinheim, 1954.

Mellor, J. W., *Modern Inorganic Chemistry*, Longmans Green, London, 1916 (often reprinted).

Mellor, J. W., *Comprehensive Treatise on Inorganic and Theoretical Chemistry*, 15 vols. Longmans Green, London, 1923.

Moissan, H., *Traité de Chimie Minérale*, 5 vols. Masson, Paris, 1904.

Muccioli, M, "Intorno ad una Memoria di Giulio Klaproth sulle 'Conoscenze Chimiche dei Cinesi nel 8 Secolo'," *Archeion*, 1926, *7*, 382.

Needham, Joseph (with the collaboration of Wang Ling, K. Robinson, Lu Gwei-Djen, Ho Ping-Yü et al.), *Science and Civilisation in China*, 7 vols. in 12 or more parts, Cambridge, 1954-, (six parts published, the eighth to eleventh now passing through the press).

Partington, J. R., *A History of Chemistry*, Vol. 1, "Earliest Period to +1500" (partly still in press); Vol. 2, "+1500 to +1700"; Vol. 3, "+1700 to 1800" Vol. 4, "1800 to the Present Time." Macmillan, London, 1961-.

Partington, J. R., *General and Inorganic Chemistry...*, 2nd ed. Macmillan, London, 1951.

Read, Bernard E. & Pak, C. (Pak Kyebyong), "A Compendium of Minerals and Stones used in Chinese Medicine, from the *'Pên Tshao Kang Mu'*," *Peking Nat. Hist. Bull.*, 1928, *3* (no. 2), i-vii, 1-120; issued separately, revised and enlarged. Peiping, 1936 (2nd ed.) Serial nos. 1-135—corresponding with chapters 8, 9, 10, 11 of *Pên Tshao Kang Mu*.

Sivin, N., *Preliminary Studies in Chinese Alchemy; the 'Tan Ching Yao Chüeh' attributed to Sun Ssu-Mo (+581? to after +674)*, Inaug. Diss., Harvard University Press, Cambridge, Mass., 1968 (Harvard Monographs in the History of Science, no. 1). Ch. 1 sep. pub., *Jap. Studies in the Hist. of Sci.*, 1967, 6, 60.

Sun Jen I-Tu & Sun Hsüeh-Chuan (tr.), *'Thien Kung Khai Wu'; Chinese Technology in the Seventeenth Century, by Sung Ying-Hsing*. Pennsylvania State Univ. Press; University Park and London, Penn. 1966.

Weeks, M. E. *The Discovery of the Elements*. Collected Reprints of a series of articles published in the *Journal of Chemical Education;* with Illustrations collected by F. B. Dains. Mack, Easton, Pa., USA, 1933.

Yü Fei-An. *Chung-kuo Hua Yen-sê-ti Yen-Chiu* (A Study of the Pigments Used by Chinese Painters). Chao-Hua Mei-Shu, Peking, 1955, 1957.

Yuan Han-Chhing. *Chung-Kuo Hua-Hsüeh Shih Lun Wên Chi* (Collected Papers on the History of Chemistry in China). San-Lien, Peking, 1956.

# 38

## The Problem of Generation in Bonnet and in Buffon: A Critical Comparison

### CARLO CASTELLANI

O CCURRING almost contemporaneously, the discovery of the "egg" of mammals and the constant presence of the "little animals of the sperm" in the seminal fluid of adult males of all species had caused in the second half of the seventeenth century a serious crisis in the biological sciences.[1]

The ancient schemata, had followed either the Aristotelian principle of the menstrual blood as the "substance" and the sperm as the "organizing agent" for the formation of the fetus, or the Hippocratic principle of the mixture of the two seeds. These were now irremediably shown to be false. Harvey had indeed, some decades before, struck a first blow at both of these theories with his treatise on reproduction.[2] But aside from the fact that his work had had scant attention on publication, the discoveries of Leeuwenhoek and of De Graaf had been necessary to revolutionize this chapter of biology and to bring the attention of the scholars back to the Harveyan *Exercitationes*.

The new prospects opened to the natural sciences by the discoveries of the two Hollanders gave rise to violent discussions among the physiologists and to an indiscriminate flourishing of theories and "systems" of procreation, each of which claimed to give the most satisfactory explanation of the phenomena observed. Whereas the seventeenth century had seen the intense and profitable spread of microscopic research applied to biology accompanied by an equally punctilious experimental research in physiology, the eighteenth century seemed, during its first fifty years, to forget the usefulness of these auxiliary techniques. There is no need to seek a precise date since the various naturalists continued along the way begun by Malpighi, Leeuwenhoek, and De Graaf. Our intention here is rather to show how the attempt to achieve a purely theoretical elaboration and arrangement of the "facts" already acquired in the preceding century had, in large measure, got the better of experimental research—almost as though the scholars of that time consciously paused for reflection before proceeding further.

265

In the atmosphere generated by this new approach to science, one might observe from the beginning the affirmation of the "animal-culist" or microscopic animal theory which seemed successfully to prove correct both the "sperm animalcules" and the "mammalian egg." To the first, in fact, was assigned the mission of introducing the embryo into the egg (which would have provided for the embryo's nourishment). Subsequently, other naturalists ventured grave doubts concerning the specific nature and the constant presence of the "little animals" in the sperm, and—along with these doubts—they eventually denied to the "animalcules" any participation in the reproductive processes. The objections raised by various factions to the animalculist hypothesis appeared sufficiently valid and documented, so that for a few decades it was practically eliminated from the scene and was successfully replaced by the "egg" theory.

In accordance with this hypothesis, the principal factor of reproduction was considered to be the egg, on which the spermatic fluid supposedly acted at the time of copulation, thus establishing the development of the embryo. In comparison with the ever-decreasing defenders of the "animalcules," the egg-theory proponents constituted a compact formation in appearance only. However, they were in reality subdivided into a myriad of individual positions. The predominance attributed to the egg constituted only a kind of approximate common platform since almost every one of the biologists who was interested in the problem had formulated his own "system" or hypothesis to explain "how" the embryonic elements are present in the egg, and how the mechanism through which the sperm would carry out its fertilizing activity functions.[3]

The middle years of the eighteenth century were a period of crisis in the biological sciences and it was just at this time that the Genevan naturalist, Charles Bonnet, became interested in the phenomena of reproduction.[4] The precociousness of his active participation in naturalistic studies is well-known; indeed so well known that it is not necessary to recall the esteem which he succeeded in enjoying in the scientific milieu as a very young man.

Unfortunately, a weak constitution forced him very early to abandon active research and dedicate himself instead to those long "meditations" from which was born the voluminous body of his writings, the result more of theoretical construction than of direct observation—at least those published after 1755. In the many volumes devoted to natural history, Bonnet reserved much space for his "system of generation." This system was to be adopted by a number of illustrious European scholars and biologists.

In the course of a systematic re-reading of his works, it appeared, therefore, of interest to make a contextual comparison between the ideas maintained by Bonnet on this problem and analagous ones held by Buffon.[6] The chronological proximity, the identical character of the cultural substratum on which their works rested, and especially the curious mutual bond of admiration-aversion which united the two men,[7] contribute to increase the importance of this comparative analysis. It is also of interest that the two scholars succeeded in formulating their theories almost contemporaneously, and independently from each other. Bonnet declares in fact:

> Je composis le chapitre précédent [*the one in which he states his theories on reproduction*] lorsque le second volume de l'Histoire Naturelle m'est tombé entre les mains.[8]

The chapter to which he alludes, together with the other pages of those *Méditations sur l'Univers* from which the Genevan naturalist supposedly later derived part of his books, was composed between 1748 and 1753.[9] This appeared in the volume on the *Considérations sur les corps organisés*[10] published in 1762. However, the point that interests us most is the near-coincidence of the time of his first writing on the subject with that in which Buffon developed the portion of the *Historie Naturelle* concerning reproduction (dated 27 May 1748).[11]

The unconscious meeting, on partly common ground, between two authors who started from embryological concepts so far apart and directly opposed, as the preformism on the part of Bonnet and the epigenesis defended by Buffon, evidently originates from a cultural, scientific, and philosophical background common to both. In accordance with correct historical methodology, we must take this common ground into consideration. This may seem all the more important since it is generally agreed that both theories arose from detailed studies that were more characteristically philosophical than biological.

We have, however, by choice focused our attention exclusively on the two texts under discussion, in order not to enlarge our study excessively, and we have sought to maintain it on a rigorously biological level. Our research seeks to determine to what extent the systems of the two men agree with modern views of reproduction as well as determine evident similarities between them. It is especially important to us to establish what validity and what importance can be attributed to these systems in relation to the period in which they were divulged, and finally, whether and to what extent the theories of the two authors do constitute a valid starting-point for further developments of biology.[12]

Although we are aware of the limits of using modern scientific terminology, we believe that such usage offers the advantage of simplifying the subject. At the same time, when proper care is employed, it permits us to focus attention on analogies that would otherwise escape us.

Furthermore, we consider ourselves justified in having disregarded the "philosophical" aspect of the question, since not all the scholars of the eighteenth century were accustomed to giving an interpretation of this type to their works and researches. During the same period, Haller, Spallanzani, and Caldani, all biologists whose views were close to those of Bonnet, avoided all mystical or philosophical connections[13] in their writings on natural history, so that they might concentrate on the facts of experimental research. We should like to observe again that, even though the theories of Bonnet and Buffon unquestionably had deep philosophical roots, they still had as their prime objective the solution of a strictly biological problem. It has therefore seemed to us permissible, in this instance, to judge them in this light. If, for example, one can accept on the philosophical and epistemological scale the concept that

> ...les molécules organiques reflètent surtout une sorte d'atomisme bio-ligique, qui exprime à sa manière l'embaras d'un mécanisme mal satisfait de ses images...[14]

it appears to us, as we shall try to show, that the "molécules organiques" can assume a different appearance when seen within the framework of biology.

In the mid-eighteenth century neither the concepts of "cell" or "tissue" had been formulated. We have come to accept these as the foundation of modern cytology. Nevertheless, the necessity to postulate some elements on which to construct adequate work hypotheses was felt very early. Thus, the Hallerian concept that the simplest component of the living organism was the *fiber* had been accepted with relative ease. Bonnet, linked both by close scientific bonds and by personal friendship with Haller, had not hesitated to assimilate this concept himself.

> Les vaisseaux, ainsi que tous les autres organes, sont originairement formés de fibres simples, c'est à dire, qui ne sont pas elles mêmes composées d'autres fibres, ce qui iroit à l'infini, mais d'élémens particuliers.[15]

The Geneva naturalist had then further split the fiber by subdividing it in turn into "éléments particuliers." This is similar to the way in which modern cytologists have gone far beyond the cell, in the process of the subdivision and simplification of living organisms, isolating in certain aminoacids or other biochemical compounds the substance of which protoplasmatic material is made. Unfortunately, Bonnet enlightens us very little on the characteristics and nature of these "éléments particuliers." On the basis of the text we can advance the hypothesis that in his thoughts they were not very distant from the "atomic elements" of modern chemistry.

> La chymie…nous offre dans son terre, dans son sel, dans son soufre, dans son esprit, dans son flegme, les élémens de tous les mixtes.[16]

The knowledge of chemistry at the disposal of scholars at that time was not only scant, but also coarse and approximate when examined in the light of modern knowledge. Our interest here, however, is just to point out the similarity of the concepts. It does not seem relevant to us that further studies have brought to light how some of the "elements" which Bonnet included in his list were a pure illusion, or that many of his supposed "basic elements" were in reality compounds. For our purpose, it is only important that he considered them perfectly capable of being superimposed on those which today we designate as atomic elements.

This point once made evident, one can observe how his thoughts followed a line that is much more "modern" than that which we might expect. His hypotheses on the constitution of the living organism are descended from the postulate to which is joined the assertion that

> Le monde physique est composé d'élémens dont le nombre est déterminé.[17]

The said elements are invariable and do not change in character in the continuous passage from animal to vegetable; only the manner in which they combine changes.

> Il n'est point de vraie métamorphose dans la nature. Les élémens sont invariables. Les mêmes particules qui entrent aujourd'hui dans la composition d'une plante, entreront demain dans celle d'un animal. Ce passage ne changera point leur nature, il ne fera que leur donner un autre arrangement.[18]

In other words, the living substance, whether of animal or vegetable nature, whose fundamental biochemical identity Bonnet emphasizes repeatedly, is made up of the same elements; that is, in the terminology of that period, of

> un mélange d'air, d'eau, de terre, de sels, de huiles, de soufres et de plusieurs autres principes différement combinés.[19]

For this reason that continuous passage "from the animal to the vegetable" and vice versa which Needham, even though in a different meaning, deduced almost during the same years from his experiments,[20] appeared to find here a certain correspondence with the theories of Bonnet. He believed that the "elements" which come together to form the living fiber are simply juxtaposed in such a manner that, between one and the other, space is left in which the "atoms" of the alimentary substances easily succeed in insinuating themselves.[21]

It is worth pointing out that the histological differentiation between the tissues of the various organs depends, according to the Geneva naturalist, not on the diversity of the "fibers" which compose them, but directly on the variety of the constituent elements of the various types of fiber. To these correspond, for the reasons already stated, the elements which converge to form the substances from which the living body is fed, whether these substances come from the animal kingdom or the vegetable kingdom. It follows that the ingested foods, after having undergone a preliminary separation produced by the digestive processes, pass into the blood vessels where "three principal operations" occur successively.[22]

> La séparation du superflu; la décomposition d'une partie des principes et la réunion de plusieurs dans une même masse analogue à la nature du corps organisé.[23]

Nutrition and growth of the protoplasmatic substance are therefore tied in with the influx of alimentary substances, duly disintegrated and selected, and continuously carried in circulation by the blood stream in animals and by the sap in plants. The components of the various fibers (that is, of the various tissues) extract, from this polymorphous mass, the homologous elements that each one needs, thanks to the circumstance that the attractive force of chemical nature among the constituent "elements" of the fibers and the "minute particles," set free by digestion, favor their uniting and penetration.[24] For this reason, after all, every tissue selects and captures exclusively the "minute particles" that present a higher degree of analogy with those of which it is formed, and with which it can more easily unite.

It is a question, in short, of a concept that seems to approach in an astonishing manner certain facts of modern biochemistry, even though obviously expressed in the faltering terminology of that period. It is interesting in any case to point out the clean division which Bonnet draws between *primary or inorganic elements* and *secondary or organic elements;* to the first category belong those we would define as "chemical elements," while the second is constituted by the uniting of several heterogeneous elements, which give rise to the "germs," "formés dès le commencement d'atomes inorganiques."[25]

One would think—and an authoritative historian of science has in effect claimed[26]—that if one continued the task of "reading" Bonnet's texts in modern code, one could succeed in establishing the equation germ = cell. The equivalence could at first seem perfectly tenable, in view of the flexibility of usage that the Swiss biologist assigned to the word "germ," attributing to it even the ability to provide for the re-creation of animal parts deliberately or accidentally amputated, which phenomenon is verified with certain species.

Still, in our judgement, a more profound examination of the concept of "germ'„ as Bonnet intended it, will easily convince us that this is far from what is understood today by "cell." Germs, fundamental postulate of Bonnetian thinking, to which the mission of procreation is principally assigned, exist *ab initio*. They were molded directly by God at the time of the creation of the universe, in sufficient quantity to provide for the preservation of the species until the end of the world, from generation to generation.[27] They are composed of an approach or juxtaposition of inorganic substances, unchangeable and incorruptible, which remain inert (and, therefore, not living) until the moment when the masculine sexual element (sperm or pollen) has fertilized them. Until this meeting, the feminine gamete (we have used this term simply in opposition to the masculine element—strictly speaking, the "germ" is not *produced,* but only *received hospitably* by the femine organism)

> ...n'est composé que des seules particules élémentaires, et...les mailles qu'elles forment y sont aussi étroites qu'il est possible.[28]

Such particles constitute a complete collection of the constituent elements of the various tissues that will form the fetus, and their arrangement is such that the germ

> ...contient actuellement en raccourci toutes les parties essentielles à la Plante ou à l'Animal qu'il represente.[29]

In other words, the organs and the limbs are not present in the gamete "potentially," as modern embryology teaches us, but "actually," performed and subjected to such a miniaturization that it is practically beyond imagination. It follows that (at least in the hypothesis of "semination") the procreation-parent relationship comes to be purely accidental. One might say that the only biological bond that unites the germ to those whom, for convenience of terminology, we shall call the father and the mother, is the nourishment that they furnish it to start it off and aid its development. In a system so designed the necessity is lacking for the masculine sexual element to contribute to the organization of the protoplasmatic material contained in the feminine gamete (here represented by the "preformed" germ). As a result, the phenomenon of fertilization is reduced to a simple process of stimulation and of nourishment of the germ:

> L'acte de la génération peut donc n'être que le principe du développement des germes.[20]

On the one hand, therefore, the mission of the "procreating" organisms is limited to furnishing the "fibers" of which the germ is composed with the "nutritive atoms" essential to its growth. On the other hand, the elementary particles which form the germ have no other function than to select the atoms themselves, and to regulate their spatial distribution in such a manner that they become "parties du tout organique" and therefore transform, by means of a mechanism that is not described, that agglomeration of inorganic matter which is the original germ, into a compound of living organic matter. In the interest of hazarding a comparison (whose limits and approximation we are well aware of), we would say that the germ would constitute a distant ancestor of that "genetic code" which modern science has isolated in the cell.

The activity of the seminal fluid in respect to the germ was necessarily included in the hypothetical plan. Nevertheless, although he accepted the conjectures of the egg-proponents, Bonnet refused positively to believe that the "little animals of the sperm" had any importance whatsoever in the effects of fertilization. If "the act of procreation is none other than the starting of the development of the germ," it was logical to ascribe to the masculine element the assignment of "nourishing" the germ.

> Les poussières des étamines et la liqueur séminale ne contiendroient-elles point les sucs nourriciers, destinés par leur subtilité et par leur activité

extrèmes, à ouvrir les mailles du germe, et à y faire naître un développement que les sucs moins fins et moins élaborés n'avoient pu commencer,
mais qu'ils peuvent continuer et amener à son dernier terme?[31]

It has been seen that the adult organism is able, through the digestive
processes, to disintegrate the alimentary substances in the elements which
comprise them. Further, this makes it possible for every tissue to capture
the atoms endowed with greater chemical affinity to its constituent
molecules. Since the germ, at the moment of fertilization, is no more
than a pure aggregate of inorganic substances and therefore deprived
of life,[32] it could evidently not develop such a complex activity of division
and selection. Bonnet resolved the difficulty neatly, presuming that

> 1) Il y dans la liqueur séminale autant d'espèces d'élémens qu'il en entre
> dans la composition du germe. 2) Que les mailles de chaque partie
> observant une certaine proportion avec les molécules rélatives à la
> sémence. 4) Que l'efficace de la liqueur séminale dépend du degré de
> son mouvement et de la chaleur, et du nombre des particules élémentaires
> de chaque espèce.[33]

In other words, the biochemical composition of the sperm is postulated to be exactly equivalent to that of the blood in order to be able to
satisfy all the requirements for "elements" different one from the other
and necessary for the various embryonic tissues. To explain how this
impressive collection of "elementary particles" collects in the testicle,
Bonnet imagined an anatomical-biological situation curiously close to
that imagined by Buffon, called upon in his turn to resolve a problem
in some ways analogous.[34]

> J'ai pensé qu'il y avoit dans les testicules des vaisseaux rélatifs à cette
> partie du cerveau qui filtre le fluide nerveux; d'autres qui répondoient
> au foie par leur fonction, et qui séparoient des particules analogues à
> la bile; d'autres qui répondoient au système lymphatique, et séparoient
> une matière analogue à la lymphe etc.[35]

The coincidence with the Buffonian system became still more marked,
inasmuch as the Swiss naturalist asserted:

> J'admettrois ici le concurs des deux liqueurs [*masculine and feminine;
> that which represented a return to biological concepts that had by then
> been overcome for some time*] dans l'acte de génération et je supposerois
> que les molécules dominantes de celle du mâle ou de celle de la femelle,

déterminent les rapports plus ou moins marqués d l'un ou de l'autre
avec la production qui leur doit le jour.[36]

The transmission of hereditary characteristics, and even the determination of the sex of the embryo (although Bonnet does not explicitly
mention this), would then be tied in with the greater or lesser abundance
of "molecules" in the male or female seminal fluid. Such molecules,
supplying a variable quantity of nourishment to the various regions of
the embryonic organism which are already roughly delineated in that
sort of mold which the germ constitutes, orient its somatic features in
a paternal or maternal direction. It would appear difficult to avoid the
suggestion that these "molecules," transmitted from parents to children
by way of the respective sexual elements and which compete in such a
precise manner in the determination of their hereditary characteristics,
might be interpreted as an advance notice of the "chromosomes." The
difference between the two concepts, however, becomes immediately
evident when one bears in mind the fact that the "elements" or molecules
theorized by Bonnet are none other than pure and simple nutritional
substances. These have been selected and preserved in the sexual glands
of the parents in order to provide for the very first alimentary necessities
of the embryo.

Reference has been repeatedly made, in the course of this study,
to the analogies which link the "systems" of Bonnet and Buffon. We
shall now try to analyze the text of the French naturalist in order to probe
more deeply in our critical comparison.

Bonnet ascribed to the organism the task of breaking up the complex
organic substances introduced as nourishment into basic (in effect inorganic) "elements." In that manner the matter was made available for a
new utilization. In his turn, Buffon, also starting from an analogous
concept of the disintegration of the foods, believed that the digestive
processes liberate and transmit to the blood not inorganic "elements" but
"organic molecules." These are real "prefabricated" compounds which
Nature furnishes to the living organism, which can then use them without
the necessity for further elaboration. We would like to observe, nevertheless, that, for the sake of being objective, a fine but conclusive difference
exists between the concepts of the two authors: at most, Bonnet's "organism," beginning with the germ stage, is made up practically of pure
inorganic substances.

The germ itself, as has been seen, is formed—up to the moment of
fertilization—of inorganic "elements," assembled in accordance with a

specific schema, which subsequently amplifies itself and increases in volume through the simple addition or insertion of other elements. These are also inorganic, having been extracted first from the seminal fluids of the parents and subsequently from the placental blood. Thus, although the Geneva naturalist considered germs as "organic elements" and fibers as also "organic," both the former and the latter are in reality made up of simple aggregates of inorganic substances. In no phase of the processes described by him is the passage from the inorganic to the organic referred to or justified.

In the system elaborated by Buffon, on the contrary, the vital processes are expressed in these propositions:

1) All living creatures are composed of "organic particles," whose number in Nature is practically infinite, in continuous increase; common (and therefore freely interchangeable) to the animal kingdom and to the vegetable kingdom.[37]

2) Nutrition, through which the organism provides for its own metabolic necessities and reproduction, is composed in its turn of three phases:

a) Disintegration of the animal or vegetable matter into its constituent parts [*organic molecules*].[38]

b) Separation of the organic substances, immediately usable by the organism, which enter into the chyle, and from there pass into the circulatory stream. The inorganic substances, unusable by living beings, are on the other hand eliminated through the excretory routes.[39]

We shall note incidentally how Buffon here anticipates the modern concept of feeding as "burning":

Les animaux semblent participer aux qualités de la flamme, leur chaleur intérieure est une espèce de feu: aussi, après la flamme, les animaux sont les plus grands destructeurs, et ils assimilent et tournent en leur substance toutes les matières qui peuvent leur servir d'aliments.[40]

c) The organic molecules extracted from the decomposition of the alimentary substances, and which have the same biochemical structure as the organism which is to assimilate them—identical in all living beings —are subsequently presented to the various organs, each of which takes unto itself the molecules that present a greater affinity to the tissue of which it is composed.

…dans ces parties organiques [*those extracted from the breaking up of the alimentary substances*] il doit y avoir beaucoup de varieté, et des espèces de parties très différentes les unes des autres; et…chaque partie du corps organisé reçoit les espèces qui lui conviennent le mieux, et dans un nombre et une proportion assez égales.[41]

At this point a typical concept of the Buffonian system slips in: the *moule intérieur.* The entire organism and every one of its individual parts can be likened to

…une espèce de moule intérieur, dans lequel la matière qui sert à son accroissement se modèle et s'assimile au total; de manière que, sans qu'il arrive aucun changement à l'ordre et à la proportion des parties, il en résulte une augmentation dans chaque partie prise séparement…mais cette augmentation, ce développement…comment peut-il se faire, si ce n'est en considérant le corps de l'animal, et même chacune de ses parties qui doivent se développer, comme autant de moules intérieurs qui ne reçoivent que la matière accessoire que dans l'ordre qui résulte de la position de toutes leurs parties?[42]

The organic molecules have an affinity to the various tissues which draw them out from the blood mass and penetrate into the *internal mold.* This incorporates them in the pre-existing tissue, to assure their growth and to satisfy the metabolic necessities by means of an "intimate assimilation and one which penetrates to mass."[43] Such a process of penetration and fusion between living tissue and contributory material is regulated by a force inherent in the material, concerning whose nature Buffon is obviously unable to comment.

Before proceeding further in our exposition of the thoughts of the French naturalist, it would seem worthwhile to pause for a moment on two key problems which always have been of particular interest to modern critics. We refer to the question of the "organic molecules" and of the "internal mold."

Buffon has been reproached for not having known how or not having wanted (at least in this first phase of his doctrinal elaboration) to indicate through what mechanism the transformation of "rough matter" *(inorganic),* into matter, or rather, into *organic* "molecules"[44] occurs. In our viewpoint, these criticisms arise from having neglected some fundamental facts. In the first place, it is forgotten that the concept of "inorganic" and "organic," as we understand it, would only emerge a few decades later, and that, when Buffon laboriously constructed his hypothetical explanation of how the fundamental life processes develop, the distinction between *living matter* and *inert or inorganic matter* was entirely empirical and intuitive. For this reason Bonnet could tranquilly accept the hypothesis that inorganic matter enters, without any change, into the context of organic matter.

The French naturalist also rejected this hypothesis intuitively, believing that a certain biochemical homology was necessary between living substance and anabolic materials. Neither does it appear to us that he can be blamed for not having known how to clarify the mechanism through which the *inorganic* becomes transformed into the *organic*.[45] Nature, he affirms, places at the disposal of the living organisms an ever-increasing number of "organic molecules" extracted from this transformation or synthesis of the rough material. It would be just as worthwhile to reproach Leonardo for his inability to put into flight—through lack of a motor—the "flying machine" that he so ingeniously projected.

To us it seems important, as borne out by subsequent developments in biology, that Buffon had stated the problem both of the distinction between organic and inorganic, and of a biochemical affinity between anabolic material and tissue destined to receive it. We know today (two centuries later!) that the organism provides directly, within certain limits, for this transformation. But through how many intermediate stages of scientific knowledge, from Buffon to today, have we come to reach this understanding of biological phenomena? We are trying to say, in other words, that the position of the French naturalist, in this light, appears to us clearly more advanced and productive than that of Bonnet.

It is obvious that both were very far from the truth, as we know it today. However, in respect to the scientific progress since made, the position of Buffon appears to us to have indicated with greater clarity the way to proceed. One of the first problems to be resolved was exactly the clarification of this distinction and of this direction.

It was said later that the concept of *internal mold* constitutes a real contradiction in terms, inasmuch as a mold—it is argued—shapes the material *externally* and not *internally* as Buffon would have it.[46] He was, however, perfectly aware of this contradiction which has, in fact, a purely semantic character. Indeed, he advised explicitly that he is using the term "mold" for lack of a word capable of indicating with greater clarity that which he wishes to define.[47] The *internal mold,* would seem to be an "organizer," to which is assigned the mission of regulating the flow of photoplasmatic material furnished by the digestive processes, and of controlling its distribution in accordance with the schemata inherent in the "biological memory" of the specific organ, and of each of its individual parts. For this season these protoplasmatic or organic materials come to assume automatically the typical architecture of the various corporeal tissues. At a higher level a special "biological memory" will organize the various tissues; another will supervise the growth of the organs; and, at the top of the pyramid, a sort of "supreme coordinator" (the *internal mold* constituted by the organism as a whole) will watch over the orderly development of the vital functions.

We had occasion to observe, in reading of Bonnet's work, how the eighteenth century naturalists would point out the necessity of deriving as a hypothesis a fundamental morphological element as a primary constituent of the organism, and from whose aggregation tissue would originate. Although for the Swiss biologist this basic element is the fiber, Buffon appeared to be nearer to the modern concept of the cell:

> ...nous pouvons supposer et croir qu'un être organisé est un tout composé de parties organiques semblables, aussi bien que nous supposons qu'un cube est composé d'autres cubes...de la même façon que nous voyons qu'un cube de sel marin est composé d'autres cubes, nous voyons aussi qu'un orme n'est qu'un composé d'autres petits ormes, puisqu' en prenant un bout de branche, ou un bout de racine, ou un morceau de bois separé du tronc, ou la graine, il en vient également un orme...[48]

This cellular definition in his thoughts becomes more evident in this passage:

> Un individu n'est qu'un tout uniformement organisé dans toutes ses parties intérieures, un composé d'une infinité de figures semblables et de parties similaires, un assemblage de germes ou de petits individus de la même espèce, lesquels peuvent tous se développer de la même façon, suivant les circonstances, et composer de nouveaux tous composés comme le premier.[49]

This "germ," formed by the meeting of a certain number of "organic molecules," enjoys—as do the cells of modern biology—an ample typological variety. For this reason, inferior organisms, those which reproduce by simple division, or—as in the case of certain plants—by sprouting, are individuals constituted by the:

...répétition de la même forme, et une composition de figures semblables toutes organisées de même; et c'est par cette raison que les corps les plus simples...se reproduisent le plus aisement et le plus abondamment.[50]

In other words, living beings with low histological differentiation are able to reproduce through simple division or duplication of the "germs" (or cells) of which they are formed. On the other hand, living beings with high morphological and tissue specialization, whose organism comprises the meeting of various cytological series, cannot preclude—in reproducing—this variety of elements. Their generative processes involve a much more complex physiological activity, which rests upon a similarly complex anatomical organization.

d) When the organism has arrived at maturity and its complete development, that is, when the metabolic necessities have reached a phase of equilibrium having to provide only for the maintenance of the body, there gathers a collection of the various organic molecules that make up the various tissues of the individual in the genital organs.[51] In the testicle or in the ovary these molecules undergo a primary elementary process of fusion and organization giving rise to a "germ" *sui generis,* a kind of "gamete" in which are present the biochemical constituents necessary for the formation of the embryo. For this reason, when the meeting and fusion of the gametes coming from the two sexes takes place, the inherent regulating force *(anima)* of the embryological development gradually organizes the protoplasmatic materials of the zygote into an embryonic outline which will complete and develop its own formation with the contribution of the "organic molecules" furnished to it by the placental blood.[52]

There has been a tendency to see in the Buffonian "germ" a simple replica of the germ as Bonnet imagined it; that is, an embryo in miniature. The only difference would consist in the fact that, whereas the Swiss naturalist called for this germ to be completely pre-formed and pre-existent *ab initio,* Buffon supposedly imagined it substantially identical to that of Bonnet but "constructed" little by little, by epigenesis. Buffon has also been reproached for not having had the courage to take this ultimate step: to admit frankly the preformation of the germ which was badly camouflaged by his system.[53]

In our viewpoint, there is a noteworthy and conclusive difference between the concepts of the two authors. The only element common to the two can be found in the collection of "elements" or "organic molecules" which supposedly form in the sexual glands, and which both biologists admit in different ways. Nevertheless, while for Bonnet such a collection has the pure function of feeding the "germ" at the time of fertilization, Buffon assigns to his "molecules" the task of furnishing the new creature with the basic materials for its formation *as a new entity*. He directly attributes to them the capability of self-organizing for the purpose of giving life to the embryo. Bonnet's germ, on the other hand, is complete within itself, inasmuch as it "presently contains in miniature all the parts essential to the Plant or Animal that it represents." For this reason, to the masculine sexual factor there is reserved exclusively the task of exciting the heart of the embryo and of putting it into movement. Only secondarily does this factor offer the embryo a certain quantity of "elements" that would provide for its more immediate necessities for development. Therefore, to exaggerate, fertilization could take place without the intervention of the male, inasmuch as it would be possible to induce action in the germ through a sufficiently active stimulus.[54]

Buffon takes a stand in a completely different position. Beginning with the premise that life originates from the fusion and organization in precisely defined circumstances of a certain number of "organic molecules" (organic matter, but not yet living), his "germ" constitutes a sort of joining ring between the organic material not yet endowed with life and the organism itself, which originates from the organization and fusion of the germs in which there is precisely present—besides life— an embryonic organization.[55] We would support *this* as our interpretation, particularly, based on the description he gives of gametes:

> Ces petits corps mouvants, auxquels on a donné le nom d'*animaux spermatiques*…sont peut-être des petits corps organisés provenant de l'individu qui les contient, mais qui, d'eux mêmes, ne peuvent se développer ni rien produire.

And again:

> Nous nous contenterons de remarquer que les prétendus animaux spermatiques…pourroient n'être que très peu organisés: qu'ils ne sont tout au plus que l'ébauche d'un être vivant: ou pour le dire plus clairement, ces prétendus animaux ne sont que les parties organiques vivantes dont nous avons parlé, qui sont communes aux végétaux, ou tout au plus qu'ils ne sont que la première réunion de ces parties organiques.[56]

Such a definition is applied also to the feminine gamete, inasmuch as, in the course of some laboratory experiments, Buffon and Needham were convinced that they had discovered formations identical to spermatozoa in the *corpora lutea* of females.[57] For this reason, biologically speaking, the French naturalist considered both the male and the female "sexual germs" (gametes) to be substantially identical.

We should also like to emphasize the importance of certain aspects of the definition given by Buffon to this problem. In the first place, so far as we know, this is the first time that a clear negation of the "animal aspect" of spermatozoa appears. We must not lose sight of the fact that it was not until the first decades of the nineteenth century that it was recognized that "spermatozoa" are not a particular type of parasite of the sperm.[58] Secondly, the schema and the whole group of theories formulated by Buffon appeared to give a (temporarily) satisfactory explanation of the phenomena of reproduction since it reconciled the positions of the "ovists" and the "animalculists."

To the latter, the objection had been raised that embryological observation had never supported the theory that the "tadpole" (spermatozoon, bearer of the embryo) transforms itself into the fetus.[59] Also disturbing was the thought that Nature would consent to the waste of millions of potential lives, since only one "animalcule" succeeded in penetrating into the egg and developing there.

On the other hand, the adversaries of the egg theory had had a large share in demonstrating that the Graafian follicle (which the first observers identified with the real egg) could not detach itself from the ovary, much less pass through the tubes. No naturalist had ever succeeded in seeing the female gamete prior to fertilization at the moment in which it leaves the gland.

Buffon's system appeared to reconcile the two theories in an acceptable manner. The difficulties appeared overcome through elimination of the animal-aspect of the spermatozoon (recognized as an aggregate of protoplasmatic molecules and conceptually not very far from the "gamete" of modern embryology) and through transfer to the luteous body the capacity of liberating at the opportune moment a "germ" exactly equal to the male germ. The zygote produced by the fusion of the two gametes furnished the constructive element for the formation of the embryo and has the inherent capacity to organize these materials.

Other scholars have emphasized that Buffon could not escape the accusation of preformism in its reference to the "organic molecules" since he affirms that they reach the living organism already synthesized or "performed" through the handiwork of Nature. His was then a real stride

forward. In his attempt to avoid the necessity of admitting the preformation of the germ, he transferred this characteristic from the germ
to the molecule. Still, in the area of modern criticism, the clearly philosophical inspiration of his concept has been especially evident.[60]

We have already tried to clarify how the hypothesis of this "molecular
synthesis" performed outside the organism. The discussion is complex
because of the necessity of explaining how the inert material (inorganic)
can change itself into organic material. The almost total lack of biochemical and histological knowledge required Buffon to search for a
"force" present in the cosmos, which was the necessary means for this
fundamental change. From this, it was pointed out, the "germ" in which
the molecules initiate their organization constitutes the second stage.
Finally, the formation through epigenesis of the embryo is regulated by
the intervention of the soul which guides the arranging of the molecules
coming from the two gametes. One alternative much less satisfactory
would have been to ascribe this organization, as other authors had maintained, to an equally ill-defined chemical precipitation or coagulation
effected by the sperm in the substance of the egg.[61]

The "soul" postulated by Buffon serves temporarily to define the
essence of this "commanding force." Others would call it variously "nisus
formativus," "vis essentialis,"[62] or, in our time, "regulator"—likewise titles
which serve simply to hide the ignorance of the exact nature of a phenomenon whose existence is recognized but whose fundamental nature
is unknown.

A final consideration militates against the presumed preformism
attributed to the french naturalist. If such preformism had truly been
present it cannot be understood how Bonnet, a man who was extremely
sensitive to criticism, would have attacked Buffon's views so strongly
both publicly and privately.[63]

We have already stated the reasons why we believe it more useful
for the purposes of a history of biological thought to avoid the indisputable *philosophical* matrixes from which there arose the thoughts of
the two authors considered here and which can be better evaluated in an
epistemological light. In particular, these reasons seem valid to us in
examining the thoughts of the French naturalist. Contemporary naturalists were able to transform his work immediately into spendable coin
in the area of their research, without worrying about the philosophical
"minting-die" with which it had been struck. This chapter of the *Histoire
Naturelle* constituted, in short—at a particularly delicate moment for the

history of the natural sciences—a solid *ubi consistam* for the epigenetic theory. It opened the road to the subsequent, conclusive contributions of Wolff,[64] from which, by unanimous consent, modern critics attribute the birth of modern embryology. The work was published at a time when authoritative support given to the preformist theories by scholars of no mean importance (Bonnet, Haller, Spallanzani) threatened to provoke a worrisome stagnation in biological research.

Buffon had formulated a complex mosaic of hypotheses and theories, from which emerged with sure evidence the plan of an explanation of the processes of reproduction. This plan was in certain ways decisively modern, and in any case—for his time—it was more satisfactory than the others. Many mosaic forms were put together in an incorrect manner; others were (from a modern view) evidently erroneous. But this mosaic could constitute more than one point of reference, or a simple work hypothesis for whoever chose to follow the road indicated by him. The master lines which emerged from it were precise: the "cellular" formation of the organism; the histological differentiation of the tissues; the substitution of a germ (seen as a sketch of cellular organization), to the "animalcules of the sperm" and to the egg understood as "preformed" embryo, from whose fusion the fetus originates in a real "zygote." There are also data points which the subsequent development of science used. For it is certainly easier to rectify, with a series of progressive adjustments, the erroneous placement of a mosaic, or to substitute for one of its errors, than to have to demolish a complex of erroneous theories and replace it with a radically new system.

Again, the ideas of Buffon appeared to be supported by a rather nutritive series of direct observations and laboratory experiments, carried out in collaboration with Needham.[65] We must not lose sight of the fact that, although for the modern scientist biological research is inconceivable without the continuous laboratory work, Bonnet had constructed his system almost exclusively through study. The pieces of his mosaic hypotheses were constructed by himself, or they were facts accepted on the simple authority of other researchers. For this reason, he had no difficulty in admitting that the crossing of chickens and ducks would produce strange monsters, or that between cattle and horses would produce the legendary *Jumarts* in whose existence he still believed, notwithstanding the most circumstantial demonstrations to the contrary.[66] In like manner, one of the fundamental pillars of his preformist theory still remained the "discovery" by Haller (fortunately contradicted by Wolff) that the intestinal membrane of the chicken is continuous with the membrane of the egg.

It does not appear very relevant to us that the indisputable errors of observation and interpretation of the experiments which invalidated these experimental researches of Buffon and Needham, eventually assisted Bonnet and Spallanzani to reject the entire system.[67] The French naturalist and his collaborator had brought back to the laboratory an environment better adapted to the problem's solution. That is, he endeavored to obtain an experimental proof of a theory established beforehand. Buffon, more-over, had indicated a rational schema for explaining reproduction, through the epigenetic route, in the case of higher organisms.

It was precisely the act of remaining in the mainstream of these two general plans of principle that success was finally achieved in resolving that which Bonnet defined as "the mystery of procreation."

## References

[1]For the history of these discoveries, see C. Castellani, "Appunti per uno studio sulla scoperta delle 'ova viviparorum,' e degli spermatozoi, e sui primi sviluppi di essa," *Atti Mem. Accad. Arte San., 3* (1962), 107-125; C. Castellani, "La scoperta degli spermatozoi e gli studi di A. van Leeuwenhoek sullo sperma maschile," *Riv. Stor. Med., 1* (1961), 18-43.

[2]W. Harvey, *Exercitationes de generatione animalium* (London, 1651).

[3]For an analysis of these problems, see C. Castellani, *La Storia della Genera-zione* (Milano: Longanesi, 1965).

[4]Charles Bonnet was born at Geneva in 1720. Starting out on law studies, he abandoned them to dedicate himself to research of a naturalistic and biological character. Having entered into correspondence with Réaumur, the latter encouraged him. He soon acquired considerable fame through his studies on parthenogenetic reproduction among the plant aphides and other entomological research. While still young, he was named Corresponding Member of the Académie des Sciences of Paris. Very soon, however, his poor health, particularly an eye condition, forced him to abandon the microscope and experimental research almost completely and to dictate to the secretary his works of a philosophical and naturalistic character. He died at Genthod in 1793.

[5]Among others, beside Haller and Needham, we may refer to Euler, Spallanzani, and Caldani.

[6]George Louis Leclerc, comte du Buffon, famous French naturalist, born at Montbard in 1707, owes his fame especially to his monumental *Histoire Naturelle*, which appeared in stages between 1749 and 1779. Having entered the *Académie des Sciences* in 1752, he was director of the *Jardin du Roi* where he built up a very valuable museum. He died in 1788.

[7]In the letters from Bonnet to Spallanzani (see Ch. Bonnet, *Lettres à Mr. l'Abbé Spallanzani*, Milano: Episteme, 1971) are found recurring attacks on the theories of Buffon, who refused to accept the "marvelous" theory of the "pre-existent germs." The issuance of the various volumes of the *Histoire Naturelle* is promptly commented upon by the Swiss naturalist with irony that was sometimes rather heavy. But at the same time it is clear that Bonnet did not succeed in escaping the fascination of this fundamental work. A few words of esteem and appreciation from the French naturalist, arranged to reach Bonnet, filled him with pride.

[8]Ch. Bonnet, *Considérations sur les Corps organisés*, éd. Oeuvres d'hist. nat. et de phil. (Neuchatel, 1779-83), T. V 8°, part I, 174.

[9]R. Savioz, *Mémoires autobiographiques de Ch. Bonnet* (Paris, 1948).

[10]Ch. Bonnet, *Considérations sur les Corps organisés* (Amsterdam, 1762). As already indicated, we have used the edition of Neuchatel, 1779-83.

[11]G. L. L. Buffon, *Histoire Naturelle* (Paris, 1749-1779). We have used the edition *Oeuvres complètes de Buffon,* Paris, 1837, Vol. II, 379-509.

[12]For an examination of the same problem as regarded by the philosophical milieu, we refer to the excellent essay of J. Roger, *Les sciences de la vie dans la penséè française du XVIII siècle,* (A. Colin, 1963).

[13]See especially the correspondence from Spallanzani to Bonnet (*Epistolario,* ed. B. Biagi and D. Prandi, Firenze, 1949-1954); and from Bonnet to Spallanzani (see note 7); that of Caldani-Bonnet and Bonnet-Caldani (*Carteggio di Leopoldo Marc'Antonio Caldani con Charles Bonnet e Lazzaro Spallanzani,* ed. C. Castellani and G. Ongaro, Antenore, Padova (in prep.).

[14]J. Roger, *La pensée...,* 550.

[15]Ch. Bonnet, *Op. cit.,* I, 89.

[16]*Ibid.,* 150.

[17]*Ibid.,* 154.

[18]*Ibid.,* 154.

[19]*Ibid.,* 89.

[20]J. T. Needham, *Nouvelles Observations microscopiques, avec des Découvertes interéressantes sur la composition et décompositions des Corps organises* (Paris, 1750), 172.

[21]Ch. Bonnet, *op. cit.,* I, 84. "On peut se représenter une fibre simple comme une espèce d'ouvrage à reseau. Les atomes nourriciers s'insinuent dans les mailles, et les agrandissent en tous sens."

[22]The studies of Spallanzani on digestion appeared after the work of Bonnet. They were published in *Dissertationi di Fisica Animale, e Vegetabile* (Modena, 1780).

[23]Ch. Bonnet, *op. cit.,* I, 107.

[24]*Ibid.,* 90.

[25]*Ibid.,* 89-90.

[26]J. Rostand, *Un grand biologiste: Ch. Bonnet* (Palais de la Découverte, D 107, Paris, 1966), 21.

[27]In the *Considérations,* Bonnet admitted two possibilities in regard to germs: either they were scattered at random on the earth and penetrate only accidentally into a female of their species (*semination*), or the germs themselves are enclosed each one within the other, in an almost infinite set (*emboîtement*). For an analysis of this problem see: C., Castellani, "Il 'Mistero della generazione' nell'opera di Ch. Bonnet." *Rev. Soc. Mexicana Hist. Nat.,* XXX, (1969), 345-371.

[28]Ch. Bonnet, *op. cit.,* I, 106.

[29]*Ibid.,* 106.

[30]*Ibid.,* 100.

[31]*Ibid.,* 101.

[32]Later, Bonnet, who finally directed his preferences toward the theory of *emboîtement,* came to admit that in this "system" the germs were already endowed with a sort of latent life and grew from generation to generation. On this subject, see C. Castellani, "Il 'Mistero della generazione'," quoted in note 27.

[33]Ch. Bonnet, *op. cit.,* I, 108-9.

[34]Caldani, in his work *Institutions Physiologiae* (Patavii, 1773), having misunderstood the exact thought of Bonnet in this respect, affirmed that the choice of the "elements" to be transferred to the testicle occurs by action of the individual organs (on the model which Buffon had supported). Bonnet was horrified with this involuntary *contaminatio,* and politely reproached Caldani both through Spallanzani and directly in his letters to the physiologist of Padua. The latter apologized for the error and promised to correct it in a future reprinting of his work.

[35]Ch. Bonnet, *op. cit.,* I, 170.

[36]*Ibid.,* 171.

[37]G. L. L. Buffon, *op. cit.,* II, 380-81, "Il y a dans la nature une infinité de parties actuellement existantes, vivantes et dont la substance est la même que celle des êtres organisés...Ces petits êtres organisés sont composés de parties organiques qui sont commune aux animaux et aux végétaux."

[38]*Ibid.,* 386, "Détruire un être organisé, n'est...que séparer les parties organiques dont il est composé."

[39]*Ibid.,* 392, "Je conçois donc, que dans les aliments que nous prenons il y a une grande quantité de molécules organiques; et cela n'a pas bésoin d'être prouvé; puisque nous ne vivons que d'animaux ou de végétaux, lesquels sont des êtres organisés; je crois que dans l'estomac et les intestins il se fait une séparation des parties grossiéres et brutes qui sont rejettées par les voies excretoires; le chyle, que je regard comme l'aliment divisé, et dont la dépuration est commencée, entre dans les veines lactées, et de là est porté dans le sang, avec lequel il se mêle; le sang transporte ce chyle dans toutes les parties du corps; il continue à se dépürer,

par le mouvement de la circulation, de tout ce que lui restoit de molécules non organiques: cette matière brute et étrangère est chassë par ce mouvement, et sort par les voies des sécretions et de la transpiration; mais les molécules organiques restent, parce qu'en effet elles sont analogues au sang, et que dès lors il y a une force d'affinité que les rétient."

[40]*Ibid.*, 385.

[41]*Ibid.*, 386.

[42]*Ibid.*, 386.

[43]*Ibid.*, 386.

[44]J. Roger, *op. cit.*, 548-49.

[45]*Ibid.*, 550.

[46]P. Flourens, *Buffon, histoire de ses travaux et de ses idées* (Paris, 1844), 74.

[47]G. L. L. Buffon, *op. cit.*, II, 384.

[48]*Ibid.*, 381.

[49]*Ibid.*, 379.

[50]*Ibid.*, 387.

[51]*Ibid.*, 388.

[52]The idea of this collection of "molecules" in the sexual organs is not original with Buffon. Under various forms it had already been advanced by various authors. (See C. Castellani, *La Storia della Generarione*, 253-278). That of Buffon remains, however, in our opinion, the most original and modern interpretation of this old theory.

[53]Flourens, P.; *op. cit.*, 67-68.

[54]On August 15, 1778, he was in fact writing to Spallanzani: "Je voudrais donc, mon cher Malpighi, que vous soubstituassiez le fluide électrique à la liquer sèminale des grenouilles et des crapauds pour féconder leurs oeufs." (See Ch. Bonnet, *Lettres à Mr. l'Abbé Spallanzani*, 370).

On January 13, 1781, he returned to the subject: "Qui sait si la poussière des étamines de certaines plantes ne pourroient point faire quelque impression sur certains germes du règne animal?" (*Ibid.*, 431).

[55]These *organic molecules*, although constructed of protoplasmatic material, identical to that of which living beings are formed, are not yet endowed with life in that they would seem to lack some fundamental attributes of life itself. They lack the capability of reproducing, of feeding themselves through aggregation of other material—capabilities which the "molecules" would acquire only after having united with other molecules similar to themselves, or entering to become part of a living organism. In our opinion, in the thought of Buffon the distinction between "organic" (that is, constructed of the same substances that form living organisms) and "living" is extremely fine, but nevertheless clearly outlined.

[56]G. L. L. Buffon, *op. cit.*, II, 391.

[57]*Ibid.*, 431-32.

[58]Sufficient to recall that, according to the opinion of von Baer (the discoverer of the egg of mammals), the "animalcules of the sperm" were ascribed to the group of infusoria—and that was in 1826. Analogous ideas were supported in the same years by various naturalists: Cloquet, Bory de Saint-Vincent, etc. Moreover, the term which we still use today has remained to indicate the "animality" of the male sexual cells. See C. Castellani, *La Storia della generazione*, 348-49.

[59]In his letters to the Royal Society, Leeuwenhoek himself had already clearly affirmed that he did not believe that the spermatozoon contains the preformed embryo, but rather its constituents.

[60]J. Roger, *op. cit.*, 556-58.

[61]Zypaeus, *Fundamenta Medicinae*, quoted by M. Schurig, *Syllepsilogia historico-medica* (Dresdae et Lipsiae, 1731), 9.

[62]The "nisus formativus" had been placed by Blumenbach at the basis of his system of epigenesis. The "vis essentialis" is the name that Wolff had attributed to the plastic force that supposedly determined the epigenetic development of the embryo.

[63]Bonnet developed his criticism—rather weak, in truth—of the system of Buffon, in pages 199 to 202 of his *Considérations* (edition cited). The gist of these objections is the following: 1) he finds it difficult to understand how the uniting of the organic molecules can give rise to a variety of tissues and organs that are encountered in the living organism; 2) he cannot agree that the "organic molecules," unalterable, can be formed in such a manner as to represent in miniature the various organs (here it becomes evident that Bonnet had not exactly grasped the Buffonian concept); 3) Buffon does not explain how it is possible that individuals coming from different species are endowed with organs that do not appear in either of the two parents; 4) the offspring of mutilated parents are normally endowed with whole members, whereas, lacking in the genital organs the "molecules" coming from these organs, they should be deprived of them.

[64]J. Needham, *A History of Embryology* (Cambridge, 1959), 201ff.

[65]The experimental part is shown in Buffon, *op. cit.*, 422-40.

[66]See Ch. Bonnet, *op. cit.*

[67]L. Spallanzani, *Saggio di osservazioni microscopiche concernenti il sistema della generazione de' sigg. Needham e Buffon—in Dissertazione due*...(Modena, 1765). 1765).

For the long controversy that ensued among Spallanzani, Needham, and Bonnet, see C. Castellani, "L'origine degli infusori nella polemica Needham-Spallanzani-Bonnet," *Episteme* III (1969): 3; idem, IV, (1970): 1.

# A Bibliography of the Writings
# of Walter Pagel

Compiled by Marianne Winder
Assistant Librarian
Wellcome Institute of the History of Medicine
London, England

1922 A1    Ueber Hydranenzephalie (Cruveilhier). *Mschr. Psychiatr. Neurol.*, 1922, Heft 51, 161-187.

1923 A2    Die gekreuzte Dystopie der Nieren. *Virchows Arch. path. Anat.*, 1923, 240, 508-529.

1924 A3    Zur Morphologie der cirkumfokalen Veränderungen bei Lungentuberkulose. *Beitr. Klin. Tuberk.*, 1924, 59, 261-265.

A4    Zur Kenntnis der Duodenaltuberkulose. Zugleich ein Beitrag zur Pathogenese des Ulcus duodeni. *Virchows· Arch. path. Anat.*, 1924, 251, 628-637.

1925 A5    Zur Frage der Pubertätsphthise. *Beitr. Klin. Tuberk.*, 1925, 60, 312-324.

A6    Zur Frage der Abstammung der grossen Exsudatzellen bei käsiger Pneumonie. *Beitr. Klin. Tuberk.*, 1925, 61, 221-229.

A7    (With Magda Pagel) Zur Histochemie der Lungentuberkulose, mit besonderer Berücksichtigung der Fettsubstanzen und Lipoide. *Virchows Arch. path. Anat.*, 1925, 256, 629-640.

A8    Ueber eine einfache Darstellung der Lungencapillaren am Gewebsschnitt. *Beitr. Klin, Tuberk.*, 1925, 61, 301-302.

A9    Beiträge zur Histologie der Exsudatzellen bei käsiger Pneumonie. *Virchows Arch. path. Anat.*, 1925, 256, 641-648.

A10   Ueber ausgedehnte Xanthomzellablagerungen in organisierten Pfröpfen der Lungenschlagader. *Virchows Arch. path. Anat.*, 1925, *258*, 414-418.

A11   Die Gewebsreaktionen des Meerschweinchens bei der experimentellen Infektion mit Tuberkelbacillen. Beiträge zur Pathohistologie der Meerschweinchentuberkulose. *1. Mitteilng. Beitr. Klin. Tuberk.*, 1925, *61*, 641-677.

A12   Untersuchungen über die Histologie des tuberkulösen Primäraffektes der Meerschweinchenlunge. Beiträge zur Pathohistologie der Meerschweinchentuberkulose. 2. *Mitteilng. Beitr. Klin. Tuberk.*, 1925, *61*, 678-688.

A13   Ueber Beteiligung des Zwölffingerdarms am Sekundärstadium der Tuberkulose. *Frankfurt. Z. Path.*, 1925, *33*, 159-164.

A14   Ueber eine eigentümliche Erscheinungsform des mutmasslichen "Superinfektionsherdes" der Lunge bei Tuberkulose. *Beitr. Klin. Tuberk.*, 1925, *62*, 614-620.

A15   Der tuberkulöse Primäraffekt der Meerschweinchenlunge. *Krankheitsforsch.*, 1925-6, *2*, 263-286; also *Brauers Beitr.*, 1925, 61, 6.

1926 A16   Bemerkungen über Versuche einer Beeinflussung der Meerschweinchentuberkulose, gemessen am histologischen Bilde, mit besonderer Berücksichtigung der Kavernenfrage und der Gefässwandreaktionen (Siegmundschen Intimagranulome.) Beiträge zur Pathohistologie der Meerschweinchentuberkulose. *3. Mitteilng. Beitr. Klin. Tuberk.*, 1926, *63*, 160-178.

A17   Zur Entstehungsgeschichte des Milztuberkels. *Zbl. allg. path. Anat.*, 1926, *38*, 195-204.

A18   Meerschweinchentuberkulose und Metallvergiftung. *Kr. forsch.*, 1926, *3*, 372-398.

A19   Allgemein-pathologisch bemerkenswerte Züge im Bilde der experimentellen Meerschweinchentuberkulose. *Verh. dtsch. path. Ges.*, 1926, *21*, 347-352.

A20   Normale Anatomie und Entwicklungsgeschichte. *Jber. ges. Tuberk. forsch.*, 1926, 12-19.

A21    Pathologische Anatomie der Tuberkulose. *Jber. ges. Tuberkforsch.*, 1926, 219-237.

A22    Spezielle pathologische Anatomie der einzelnen Organmanifestationen. *Jber. ges. Tuberkforsch.*, 1926, 242-248.

A23    Allgemeine pathologische Anatomie und spezielle pathologische Anatomie der Grenzgebiete. *Jber. ges. Tuberkforsch.*, 1926, 98-111.

A24    Ueber den Zusammenhang von ungewöhnlichen Wucherungen atypischen und ortsfremden Epithels der Bronchien mit Bronchiektasien. Untersuchungen über adenomartige Verästelungen der Bronchien des Meerschweinchens. *Virchows Arch. path. Anat.*, 1926, 262, 583-594.

1927 B1    Die allgemeinen patho-morphologischen Grundlagen der Tuberkulose. Berlin, J. Springer. 1927.

A25    Bemerkungen zur Abhandlung von Kurosu über einen histochemischen Goldnachweis usw. in Band 57, Heft 1-2 dieser Zeitschrift. *Z. ges. exp. Med.*, 1927, 58, 642-644.

A26    Vergleichende Betrachtungen zur Tuberkulosemorphologie beim Menschen und Versuchstier. *Frankfurt. Z. Path.*, 1927, 35, 375-400.

A27    Nutzen und Notwendigkeit der Tuberkulosekrankenhaus-Prosektur. *Z. ges. Krankenhauswesen*, 1927, 23, 755-757.

A28    Die Krankheitslehre der Phthise in den Phasen ihrer geschichtlichen Entwicklung. *Beitr. Klin. Tuberk.*, 1927, 66, 66-98.

A29    Ueber die tuberkulöse Herdbildung bei intratrachealer Infektion des Kaninchens. Beiträge zur Pathohistologie der Meerschweinchentuberkulose; 4. *Mitteilng. Beitr. Klin. Tuberk.*, 1926, 66, 423-440.

A30    Ueber parafokale Hohlräume bei Lungentuberkulose. *Beitr. Klin. Tuberk.*, 1927, 66, 545-549.

A31    Zur Pathogenese der Lungenblutung bei Tuberkulose. *Beitr. Klin. Tuberk.*, 1927, 66, 631-634.

A32    Zum 450 jährigen Jubiläum der Tübinger Medizinischen Fakultät. *Dtsch. med. Wschrift.* 1927, 53, 1270-1273. (Sonderabdruck Nr. 30, 1-10).

A33 Ueber die Herdbildung bei intratrachealer Infektion des Kaninchens u. Meerschweinchens. *4. Mitteilng. Beitr. Klin. Tuberk.*, 1927, 66, 432-440.

A34    Ueber die Morphologie des durch intratracheale Infektion erzeugten Lungenherdes bei Meerschweinchentuberkulose. *5. Mitteilng. Beitr. Klin. Tuberk.*, 1927, 66, 588-598.

A35    Das histologische Bild der Tuberkulose. *Verb. techn. Assist.-Bl.*, 1927, 2, 1-3.

1928 B2    (With Magda Pagel-Koll) Karl Ernst Rankes Ausgewählte Schriften zur Tuberkulosepathologie eingeleitet und herausgegeben. Tuberkulose in Einzeldarstellungen, Band 6. Berlin, J. Springer, 1928. Einleitung: pp. 1-36.

A36    Spezielle pathologische Anatomie der einzelnen Organmanifestationen. Uebersichtsreferat. *Jber. Tuberkforsch.*, 1928, 184-189.

A37    Ueber die Rolle der Allergie beim Abbau in die Bauchhöhle überpflanzter Gewebsteile. *Kr. forsch.*, 1928, 6, 337-377.

A38    Zur Geschichte der Lungensteine und der Obstruktionstheorie der Phthise. *Beitr. Klin. Tuberk.*, 1928, 69, 315-323.

A39    Stadien und Phasen im tuberkulösen Geschehen. *J. kurse ärztl. Fortb.*, 1928, *19*, Heft *1*, 9-30.

A40    Allgemeine pathologische Anatomie u. spezielle pathologische Anatomie der Grenzgebiete. Uebersichtsreferat. *Jber. Tuberk. forsch.*, 1928, 70-75.

A41    Tuberkuloseallergie und Reticuloendothel. *Klin. Wschr.*, 1928, 7, 700.

A42    Reticuloendothel—Amyloid—Tuberkulose. *Zbl. ges. Tuberk. forsch.*, 1928, 29, 257-275.

A43    Pathologische Anatomie der Tuberkulose (einsschliesslich experimentelle Pathologie). Uebersichtsreferat. *Jber. Tuberk. forsch.,* 1928, 167-179.

1929 B3    Die anatomischen Grundlagen der Immunitätsvorgänge. In: St. Engel *and* Clemens von Pirquet: Handbuch der Kindertuberkulose. Band 1. 1929. Leipzig, G. Thieme, 213-252.

B4    Missbildungen der Nebennieren. In: Schwalbe, Ernst *and* Gruber, Georg Benno: Morphologie der Missbildungen, Jena, G. Fischer, 1906-37, 3, 3 (1929), 525-563.

A44    Zum Wesen der tuberkulösen Erweichung. Nach einem Modellversuch. *Klin. Wschr.,* 1929, 8, 1352-1354.

A45    (With W. Roloff) Zur Virulenz der Tuberkelbazillen bei der Lungentuberkulose. *Beitr. Klin. Tuberk. spezif. Tuberkforsch.,* 1929, 72, 685-699.

A46    Tuberkuloseallergie u. Bazillenvirulenz. *Dtsch. path. Ges., 24. Tagung in Wien.* Jena, G. Fischer, 1929, 164-170, 238-254.

A47    Ueber Entstehung u. Bedeutung der Miliartuberkulose. *Fortschr. Med.,* 1929, 47, No. 14, 1-11.

A48    Zur pathologischen Anatomie des infraklavicularen Infiltrates. *Dtsch. med. Wschr.,* 1929, No. 10, 1-3.

A49    Tuberkuloseallergie u. Bacillenstamm. Zugleich ein Beitrag zur Biologie des BC6-Bacillus. *Klin. Wschr.,* 1929, 8, 170-171.

A50    Tuberkuloseallergie und Serumanaphylaxie. *Klin. Wschr.,* 1929, 8, 742-743.

A51    Die deutsche Aerztebücherei. *Klin. Wschr.,* 1929, 8, 1887-8.

1930 B5    J. B. van Helmont. Einführung in die philosophische Medizin des Barock. Berlin, J. Springer, 1930.

B6    Lungentuberkulose. *In: Handbuch der speziellen pathologischen Anatomie u. Histologie.* Herausgegeben von F. Henke u. O. Lubarsch. Band III/2, Berlin, J. Springer, 1930-1, 139-528.

A52    (With J. E. Garcia-Frias) Ueber das Verhältnis der Uferzellenspeicherung and Serumüberempfindlichkeit zur experimentellen Tuberkulose. *Virchows Arch. path. Anat.*, (Festchrift Lubarch), 1930, 275, 479-504.

A53-4    Der Beginn der Lungentuberkulose und die Rankesche Stadienlehre. *Klin. Wschr.*, 1930, 9, 51-58.

A55    Immunitätsvorgänge. Ihre anatomischen Grundlagen und ihre Bedeutung für den Ablauf der menschlichen Tuberkulose. *Dtsch. med. Wschr.*, 1930, No. 50, 1-12.

A56    Megjegyzesek a tüdötuberkulózis kezdeteník problémájához (Notes on the problem of the first onset of tuberculosis) *Ther. Hung.*, 1930, No. 4, 1-7.

A57    Zur Frage der Histogenese tuberkulöser Prozesse. Bemerkungen zur gleichnamigen Arbeit von Hübschmann in dieser Zeitschrift Bd. 58, Heft. 5. *Z. Tuberk.*, 1930, 59, 124-8.

1931 B7    Virchow und die Grundlagen der Medizin des XIX. Jahrhunderts. *Jena. med. hist. Beitr.*, Heft 14, Jena, G. Fischer, 1931.

A58    Helmont—Leibniz—Stahl. *Sudhoffs Arch. Gesch. Med.*, 1931, 24, 19-59.

A59    Zur Morphologie der Ueberempfindlichkeit und Immunitätserscheinungen. *Z ges. exp. Med.*, 1931, 77, 396-409.

A60    Studien über die tuberkulöse Erweichung. *Beitr. Klin. Tuberk.*, hrsg. v. Ludolph Brauer, 1931, 76, 414-458.

A61    Pathologisch-anatomisches zum Beginn der chronischen Lungenphthise. *Dtsch. med. Wschr.*, 1931, No. 50, 2094-2097.

A62    Ein Gang durch die älteren medizinischen Lehrsysteme. *Med. Welt*, 1931, Nos. 9 & 13, Sonderabdruck, 1-14.

1932 A63    Geschichte der runden Magengeschwürs. *Sudhoffs Arch. Gesch. Med.*, 1932, 25, 330-348.

A64    Zur Entstehungsgeschichte und Kasuistik der Lungentuberkulose. *Beitr. Klin. Tuberk.*, 1932, 79, 383-400.

A65 (With M. Gundel and P. György) Experimentelle Beobachtungen zu der Frage der Resistenzverminderung und Infektion. *Z. Hyg. Infektkr.*, 1932, *113*, 629-644.

A66 Hämatogene Streuungsformen der Tuberkulose. Naturhistorischmedizinischer Verein Heidelberg. Sitzung vom 7. Juni 1932. *Klin. Wschr.*, 1932, *11*, No. 42, 1772-3.

A67 (With A. Klopstock *and* A. Guggenheim). Zum Problem der Beziehungen zwischen allergischer Entzündung u. tuberkulöser Infektion. *Klin. Wschr.*, 1932, *11*, 1826-8.

A68 Pathologie der experimentellen Meerschweinchentuberkulose. Uebersichtsreferat. *Zbl. ges. Tuberkforsch.*, 1932, 37, 305-315.

A69 Zur Pathologie des Asthma bronchale. *Virchows Archiv path. Anat.*, 1932, *286*, 580-590.

A70 Die hämatogenen Tuberkulosen. Leitsätze. *Z. Tuberk.*, 1932, *65*, 197-202.

1933 A71 Pathologische Anatomie der haematogenen Streuungs-Tuberkulose. *Ergebn. ges. Tuberkforsch.*, 1933, 5, 231-350.

A72 Pathologisch-anatomische Grundlagen von Allergie und Immunität. *Kinderärztl. Prax.*, 1933, 4, 373-385.

A73 Ueber die Beteiligung der Zunge an inneren Organerkrankungen. Pathologisch-anatomische Untersuchungen. *Klin. Wschr.*, 1933, *12*, 1496-99.

A74 Neuere Ergebnisse der pathologischen Anatomie des Kindesalters. *Kinderärztl. Prax.*, 1933, 522-9, 564-570.

A75 Ergebnisse der Tuberkulosepathologie. *Beiheft z. Med. Klin.*, *1933*, 1-32.

A76 (With M. Gundel and F. Süssbrich) Untersuchungen zur Aetiologie der Appendicitis und postappendiculären Peritonitis. *Beitr. path. Anat.*, 1933, *91*, 399-438.

1934 A77 Importance of local factors in the onset of pulmonary tuberculosis. *Brit. med. J.*, 1934, 2, 1024-5.

A78 Histological studies on the variability of the Tubercle Bacillus. *J. Path. Bact.*, 1934, 39, 689-701.

A79     (With L. B. Stott) A simple method of estimation of the proteins of blood-serum and its value in tuberculosis. *Tubercle* (Edinb.), 1934, *15*, 454-9.

1935 A80     Religious motives in the medical biology of the XVIIth century. *Bull. Hist. Med.*, 1935, *3*, 97-128, 213-231, 265-312.

A81     The production of Koch's phenomenon with various strains of Tubercle Bacilli. *J. Path. Bact.*, 1935, *41*, 89-96.

A82     On endogenous origin of early pulmonary tuberculosis. The anatomic view of its clinical diagnosis. *Amer. J. med. Sci.*, 1935, *189*, 253-264.

A83     On allergy and immunity. Investigations in morbid anatomy and experimental pathology. *Acta med. scand.*, 1935, *84*, 422-438.

A84     The bactericidal power of blood serum as a means of differentiating a certain type of pulmonary tuberculosis. *Tubercle* (Edinb.), 1935, *16*, 256-266.

A85     Funnel-chest and pulmonary tuberculosis. *Brit. med. J.*, 1935, i, 922-3.

1936 A86     (With E. Weichherz) Intestinal tuberculous limited to the appendix. *Brit. med. J.*, 1936, ii, 1305-6.

A87     (With E. Brieger) "Primary" laryngeal and intestinal tuberculouis. *Papworth Research Bull.*, 1936, *I*, 43-49.

A88     The role of the bacillus and of "hetero-allergy" in tuberculous liquefaction. *J. Path. Bact.*, 1936, *42*, 417-424.

A89     Experimental studies on early pulmonary tuberculosis of the "adult" type. *Brit. J. Tuberc.*, 1936, *30*, 204-218.

A90     New paths in tuberculosis pathology. *Papworth Res. Bull.*, 1936, *1*, 1-13.

A91     The reproduction of early pulmonary tuberculosis of the adult type by exogenous and endogenous reinfection. *Papworth Res. Bull.*, 1936, *1*, 33-36.

A92     (With H. J. Robinson) Spontaneous cavity healing. *Papworth Res. Bull.*, 1936, *1*, 37-41.

A93    New experiments on the "dissociation" of allergic hypersensitiveness and immunity. *Papworth Res. Bull.*, 1936/37, *1*, 62-80.

A94    (With D. MacCallum) On perifocal and traumatic haemorrhages in pulmonary tuberculosis. *Brit. J. Tuberc.*, 1936, *30*, 25-32.

1937 B8a    Immunität. In: J. Berberich and P. Spiro: Therapie der Tuberkulose. Leiden, A. W. Sijthoff, 1937, 105-136.

B8b    Pathogenese, Morphologie und Allergiebeziehungen der Heilungsvorgänge bei Tuberkulose. In: J. Berberich and P. Spiro: Therapie der Tuberkulose. Leiden, A. W. Sijthoff, 1937, 137-170.

B8c    Anatomische und experimentelle Befunde bei therapeutischen Eingriffen. In: J. Berberich and P. Spiro: Therapie der Tuberkulose. Leiden, A. W. Sijthoff, 1937, 171-190.

A95    Experiments on dissociation of allergic hyptersensitiveness and immunity. *J. Path. Bact.*, 1937, *44*, 643-659.

A96    The reproduction of early pulmonary tuberculosis of the adult type of bronchogenic and haematogenous re-infection. *J. State. Med.*, 1937, *45*, 63-73.

A97    Reactivation of a tuberculosis focus by micro-organisms other than the tubercle bacillus. *Lancet*, 1937, i, 1279-81.

A98    (With P. Kallós) Experimentelle Untersuchungen über Asthma bronchale. *Acta med. scand.*, 1937, *91*, 292-305.

A99    (With R. Passmore and L. J. Harris) Vitamin C and infection: Influence of infection on vitamin C content of tissues of animals. *Lancet*, 1937, ii, 183-6.

A100    The evolution of tuberculosis in Man. *Irish J. med. Sci.*, 1937, 735-741.

1938 B9    Background to modern science. Ten lectures at Cambridge arranged by the History of Science Committee, 1936. By F. M. Cornford, Sir W. Dampier, Lord Rutherford (and others). Edited by Joseph Needham and Walter Pagel. Cambridge, University Press. 1938.

A101   (With Laurence Roberts) Behaviour of tuberculous cavities in the lung under artificial pneumothorax treatment. *Brit. med. J.*, 1938, ii, 1258-9.

A102-3  (With R. H. Fish) The morbid anatomy of epituberculosis. *J. path. Bact.*, 1938, 47, 593-601.

A104   (With F. A. H. Simmonds) Chronic disseminated tuberculosis illustrated by a case of cortico-pleural disease. *Brit. med. J.*, 1938, i, 15-16.

R1-23  Collective Review of the following items: Max Neuburger: The doctrine of the healing power of nature throughout the course of time; George Sticker: Entwicklungsgeschichte der medizinischen Facultät an der Alma Mater Julia; Henry E. Sigerist: Grosse Aerzte; Wilhelm Haberling: Wer war der Vater der Aseptik? Hans Haustein: Kannten Mittelalter und Altertum die Syphilis. Warren F. Dawson: Manuscripta medica; E. D. Oosterbeek: Der Wahnsinn der Io, in *Sudhoffs Arch. Gesch. Med.*, 1932, 25, 307-14; St. Bezdechi-Cluj: Das psychopathische Substrat der "Bacchantinnen" Euripides, in *Sudhoffs Arch. Gesch. Med.*, 1932, 25, 279-306; W. Riemschneider: Ein Krankenbett auf der antiken Bühne, in *Janus*, 37, 1933, 275-80; Ernst Darmstaedter: Ptisana. Ein Beitrag zur Kenntnis der antiken Diätetik, in *Archeion*, 1933, 15, 181-201; R. Koch: Warum kamen die hippocratischen Aphorismen zu klassischer Bedeutung? in *Münch. med. Wschr.*, 1933, 5, 189-191; Owsei Temkin: Geschichte des Hippokratismus im ausgehenden Altertum, in *Kyklos*, 1932, 4, 1-80; Rafaelle Cantarella: Una tradizione ippocratica nella scuola Salernitana: Il giuramento dei medici, in *Archeion*, 1933, 15, 305-20; Karl Bräunig: Hippokrates u. die heutige Medizin, in *Human. Gymn.*, 1932, 43, 25-44; Max Meyerhof: La fin de l'école d'Alexandrie d'après quelques auteurs arabes, in *Archeion*, 1933, 15, 1-15; Max Meyerhof: Ibn an-Nafis und seine Theorie des Lungenkreislaufs, in: *Quellen Stud. Gesch. Naturw.*, 1933, 4, 37-88; Karl Sudhoff: Constantin, der erste Vermittler muslimischer Wissenschaft ins Abendland u. die beiden Salernitaner Frühscholastiker Maurus u. Urso, als Exponenten dieser Vermittlung, in *Archeion*, 1932, *14*, 359-69; Hugo Schulz: Der Aebtissin Hildegard von Bingen Ursachen u. Behandlung der Krankheiten. München, 1933; Ernst Windler: Das Bremer mittelniederdeutsche Arzneibuch des Arnoldus Doneldey; Walter Artelt: Costanzo Landi u. sein "Methodus de bona valetudine tuenda" in *Sudhoffs Arch. Gesch. Med.*, 1932, *25*, 315-29; Walter Artelt: Paracelsus im Urteil der Medizinhistorik, in *Fortschr. Med.*, 1932, *50*, 929-33; E. Darmstaedter: Paracelsus De natura rerum, in *Janus*, 1933, *37*, 1-18, 48-62, 109-15; Wilhelm Haberling: Johann Winter von Andernach, in *Klin. Wschr.*, 1932, *11*, 1616-20, in *Kulturwiss. Bibliogr. Nachleben Antike*, 1938, 2, London, Warburg Inst., 71-8.

R24    Review of: Franz Strunz: Theophrastus Paracelsus. Idee und Problem seiner Weltanschauung, 2. Auflage, Band II, Salzburg, 1937. *Isis*, 1938, *28*, 469-471.

R25    Review of R.A.B. Oosterhuis: Paracelsus en Hahnemann, een Renaissance der geneeskunst, Leiden, 1937. *Isis*, 1938, *28*, 471-3.

R26    Review of: R. Hoenigswald: Denker der italienischen Renaissance. Gestalten und Probleme, Basel, 1938. *Isis*, 1938, *29*, 453-7.

1939 B10    Pathologie und Histologie der allergischen Erscheinungen. In: *Fortschritte der Allergielehre* herausgegeben von P. Kallos. Vol. *1*, 73-146, Basel-New York, 1939.

B11    Pulmonary tuberculosis. Pathology, diagnosis, management and prevention. 1st Edition, jointly with George Gregory Kayne and L. O'Shaughnessy. Oxford, Univ. Press, 1939.

A105    (With F.A.H. Simmonds) The healing of cavities. *Amer. J. med. Sci.*, 1939, *197*, 281-286.

A106    (With A. S. Griffith) Susceptibility of Golden hamster (cricetus auretus) to bovine, human and avian tubercle bacilli and to Vole strain of acidfast bacillus (Wells) with histological observations. *J. Hyg.*, 1939, *39*, 154-160.

A107     The lung lesion in extrapulmonary tuberculosis; morbid anatomical aspects. *Papworth Res. Bull.* (1938), 1939, 2, 57-71.

A108-9   Rheumatism, allergy, tuberculosis. *Papworth Res. Bull.,* (*1938*), 1939, 2, 95-112.

A110     Prognosis und diagnosis: a comparison of ancient and modern medicine. *J. Warburg Inst.*, 1939, 2, 382-398.

R27     Review of: D. Mahnke: Unendliche Sphäre und Alltmittelpunkt. Beiträge zur Genealogie der mathematischen Mystik, Halle, 1937. *Isis*, 1939, *30*, 121-4.

1940 A111     The effect of blood serum on the growth of tubercle bacilli in the depth of liquid media. *J. Path. & Bact.*, 1940, *50*, 111-9.

A112     Experimental tuberculosis; observations on tissue reaction and natural resistance. *Amer. Rev. Tuberc.*, 1940, *42*, 58-69.

1941 A113     John Baptist van Helmont: *De Tempore* and the history of the biological concept of time. *Isis*, 1941-2, *33*, 621-3.

A114     The effect of seal oil and Glycerol Broth Treatment on anti-tuberculous vaccination. *J. Path. Bact.*, 1941, *52*, 383-5.

1942 A115     (With F.A.H. Simmonds) Cavity healing and bronchial occlusion. *Amer. J. med. Sci.*, 1942, 203, 177-187.

A116     Primary tuberculosis of the tonsils. *Pract. oto-rhino-laryng.*, 1942, 4, 279-284.

A117     Tubercles and foreign-body granulomata; experiments in mice and guinea pigs. *Amer. Rev. Tuberc.*, 1942, *46*, 295-303.

A118     (With G. G. Kayne) Discussion on primary tuberculosis in adolescents and adults. *Proc. Roy. Soc. Med.*, 1942, *35*, 489-494.

1943 A119     (With D. S. Price) An early primary tuberculous pulmonary focus, about four to eight weeks old. *Amer. Rev. Tuberc.*, 1943, *47*, 614-617.

A120    The debt of science to a devout belief in God as illustrated by the work of J. B. van Helmont. *J. Trans. Victoria Inst.*, 1943, 74, 99-115.

A121    Pathological aspects of pleurisy in young adults. *Tubercle* (Edinb.) 1943, 24, 68-72.

1944 A122    The religious and philosophical aspects of Van Helmont's science and medicine. *Bull. Hist. Med. Suppl. 2,* 1944, 1-44.

A123    William Harvey: Some neglected aspects of medical history. *J. Warburg Courtauld Inst.*, 1944, 7, 144-153.

A124    The origin of bronchogenic tuberculosis in the adult; pathological aspects of "exogenous and endogenous reinfection." *Brit. med. J.*, 1944, ii, 791.

A125    (With I. James) Miniature scar-carcinoma of the lung and the "Upper Sulcus Tumour" of Pancoast. *Brit. J. Surg.*, 1944, 32, 85-90.

A126    J. B. van Helmont (1579-1644). *Nature*, 1944, *153,* 675-6.

1945 A127    The speculative basis of modern pathology: Jahn, Virchow and the philosophy of pathology. *Bull. Hist. Med.*, 1945, *18,* 1-43.

A128    The vindication of "rubbish." *Middx. Hosp. J.*, 1945, *45,* 42-45.

A129    (With J. D. Fergusson) Some observations on carcinoma of prostate treated with oestrogens—as demonstrated by serial biopsies. *Brit. J. Surg.*, 1945, *33,* 122-130.

A130    Van Helmont: the 300th anniversary of his death. *Brit. med. J.*, 1945, i, 59.

R28    Review of Pathogenesis of Tuberculosis" by A. R. Rich, in *Tubercle* (Edinb.), 1945, 26, 154-160; 190-5; 1945, 27, 19-24.

R29    Review of: O. Temkin: The falling sickness, Baltimore, 1945. *Isis*, 1945-6, *36,* 275-8.

1946 A131   (With S. Hall) Aspiration type of congenital tuberculosis. *Tubercle* (*Edinb.*), 1946, 27, 153-158.

A132   Relationship between primary and adult pulmonary tuberculosis. *Lancet,* 1946, ii, 471.

R30   Review of: Sir C. Sherrington: The endeavor of Jean Fernel, Cambridge, 1946. *Bull. Hist. Med.,* 1946, 20, 587-9.

1947 A133   (With E. J. Blair) Fulminant tuberculous septicaemia and other atypical forms of abdominal tuberculosis. *Tubercle* (Edinb.), 1947, 28, 115-123.

R31   Review of: H. Bailey and W. J. Bishop: Notable names in medicine and surgery. Short biographies, London, 1946. *Bull. Hist. Med.,* 1947, 21, 128-9.

R32   Review of: S. Vere Pearson: Men, medicine and myself. London, 1946. *Bull. Hist. Med.,* 1947, 21, 129-131.

R33   Review of: R. Scott Stevenson: Morell Mackenzie. The story of a Victorian tragedy. *Bull. Hist. Med.,* 1947, 21, 131-3.

R34   Review of: Sir Walter Langdon-Brown. Some chapters in Cambridge medical history, *Bull. Hist. Med.,* 1947, 21, 630-2.

R35   Review of: H. de Waele: J. B. Van Helmont, Brussels, n.d. *Isis,* 1947-48, 38, 248-9.

1948 B12   Pulmonary tuberculosis. Pathology, diagnosis, management and prevention. 2nd Ed. Revised and partly rewritten by Walter Pagel, F.A.H. Simmonds, N. Macdonald and L. Fatti. Oxford, University Press, 1948.

A134   (With S. Hall) Aspiration type of congenital tuberculosis. Further communication. *Tubercle,* (Edinb.) 1948, 29, 32-33.

A135   (With A. L. Woolf) Aseptic necrosis of pancreas. Due to Arterial thrombosis in malignant hypertension. *Brit. med. J.,* 1948, i, 442-3.

A136    "Circulatio"—its unusual connotations and William Harvey's philosophy. In: *Festschrift zum 80. Geburtstag Max Neuburgers.* Vienna, W. Maudrich, 1948, 358-362.

A137    (With C.H.C. Toussaint) Pathology of reinfection; some sources of diagnostic errors. *Amer. Rev. Tuberc.,* 1948, *58,* 85-97.

A138    Julius Leopold Pagel (1851-1912). In: *Victor Robinson Memorial Volume.* Essays on hist. of medicine, 1948, New York, Froben Press, 273-297.

A139    A background study to Harvey: *Med. Bookman,* 1948, *2,* 407-410.

A140    Some morbid anatomical aspects of the origin of bronchogenic phthisis. *Pneumonologia Danubiana* (Budap.), 1948, 1-3.

A141    Historical notes on haemoptysis due to vicarious menstruation. In: *Victor Robinson memorial volume,* New York, Froben Press, 1948, 299-312.

A142    Jung's views on alchemy. *Isis.* 1948, *39,* 44-8.

R36     Review of: J. R. Marcus: Communal sick-care in the German ghetto, Cincinatti, 1947. *Bull. Hist. Med.,* 1948, *22,* 343-4.

R37     Review of: N. Steno: Opera theologica. *Ed.* K. Larsen *and* G. Scherz, Copenhagen, 1944-7. *Bull. Hist. Med.,* 1948, *22,* 720-2.

R37a    Review of: John Francis: Bovine tuberculosis including a contrast with human tuberculosis. *Med. Bookman,* 1948, 137-8.

1949 A143    (With A. L. Woolf) On fulminant tuberculous septicemia with leukopenia. *Amer. Rev. Tuberc.,* 1949, *59,* 311-316.

A144-5  J. B. Van Helmont, *De Tempore,* and biological time. *Osiris,* 1949, *8,* 346-417.

A146    Acronecrosis due to Fibrin Thrombi and Endothelial Cell Thrombi. *Amer. J. med. Sci.,* 1949, *218,* 425-431.

A147   (With J. H. Humphrey) The tissue response to heat-killed streptococci in the skin of normal subjects, and in persons with rheumatic fever, rheumatoid arthritis, subacute bacterial endocarditis and erythema nodosum. *Brit. J. exp. Path.*, 1949, *30*, 282-288.

A148   (With A. L. Woolf and R. Asher) Histological observations on dermatomyositis. *J. Path. Bact.*, 1949, *61*, 403-411.

R38   Review of: B. J. Ficcarra: Essays on historical medicine. *Bull. Hist. Med.*, 1949, *23*, 521-2.

R38a   Review of: Aroldo Baffoni: Storia delle pleuriti da Ippocrate a Laennec. *Medicine illustrated*, 1949, *3*, 15.

R38b   Review of: Anton Sattler: Frühdiagnose der Lungentuberkulose durch den praktischen Arzt. *Medicine illustrated*, 1949, *3*, 93.

R38c   Review of: Victor Robinson Memorial Volume. *Medicine illustrated*, 1949, *3*, 187-8.

R38d   Review of: H. Glaser: Das Weltbild der Medizin von heute. *Medicine illustrated*, 1949, *3*, 238.

R38e   Essay Review of: George Sarton: Introduction to the history of science, vol. III: Science and learning in the fourteenth century. *Medicine illustrated*, 1949, *3*, 271-2.

R38f   Review of: S. L. Cummins: Tuberculosis in history from the seventeenth century to our own times. *Medicine illustrated*, 1949, *3*, 526-7.

1950 A149   Harvey's role in the history of medicine. *Bull. Hist. Med.*, 1950, *24*, 70-73. (Comment on Peller's article in Bull. Hist. Med. 1949, 213.)

A150   The circular motion of the blood and Giordano Bruno's philosophy of the circle. *Bull. Hist. Med.*, 1950, *24*, 398-9.

R39   Review of: E. R. Curtius: Europäische Literatur und Lateinisches Mittelalter, Bern, 1948. *Isis*, 1950, *41*, 247-8.

R40   Review of: E. Berghoff: Max Neuburger, Vienna, 1948. *Bull. Hist. Med.*, 1950, *24*, 91-2.

R41     Review of: A. van Leeuwenhoek: The collected letters. Ed. by a committee of Dutch scientists. Vol. III. Amsterdam, 1948. *Bull. Hist. Med.,* 1950, *24,* 92-3.

R42     Review of: H. A. Skinner: The origin of medical terms, Baltimore, 1949. *Bull. Hist. Med.,* 1950, *24,* 404-5.

R43     Review of: William Clowes (1544-1604). Selected writings. Ed. F. N. L. Poynter, London, 1948. *Isis,* 1950, *41,* 109.

R44     Review of: F. Saxl and R. Wittkower: British art and the Mediterranean, London, 1948. *Isis,* 1950, *41,* 143-4.

R45     Review of: E. H. Ackerknecht: Malaria in the Upper Mississippi Valley, 1760-1900, Baltimore, 1945. *Arch. int. Hist. Sci.,* 1950, *29,* 470-1.

R46     Review of: Abraham Levinson Anniversary Volume, New York, 1949. *Bull. Hist. Med.,* 1950, *24,* 591-2.

R47     Review of: E. Harding: Das Geheimnis der Seele. Ursprung und Ziel der phychischen Energie, Zurich, 1948. *Isis,* 1950, *41,* 137-8.

R48     Review of: Eranos-Jahrbuch 1947. Vol. XV: 'Der Mensch,' ed. O. Froebe—Kapteyn, Zürich, 1948. *Isis,* 1950, *41,* 138.

1951 A152     Giordano Bruno, the philosophy of circles and the circular movement of the blood. *J. Hist. Med.,* 1951, *6,* 116-124.

A153     Julius Pagel and the significance of medical history for medicine. *Bull. Hist. Med.,* 1951, *25,* 207-225.

A154     William Harvey and the purpose of circulation. *Isis,* 1951, *42,* 22-38.

A155     (With E. Nassau) The early changes of pulmonary tuberculosis in lobectomy specimens. *Tubercle* (Edinb.), 1951, *32,* 120-127.

A156     Polyarteritis nodosa and "rheumatic" diseases. *J. clin. Path.,* 1951, *4,* 137-157.

A157   (With K. Ball, and H. Joules) Acute tuberculous septicaemia with leucopenia. *Brit. med. J.*, 1951, ii, 869-873.

A158   (With S. Jackson) Pyogenic brain abscess as complica-
tion of cavitated phthisis. *Tubercle* (Edinb.), 1951, *32*,
168-170.

A159   (With T. G. I. James) Oligodendroglioma with extra-
cranial metastases. *Brit. J. Surg.*, 1951 *39*, 56-65.

A160   Then and now. (Letter re Keevil and Payne to the
*Lancet,* 1951, i, 966.

R49   Review of: F. A. Willius and J. J. Dry: A history of
the heart and the circulation, Philadelphia—London,
1948. *Arch. int. Hist. Sci.,* 1951, *30,* 1038-9.

R50   Review of: Ernst Hoffmann: Plato, Zürich, 1950. *Arch.
int. Hist. Sci.,* 1951, *30,* 186-7.

R51   Review of: R. Meister: Geschichte der Akademie der
Wissenschaften in Wien 1847-1947, Vienna, 1947.
*Arch. int. Hist. Sci.,* 1951, *30,* 203.

R52   Review of: J. B. Van Helmont: Dageraad ofte nieuwe
opkomst der geneeskonst in verborgen grondregulen
der Natur, Rotterdam, 1660. Facsimile editie Brussels,
1944. *Arch. int. Hist. Sci.,* 1951, *30,* 262-3.

R53   Review of: Ernst Hoffman: Nicolaus von Cues, Zwei
Vorträge, Heidelberg, 1940. *Arch. int. Hist. Sci.,* 1951,
*30,* 508-9.

R54   Review of: J. B. Conant: Robert Boyle's experiments in
pneumatics, Cambridge (Mass.), 1950. *Arch. int. Hist.
Sci.,* 1951, *30,* 793.

R55   Review of: H. E. Sigerist: A history of medicine. Vol. I.
Primitive and archaic medicine. New York, 1951. *Arch.
int. Hist. Sci.,* 1951, *30,* 812-3.

R56   Review of: A. Vesalius: Das Epitome ofte cort begriip
der Anatomien. In nederduudsch van J. Wouters, Bruges,
1569. Facsimile ed. Brussels, 1947. *Arch. int. Hist. Sci.,*
1951, *30,* 821-2.

R57    Review of: Hugh Clegg, ed.: Fifty years of medicine. A symposium from the British Medical Journal, London, 1950. *Arch. int. Hist. Sci.,* 1951, *30,* 1069.

R58    Review of: G. Urdang: Pharmacy's part in society, Madison, 1946. *Arch. int. Hist. Sci.,* 1951, *30,* 829.

R59    Review of: H. J. C. Gibson: Dundee Royal Infirmary, 1798-1948, Dundee, 1949. *Bull. Hist. Med.,* 1951, *25,* 402-3.

R60    Review of: Caelius Aurelianus: On acute diseases *and* On chronic diseases. *Ed. and transl.* I. E. Drabkin, Chicago, 1950. *Bull. Hist. Med.,* 1951, 590.

R61    Review of: H. M. Pachter: Paracelsus. Magic into science, New York, 1951. *Isis,* 1951, *42,* 244-6.

R62    Review of: W. C. Dampier: A history of science and its relations with philosophy and religion, Cambridge, 1948. *Arch. int. Hist. Sci.,* 1951, *30,* 178-180.

1952 A161    Medical history at the end of the nineteenth century. To commemorate Julius Pagel (1851-1912) and his discovery of mediaeval sources. *Proc. Roy. Soc. Med.,* 1952, *45,* 303-6.

A162    Recrudescence in early phthisis. *Amer. Rev. Tuberc.,* 1952, *65,* 673-691.

A163    An outline of the principal forms of tuberculosis in Man; primary, disseminated and bronchogenic tuberculosis. *Postgrad. med. J.,* 1952, *28,* 606-614.

R63    Review of: Paracelsus: Selected writings, ed. J. Jacobi, New York, 1951. *Isis,* 1952, *43,* 64.

R64    Review of: I. B. Cohen: E. A. Hitchcock. Discoverer of of the "true subject" of the hermetic art, Worcester, Mass., 1952. *Isis,* 1952, *43,* 374-5.

R65    Review of: E. Lesky: Die Zeugungs—und Vererbungslehren der Antike und ihr Nachwirken, Mainz, 1950. *Bull. Hist. Med.,* 1952, *26,* 389-390.

R66    Review of: J. F. Callahan: Four views of time in ancient philosophy. Cambridge (Mass.), 1948. *Arch. int. Hist. Sci.,* 1952, *31,* 117.

R67 Review of: W. C. Till: Die Arzneikunde der Kopten, Berlin, 1951. *Arch. int. Hist. Sci.,* 1952, *31,* 159.

R68 Review of: J. B. de C. M. Saunders and C. D. O'Malley: The illustrations from the works of Andreas Vesalius of Brussels, Cleveland, 1950. *Arch. int. Hist. Sci.,* 1952, *31,* 170-1.

R69 Review of: Galen: Compendium Timaei Platonis, ed. P. Kraus and R. Walzer, London, 1951. *Arch. int. Hist. Sci.,* 1952, *31,* 427-8.

R70 Review of: K. D. Keele: Leonardo da Vinci on movement of the heart and blood, London, 1952. *Arch. int. Hist. Sci.,* 1952, *31,* 429-430.

R71 Review of: K. D. Keele: Leonardo da Vinci on movement of the heart and blood, London, 1952. *Isis,* 1952, *43,* 270-1.

R72 Review of: Paracelsus: Sozialethische und sozialpolitische Schriften, ed. K. Goldammer, Tübingen, 1952. *Isis,* 1952, *43,* 272.

R73 Review of: F. N. L. Poynter *and* W. J. Bishop: A seventeenth century doctor and his patients: John Symcotts (1592 (?)-1662), Streatley, 1951. *Isis,* 1952, *43,* 66.

1953 B13 Pulmonary tuberculosis. 3rd ed. (With F. A. H. Simmonds, and N. Macdonald) London, Oxford University Press. 1953.

A164 The reaction to Aristotle in seventeenth century biological thought. Campanella, van Helmont, Glanvill, Charleton, Harvey, Glisson, Descartes. In: *Science, Medicine and History.* Essays on the evolution of scientific thought and medical practice written in honour of Charles Singer. Oxford, University Press, 1953, I, 489-509.

A165-6 Die Stellung Caesalpins und Harveys in der Entdeckung und Ideologie des Blutkreislaufes. *Sudhoffs Arch. Gesch. Med.,* 1953, *37,* 319-328.

R74 Review of: C. Raimer Smith: The physician examines the Bible, New York, 1950. *Bull. Hist. Med.*, 1953, 27, 85-60.

R75 Review of: S. R. Kagan: Jewish medicine, Boston (Mass.), 1952. *Bull. Hist. Med.*, 1953, 27, 288-290.

R76 Review of: H. Zoske: Die Osteologie Vesals, Hannover, 1951. *Bull. Hist. Med.*, 1953, 27, 396-7.

R77 Review of: S. Bornhauser: Zur Geschichte der Schilddrüsen- und Kropfforschung im XIX. Jahrundert, Aarau, 1951. *Bull. Hist. Med.*, 1953, 27, 500-1.

R78 Review of: C. D. Leake: The Old Egyptian medical papyri, Kansas, 1952. *Bull. Hist. Med.*, 1953, 27, 578.

R79 Review of: Hippokrates: Die anatomischen Schriften. *Transl. and ed.* R. Kapferer, Stuttgart, 1951. *Bull. Hist. Med.*, 1953, 27, 579.

R80 Review of: G. M. Lancisi: De aneurysmatibus. With transl. and notes by W. Cave Wright, New York, 1952. *Isis*, 1953, 44, 392-3.

R81 Review of: R. Herrlinger: Volcher Coiter, 1534-1576, Nuremberg, 1952. *Isis*, 1953, 44, 283.

R82 Review of: H. W. Jansen: Apes and ape lore in the Middle Ages and the Renaissance, London, 1952. *Arch. int. Hist. Sci.*, 1953, 32, 336-8.

R83 Review of: Theophrastus von Hohenheim genannt Paracelsus. Sämtliche Werke, Ed. J. Strebel, St. Gallen, 1944-9. *Bull. Hist. Med.*, 1953, 27, 276-281.

R84 Review of: Sir C. Sherrington: Man on his nature, Edinburgh, 1937-8, Cambridge, 1951. *Bull. Hist. Med.*, 1953, 97-8.

R85 Review of: H. L. Gordon: The Maggid of Caro, New York, 1949. *Arch. int. Hist. Sci.*, 1953, 32, 493.

R86 Review of: H. J. Zimmels: Magicians, theologians and doctors. Studies in folk-medicine and folk-lore as reflected in the Rabbinical Responsa (12th-19th centuries), London, 1952. *Arch. int. Hist. Sci.,* 1953, *32,* 524-5.

1954 R87    Review of: Sir. G. Keynes: A bibliography of the writings of Dr. William Harvey, Cambridge, 1953. *Arch. int. Hist. Sci.,* 1954, *33,* 102-3.

R88    Review of: R. Montraville Green: A translation of Galen's Hygiene (De sanitate tuenda), Springfield, 1951. *Bull Hist. Med.,* 1954, *28,* 577-8.

R89    Review of: E. H. Ackerknecht: Rudolf Virchow. Doctor, statesman, anthropologist, Madison, 1953. *Bull. Hist. Med.,* 1954, *28,* 194-8.

R90    Review of: W. Artelt: Index zur Geschichte der Medizin, Naturwissenschaft und Technik, Munich, 1953. *Isis,* 1954, *55,* 109.

R91    Review of: E. H. Ackerknecht: Rudolf Virchow, Madison, 1953. *Arch. int. Hist. Sci.,* 1954, *33,* 105-8.

R92    Review of: K. Goldammer: Paracelsus. Natur und Offenbarung, Hannover, 1953. *Arch. int. Hist. Sci.,* 1954, *33,* 214-7.

R93    Review of: W. Brockbank: Portrait of a hospital, 1782-1948. Bicentenary of the Royal Infirmary, Manchester, London, 1952. *Bull. Hist. Med.,* 1954, *28,* 98.

R94    Review of: F. N. L. Poynter: A catalogue of incunabula in the Wellcome Historical Medical Library, London, 1954. *Arch. int. Hist. Sci.,* 1954, *33,* 353.

R95    Review of: N. Steno: Epistolae et epistolae ad eum datae. *Ed.* G. Scherz, Copenhagen, *1952.* Bull. Hist. Med., 1954, *28,* 287-9.

R96-7    Review of: K. E. Rothschuh: Geschichte der Physiologie, Berlin, 1953, *and* K. E. Rothschuh: Entwicklungsgeschichte physiologischer Probleme in Tabellenform, Munich, 1952. *Isis,* 1954, *45,* 104-6.

1955 A167    Humoral pathology: A lingering anachronism in the history of tuberculosis. *Bull. Hist. Med.,* 1955, *29,* 299-308.

A168    J. B. Van Helmont's reformation of the Galenic doctrine of digestion—and Paracelsus. *Bull. Hist. Med.,* 1955, *29,* 563-8.

A169    Collagen disease; transitional features between various types ("Viscero-cutaneous collagenosis"). *Int. Arch. Allergy,* 1955, *6,* 279-292.

A170    Max Neuburger, M.D., Ph.D., *Brit. med. J.,* 1955, i, 793-4.

A171    (With F. A. H. Simmonds): Chemotherapy and cavity wall. Histological observations. *Tubercle,* (Edinb.), 1955, *36,* 2-14.

A172    (With C. S. Treip) Viscerocutaneous collagenosis. A study of intermediate forms of dermatomyositis, scleroderma, and disseminated lupus erythematosus. *J. clin. Path.,* 1955, *8,* 1-18.

R98    Review of: J. F. F. Fulton: Michael Servetus, humanist and martyr, New York, 1953, *Bull. Hist. Med.,* 1955, *29,* 85-6.

R99    Review of: E. O. von Lippmann: Beiträge zur Geschichte der Naturwissenschaften und der Technik, vol. II, Weinheim, 1953. *Bull. Hist. Med.,* 1955, *29,* 280-2.

R100    Review of E. O. von Lippmann: Entstehung und Ausbreitung der Alchemie, 3. Band, Weinheim, 1954. *Bull. Hist. Med.,* 1955, *29,* 580-1.

R101    Review of: Bruno Kisch: Forgotten leaders in modern medicine: Valentin, Remak, Auerbach, Philadelphia, 1954. *Bull. Hist. Med.,* 1955, *29,* 484-7.

R102    Review of: F. Saxl and H. Meier: Catalogue of astrological and mythological illuminated manuscripts of the Latin Middle Ages, part III; manuscripts in English libraries, London, 1953. *Arch. int. Hist. Sci.,* 1955, *34,* 75-6.

1956 A173    (With C. S. Treip): The influence of cortisone on the disposal of heat-killed tubercle bacilli by the sensitised guinea-pig. *Int. Arch. Allergy,* 1956, *9,* 1-14.

A174   Van Helmont's ideas on gastric digestion and the gastric acid. *Bull. Hist. Med.,* 1956, *30,* 524-536.

A175   (With E. Nassau) Heilungsvorgänge bei der Lungentuberkulose gestern und heute. Eine vergleichende Betrachtung der spontanen und auf Collaps—und Chemotherapie beziehbaren anatomischen Heilungsbilder. *Fortschr. Tuberkforsch.,* 1956, 7, 212-253.

R103   Review of: J. J. Izquierdo: El Brownismo en Mexico, Mexico, 1956. *Arch. int. Hist. Sci.,* 1956, *35,* 288-9.

R104   Review of F. A. Yates: The art of Ramon Lull, London, 1954. *Isis,* 1956, 47, 199-200.

R105   Review of: The surgery of Theodoric, ca. A.D. 1267. Trl. E. Campbell and J. Colton, New York, 1955. *Isis,* 1956, 47, 444-5.

R106   Review of: G. B. Gruber: Historisches und Aktuelles über das Sirenen—Problem in der Medizin, Leipzig, 1955. *Sudhoffs Arch. Gesch. Med.,* 1956, 40, 187.

R107   Review of: Theophrast von Hohenheim genannt Paracelsus. Sämtliche Werke. Theologische und religionsphilosophische Schriften. Band IV. Bearb. K. Goldammer, Wiesbaden, 1955. *Arch. internat. Hist. Sci.,* 1956, *35,* 253-4.

R108   Review of: W. Katner: Das Rätsel des Tarentismus, *Sudhoffs Arch. Gesch. Med.,* 1956, 40, 377.

R109   Review of: Johannes Karcher: Theodor Zwinger und seine Zeitgenossen, Basel, 1956. *Sudhoffs Arch. Gesch. Med.,* 1956, 40, 379.

R110   Review of: R. Montraville Green: Asclepiades. Transl. of Cocchi's Life of Asclepiades and Gumpert's Fragments of Asclepiades, New Haven, 1955. *Bull. Hist. Med.,* 1956, *30,* 279-280.

R111   Review of: J. Ferguson: Bibliotheca chemica. A catalogue of the alchemical, chemical and pharmaceutical books in the collection of the late James Young. Reprinted London, 1954. *Arch. int. Hist. Sci.,* 1956, *35,* 155-6.

1957 A176 The philosophy of circles—Cesalpino-Harvey, a penultimate assessment. *J. Hist. Med.,* 1957, *12,* 140-157.

A177 (With C. S. Treip) Cortisone and the dissociation of hypersensitivity and acquired resistance; experiments with heat-killed tubercle bacilli. *J. Mount Sinai Hosp.,* 1957, *24,* 1093-9.

A178-9 Henry E. Sigerist (1891-1957). *Med. Hist.,* 1957, *1,* 285-9.

R112 Review of: Hildegard von Bingen. Gesamtausgabe. Vol. I. Wisse die Wege—Scivias. Salzburg, 1956. *Arch. int. Hist. Sci.,* 1957, *10,* 153-5.

R113 Review of: M. Schrader and A. Führkötter: Die Echtheit des Schrifttums der Heiligen Hildegard von Bingen. Köln-Graz, 1956. *Arch. int. Hist. Sci.,* 1957, *10,* 153-5.

R114 Review of: A. Vogt: Theophrastus Paracelsus als Arzt und Philosoph. Stuttgart, 1956. *Bull. Hist. Med.,* 1957, *31,* 194.

1958 B14 Paracelsus. An introduction to philosophical medicine in the era of the Renaissance. Basle and New York, S. Karger. 1958.

A180 (With C. S. Treip) Notes on the histological criteria of hypersensitivity. *Int. Arch. Allergy,* 1958, *12,* 113-124.

A181 Medieval and Renaissance contributions to knowledge of the brain and its functions. In: F. N. L. Poynter: The history and philosophy of knowledge of the brain and its functions. An Anglo-American Symposium London, July 15th-17th, 1957. Oxford, Blackwell, 1958, 95-114.

A182 The position of Harvey and Van Helmont in the history of European thought. To commemorate H. E. Sigerist's essay on Harvey (1928). *J. Hist. Med.,* 1958, *13,* 186-199.

R115 Review of: W. Ganzenmüller: Beiträge zur Geschichte der Technologie und der Alchemie, Weinheim, 1956, *Isis,* 1958, *49,* 84-6.

R116 Review of: K. Goldammer: Vorträge über Paracelsische Quelleneditionen. (Paracelsus Schriftenreihe der Stadt Villach. No. VII), Klagenfurt, 1957. *Arch. int. Hist. Sci.,* 1958, N.S. *11,* 190.

R117    Review of: D. Brinkmann: Augustin Hirschvogel und Paracelsus. (Paracelsus Schriftenreihe der Stadt Villach. No. VI), Klagenfurt, 1957, *Arch. int. Hist. Sci.*, 1958, N.S. *11*, 190.

R118    Review of: P. I. Betschart: So spricht Paracelsus, München Planegg, 1956, *Arch. int. Hist. Sci.*, 1958, N.S. *11*, 191.

R119    Review of: Theophrast von Hohenheim Paracelsus. Saemtliche Werke, II. Abt., Teil II: Kommentar zu den Psalmen 103-117. Ed. K. Goldammer, Wiesbaden, 1957. *Arch. Int. Hist. Sci.*, 1958, N.S. *11*, 191.

R120    Review of: M. Steinschneider: Die europaeischen Uebersetzungen aus dem Arabischen bis Mitte des Siebzehnten Jahrhunderts, Reprint, Graz, 1956. *Arch. int. Hist. Sci.*, 1958, N.S. *11*, 47-8.

R121    Review of: Hildegard von Bingen: Heilkunde. *Trl. and ed.* H. Schipperges, Salzburg, 1957. *Arch. int. Hist. Sci.*, 1958, N.S. *11*, 313-5.

R122    Review of: G. Sarton: Six wings; men of science in the Renaissance, Bloomington, 1957. *Bull. Hist. Med.*, 1958, 575-6.

R123    Review of: R. M. Green: Asclepiades, his life and writings, New Haven, 1955, *Isis*, 1958, *49*, 456-7.

R124    Review of: Soranus: Gynecology. *Trl. and introd.* O. Temkin, Baltimore, 1956. *Isis*, 1958, 456-7.

1959 A183-5    Paraclesus. In: J. Hoffer et al: Lexikon für Theologie und Kirche, Freiburg, Herder, 1959, 66-7.

R125    Review of: E. Wind: Pagan mysteries in the Renaissance, London, 1958, *Isis*, 1959, *50*, 276-8.

R126    Review of: Karl Sudhoff: *Bibliographia Paracelsica*. Besprechung der unter Hohenheims Namen 1527-1893 erschienenen Druckschriften, Graz, 1958, *Bull. Hist. Med.*, 1959, *33*, 480-2.

R127    Review of: Paracelsus. Die Kaerntner Schriften, *ed.* K. Goldammer, Klagenfurt, 1955. *Isis*, 1959, *50*, 174-5.

R128 A founder of scientific medicine. Review of: Disease, life and man. Selected essays by Rudolf Virchow, trl. L. J. Rather, *New Scientist,* 1959, 5, No. 127, 925.

R129 Biology to the aid of archeology. Review of: G. E. W. Wolstenholme and C. M. O'Connor: Medical biology and Etruscan origins, J. & A. Churchill, 1959, *New Scientist,* 1959, 5, 1204.

R130 Review of: L. Thorndike: A history of magic and experimental science, vols. VII and VIII, New York, 1958. *Bull. Hist. Med.,* 1959, 33, 84-6.

1960 A186 F. S. Bodenheimer (1897-1959). *J. Hist. Med.,* 1960, 15, 96-7.

A187 Paracelsus and Techellus the Jew. *Bull. Hist. Med.,* 1960, 34, 274-7.

A188 Some Anglo-German medical relations in historical perspective. (German and English parallel versions). *Anglo-Germ. med. Rev.,* 1960, 1, 11-36, 1961, 299-300.

A189 Paracelsus and the Neoplatonic and Gnostic Tradition. *Ambix,* 1960, 8, 125-166.

A190 (With F. N. L. Poynter). Harvey's doctrine in Italy: Argoli (1644) and Bonaccorsi (1647) on the circulation of the blood. *Bull. Hist. Med.,* 1960, 34, 419-429.

A191 (With S. Goldfarb) The diagnostic value of pleural biopsy in bronchopulmonary carcinoma. *J. clin. Path.,* 1960, 13, 425-431.

R131 Review of: Hildegard von Bingen: Naturkunde. *Trl. and ed.* P. Riethe, Salzburg, 1959, *Arch. int. Hist. Sci.,* 1960, N.S. 13, 180.

R132 Review of: W. Harvey: De motu locali animalium. *Ed. and trl.* G. Whitteridge, Cambridge, 1959. *Med. Hist.,* 1960, 4, 361-2.

1961 A192 The prime matter of Paracelsus. *Ambix,* 1961, 9, 117-135.

A193 Note on Anglo-German medical relations in historical perspective. *Anglo-Germ. med. Rev.,* 1961, 1, 299-300.

R133    Review of: Registerband zu Sudhoffs Paracelsus-Gesamt-
        ausgabe, Basel, 1960. *Med. Hist.*, 1961, *5*, 299-300.

R134    Review of: Registerband zur Sudhoffs Paracelsus-Gesamt-
        ausgabe, Basel, 1960. *Ambix*, 1961, *9*, 51-52.

R135-6  Review of: Hildegard von Bingen: Naturkunde, *transl.*
        P. Riethe, Salzburg, 1959, *Arch. int. Hist. Sci.*, 1961,
        *14*, 180.

1962 B15    Das medizinische Weltbild des Paracelsus. Seine Zusam-
            menhänge mit Neuplatonismus und Gnosis. (Kosmo-
            sophie, Forschungen und Texte zur Geschichte des
            Weltbildes, der Naturphilosophie, der Mystik und des
            Spiritualismus vom Spätmittelalter bis zur Romantik
            herausgegeben von Kurt Goldammer. Band I.) Wies-
            baden, F. Steiner, 1962.

A194    The "Wild Spirit" (Gas) of John Baptist van Helmont
        (1579-1644) and Paracelsus. *Ambix*, 1962, *10*, 1-13.

R137    Review of: Paracelsus: Sämtliche Werke, 2. Abteilung,
        Band IV-V Auslegung des Psalters David, *ed.* K. Goldam-
        mer, 1955-9. *Isis*, 1962, *53*, 527-528.

R138    Review of: Paracelsus. Sämtl. Werke, *ed.* Sudhoff, Regis-
        terband, Einsiedeln, 1960, *Isis*, 1962, *53*, 528-9.

R139    Review of: Paracelsus: Liber de nymphis, sylphis, pyg-
        maeis et salamandris et de caeteris spiritibus, *ed.* R.
        Blaser, Bern, 1960. *Isis*, 1962, *53*, 529-530.

R140    Review of: R. Blaser: Himmel und Erde machen den
        Menschen. Weisheit des Paracelsus ausgewählt und
        übertragen, Salzburg, 1958, *Isis*, 1962, *53*, 530.

R141    Review of: K. Goldammer *and* K.-H. Weimann: Para-
        celsus, Eine Auswahl, Stuttgart, n.d. *Isis*, 1962, *53*, 530.

R142    Review of: G. E. Stahl: Ueber den mannigfaltigen Ein-
        fluss von Gemütsbewegungen auf den menschlichen
        Körper, *trl. and introd.* B. J. Gottlieb, Leipzig, 1961.
        *Med. Hist.*, 1962, *6*, 292-3.

R143    Review of: David Edwardes: Introduction to Anatomy
        1542. Facsimile reproduction *trl.* C. D. O'Malley and
        K. F. Russell, London, 1961. *Med. Hist.*, 1962, *6*, 295-6.

R144    Review of: J. R. Partington: A history of chemistry, 1961. *Med. Hist.*, 1962, *6*, 189-191.

R145    Review of: Valentin Weigel, Sämtliche Schriften. Erste Lieferung: Vom Ort der Welt, Stuttgart, 1962. *Ambix*, 1962, *10*, 37.

R146    Review of: Leslie G. Matthews: History of pharmacy in Britain, London, 1962. *Ambix*, 1962, *10*, 103-4.

R147    Review of: Preface d'André Vesale à ses livres sur l'anatomie, suivie d'une lettre a Jean Oporinus. *Ed.* L. Bakelants, Brussels, 1961. *Ambix*, 1962, *10*, 104-5.

R148    Review of: F. Lieb: Valentin Weigels Kommentar zur Schöpfungsgeschichte und die Schriften seines Schülers Benedikt Biedermann, Zürich, 1962, *Ambix*, 1962, *10*, 145-6.

1963 B16    Paracelse. Introduction à la médecine philosophique de la Renaissance. (Translation of: Paracelsus. An Introduction to philosophical medicine in the era of the Renaissance, 1958). Paris, Arthaud, 1963.

R149    A Harveyan prelude to Harvey. Essay review of Harvey's Lectures on the whole of anatomy; an annotated translation of *Praelectiones anatomiae universalis* by C. D. O'Malley, F. N. L. Poynter, and K. F. Russell, Los Angeles, 1961. *Hist. Sci.*, 1963, *2*, 114-125.

R150    Review of: Catalogue of Western manuscripts on medicine and science in the Wellcome Historical Medical Library. I.: S. A. J. Moorat: Manuscripts written before A.D. 1650. *Med. Hist.* 1963, *7*, 280-1.

R151    Review of: K.-H. Weimann: Paracelsus-Bibliographie, 1932-1960. Mit einem Verzeichnis neu entdeckter Paracelsus-handschriften (1900-1960). *Med. Hist.*, 1963, *7*, 394.

R152    Review of: H. E. Sigerist: A history of medicine. Vol. II, New York, 1961. *Isis*, 1963, *54*, 499-501.

R153    Review of: K.-H. Weimann: Paracelsus-Bibliographie 1932-1960, Wiesbaden, 1963. *Ambix*, 1963, *11*, 52.

R154    Review of: G. Arnold: Das Geheimnis der Göttlichen Sophia, *Reprint ed.* W. Nigg, Stuttgart, 1963, *Ambix,* 1963, *11,* 52-3.

R155    Review of: B. Lawn: The Salernitan questions, Oxford, 1963. *Ambix,* 1963, *11,* 97.

R156    Review of: H. Kopp: Die Alchemie in älterer und neuerer Zeit, Reprint, Hildesheim, 1962. *Ambix,* 1963, *11,* 97-8.

R157    Review of: H. Schelenz: Geschichte der Pharmazie, Reprint, Hildesheim, 1962. *Ambix,* 1963, *11,* 159.

1964 B17    Pulmonary tuberculosis. 4th Edition, jointly with F. A. H. Simmonds, Norman Macdonald and E. Nassau. Oxford, University Press. 1964.

A195    (With Pyarali Rattansi) Vesalius and Paracelsus. *Med. Hist.,* 1964, *8,* 309-328.

A195a    Vesalius and the pulmonary transit of venous blood. *J. Hist. Med.,* 1964, *19,* 329-341.

A196    (With Pyarali Rattansi) Harvey meets the 'Hippocrates of Prague' (Johannes Marcus Marci of Kronland) — 1636. *Med. Hist.* 1964, *8,* 78-84.

A197    Paracelsus' ätherähnliche Substanzen und ihre pharmakologische Auswertung an Hühnern. Sprachgebrauch (henbane) und Konrad von Megenbergs "Buch der Natur" also mögliche Quellen. *Gesnerus,* 1964, *21,* 113-125.

R158    Review of: Collection des anciens alchimistes grecs, by P. E. M. Berthelot. Reprinted from the Paris (1888) edition. *Ambix,* 1964, *12,* 77-80.

R159    Review of: Giordano Bruno and the Hermetic tradition, by Frances A. Yates. *Ambix,* 1964, *12,* 72-6. (with appendix).

R160    Review of: Catalogue of the Wellcome Historical Medical Library. I. Books printed before 1641. *Isis,* 1964, *55,* 107-109.

R161    Review of: Brian Lawn: The Salernitan questions. An introduction to the history of medieval and Renaissance problem literature. *Med. Hist.*, 1964, *8*, 87-89.

1965 A198    (With P. Rattansi) Vesalius and Paracelsus. *Filosofia*, 1965, *16*, 739-742.

R162    Review of: The anatomical lectures of William Harvey, Praelectiones anatomie universalis. De musculis, edited with an introduction, translation and notes by Gweneth Whitteridge, Edinburgh, London, E. & S. Livingstone, 1964. *Med. Hist.*, 1965, *9*, 187-190.

R163    Review of: R. Klibansky, E. Panofsky, F. Saxl: Saturn and Melancholy: Studies in the history of natural philosophy, religion and art, London, Nelson, 1964. *Med. Hist.*, 1965, *9*, 293-4.

R164    Review of: E. Schöner, M. R. Herrlinger: Das Viererschema in der antiken Humoralpathologie, Archiv. f.d. Geschichte der Medizin, 1964, Beiheft 4. *Med. Hist.*, 1965, *9*, 298.

1966 A199    Harvey, foetal irritability—and Albertus Magnus. *Med. Hist.*, 1966, *10*, 409-411.

A200    Paracelsus. In: R. Dumesnil and H. Schadewaldt: Die berühmten Aerzte, Düsseldorf, Aulis Verlag, 1966, 63-5.

R165    Transition in chemistry. Review of: Allen G. Debus: The English Paracelsians, London, Oldbourne, 1966, *Hist. Sci.*, 1966, *5*, 100-104.

R166    Review of: Lynn Thorndike: Michael Scot, London, T. Nelson, 1965. *Brit. J. Hist. Sti.*, 1966, *3*, 189-190.

R167    Review of: Quaderni di storia della scienza e della medicina. Universita degli Studi de Ferrara 1963-65. Robert Blaser: Il Fenomeno Paracelso, 1963.

R168    *and* P. Rocco: Giovanni Pico della Mirandola nei suoi rapporti de amicizia con Gerolamo Savonarola, 1964.

R169    *and* F. Pierro: Arcangelo Piccolomini Ferrarese (1525-86) e la sua importanza nell' anatomia postvesaliana, 1965. *Med. Hist.*, 1966, *10*, 99-100.

R170   Review of: Gerhard Eis: Vor und nach Paracelsus. Untersuchungen über Hohenheims Traditionsverbundenheit und Nachrichten über seine Anhänger, Stuttgart, 1965. *Med. Hist.*, 1966, *10*, 210-2.

R171   Review of: Andreas Libavius: Die Alchemie. Ein Lehrbuch der Chemie aus dem Jahre 1597. Hrsg. Gmelin-Institut für anorganische Chemie (und) Gesellschaft deutscher Chemiker, Weinheim, 1964. *Ambix*, 1966, *13*, 118-120.

R172   Review of: Ernst H. F. Meyer: Geschichte der Botanik, Amsterdam, 1965. *Ambix*, 1966, *13*, 190-2.

1967 B18   William Harvey's biological ideas. Selected aspects and historical background. Basel and New York, S. Karger, 1967.

A201   Harvey and Glisson on irritability, with a note on Van Helmont. *Bull. Hist. Med.*, 1967, *41*, 497-514.

A202   Bazilläre und allergische Faktoren bei der Gewebsreaktion und dem Infektionsablauf der Tuberkulose. *Ergebn. ges. Lungen-Tuberk. forsch.*, 1967, *16*, 69-115.

R173-4   Keynes on William Harvey. Essay review (of Sir Geoffrey Keynes: The life of William Harvey, Oxford, 1966). *Med. Hist.*, 1967, *11*, 201-5.

R175   Review of: M. Berthelot: La chimie au Moyen Age, reprint of 1893 ed., Amsterdam, 1967. Ambix, 1967, *14*, 203-6.

R176   Review of: H. B. Adelmann: Marcello Malpighi and the evolution of embryology, Ithaca and Oxford, 1966. *Brit. J. Hist. Sci.*, 1967, *3*, 395-6.

R177   Review of: H. B. Adelmann: Marcello Malpighi and the evolution of embryology, Ithaca and Oxford, 1966. *Clio. med.*, 1967, *2*, 149-152.

R178   Review of: G. Eis: Vor und nach Paracelsus, Stuttgart, 1965. *Arch. int. Hist. Sci.*, 1967, *20*, 123-4.

R179   Review of: G. Eis: Vor und nach Paracelsus, Stuttgart, 1965. *Dtsch. Lit. ztg.*, 1967, *88*, 160-2.

R180 Review of: Elias Ashmole. His autobiographical and historical notes. Ed. C. H. Josten, Oxford, 1966. *Clio med.*, 1967, *2*, 265-6.

R181 Review of: Current problems in history of medicine. (Proceedings of the XIXth International Congress for the History of Medicine, Basel, 1964), *ed.* R. Blaser and H. Buess, Basle and New York, 1966. *Med. Hist.*, 1967, *11*, 319.

R182 Review of: Chemical, medical and pharmaceutical books printed before 1800. A catalogue of holdings in the University of Wisconsin Library, *ed.* J. Neu, Madison, 1965. *Med. Hist.*, 1967, *11*, 108.

R183 Review of: Theophrastus Paracelsus von Hohenheim: Theologische und religionsphilosophische Schriften. Vol. II. *Ed.* K. Goldammer, Wiesbaden, 1965. *Ambix*, 1967, *14*, 63.

R184 Review of: A. G. Debus: The English Paracelsians, London, London, 1965. *Ambix*, 1967, *14*, 63-4.

R185 Review of: H. Jonas: Gnosis und spätantiker Geist, Göttingen, 1964-6. *Ambix*, 1967, *14*, 146-8.

R186 Review of: V. Weigel: Sämtliche Schriften. 3. Lieferung. Zwei nützliche Traktate, Stuttgart, 1966. *Ambix*, 1967, *14*, 208-9.

R187 4. Lieferung. Dialogus de Christianismo, Stuttgart, 1967. *Ambix*, 1967, *14*, 210.

R188 Review of: Raimundus Sabundus: Theologia naturalis, Reprint, Stuttgart, 1966. *Ambix*, 1967, *14*, 210-1.

1968 A203 Paracelsus: Traditionalism and medieval sources. In: *Medicine, Science and Culture. Historical essays in honor of Owsei Temkin.* Baltimore, Johns Hopkins Press. 1968. 51-75.

A204 (With Marianne Winder) Gnostisches bei Paracelsus und Konrad von Megenberg. In: *Fachliteratur des Mittelalters. Festschrift für Gerhard Eis.* Stuttgart, J. B. Metzler. 1968. 359-371.

A205    (With Marianne Winder) Harvey and the "modern" concept of disease. *Bull. Hist. Med.,* 1968, *42,* 496-509.

R189    Review of: Walter L. von Brunn: Kreislauffunktion in William Harveys Schriften, Berlin, New York, Springer, 1967, *Med. Hist.,* 1968, *12,* 416-8.

R190    Review of: Medizingeschichte im Spektrum. Festschrift zum 65. Geburtstag von Johannes Steudel hrsg. v. Gernoth Rath u. Heinrich Schipperges, Wiesbaden, F. Steiner, 1966. *Med. Hist.,* 1968, *12,* 209-210.

R190a   Review of: Wilhelm Knappich: Geschichte der Astrologie. *Clio med.,* 1968, *3,* 291.

R190b   Review of: W.-E. Peuckert: Pansophie. Ein Versuch zur Geschichte der weissen und schwarzen Magie, 2. Auflage. W.-E. Peuckert: Gabalia. Ein Versuch zur Geschichte der magia naturalis im 16. bis 18. Jahrhundert. *Clio med.,* 1968, *3,* 294-7.

1969 A206   (With Marianne Winder) The eightness of Adam and related "Gnostic" ideas in the Paracelsian corpus. *Ambix,* 1969, *16,* 119-139.

R191    Chemistry at the cross roads: the ideas of Joachim Jungius. Essay review of: Joachim Jungius' Experimente und Gedanken zur Begründung der Chemie als Wissenschaft, by Hans Kangro. *Ambix,* 1969, *16,* 100-108.

R192    Review of: reprint of Elias Ashmole: Theatrum chemicum Britanicum, introduction by Allen G. Debus, New York, Johnson Reprint Corporation, 1966, *Med. Hist.,* 1969, *13,* 99.

R193    Review of: Allen G. Debus: The chemical dream of the Renaissance, (Churchill College Overseas Fellowship Lecture No. 3), Cambridge, Heffer, 1968, *Med. Hist.,* 1969, *13,* 209-210.

R194    Review of: Hans Kangro: Joachim Jungius' Experimente und Gedanken zur Begründung der Chemie als Wissenschaft. Ein Beitrag zur Geistesgeschichte des siebzehnten Jahrhunderts (Boethius. Texte u. Abhandlungen zur Geschichte der exakten Wissenschaften, vol.

7). Wiesbaden, F. Steiner, 1968, *Brit. J. Hist. Sci.*, 1969, 4, No. 16, 409-411.

R195 Spagyric purification and redemptive clarification. Review of: Ian Macphail: Alchemy and the occult. A catalogue of books and manuscripts from the Mellon Collection, New Haven, *Times Lit. Suppl.* 17.7. 69, 784.

A207 William Harvey revisited. Part I. *Hist. Sci.*, 1969, 8, 1-31; part II, *Hist. Sci.*, 1970, 9, 1-41.

1970 R196 Review of: Steno and brain research in the seventeenth century, *ed.* G. Scherz, 1968, *Med. Hist.*, 1970, *14*, 213-6.

R197 Review of: Valentin Weigel: Sämtliche Schriften, *ed.*, W.-E. Peuckert *and* W. Zeller, 5. Lieferung: Ein Büchlein vom wahren seligmachenden Glauben, Stuttgart, 1969. *Ambix*, 1970, *17*, 61-2.

R198 Review of: K. H. Burmeister: Georg Joachim Rheticus, 1514-1574. Eine Bio-Bibliographie, Wiesbaden, 1961-8. *Ambix*, 1970, *17*, 62-3.

R199 Review of: M. Mersenne: La verité des sciences contre les sceptiques ou pyrrhoniens, Paris, 1625, facsimile reprint Stuttgart, 1969. *Ambix*, 1970, *17*, 64-5.

R200 Review of: E. W. von Tschirnhaus: Gründliche Anleitung zu nützlichen Wissenschaften, Frankfurt, 1729, facsimile reprint introd. E. Winter, Stuttgart, 1967. *Ambix*, 1970, *17*, 64-5.

R201 Review of: Theophrastus Paracelsus. Werke. Studien-Ausgabe, *ed.* W.-E. Peuckert, 5 vols., Basel, 1965-8. *J. Hist. Med.*, 1970, 25, 95-7.

R202 Review of: Galen: On the usefulness of the parts of the body (de Usu partium), *trans. and introd.* M. Tallmadge, Ithaca, 1968. *Med. Hist.*, 1970, *14*, 406-8.

1971 B19 J. B. Van Helmont. Seine Lehre und seine Stellung in der heutigen Wissenschaftsgeschichte. Aufgang der Artzney-Kunst, *trl.* Christian Knorr von Rosenroth, Munich, Kösel-Verlag, 1971, III-XIX.

A208    *Article on* Thomas Erastus. In: Dictionary of scientific biography. ed. C. C. Gillespie, New York, Scribner, vol. iv, 1971, 386-8.

A209    (With J. Bylebyl): The chequered career of Galen's doctrine on the pulmonary veins. *Med. Hist.,* 1971, *15,* 211-229.

A210    Julius Pagel (29.5.1851—31.1.1912) und die Medizin-geschichte in Berlin. *Deut. med. J.,* 1971, *22,* 567-570.

R203    Review of: Correspondance du P. Marin Mersenne, ed. Paul Tannery and Cornelis de Waard, vol. III (1631-33). *Med. Hist.,* 1971, *15,* 312.

R204    Review of: James Riddick Partington: A history of chemistry. Vol. I, 1971. *Brit. J. Hist. Sci.,* 1971, *5,* 397-9.

R205    Review of: James Riddick Partington: A history of chemistry. Vol. I, 1971. *Med. Hist.* 1971, *15,* 406-7.

R206    Review of: J. Reuchlin: De verbo mirifico (1494). De arte cabalistica (1517), facsimile reprint, Stuttgart, 1964. *Ambix,* 1971, *18,* 217.

R207    Review of: Sir Kenelm Digby: Two treatises. Facsimile reprint of the Paris 1644 edition, Stuttgart, 1970. *Ambix,* 1971, *18,* 217-9.

R208    Review of: K. H. Burmeister: Achilles Pirmin Gasser, 1505-1577. Arzt und Naturforscher, Historiker und Humanist. 2 vols. publ. to date, Wiesbaden, 1970. *Ambix,* 1971, *18,* 219-220.

1972 A211    Van Helmont's concept of disease—to be or not to be? The influence of Paracelsus. *Bull. Hist. Med.,* 1972, *46.* In Press.

## In preparation

A212
213
214
         *Articles on:* J. B. Van Helmont, Hildegard von Bingen (Bermersheim) and Paracelsus. In: Dictionary of scientific biography, ed. C. C. Gillespie, New York, C. Scribner, vol. V.

A215  *Articles on* Paracelsus *and* J. B. Van Helmont. In: His-
216  toria de la medicina, *ed.* P. Lain Entralgo, Barcelona,
Salvat Editores.

A217  *Article on* William Harvey. In: Encyclopedia Ameri-
cana, New York.

A218  The spectre of J. B. Van Helmont and the idea of continuity in the history of chemistry. In: *Perspectives in the
history of science. Essays dedicated to Joseph Needham,*
ed. Robert Young and M. Teich. In Press.

## Tributes to Professor Dr. Walter Pagel

1961  Neue Ehrendoktoren der Universität. *Basler National-
Zeitung,* 1961, Nr. 548, 25 November.

Der Dies Academicus der Universität Basel. Ehrenpro-
motionen. *Basler Nachrichten,* 1961, Nr. 503, 25 November, 6 Beilage.

1962  We present Walter Pagel. Karger-gaz., 1962, nr. 2,
(15.5), 4.

1963  W. Gürich: Walter Pagel zum 65. Geburtstag. *Tuberk.
facharzt,* 1963, *17,* 228-9.

W. Artelt: Walter Pagel zum 65. Geburtstag. *Nachrbl.
dtsch. Ges. Gesch. Med. Naturwiss.,* 1963, 50-1.

E. Uehlinger: Walter Pagel zum 12. November 1963.
*Dtsch. med. Wschs.,* 1963, 88, 2437-8.

1966  W. Doerr: Zur Einweihung des Pathologischen Instituts der Universität am 25. April 1966 und Ehrenpromo-
tion. *Ruperto-Carola,* 1966, *39,* 272-280 (esp. 277).

1968  W. Artelt: Walter Pagel zum 70. Geburtstag. *Nachrbl.
dsch. Ges. Gesch. Med. Naturwiss.,* 1968, 82.

*University of Leeds Reporter,* 1968, 13.

H. Buess: Gedenktage. Walter Pagel—Septuagenarius.
12. November 1968. *Dtsch. med. Wschr.,* 1968, *93,*
2186-8.

H. Buess: Walter Pagel—Septuagenarius 12. November 1968. *Gesnerus*, 1968, 25, 223-5.

1970        Notice of conferment of honorary membership of the Paracelsusgesellschaft. *Paracelsusbrief*, Salzburg, December 1970.

1971        Award of Sarton Medal by History of Science Society, Chicago. *Isis*, 1971, 62, 97.

Mellizo, Felipe: Los cazadores de recuerdos, no. 13: Paracelso. *Tribuna medica* (Madrid), 1971, 8, no. 402, 14-15.

Sarton Medal for Walter Pagel. *Ambix*, 1971, 18, 214.

Julius Pagel medal conferred December 1971 by *Berlin Gesellschaft für Geschichte der Medizin und Naturwissenschaften.*

# The Contributors

JEROME J. BYLEBYL is Assistant Professor of the History of Medicine in the Department of History and the Morris Fishbein Center for the Study of the History of Science and Medicine at The University of Chicago. His research has centered on the early history of cardio-vascular physiology, and he has also published on William Beaumont.

CARLO CASTELLANI, Professor at Parma, is the author of several studies on the history of medicine and biology, among them the *Storia della Generazione* (1965) and his critical edition of the *Lettres de Charles Bonnet à Lazzare Spallanzani* (1971). He is also the editor of *Episteme. Revista critica di Storia delle Scienze mediche e biologiche*.

I. BERNARD COHEN is Professor of the History of Science at Harvard University. He has produced (in collaboration with the late Alexandre Koyré) an edition of Newton's *Principia* with variant readings (1971), and an accompanying Introduction to Newton's *Principia* (1971). Among his other works may be noted *Some Early Tools of American Science* (1950), *The Birth of a New Physics* (1960), *Franklin and Newton: An Inquiry into Speculative Newtonian Experimental Science* (1954, 1964; revised edition 1972), *Benjamin Franklin's Experiments* (1941), *Roemer and the First Determination of the Velocity of Light* (1942, 1944).

PAUL F. CRANEFIELD, Associate Professor at the Rockefeller University, is a cardiac physiologist and Editor of the *Journal of General Physiology*. As a medical historian he is the author of studies of the history of biophysics and physiology, the history of psychoanalysis and the history of mental retardation.

AUDREY B. DAVIS is Curator of Medical Sciences at the Smithsonian Institution. Her research emphasizes problems in seventeenth century medicine and science and her book, *The Circulation of the Blood and Medical Chemistry in England, 1650-1680*, will appear in 1972.

ALLEN G. DEBUS is Professor of the History of Science and Director of The Morris Fishbein Center for the Study of the History of Science and Medicine at The University of Chicago. His research has centered on sixteenth and seventeenth century science and medicine. He is the author of *The English Paracelsians* (1965) and *Science and Education in the*

*Seventeenth Century—The Webster Ward Debate* (1970). He has also prepared a new edition of Elias Ashmole's *Theatrum Chemicum Britannicum* (1967) and edited the *World Who's Who in Science: A Biographical Dictionary of Notable Scientists from Antiquity to the Present* (1968).

KURT GOLDAMMER is Professor of the Comparative History of Religion and the History of Religious Art at the Philipps-Universität at Marburg an der Lahn. He is also President of the Internationale Paracelsus-Gesellschaft at Salzburg, Chairman of the Paracelsus-Kommission and Editor of the theological and religious writings of Paracelsus. He is the author of *Paracelsus, Sozialethische und sozialpolitische Schriften* (1952), *Paracelsus—Natur and Offenbarung* (1953), *Paracelsus-Studien* (1954), *Die Formenwelt des Religiösen* (1960), *Kultsymbolik des Protestantismus* (1960-67) and numerous studies related to Paracelsus and the history and phenomenology of religion.

HENRY GUERLAC, Goldwin Smith Professor of the History of Science at Cornell University, is Director of Cornell's Society for the Humanities. He is author of *Lavoisier—The Crucial Year* (1961) and of numerous articles on eighteenth century chemistry, Newtonianism and the Enlightenment, and other subjects in the early history of science.

WLODZIMIERZ HUBICKI is Professor of Chemistry at the Marie Curie Sklodowskiej University Lublin. He has published broadly in the history of chemistry, but his special interests are related to alchemy and Paracelsian thought in Central and Eastern Europe in the sixteenth and the seventeenth centuries.

A. G. KELLER is a Lecturer in the History of Science at Leicester University, England. His research has centered on the connections between technological change and contemporary social and intellectual movements and he has written *A Theatre of Machines* (1964), a work which deals with the early printed literature of mechanical invention.

SAUL JARCHO formerly taught pathology at Johns Hopkins and Columbia Universities and is now a practising internist in New York. He is immediate past president of the American Association for the History of Medicine and editor-in-chief of the *Bulletin of the New York Academy of Medicine*.

FRIDOLF KUDLIEN is Professor of the History of Medicine at the Institut für Geschichte der Medizin und Pharmazie der Christian-Albrechts-Universität, Kiel. Among his works on ancient medicine may be cited *Der Beginn des medizinischen Denkens bei den Griechen* (1967) and *Die Sklaven in der griechischen Medizin der klassischen und hellenistischen Zeit* (1968).

OTTO KURZ is Professor of the History of the Classical Tradition with special reference to the Near East at The Warburg Institute, University of London. He is the author of numerous papers dealing with the history of cultural contacts, art history and archaeology.

ERNA LESKY, Professor of the History of Medicine at the University of Vienna, is the author of several books on the history of Viennese medicine, the history of social and Greek medicine. Among them may be cited *Die Zeugungs- und Vererbungslehren der Antike* (1950), *Arbeitsmedizin im 18. Jahrhundert* (1956), *Osterreichisches Gesundheitswesen im Zeitalter des aufgeklärten Absolutismus* (1959), *Semmelweis und die Wiener medizinische Schule* (1964), and *Die Wiener medizinische Schule im 19. Jahrhundert* (1965).

DAVID C. LINDBERG, Associate Professor of the History of Science at the University of Wisconsin, has worked principally on the history of Medieval and Renaissance optics. His publications include *John Pecham and the Science of Optics* (1970) and a critical edition of Pecham's *Tractatus de perspectiva* (in press). He is presently engaged in writing a history of Medieval and Renaissance theories of vision.

ROBERT P. MULTHAUF occupies a senior research position at the Smithsonian Institution. He is editor of *Isis* and past Director of the Museum of History and Technology. His *Origins of Chemistry* appeared in 1967.

JOSEPH NEEDHAM, F.R.S., Master of Gonville and Caius College, Cambridge, was for many years Sir William Dunn Reader in Biochemistry in the University. His *History of Embryology* (1934) was written during the time of his activity as a working scientist. Since the second World War he has been an orientalist, and his *Science and Civilisation in China* (1954-) is in course of publication (7 vols. in 11 parts). Ancillary works include *The Development of Iron and Steel Technology in China* (1958), *Heavenly Clockwork* (1960) and *Clerks and Craftsmen in China and the West* (1970). He collaborated with Walter Pagel in editing *Background to Modern Science* (1938).

PETER H. NIEBYL is Assistant Professor in the Institute of the History of Medicine, School of Medicine, The Johns Hopkins University. His research and publications have centered on various problems of seventeenth century medicine.

LEO NORPOTH is Professor of the History of Medicine at the Klinikum Essen of the Ruhr-University in Bochum. He is the author of numerous studies of medieval philosophy and medicine and Paracelsism. He was chief clinician (internal medicine) of the Elisabeth-Hospital in Essen (1949-1969) and he has written several clinical studies concerning the physiology and pathology of the intestinal tract.

CHARLES DONALD O'MALLEY (1907-1970) was Professor and Chairman of the Department of Medical History at the University of California at Los Angeles. He published numerous articles and monographs on all aspects of Renaissance science and medicine, but he is perhaps best known for his critical editions of the medical texts of the sixteenth and seventeenth centuries and his book, *Andreas Vesalius of Brussels 1514-1564* (1964).

NOEL POYNTER is Director of the Wellcome Institute of the History of Medicine in London, editor of the quarterly journal, *Medical History*, author of several books (of which *Medicine and Man*, 1971, is the most recent) and of many papers on the history of medicine.

P. M. RATTANSI is Professor and Head of the Department of the History and Philosophy of Science at University College, London. His research and publications have centered on science in seventeenth century England.

JEROME R. RAVETZ is Senior Lecturer in the History and Philosophy of Science at the University of Leeds. His research interests are divided between the history of the mathematical sciences and the social and ethical aspects of science, past and present. In the former line he has worked on Fourier, Galileo and Copernicus; on the latter, he has published *Scientific Knowledge and its Social Problems* (1971).

WALTHER RIESE is Emeritus Associate Professor of Neurology, Psychiatry and the History of Medicine at the Medical College of Virginia and Professor Emeritus on the Medical Faculty of the Johann Wolfgang Goethe University in Frankfurt a.M. Formerly he was Chargé de Recherches du Centre National de la Recherche Scientifique (Paris) and

Consulting Neuropathologist to the Department of Mental Hygiene and Hospitals of the Commonwealth of Virginia. In the course of his long career he has written many books among which may be cited *The Conception of disease, its History, its Versions, and its Nature* (1953), *A History of Neurology* (1954), and, most recently, *The Legacy of Pinel. An Inquiry into Thought on Mental Alienation* (1969).

PAOLO ROSSI is Professor of the History of Philosophy at the University of Florence. His main interests are in the history of sixteenth and seventeenth century philosophical and scientific thought. Among his publications are *Francis Bacon: From Magic to Science* (1957, English translation, 1968), *Clavis universalis: arti mnemoniche e logica combinatoria da Lullo a Leibniz* (1960), *Philosophy, Technology and the Arts in the Early Modern Era* (1962, English translation, 1970), *Le sterminate antichità: studi vichiani* (1969), *Storia e filosofia: saggi sulla storiografia filosofica* (1969) and *Aspetti della rivoluzione scientifica* (1970).

KARL EDUARD ROTHSCHUH is Professor of the History of Medicine at the University of Münster/Westfalen, F.R.G. Among his most important books on Biology, Medicine and the History of Physiology may be cited the following: *Theorie des Organismus* (1959, 1963), *Prinzipien der Medizin* (1965), *Entwicklungsgeschichte physiologischer Probleme in Tabellenform* (1952), *Geschichte der Physiologie* (1953), *Physiologie. Der Wandel ihrer Konzepte, Probleme und Methoden vom 16. bis 19. Jahrhundert* (1968), *Physiologie im Werden* (1969), *René Descartes. Uber den Menschen* (Editor, 1969), and Claude Bernard, *Einführung in das Studium der experimentellen Medizin*, Paris, 1865 (Editor, 1961).

CHARLES B. SCHMITT is Lecturer in the History of Science and Philosophy, The Warburg Institute. Among his publications are *Gianfrancesco Pico della Mirandola and His Critique of Aristotle* (1967), *A Critical Survey and Bibliography of Studies on Renaissance Aristotelianism, 1958-1969* (1971), and "Theophrastus" in *Catalogus translation, 2* (1971). His *Cicero Scepticus: A Study of the Influence of the Academica in the Renaissance* is to be published shortly.

WOLFGANG SCHNEIDER is Professor and Head of the *Seminar of the History of Pharmacy* at the Technical University at Braunschweig. He is the author of numerous studies on the history of pharmacy and chemistry, among them the following books: *Lexicon alchemisch-pharmazeutischer*

*Symbole* (1962), *Geschichte der Deutschen Pharmazeutischen Gesell-schaft* (1965), *Lexicon zur Arzneimittelgeschichte* (since 1968); *1, Tierische Drogen, 2, Pharmakologische Arzneimittelgruppen, 3, Pharmazeutische Chemikalien und Mineralien, 4, Geheimmittel und Spezialitäten*).

HARRY J. SHEPPARD is Head of the Chemistry Department, Warwick School, England. He is the author of numerous papers on alchemy, symbolism and chemistry.

RUDOLPH E. SIEGEL is Clinical Assistant Professor of Medicine at the State University of New York at Buffalo, School of Medicine. He has written a number of papers on various topics in the history of science and medicine and also two books on Galen: *Galen's System of Physiology and Medicine, an Analysis of His Doctrines and Observations on Blood Flow, Respiration, Humors and Internal Diseases* (1968) and *Galen on Sense Perception; His Doctrines, Observations, and Experiments on Vision, Hearing, Smell, Taste, Touch, and Pain, and their Historical Sources* (1970).

JERRY STANNARD is Professor of History of Science, Department of History, at the University of Kansas. He is the author of many papers in ancient and medieval botany, medicine, and philosophy and is presently working on a history of botany to the year 1500.

NICHOLAS H. STENECK is Assistant Professor of History at the University of Michigan. His research interests are centered on medieval and Renaissance psychology, and he is currently pursuing a study of the natural philosophy of Henry of Langenstein.

OWSEI TEMKIN is William H. Welch Professor Emeritus at The Johns Hopkins University School of Medicine. His publications extend over various periods and include "Geschichte des Hippokratismus im ausgehenden Altertum" (*Kyklos, 4* (1932), 1-80); *The Falling Sickness* (1945, revised edition 1971); *Soranus' Gynecology* (1956, with N. J. Eastman, L. Edelstein, A. F. Guttmacher).

RICHARD TOELLNER is Professor of Medical History and Director of the Institut für Geschichte der Medizin at the Free University of Berlin. He has devoted much time to the study of the medical history of Württemberg and his special field of research is the origin and development of modern medicine in its relation to the history and philosophy of science. He has recently published *Uber die Einheit im Denken Albrecht von Hallers* (1971).

HUGH TREVOR-ROPER is Regius Professor of Modern History in the University of Oxford: a post which he has held since 1957. His published work includes a biography of Archbishop Laud, *The Last Days of Hitler,* and *Religion, The Reformation and Social Changes* (U.S. title, *The Crisis of the 17th Century*). He is a Fellow of the British Academy and a Foreign Honorary Member of the American Academy of Arts and Sciences.

DANIEL PICKERING WALKER is Reader in Renaissance Studies in the University of London at the Warburg Institute. He has written on various aspects of the intellectual history of the fifteenth to the seventeenth centuries. He has published two books: *Spiritual and Demonic Magic from Ficino to Campanella* (1958), *The Decline of Hell* (1964), and has just completed a third, *Essays on the Ancient Theology.*

CHARLES WEBSTER is Wellcome Reader in the History of Medicine at the University of Oxford. He is the author of several articles on medicine and science in the seventeenth century and he is the editor of *Samuel Hartlib and the Advancement of Learning* (1970).

RICHARD S. WESTFALL is Professor of the History of Science at Indiana University. He has published a number of articles dealing with science in the 17th century and with Isaac Newton in particular. He is also the author of *Science and Religion in Seventeenth Century England* (1958), *Force in Newton's Physics* (1971) and *The Construction of Modern Science* (1971).

RONALD S. WILKINSON, Manuscript Historian at the Library of Congress, has published a number of studies in seventeenth century chemistry, alchemy, Renaissance medicine and pharmacy. He is presently writing an account of the scientific endeavours of John Winthrop.

MARIANNE WINDER is Assistant Librarian and Assistant Keeper of Manuscripts at the Wellcome Institute of the History of Medicine. She has published a number of articles, among them several with Walter Pagel as co-author. Her *Tibetan Medicine Illustrated in Original Texts* (with Ven. Rechung Rimpoche) will be published shortly.

# Editor's Acknowledgments

It is not possible to name all those who have contributed of their time and effort to the completion of these volumes during the past four years. Nevertheless, it would be unforgiveable not to mention at least a few whose work might go otherwise unrecorded. The attention paid to the original texts by Dr. Christine Schofield in England and Miss Rose Jacobowitz in New York has lightened the burden on the Editor considerably. In addition, Miss Selene Fung is to be thanked for the Chinese calligraphy that is incorporated in the article by Dr. Joseph Needham. Miss Marianne Winder was responsible not only for the preparation of the long and complex biliography of the works of Walter Pagel, but also for helping to choose and arrange for the publication of many of the illustrations that are included in these pages from the collection of the Wellcome Historical Library in London. The Editor is indebted to Mrs. Helen Little who typed and mailed many hundreds of letters to the contributors and at the same time managed to keep in order the almost bewildering number of galley and page proofs that have crossed our desks.

Full credit for the appearance of the books must be given to Ted Gensamer who was in charge of the total book design and production—and the Editor is fully convinced that the final publication of these volumes would not have been feasible without the genuine interest first of Dr. Michael Hoskin of Churchill College, Cambridge, and later, Mr. Neale Watson of New York. Dr. Hoskin completed many of the original arrangements for the publication of these essays while Mr. Watson's concern for the history of science and the history of medicine—coupled with his appreciation of the importance of Professor Pagel's contribution to these fields—has ensured his total dedication to the publication of these volumes.

Finally, the Editor wishes to acknowledge the support of the National Institutes of Health (Research Grant LM-00046) and the National Science Foundation (Research Grant GS-29189) at different times during the period when these volumes were prepared.

Allen G. Debus
The Institute for Advanced Study
Princeton, New Jersey

13 October 1972

335

# Illustration Acknowledgments

## Volume One

iv Frontispiece   9 Introduction   Both from the private collection of the editor.

54 Maier, Michael. 1568?-1622. Title page *Viatorium*. Oppenheim: H. Galler for J. T. de Bry. 1618. By courtesy of "The Wellcome Trustees."

56 Maier, Michael. 1568?-1622. Title page *Atlanta fugiens, hoc est emblemata nova de secretis natura chymica*. Oppenheim: H. Galler for J. T. de Bry. 1618. By courtesy of "The Wellcome Trustees."

68 Joubert, Laurent. 1529-1583. *Opuscula*. Lugduni, apud Salamandram. 1571. By courtesy of "The Wellcome Trustees."

72 Fernel, Jean. 1497-1558. Printers device from Title page *Universa Medicina....*Paris: A. Wechel. 1567. By courtesy of "The Wellcome Trustees."

82 Courtesy of Museum f. Völkerkunde, Wien.

103 Detail from The chemical laboratory of the Jardin des Plantes. Vignette by Sébastien Le Clerc. *Mémoires pour servir à l'histoire des plantes:* Dodart. Paris: 1676. Reproduced from the Collection of the Library of Congress.

150 Paracelsus, Bombastus ab Hohenheim, Aureolus Philippus Theophrastus. 1493-1541. From *Paracelsus Medici libelli....*Cologne: G. Vierendunck for heirs of A. Byrckman. 1567. By courtesy of "The Wellcome Trustees."

182 Title page *De la nature des plantes*. Guy de la Brosse. Paris: Rollin Baragnes. 1628. Courtesy University of Michigan.

183 Frontispiece from above.

190 Vignette by Sébastien Le Clerc. *Mémoires pour servir à l'histoire des plantes:* Dodart. Paris: 1676. Reproduced from the Collection of the Library of Congress.

204 Title page *Medici systematis harmonici....*Simeonis Partlicii de Spitzberk (Partlicius, Simeon). Frankfurt: Danielis & Dauidis. 1625. By courtesy of "The Wellcome Trustees."

205 Partlicius, Simeon. Title page *A New method of physick....*Trans. by Nicholas Culpeper. London: P. Cole. 1654. By courtesy of "The Wellcome Trustees."

210 Culpeper, Nicholas. 1615-1654. *Mr. Culpepper's treatise of Arurum Potabile*. London: G. Eversden. 1657. By courtesy of "The Wellcome Trustees."

216 Culpeper, Nicholas. 1615-1654. *Mr. Culpeper's Ghost*....London: P. Cole. 1656. By courtesy of "The Wellcome Trustees."

275 Galen demonstrates the uses of the bodily parts of man and elephant. Miniaturen der lateinischen Galenos-Handschrift der Kgl. Oeffentil. Bibliothek Dresden. Phototype reproduction: E. C. Leersum and W. Martin, Leiden: A. W. Sijthoff 1910: p. 9. no. 36. By courtesy of "The Wellcome Trustees."

## Volume Two

4 Sorbait, Paul de. 1642-1691. Kupferstich von Gerhart Bouttats, Wien O. J. Courtesy of the Bildarchiv der Instituts für Geschichte der Medizin, Wien.

11 Sorbait, Paul de. 1624-1691. Kupferstich von Cor. Meyssens, Wien 1669. Courtesy of the Bildarchiv der Instituts für Geschichte der Medizin, Wien.

23 Jean Baptiste van Helmont with his son. From an etching attributed to Kanel De Moor 1. Impression in the Wellcome Institute. By courtesy of "The Wellcome Trustees."

37 Galen discusses the four elements. See listing 275 above. (p. 15. no. 81).

52 Harvey demonstrating the discovery of the circulation of the blood to Charles I. From an engraving by H. Leman after R. Hannah. Impression in the Wellcome Institute. By courtesy of "The Wellcome Trustees."

72 Guinter, Joannes. c. 1505-1574. From *De medicina veteri et nova tum cognoscenda, tum faciunda commentarii duo*. Basel: Ex off. Henric petrina, 1571. By courtesy of "The Wellcome Trustees."

89 Title page *De efficaci medicina*. Severino, Marco Aurelio. 1580-1656. Frankfurt: J. Beyer. 1646. By courtesy of "The Wellcome Trustees."

165 Illustration from *L'homme*. Descartes, René. Paris: 1664, p. 81. By courtesy of "The Wellcome Trustees."

182 Portrait of Sir Isaac Newton. By Sir Godfrey Kneller (1702). Courtesy the National Portrait Gallery.

198 Illustration from *Principia*. Newton, Sir Isaac. Glasgow: J. Maclehose, 1871, p. 328. By courtesy of "The Wellcome Trustees."